Survival in Two Worlds

MOSHOESHOE OF LESOTHO
1786–1870

Moshoeshoe at Aliwal North, 19 August 1860, aged about 74

Survival in Two Worlds

MOSHOESHOE OF LESOTHO
1786–1870

BY

LEONARD THOMPSON

OXFORD
AT THE CLARENDON PRESS
1975

Oxford University Press, Ely House, London W. 1

GLASGOW NEW YORK TORONTO MELBOURNE WELLINGTON
CAPE TOWN IBADAN NAIROBI DAR ES SALAAM LUSAKA ADDIS ABABA
DELHI BOMBAY CALCUTTA MADRAS KARACHI LAHORE DACCA
KUALA LUMPUR SINGAPORE HONG KONG TOKYO

CASEBOUND ISBN 0 19 821693 9
PAPERBACK ISBN 0 19 822702 7

© *Oxford University Press 1975*

*Printed in Great Britain
at the University Press, Oxford
by Vivian Ridler
Printer to the University*

General Sir George Cathcart, British High Commissioner and Governor of the Cape Colony:

I told you in that letter that I hoped to meet you in peace, and I still hope so, as I look to you as the great chief in this part.

Moshoeshoe:

I hope so too, for peace is like the rain which makes the grass grow, while war is like the wind which dries it up.

PREFACE

MOSHOESHOE was an African whose life extended from the old order to the new—the traditional to the colonial. He was brought up in the interior of southern Africa in an isolated society of mixed farmers, organized in small chiefdoms. As a young man he knew nothing of horses, of firearms, or of white people. During his thirties, Africans who had been displaced from Natal by Shaka invaded his homeland and triggered a series of catastrophes that caused bloodshed, social and political disintegration, and collapse of confidence. It was then that Moshoeshoe emerged as a leader. Through moral influence as much as military prowess, he rallied the survivors and built a kingdom. He had scarcely begun to do so, however, when the western world impinged upon him, reaching out from the long-established colony of the Cape of Good Hope. In quick succession there came armed Coloured horsemen, plundering; French Protestant missionaries, evangelizing; British officials, bearing impressive presents and concocting ominous documents; and Afrikaner pastoralists, appropriating land. For the rest of his long life Moshoeshoe grappled with the growing and ultimately overwhelming strength of these diverse intruders.

Moshoeshoe was a humane man. Unlike Shaka, he respected the dignity of every person, he ruled by consultation and consent, and he rarely imposed the death penalty. His was a self-disciplined and integrated personality. He abstained from drinking alcohol and smoking cannabis, for he declared that they would prevent him from making wise decisions. He was a selective innovator, quick to appreciate the advantages of guns, horses, new crops, and literary education. Above all, he was a realist and a patriot. While he accepted much evangelical Christian doctrine, he had compelling social and political reasons for rejecting several aspects of the teachings presented by the missionaries. To preserve the cohesion of his people he kept one foot in the conservative and traditionalist camp, even while placing the other in the modern and Christian. He acquired a deep understanding of the changing power relationships in the southern African state system of his day and, matching his policy to his means, he pursued an active diplomacy.

He resorted to warfare only in self-defence or under the utmost provocation, and when he did so he deployed his forces with great skill. His own mountain stronghold of Thaba Bosiu was never captured in his lifetime. He was adept in extracting political advantages from military successes, even when this required great restraint and magnanimity. It was only after he had repeatedly been deceived by British officials and his country had been ravaged by Afrikaner commandos that he himself became devious; and he was nearly eighty years of age by the time he lost control of his own more reckless subordinates.

Eventually the BaSotho suffered the fate that overtook almost every African people in the era of European imperialism. Even so, in a final diplomatic *coup* Moshoeshoe contrived to secure the lesser of the two evils that were available: he had his people annexed by Britain, which had little interest in exploiting them, rather than by the Orange Free State, which had determined to deprive them of nearly all their arable land.

After nearly a century of British over-rule, Lesotho became independent again in 1966. The problems of the new Lesotho are as intractable as those which Moshoeshoe faced. But that it exists at all as a separate entity is his enduring legacy.

Although this book is primarily biographical, I have explained the changing conditions in south-eastern Africa which were the background to Moshoeshoe's career. Chapter I includes sketches of SeSotho culture and history before the Shakan revolution. Chapter II starts with brief accounts of that revolution and its cataclysmic effects in LeSotho. Chapter III examines the initial impact of Christian missionaries on SeSotho society as well as its leader. Chapters IV, VI, and VII describe white secular pressures as well as the responses of Moshoeshoe and his people. And Chapter V is an analysis of the kingdom of LeSotho at its apogee in the mid-1850s.

The book should have something to say to historians of tropical as well as southern Africa. For example, Chapter V contributes data to the ongoing debate about the origins and early histories of African kingdoms. That debate has tended to be highly speculative because very little is known in most cases, whereas in the case of LeSotho we have relatively detailed information about the kingdom while its founder was still alive.

The tone of recent writing on Africa has ranged between the superficial and the arcane. In this book I have tried to find middle ground: to make the achievements of a remarkable human being intelligible to non-specialists without sacrificing scholarly integrity. In the first chapter, the sketches of SeSotho culture and prehistory are written in the language of a layman rather than an anthropologist, and in several places discussions of controversial questions and comments on professional literature have been relegated to footnotes. Also, throughout the book many Bantu proper names have been simplified, as explained in the note on Orthography and Pronunciation, and the modern, European-derived names of rivers have been used rather than SeSotho names which have become obsolete (e.g. Caledon rather than Mohokare, Orange rather than Senqu, Vaal instead of Lekoa).

The sources are discussed in the bibliography and, on some issues, in the text and in footnotes. As historians are well aware, it is difficult to obtain reliable evidence about the history of societies before they became literate, and difficult, too, to interpret what evidence there is. In the case of Moshoeshoe, there are no eye-witness accounts written before 1833, when he was about forty-seven years old. Moreover, although there is a great deal of documentation for the ensuing years, Moshoeshoe himself did not learn to read or write and the vast majority of the documents that have survived were written by white people. I have tried to compensate for the distortions imposed upon reality by alien minds. In this I have been assisted by BaSotho informants whom I consulted during my visits to Lesotho in 1965, 1968, and 1972. They deepened my general understanding of SeSotho culture and the major processes of SeSotho history. In addition, several informants have independent strands of tradition that include specific data about Moshoeshoe and his times. Nevertheless, the feedback from published works is already pervasive. More than one elderly informant responded to a question by producing the Revd. D. F. Ellenberger's compilation of BaSotho traditions, or some other publication derived from it.

In quoting from French, Dutch, and Afrikaans sources, I have used published English translations if they exist (as in two books by Eugène Casalis), otherwise I have made my own translations (as in the numerous quotations from the *Journal des Missions Évangéliques de Paris*). SeSotho sources were translated by Mosebi Damane, S. M. Guma, J. R. Masiea, and E. M. Sehalahala.

Yale University, January 1975   LEONARD THOMPSON

ACKNOWLEDGEMENTS

I AM grateful for the professional assistance of the staffs of the Lesotho Archives and the Archives of the Lesotho Evangelical Church and the Catholic Archdiocese, Maseru; the Orange Free State Archives, Bloemfontein; Rhodes University Library, Grahamstown; the Libraries of the University of Cape Town and the South African Museum, and the South African Public Library, Cape Town; the Archives of the Société des Missions Évangéliques, Paris; the Public Record Office and the Archives of the Wesleyan and London Missionary Societies, London; Durham University Library; the Library of the University of California, Los Angeles; and the Divinity School Library and the Sterling Memorial Library, Yale University.

The Revd. Paul Ellenberger gave me open access to the documentary collection made by his grandfather, the Revd. D. F. Ellenberger. Professor Isaac Schapera of the London School of Economics, now emeritus, provided me with genealogies he collected in Basutoland in the 1930s. Captain R. S. Webb of Paarl and Amy and Charlot Jacot-Guillarmod of Grahamstown allowed me to use rare books and documents from their private collections.

During my field research in Lesotho in 1965 and 1968 H. H. Motlohlehi Moshoeshoe II and Prime Minister Leabua Jonathan encouraged their people to talk with me, and almost without exception potential informants were most co-operative.

I have benefited greatly from discussions of parts of this work in seminars at the University of Botswana, Lesotho, and Swaziland; Natal University; Stellenbosch University; the University of Sussex; Edinburgh University; Columbia University; Indiana University; and Yale University. The discussions at the University of Sussex with Anthony Low, Peter Lloyd, Christopher Wrigley, Richard Brown, and their graduate students, were especially valuable.

For commenting on drafts of parts or all of the book I am most grateful to Jeffrey Butler, Frederick Cooper, Richard

Elphick, William Foltze, John Galbraith, Richard Gray, B. M. Khaketla, Daniel Kunene, Duncan Rice, David Robinson, Ellen Titus, Monica Wilson, and David Yudelman.

I am also greatly indebted to several other people who, in various ways, have made major contributions to the substance of this book. Mosebi Damane has a uniquely deep knowledge and sensitive appreciation of the history of his people and has been most patient, tolerant, and generous in his responses to my many inquiries, which started when we met in Paris in 1964 and continued till this book went to press. He read the first five chapters with great care and clarified many issues. Esau Moroa Sehalahala worked with me as interpreter and travelling companion during my field research with immense enthusiasm and good humour and was an invaluable intermediary because he knew personally nearly every informant we consulted. The Revd. Albert Brutsch not only placed the archives of the Lesotho Evangelical Church at my disposal but also identified many documents and illuminated several historical points. Finally, my brother Rivers Thompson, who has lived in Lesotho since 1929 and was Judicial Commissioner at the time of my visits, shared with me his intimate knowledge of Sesotho custom, arranged for me to employ Mr. Sehalahala, introduced me to informants, and, with his wife Betty and his daughter and son-in-law Margaret and Michael Everett, provided unbounded hospitality and lent me transport when my own broke down. *Khotso*! I salute them all. But the errors of fact and interpretation are, of course, mine.

The typescript was prepared by Janet Villastrigo, Paula Schneider, Cleo Thompson, and Pamela Baldwin at Yale. They have taken pains to cope with names that were strange to them and to make sense of my nearly illegible writing.

My research was made possible by a Fulbright–Hays Fellowship in 1964–5; a Yale University Senior Faculty Fellowship and a Leverhulme Visiting Fellowship at the University of Sussex in 1968–9; and grants from the Research Committee of the University of California, Los Angeles, and the Yale Concilium on International and Comparative Studies.

CONTENTS

LIST OF MAPS

LIST OF PLATES

ORTHOGRAPHY AND PRONUNCIATION[1]

THERE are two SeSotho orthographies. One is used in the Republic of South Africa and endorsed by the International African Institute; the other is the official orthography of Lesotho. In this book I have used the official orthography of Lesotho.

In my first draft of Chapter I, I used the appropriate Bantu prefixes throughout; but it was pointed out that this made for extremely difficult reading for people who are not Bantu-speakers. Consequently, I have generally followed the common practice of using the stems only of Bantu proper nouns: for example, *Koena, Khoakhoa, Ndebele,* and *Nguni* rather than (in the plural form) *BaKoena, MaKhoakhoa, AmaNdebele,* and *AbeNguni*. To this I have made an exception of the stem *Sotho,* but, to help the reader, I have capitalized the stem (a practice the early French missionaries sometimes used). Thus

SeSotho   refers to language and customs;
MoSotho refers to a member of the linguistic or political community;
BaSotho refers to members of the community; and
LeSotho refers to the territory subject to Moshoeshoe (but for the state that became independent in 1966 I use the official form, *Lesotho*).

I have also capitalized the name of the son or daughter in cases where a person was known as 'Father of . . .' or 'Mother of . . .', as in *RaMatšeatsana* and *'MaMohato*. Moreover, where I have used non-proper SeSotho nouns I have made the meaning clear and included the appropriate prefixes. For examples, see the Glossary.

---

[1] I am most grateful to Professor Daniel Kunene of the University of Wisconsin for his advice.

The accent in SeSotho falls on the penultimate syllable. Major variations from English pronunciation include:

o or *u* before *a* or *e* or open or semi-open *o* is a consonant, with the sound as in English *w* (as in *oabala*, to strike);

e before *a* or *o* or open or semi-open *e* is a consonant, with the sound as in English *y* (as in *ea*, to go);

l before *i* or *u* is pronounced much like English *d* (as in *litelu*, a beard) except when the *l* is preceded by another (syllabic) *l*, in which case each *l* is pronounced much like an ordinary English *l* (as in *molli*, one who cries);

q is a palatal click (as in *qaba*, to quarrel);

ph, *th*, and *tš* are aspirated *p*, *t*, and *ts* respectively (cf. *paka*, to bear witness, and *phaka*, to make haste; *taba*, a thing, and *thaba*, a mountain; and *tsela*, a road, and *tšela*, to cross a road);

in *'m* and *'n* the apostrophes represent syllabic *m* and *n* respectively (as in *'Ma*, mother of, and *'ngoe*, which?).

The phonetic pronunciation of Moshoeshoe is *muʃweʃwe*: or, approximately, *mushweshwe* (with the *e*'s pronounced more or less as in English *get*). The phonetic pronunciations of some other main characters in this book are:

Mokhachane (Moshoeshoe's father) *mukxhatʃhani*
Posholi (Moshoeshoe's brother) *pushudi*
'MaMohato (Moshoeshoe's senior wife) *mmamuhatᵓ*
Letsie (Moshoeshoe's senior son) *litsie*
Molapo (Moshoeshoe's second son) *mulapᵓ*
Tšapi (a renowned doctor and diviner) *tshapi*.

GLOSSARY OF SESOTHO TERMS

bohali	marriage; marriage cattle
joala	strong beer
kenela	levirate
lebollo	initiation; initiation school
lenaka (pl. *manaka, linaka*)	horn in which a chief or doctor keeps his medicine
letona (pl. *matona*)	councillor
letsema (pl. *matsema*)	communal labour performed for a chief
lifaqane (sing. *faqane*)	the wars in LeSotho in the 1820s
mafisa	animals put in charge of a person who shares their produce with the owner
malome (pl. *bo-malome*)	a maternal uncle who has a special responsibility for his nephew
mohlanka (pl. *bahlanka*)	client; servant
mophato (pl. *mephato*)	hut where initiated boys live
morena (pl. *marena*)	chief
moruti (pl. *baruti*)	teacher; missionary
mosuoe (pl. *mesuoe*)	master in an initiation school
ngaka (pl. *lingaka*)	doctor
pitso (pl. *lipitso*)	public meeting
seboko (pl. *liboko*)	totem
sechaba (pl. *lichaba*)	people; tribe; nation
sethaba-thaba	tax levied by a chief on all his people
thoko (pl. *lithoko*)	praise; praise song

LIST OF ABBREVIATIONS

Arbousset (1)	T. Arbousset and F. Daumas, *Narrative of an Exploratory Tour to the North-East of the Colony of the Cape of Good Hope* (i.e. the 1836 journey)
Arbousset (2)	Excursion Missionnaire de M. T. Arbousset dans les Montagnes Bleues (i.e. the 1840 journey) (unpublished)
AYB	*Archives Year Book for South African History*
BR	G. M. Theal, *Basutoland Records*, vols. i–iii
BR	G. M. Theal, Basutoland Records, vols. IV–VI (unpublished)
Casalis (1)	*The Basutos*
Casalis (2)	*My Life in Basutoland*
E & M	D. Fred Ellenberger (compiler) and J. C. Macgregor (translator), *History of the Basuto: Ancient and Modern*
JME	*Journal des Missions Évangéliques de Paris*
LEC	Lesotho Evangelical Church archives
LMS	London Missionary Society archives
OFS	Orange Free State archives
OHSA	*The Oxford History of South Africa*
PRO	Public Record Office
SAAR, OFS	*South African Archival Records, Orange Free State*
SME	Société des Missions Évangéliques archives
WMS	Wesleyan Missionary Society archives

I

THE YOUNG MOSHOESHOE AND THE TRADITIONAL ORDER

1. *Birth, Initiation, and Marriage*[1]

MOSHOESHOE—or Lepoqo as his parents called him—was born in the village of Menkhoaneng in the north of modern Lesotho. His father Mokhachane had been born there too and was the headman of the village. His mother Kholu had been brought up eight miles further north, near Botha Bothe mountain. She was Mokhachane's first wife and she already had a daughter, who became known as 'MaTšouenyane; but in SeSotho society to bear a son was a more important achievement.

His parents named him Lepoqo, meaning Dispute, because, as he said later, 'I was born at the moment when they were fighting in my father's village about a person accused of witchcraft.'[2] Precisely when he was born we do not know. Many years were to pass before the BaSotho met people who computed dates, and the estimates that have been made vary between 1780 and 1794. It was probably in about 1786.[3]

---

[1] The reader is referred to the List of Abbreviations, p. xxiii, and the Bibliography.

[2] Eugène Casalis, 15 July 1843, *JME* xix (1844), 124. Three informants, 14, 16, and 35, declare that the actual mother of Lepoqo was not Kholu, but a Coloured girl who had been captured by Mokhachane's people. They cite as evidence a song, which includes the words: 'Kholu refuses to nurse Lepoqo', interpreted as meaning he was not her son. The story is improbable: there is no contemporary or near-contemporary evidence to support it; nor is there any other evidence that Khoi or Griqua people were in contact with Mokhachane's people by the time of Lepoqo's birth.

[3] This is a good example of the impossibility of obtaining precision about the chronology of BaSotho history before the *lifaqane*. Casalis ((2), p. 177) said Moshoeshoe seemed to be about 45 in 1833; Andrew Smith (Andrew Smith Papers, South African Museum Library, Cape Town, vol. xii, p. 28) thought him to be about 40 in 1834; J. J. Freeman (*JME* xxv (1850), 445) estimated he was about 60 in 1850; T. Jousse ('Moshesh, roi des Bassouto', *Le Chrétien Évangélique: revue religieuse de la Suisse romande*, 1867, p. 7) said he was born in about 1785; E. Jacottet (in M. A. Boegner *et al.*, *Livre d'Or de la Mission du Lessouto*, Paris, 1912, p. 168) suggests he was born between 1786 and 1788;

Nor do we have much specific information about the childhood of Lepoqo. It was evidently a happy one, for there is no tradition of serious friction between him and his parents and he remained on good terms with them throughout the rest of their long lives. Mokhachane lived near him until he died in 1855, after which Kholu spent her final years not far from Menkhoaneng in the care of grandchildren.[1]

For his first few years Lepoqo was spoilt, in the SeSotho manner, by his mother and the other women of the village. From about his sixth year onwards he began to mix work with play, taking part in herding first the family sheep and goats and later the cattle. When he toured the Menkhoaneng area in 1840 after a long absence, he fell into a nostalgic mood and the missionary who was with him recorded that the places

were full of the memories of his childhood, the pleasant and charming kinds of memories that everyone keeps inlaid in his soul, as the best and the strongest of all. Over there, on a beautiful plateau, he had often raced with his friends, sometimes nude and as free as the gazelles of the wilderness, sometimes mounted on three-year-old calves which they had broken in to carry them across the plains.[2]

He certainly grew up in a domestic and social environment where he felt secure and relaxed. His contemporary, Shaka, on the other hand, had a miserable childhood, being rejected by his father and brought up by a quarrelsome mother in a succession of relatives' villages. Perhaps their childhood experiences contributed to the contrast between their adult behaviour as creators and rulers of kingdoms. The Zulu was a violent man; the MoSotho, a man of peace and, as was said, 'a man who loved people'.[3]

J. C. Macgregor (*Basuto Traditions*, Cape Town, 1905, p. 12) suggests 1786; E & M (p. 106) seems to agree with that; and modern BaSotho authors follow E & M (e.g. Edward Motsamai Leoatle, *Morena Moshoeshoe Mor'a Mokhachane*, Morija, 1952, ch. 1).

[1] T. Jousse, annual report for Thaba Bosiu mission station, 1855–6, *JME* xxxi (1856), 324–5; T. Jousse, 14 Aug. 1857, *JME* xxxiii (1858), 56.

[2] Arbousset (2), p. 55.

[3] On Shaka's birth and childhood, see A. T. Bryant, *Olden Times in Zululand and Natal*, London, 1929, pp. 48–9, 62–4. Many informants declare that Moshoeshoe was known as 'a man who loved people'.

Mokhachane and Kholu produced three other children after Lepoqo: two boys, who became known as Makhabane and Posholi, and another girl, later known as 'MaNtoetse. As his wealth grew Mokhachane was also able to take other wives. His second wife produced daughters only. His third gave birth to a son, Mohale, who was probably about the same age as Makhabane. His fourth had many sons, of whom the oldest, Mopeli, was to play a significant role in BaSotho history. By the end of his life Mokhachane had married several more girls.[1] Consequently as Lepoqo was growing up his mother became somewhat neglected by his father. Nevertheless Kholu's household was always regarded as the senior one and Lepoqo realized at an early age that he stood a good chance of succeeding to his father's position, provided that he proved acceptable to the people.

An essential step towards manhood for a young MoSotho was his initiation.[2] A chief would convene a *lebollo* when one of his sons had reached the appropriate age, a few years after puberty. Then the boy and his age-mates would be initiated. This was a dramatic episode in the life of a chief-dom—the village or cluster of villages that recognized the authority of a single leader. Only the chief could authorize a *lebollo* and make it effective, because it was he who appointed the *mohlabani* (distinguished warrior), the *mesuoe* (instructors), and the *thipane* (surgeon) who conducted the ceremonies. The chief also provided the crucial ingredients— a bull, butter-fat, and, most important of all, his *lenaka*. This was a horn, preferably a rhinoceros' horn, containing

---

[1] D. F. Ellenberger gives a short list of Mokhachane's wives and children in *Livre d'Or*, p. 676. See below, p. 331, Note 1, for his longer list, in a manuscript in the Ellenberger Papers.

[2] There are descriptions of traditional Basotho initiation practices in E & M, pp. 280–9; H. Dieterlin and F. Kohler in *Livre d'Or*, pp. 149–56; Paul Ramseyer, 'La Circoncision chez les Bassoutus', *Revue d'Ethnographie et des Traditions Populaires*, xxxiii (1928), 40–70; F. Laydevant, 'Les Rites de l'initiation au Basutoland', *Anthropos*, xlvi (1951), 221–54; Hugh Ashton, *The Basuto*, London, 1952, pp. 41–61; and S. M. Guma, 'Some aspects of Circumcision in Basutoland', *African Studies*, xxiv (3–4) (1965), 241–9. I have preferred the account by Dr. Guma, who has probably had access to more authentic information than his white predecessors. His account does not differ substantially from that of Father Laydevant, a Catholic missionary. Informants have corroborated and amplified the written sources.

a powder composed of a mixture of vegetable and animal materials and human flesh. The bull and the cow which produced the butter-fat were meant to have been captured from a rival chiefdom; and the human flesh should have been cut from the body of an enemy who had been killed, fighting bravely.

The first phase in initiation took place in the *lekhotla*—the men's meeting-place near the chief's hut. There the bull was slaughtered, but before it died the shoulder-blade was ripped off and cut up into small pieces. The *mohlabani* spat on each piece of meat and smeared it with a mixture of the butter-fat from the captured cow and the powder from the chief's horn. While the meat was being roasted on an open fire, a naked woman entered the *lekhotla* and made incisions on the bodies of the boys, who were also nude. The warrior then speared a piece of the cooked meat and held the spear over his shoulder, waving it from side to side; and the boy who was the most senior in the accepted genealogical order knelt behind the warrior with his hands behind his back, to be beaten by men until he had managed to bite the meat off the spear. The other boys then did the same, one by one, in strict order of genealogical seniority.

The second phase in initiation took place in open country away from the village, where the boys were circumcised by the *thipane* in the same sequence; after which they were given *sehoere*, a porridge-like food containing butter-fat, medicine from the chief's horn, and a toxic substance from the bulb *leshoma* (*boophane distichi*), which drugged the boys and dulled the pain of their operation.

Thirdly, the boys went to their *mophato*, a lodge specially built for the occasion in the countryside. They lived there for from three to six months, without any contact with their families, under the charge of the *mesuoe*, who taught them the customs and traditions of the chiefdom. Much of this took the form of learning by heart *likoma*—ancient songs in archaic SeSotho. In addition each initiate had to compose a song about himself—a praise song (*thoko*) in which he extolled his achievements, expressed his ambitions, and gave himself a new name. As long as the boys were in the *mophato* they saw no women and their teachers and even their parents were obliged to refrain from sexual intercourse, subject to severe penalties; and the *mosuoe* and his assistant beat them frequently for the slightest errors.

Finally, the boys burnt down the *mophato*, with all their childhood possessions inside it, and they returned to their village, where the entire community had a tremendous celebration, stimulated by *joala*, a strong beer made from fermented sorghum. Throughout the rest of their lives the boys who had been initiated together formed a distinct group in society under the leadership of the chief's son for whom the *lebollo* had been convened. A chief therefore had a band of devoted followers in his initiation-mates.

The purpose of these rituals, which had been built up over many generations, was to prepare the boys for their adult responsibilities as husbands and fathers, as guardians of cattle—the principal form of wealth—as warriors, and as loyal subjects of their chief. The initiates were deemed to have absorbed the heroic qualities and powers of the *mohlabani* through his spittle and of the enemy warrior through his flesh. From the *mesuoe* they learnt sexual hygiene, group solidarity, and obedience to seniors, especially the chief. The *lebollo* turned them from carefree children into *makoloane* —initiated youths.

Nineteenth-century missionaries, as we shall see, never fully probed the highly secret proceedings of the *lebollo*. Nevertheless among the first generation of missionaries in LeSotho were some who understood its social function. Initiation promoted 'national survival', wrote one of them. 'Circumcision makes the child a man. Anyone who has not experienced this rite is unequipped for war, unfitted for business, inadmissible in society. In a word, he is not a MoSotho, he lacks the distinctive mark of his race, his father and mother disavow him, his equals insult him and run away from him.'[1] Another missionary observed that its objective was 'to incorporate them into the nation, to attach them to the young chief who is part of the band'.[2]

[1] Casalis, 4 Mar. 1845, *JME* xx (1845), 283.
[2] Lemue, 4 Jan. 1854, *JME* xxix (1854), 209.

Mokhachane convened a *lebollo* for Lepoqo and his age-mates in about 1804.[1] Their *mophato* was in open country about 2 miles south-west of Menkhoaneng, his father's village. When he revisited the area in 1840, he told the missionary who was in his entourage that he was in the *mophato* 'for six full moons', during which 'he had undergone his difficult education for manhood and military activity'.[2] In his initiation song, as was the custom, he praised himself with various names, including Tlaputle (Busy or Energetic),[3] Lekhema (the Hastener),[4] and especially Letlama (the Binder),[5] and thereafter his age set was known as the *Matlama* (the Binders).[6]

He did not use Letlama as his personal name for long. Soon after his initiation he led his age-mates on a successful cattle-raid against a neighbouring village, whose chief was called RaMonaheng, and to commemorate that achievement he composed a new verse:

Ke 'na Moshoeshoe Moshoashoaila oa ha Kali,
Lebeola le beotseng Ramonaheng litelu.

(I am the sharp Shearer, the Shaver, descendant of Kali [Mona-heng]
The [barber's] blade that shaved off RaMonaheng's beard.)[7]

Thereafter Lepoqo, alias Letlama, was known as Moshoe-

[1] The date is uncertain. In 1880 Sekhonyana, a son of Moshoeshoe, wrote that his father's *lebollo* was held in the year of the *mamothohana*, when there was a severe disease among the cattle (Nehemiah [Sekhonyana] Moshesh, 'A Little Light from Basutoland', *Cape Monthly Magazine*, 3rd ser. ii (Jan.–June 1880), 203); later still D. F. Ellenberger, in his synthesis of the traditions of the BaSotho, wrote that it took place after the *sekoboto* or great famine which he dated in 1803 (E & M, p. 107); and recent authors, BaSotho as well as others, have followed Ellenberger (e.g. Leoatle, ch. 1).

[2] Arbousset (2), p. 55.

[3] Casalis (1), p. 194.

[4] Simeon F. Mlapokaze, *Leselinyana*, Mar. 1902.

[5] E & M, p. 107; Guma, p. 246; Informant 39.

[6] We cannot be sure that Lepoqo's initiation was conducted precisely as described in the preceding pages. However, such rituals are amongst the most conservative institutions in a society and there is therefore good reason to believe that Lepoqo's initiation was approximately as the institution has been described by a series of authors from D. F. Ellenberger to S. M. Guma, who consulted many different informants. See p. 3 n. 2.

[7] D. P. Kunene, *Heroic Poetry of the Basotho*, Oxford, 1971, p. 1.

shoe, the Shearer, a name derived from the sound of a razor shaving.[1]

A MoSotho was not accepted as a full adult merely because he had been initiated and had proved his manliness by raiding cattle. Marriage was also necessary. In about 1810 his father, or perhaps Peete, his grandfather, provided the *bohali* cattle for Moshoeshoe to marry the daughter of Seepheephe and his wife Makoai.[2] The marriage was fruitful. While they still lived in Mokhachane's village of Menkhoaneng, two sons and a daughter were born to them. First, in about 1811, there was Mohato, who was later to become known under his initiation praise name of Letsie; then in about 1814, Molapo, followed some three years later by their daughter Mathe. Two more boys were born of this marriage: Masopha in about 1820 and Majara in about 1829.[3]

The marriage was a happy one. In 1833 the missionary Casalis wrote that

'MaMohato [i.e. mother of Mohato] was a tall and strong woman already of somewhat ripe age, but not wanting in attractions. . . . Moshesh seated himself by her side, and took their youngest son Ntalime [Majara], a little boy between four and five, between his knees. The apparently perfect union between these two, and the perfect cordiality mingled with respect with which they addressed and offered little services to each other, greatly struck me.[4]

Long after 'MaMohato's death in 1834 Moshoeshoe continued to speak of her with affection.[5]

Moshoeshoe married many other women. His second wife was known as 'MaNneko from the name of her only son, who died young; his third, 'MaSekhonyana, was a relative of 'MaMohato. Thus Moshoeshoe soon presided over three establishments or Houses, each with its own cattle

---

[1] Kunene, op. cit.; also Samson Mbizo Guma, 'The Forms, Contents and Techniques of Traditional Literature in Southern Sotho', Ph.D. dissertation, University of South Africa, 1964, pp. 209–10; E & M, p. 107; F. Laydevant, 'La Poésie chez les Basuto', *Africa*, iii (1930) 526; Leoatle, ch. 1; A. S. Mopeli-Paulus, *Moshweshwe Moshwaila*, King William's Town, n.d., ch. 3.

[2] E & M, p. 109.

[3] These are the dates given in E & M, p. 379; except for Majara.

[4] Casalis (2), pp. 179–80.

[5] Casalis (1), p. 107.

and its own fields for cultivation. Under him, each of the three women controlled her own household.[1]

Later, as his wealth and power increased, Moshoeshoe was in a position to acquire more wives year after year, until almost the end of his long life. In 1833 a French missionary thought he had thirty or forty wives; a year later Moshoeshoe told the leader of an expedition from the Cape Colony, that 'he has twenty wives he knows well'; in 1865 the Catholic nuns who had settled at Roma, LeSotho, thought he had 140 wives; and a MoSotho author writing in 1891 estimated that the total had been 200.[2] Most of his later wives were regarded as distinctly inferior. Moshoeshoe would summon whomever he wished to spend the night with him and he undoubtedly sired a vast progeny; but he employed his junior wives mainly as domestic servants. He also offered them to visitors for the night by way of hospitality, but according to custom any children they produced were regarded as his own.[3]

2. *Moshoeshoe's World*[4]

The world that Moshoeshoe grew up in had narrow horizons. His father's village was situated in rugged country in

[1] Nehemiah [Sekhonyana] Moshesh, 'A Little Light', p. 222.

[2] Casalis (2), p. 179; Andrew Smith, vol. 12, p. 30; *Annales de l'association de la Sainte-Famille*, 10 Oct. 1865, iii (1), 105; M. Nchakala, *Leselinyana*, 15 July 1891; F. Laydevant, 'Étude sur la famille en Basutoland', *Journal de la Société des Africanistes*, i (1931), 244.

[3] Mopeli-Paulus, ch. 7; Nehemiah [Sekhonyana] Moshesh, 'A Little Light'. Casalis (1), pp. 186–8, with his religious commitment to monogamy, failed to understand that the Second and Third Houses were autonomous establishments under the Chief, each with its own cattle and its own lands, even though the succession to the chieftainship would normally go to a son of the first wife. Andrew Smith, vol. 12, pp. 16–19, made the same error, probably because he was dependent on Casalis for interpretation and information. See below, pp. 331–2, Note 2, for a list of Moshoeshoe's wives and children.

[4] For this section the basic sources are: Casalis (1), Part II, pp. 123–355, 'Manners and Customs of the Basutos', which is the first systematic account of the BaSotho, by a perceptive missionary who resided in LeSotho from 1833 to 1855; and E & M, pp. 237–304, and H. Dieterlin and F. Kohler in *Livre d'Or*, pp. 23–156, which are descriptions of pre-*lifaqane* SeSotho society by French Protestant missionaries who arrived in LeSotho in the 1860s and 1870s. Ashton, op. cit., is the standard work by a modern anthropologist, based on

the valley of the Hlotse, a left-bank tributary of the Caledon
River, nearly 6,000 feet above sea level. To the north-west
lay the grasslands of the South African high veld, inhabited
by his own sort of people; but to the east and south the
barren Maloti and Drakensberg mountains, rising to over
11,000 feet and inhabited only by a few small bands of
hunters and herders, separated the Caledon river valley
from the coastal lowlands.

Although Europeans had explored much of southern
Africa long before Moshoeshoe was born, they had never
penetrated to the Caledon valley. Moshoeshoe had never
seen a horse, a gun, or a white person until he was forty,
and as a child he was probably not aware of their existence,
though all three were to be vital influences in his later life.
His little world with its satisfactions and its hazards seemed
self-contained.

His people were mixed farmers. They owned dogs,
poultry, goats, sheep, and—above all—cattle, which were
their most prized possessions. Their staple crop was sorghum
(*mabele*) which they stored in large wicker baskets.[1] They
lived in compact villages of between 50 and 400 inhabitants.
The core of a village community was an extended family,
consisting of the headman, his uncles, his brothers, and their
wives and children and other relatives; and families who
were not related attached themselves to the dominant
patrilineage. A village controlled arable fields, which were
divided into strips for each household much as in medieval
Europe, and communal pastures and hunting-grounds.
Sorghum was planted after the first rains in September or
October and harvested after the first frost in May or June.[2]

In good seasons the standard foods were sorghum bread
and porridge, light sorghum beer (*mahleu*), and sour milk,

field research performed mainly in 1934 and 1935. F. Laydevant, 'La Famille',
op. cit., and *The Basuto*, Mazenod, Lesotho, n.d., Vernon Sheddick, *The Southern
Sotho*, London, 1953, and Monica Wilson, 'The Sotho', in *OHSA* i. 131–67,
are briefer modern studies.

[1] It is probable that maize did not reach the Caledon valley before the 1820s.
Wheat was introduced by missionaries in the 1830s.

[2] Laydevant, 'La Famille'; Casalis (1), pp. 126–8; James Walton, *African
Village*, Pretoria, 1956.

with occasional feasts of beef or mutton and strong beer (*joala*), while women and children also ate greens. This constituted a healthy and balanced diet. But prosperity depended on the summer rains. When the rains failed, as was often the case, the crops wilted, the livestock starved, and people depended on game and edible plants. *'Pula!'*—may it rain!—was the popular greeting.

Each extended family was an almost completely self-sufficient economic unit, but there were two types of specialists: iron-workers and doctors. Smiths smelted iron from surface outcrops and made hoes, knives, awls, spears, and battle-axes. There were no professional traders; but since good iron and copper ore was relatively scarce in the Caledon basin, metals and metal wares were sometimes brought in from outside, especially from beyond the mountain escarpment. The ablest smiths also came from there. Small quantities of beads of European and Asian origin reached the Caledon from the north-east, having been bartered from chiefdom to chiefdom all the way from the coast at Delagoa Bay, or Sofala, or farther north.[1]

Doctors (*lingaka*) were of several types. Many had expert knowledge of the medicinal qualities of local herbs. Others treated the sick by prescribing rituals or using divining bones to identify the witch or the sorcerer who had caused the illness. Some diviners also acquired reputations for being able to bring rain and to foretell the future.[2]

In his childhood Moshoeshoe's perceptions about his fellow human beings were derived from observing their behaviour and listening to the stories, riddles, and proverbs recounted by his parents and grandparents. The oral literature in SeSotho, as in other Bantu languages, is full of shrewd and witty comments on human nature. It stresses the social norms which were necessary for the security and

---

[1] Casalis (1), pp. 130–5; Anon., *Leselinyana*, 16 July 1911; Informants 52, 56. We know very little about trade in pre-*lifaqane* LeSotho. The missionary Eugène Casalis said glass beads were still almost unknown among Moshoeshoe's people in 1833 (4 Oct. 1833, *JME* ix (1834), 143). His colleague Thomas Arbousset wrote that the BaSotho had already exploited all the iron outcrops in the area by 1838 (17 Dec. 1838, *JME* xiv (1839), 295–6).

[2] Casalis (1), pp. 283–9; E & M, pp. 249–61; Informants 39, 52.

harmony of a patrilineal farming society. As a modern African scholar has explained:

Respect for one's elders; the maintenance of strong family ties; respect for constituted authority in the form of chiefs; respect of womanhood; hospitality towards strangers, and goodwill towards all men at all times; self-protection on the part of all, as well as the protection of one's rights and property if trampled underfoot—all these and more, are directly transmitted to us through these ancient proverbs.[1]

Later Moshoeshoe's social perceptions were sharpened by the teachings of the *mesuoe* in his *lebollo*.

Great emphasis was placed on distinctions of sex and age. At every stage in her life a woman depended on a man —a father, a husband, or (in her old age) perhaps a son, a son-in-law, or a grandson. Hence the levirate (*kenela*): when a woman's husband died she came under the protection of his brother. When a girl married, she became a member of her husband's family and to compensate her father's family for the loss of a daughter it received cattle (*bohali*) from the family of the bridegroom. Girls married soon after puberty but a man did not normally take a wife before he was about twenty-five years old.[2]

Age was respected, not merely because people older than oneself were recognized as having greater experience, but also because a family was regarded as an open-ended community. Besides its living members, it included the deceased ancestors and the children yet unborn. The ancestors influenced the lives of their descendants and the oldest among the living were the closest to the ancestors. When a person was ill, unless he was quickly cured by a herbalist, he believed that he must have annoyed his ancestors or been bewitched by a living person. He would then consult a doctor who would advise him to make a sacrifice to the shades of his ancestors—a goat, or a sheep, or, if the matter was serious

[1] Guma, 'Traditional Literature', p. 245. Dr. Guma's dissertation is a mine of valuable information. Ruth Finnegan, *Oral Literature in Africa*, Oxford, 1970, is an excellent survey of the entire field of oral literature in Sub-Saharan Africa. See also M. Damane and P. B. Sanders, *Lithoko: Sotho Praise-Poems*, Oxford, 1974.

[2] On the role of women in African societies in southern Africa see J. H. Simons, *African Women: Their Legal Status in South Africa*, London, 1968.

enough, a beast (i.e. a bull, a cow, or an ox)—or perhaps the doctor's divining bones would show that an evil-doer had bewitched him.[1]

The wealth and prestige of families varied, as did their status. When misfortune overtook a person, he attached himself to a more successful man. The patron might provide his client (*mohlanka*) with cattle, but these *mafisa* cattle remained the property of the patron. However, social stratification was not rigid, and there were opportunities for upward as well as occasions for downward mobility. Patrons treated their clients (*bahlanka*) as junior kinsmen and arranged their marriages, and within a generation or two many people of *bahlanka* antecedents merged into their patrons' families.[2]

Besides the distinctions of sex, age, and status, the young Moshoeshoe would have perceived ethnic differences in the world around him: differences between his own BaSotho people and the Nguni and the San. SeSotho and Nguni cultures were very similar. Both peoples were pastoralists and cultivators, as well as hunters. Their languages, though not mutually intelligible, were members of the same Bantu linguistic family and some BaSotho, like Moshoeshoe himself, could speak an Nguni dialect.[3] The Nguni dressed somewhat differently from the BaSotho. Their men left the penis exposed in a way that seemed immodest to BaSotho, who wore a *tšea*—a skin garment that passed through the legs and was knotted to a belt, front and back. They also had different marriage rules. Among Nguni, marriage with a member of one's father's descent group was regarded as incest: to BaSotho, the marriage of cousins was not merely permitted, it was positively preferred.[4]

[1] Casalis (1), pp. 237–99; Informant 39. Monica Wilson, *Religion and the Transformation of Society*, Cambridge, 1971, includes valuable discussions of religion in traditional societies in eastern and southern Africa.

[2] On *mafisa* as practised in recent times see Vernon Sheddick, *Land Tenure in Basutoland*, London, 1954, pp. 109–10. Mosebi Damane points out that to hold a *lefisa* was not necessarily to become the *mohlanka* (client or servant) of the owner of the cattle.

[3] Arbousset (2), p. 72, reported that Moshoeshoe was fluent in Zulu in 1840 and, pp. 62–5, he summarized Moshoeshoe's reflections on the different SeSotho dialects.

[4] The traditions of the northern Nguni were collected by A. T. Bryant,

The San, on the other hand, did not possess domesticated animals nor did they grow crops; they depended exclusively on collecting plants and insects and hunting game with poisoned arrows. Moreover, they did not live in permanent homes but moved around in small bands, and their languages were radically different from Bantu. Consequently, while BaSotho treated Nguni as people of the same kind as themselves, they regarded San as thoroughly alien. Even so, they were accustomed to incorporating individual San as well as Nguni into their own society by marriage and clientage, and bringing up their children as BaSotho.[1]

Every MoSotho had a totem (*seboko*), which he inherited from his father, like a surname in European custom. Most totems (*liboko*) were the names of animals or reptiles, such as Koena (crocodile), Khatla (monkey), Kubung (hippopotamus), Phuthi (duiker), Taung (lion), Tloung (elephant), and Tšoeneng (baboon). A MoSotho was not meant to kill or even touch a living member of his *seboko*, but he used representations of it as a symbol to mark his cattle, his clothes, and his utensils, and he swore by it.[2]

In theory everyone who had the same *seboko* was descended in the male line from a common ancestor. Anthropologists have worked out ingenious diagrams purporting to show the relationships between the different BaSotho 'clans'.[3] In fact, however, these diagrams, which are based on the

Olden Times in Zululand and Natal. See also Monica Wilson, 'The Nguni People', *OHSA* i. 75–130, especially pp. 95–102. See below, pp. 332–3, Note 3, for discussion of the terms Sotho and Nguni.

[1] On the San, whom the BaSotho called BaRoa and white settlers called Bushmen, see Arbousset (1), pp. 242–62; George W. Stow, *The Native Races of South Africa*, London, 1905; I. Schapera, *The Khoisan Peoples of South Africa*, 1930; V. Ellenberger, *La Fin tragique des Bushmen*, Paris, 1953; Marion W. How, *The Mountain Bushmen of Basutoland*, Pretoria, 1970; Monica Wilson, 'The Hunters and Herders', *OHSA* i. 40–74. There is also a considerable literature on the remarkable artistic achievements of these people, e.g. D. N. Lee and M. C. Woodhouse, *Art on the Rocks of Southern Africa*, Cape Town, 1970.

[2] On totems among the Tswana see I. Schapera, *The Ethnic Composition of Tswana Tribes*, London, 1952. The BaSotho *liboko* have not been subjected to intensive study by modern anthropologists; but see Vernon Sheddick, *Land Tenure in Basutoland*, pp. 18–19, and Monica Wilson, *OHSA* i. 162–3, as well as the works listed above, p. 8 n. 4.

[3] See, for example, Cmd. 8209 [G. I. Jones], *Basutoland Medicine Murder*, 1951, p. 4, which is set out on p. 334, Note 4, below.

genealogies taken from chiefs in the nineteenth and twentieth centuries, represent the relationships that the ruling families claimed to have existed among themselves. Whatever the origins of the *liboko* may have been, by Moshoeshoe's time a person's *seboko* did not determine where he lived. For example, there were people called Koena living far away beyond the Vaal River as well as in the Caledon valley. Nor did it necessarily determine whose political authority he accepted, for chiefdoms included people of different *liboko*. Moreover a MoSotho could change his *seboko*, and it was sometimes convenient for him to do so: for example, to adopt the *seboko* of his chief.

In Moshoeshoe's youth the two most common *liboko* in the upper Caledon valley were Koena and Fokeng (dew). Moshoeshoe's father, Mokhachane, was a Koena and so, consequently, was Moshoeshoe. His mother, Kholu, was a Fokeng, and so were his own senior wife, 'MaMohato, and his third wife, 'MaSekhonyana. This was typical of the relationship between these two clans in the area. The Fokeng were regarded as the senior clan because they were the first BaSotho inhabitants of the area, and in a *lebollo* Fokeng boys were always circumcised first; but the chief's son was the undisputed leader of the initiation group and most of the chiefs were Koena.[1]

The effective political units in Moshoeshoe's world were chiefdoms.[2] Everyone, except for the San hunter-gatherers, was the subject of a chief. Chiefdoms varied in size and population. Seventy miles north-east of Menkhoaneng (around modern Harrismith) the long-established chiefdom of the Tlokoa of Mokotleng comprised many villages and several thousand people. But in the Caledon valley itself most chiefdoms were small. This was because they frequently split. An ambitious member of a ruling family would strike out on his own with his age-mates and any other followers he could attract. At first his relationship with the chief he

[1] E & M, pp. 14–17; Macgregor, pp. 20–2; Informants 26, 27, 28, 39.
[2] On traditional political systems in southern Africa see I. Schapera, *Government and Politics in Tribal Societies*, London, 1956, which is based mainly on work among the Tswana.

had left would be ambiguous. Later, if he was successful, he would establish his independence, but some residue of doubt might remain, and claims and counter-claims might be inherited by the next generation. In practice, therefore, a chiefdom often consisted of no more than a single village, with a population of perhaps a couple of hundred people, and its fields and cattle-posts, though some other chief might claim overlordship by virtue of his genealogical seniority.

Whatever the size of a chiefdom it was governed in much the same way. The chief spent most of his time in the *lekhotla*, the open-air meeting-place near his personal hut. There he regulated the affairs of his people, listening to complaints, settling disputes, and receiving visitors. He was the wealthiest man in his territory. His subjects paid him sheep and cattle for settling their disputes, his warriors handed over to him for disposal any livestock they seized from neighbouring chiefdoms, and he had the right to summon his people to work for him (*letsema*). They cultivated the fields of his senior wives, which were regarded as the property of the chiefdom, and he used their produce to entertain guests and feed the men when they were conscripted for military purposes. Consequently a chief was wealthy enough to marry more wives and provide more generous hospitality than any of his subjects.

As we have seen, the teachings of the *mesuoe* in the *lebollo* emphasized the authority of chiefs. But it was by no means an unqualified authority. A chief depended on the co-operation of his councillors. Some of these were his kinsmen and others men of talent from other lineages, especially members of his initiation group. A chief would also convene a mass meeting of his menfolk—a *pitso*—when he had important news to communicate or problems to discuss with them, and at a *pitso* anyone could express himself freely in criticism of the chief and councillors. Moreover, in the last resort an aggrieved subject could move away from a chief's territory and place himself under another chief. This was an effective safeguard against abuse of power, because a chief's strength and prosperity depended on the number of his followers. Thus the patriarchal principle was offset by the principle of

popular consent. The balance was summed up in two proverbial sayings: *Morena ha a tentšoe moluopo* (The chief can do
no wrong) and *Morena ke morena ka batho* (A chief is a chief
because of the people).[1]

Every chiefdom and practically every village included
people of different *liboko* and families of Nguni as well as
BaSotho origin. In Mokhachane's village of Menkhoaneng,
for example, there was an Nguni called Ntšekhe whose son,
Makoanyane, became thoroughly assimilated. He was
initiated with Moshoeshoe and became his right-hand man.[2]
The nomenclature of chiefdoms followed no set rules. Sometimes people referred to a chiefdom by the *seboko* of its
ruling family, but usually they added the personal name of
the man who was deemed to have founded the chiefdom.
Mokhachane's people were known as the Koena of Mokoteli
or, for short, the Mokoteli.

3. *The Historical Background of Moshoeshoe's World*

In isolated, small-scale, pre-literate societies historical
knowledge consists mainly of the traditions of prominent
families, and the BaSotho of Moshoeshoe's day were no
exception. Today we can see their history in a broader
perspective, we can correlate the traditions of the different
chiefdoms, and we can use evidence provided by archaeologists and linguists. On the other hand the BaSotho have
experienced such profound social and political changes
since Moshoeshoe was a young man that much of what they
did know has been lost or obscured.

The hunters (San) of LeSotho were descended in the main
from people who had lived in southern Africa for many
millennia and they may undoubtedly be regarded as the
aboriginal inhabitants. They did not smelt metals nor did
they produce food by agriculture or stock-farming.

During the first millennium A.D. people were working iron,

---

[1] Guma, 'Traditional Literature', pp. 115, 119, as corrected by Mosebi
Damane. The literal meaning of the first phrase is that nobody may adjust the
loincloth of the chief.
[2] Arbousset (1), pp. 286 ff.; Anon, *Leselinyana*, 28 Sept. 1911.

growing sorghum, and herding sheep and cattle in and
near the Transvaal. Archaeologists have shown that iron
was being worked at Castle Peak in western Swaziland and
Broederstroom north of Johannesburg by the fifth century,
and near Tzaneen in the northern Transvaal probably by
the third century. The introduction of iron-working, agriculture, and stock-farming to those areas was almost certainly
connected with a gradual infiltration from the north of small
groups of negroid peoples who spoke Bantu languages.[1]

We do not know when the first Bantu-speaking farmers
settled south of the Vaal river valley: that would require
extensive archaeological work and a considerable amount of
luck in identifying occupation sites. We do know that by the
fourteenth century—and probably much earlier—Bantu-
speaking farmers had created two main, distinctive cultures
in South Africa: the SeSotho culture with its nucleus in the
Transvaal high veld and the Nguni culture with its nuclear
area in Natal.[2]

The traditions of the BaSotho chiefly lineages, which were
systematically collected after Moshoeshoe's time, show that
by A.D. 1500, if not earlier, some of the SeSotho-speaking
farmers were moving southwards from the valley of the
Vaal and spreading out across the plains of the Orange
Free State towards the Caledon valley, in small autonomous
groups. These early SeSotho-speaking settlers called themselves Fokeng, but they eventually adopted several different
liboko.

During the seventeenth and eighteenth centuries more
SeSotho-speaking farmers moved southwards into the Orange

[1] This is not the place to review the highly technical literature on the pre-
history of southern Africa. For recent summaries see D. W. Phillipson, 'Early
Iron-using Peoples of Southern Africa', Brian Fagan, 'The Later Iron Age
in South Africa', Monica Wilson, 'Changes in Social Structure in Southern
Africa', and Martin Legassick, 'The Sotho-Tswana Peoples before 1800',
in Leonard Thompson, ed., *African Societies in Southern Africa: Historical Studies*,
London and New York, 1969; R. R. Inskeep, 'The Archaeological Background',
OHSA i. 1–39; B. M. Fagan, *South Africa*, London and New York, 1965; R. J.
Mason, *The Pre-History of the Transvaal*, Johannesburg, 1962, and 'Background to
the Transvaal Iron Age—new discoveries at Olifantspoort and Broederstroom',
Journal of the South African Institute of Mining and Metallurgy, lxxiv (6) (1974).
[2] Monica Wilson, *OHSA* i. 75–107, 131–42; Fagan, in *African Societies*,
pp. 66–70.

Free State. Among them were the Hoja, who came from the north-west and, like the Fokeng before them, spread out widely and had distinctive customs; but most of the SeSotho-speaking settlers of the seventeenth and eighteenth centuries were led by members of three lineages, who claimed to be distantly related to each other and who themselves divided, time and time again, to form clusters of small, independent chiefdoms, some of which adopted new *liboko* to emphasize their autonomy. One such cluster was derived from the Taung chiefly lineage; another developed from the Khatla lineage, which spawned the Phuthing, Kholokoe, Tlokoa, and Sia chiefdoms and their offshoots; the third was the Koena lineage, which produced many chiefdoms that retained the name Koena and others that called themselves Hlakoana and Khoakhoa. By Moshoeshoe's time chiefs of these three clusters had gained control over most of the inhabitants of the plains between the Vaal River and the Maloti mountains, with the Koena predominating in the upper Caledon valley, though some of the Fokeng and Hoja remained independent under their own chiefs.[1]

SeSotho-speakers were not the only farming settlers in the area in the seventeenth and eighteenth centuries. Nguni-speakers, from their nuclear area below the mountain escarpment, also moved into the lands between the Vaal River and the Maloti mountains. A series of small groups detached themselves from the Nguni chiefdoms in the Tugela valley and crossed the watershed to the north of the Drakensberg, where it is relatively easy to do so. Some of these, such as those who became known as the Tšoeneng, settled around the valleys of the Wilge and the upper Vaal; others spread southwards along the Caledon, becoming known as the Phetla (Pioneers), the Polane, and the Phuthi.[2]

[1] The most substantial compilations of the historical traditions of the BaSotho before the *lifaqane* wars are in E & M, pp. 14–115; Macgregor, *passim*; G. W. Stow, *Native Races* (n.d.), pp. 404 ff., and 'The Intrusion of the Stronger Races', 572968 FOL-STO, South African Public Library, Cape Town. On the Hoja see also James Walton, *Early Ghoya Settlement in the Orange Free State*, Bloemfontein, 1965, and R. S. Webb, The History of the LiHoja (n.d.), Lesotho Archives, Maseru. On the interpretation of these compilations, see Martin Legassick, op. cit., pp. 87–94.

[2] E & M, pp. 21–30; Bryant, pp. 356–7; Stow, 'Intrusion'.

Initially, while the Bantu-speaking farmers were relatively small in numbers, they lived peacefully alongside the indigenous hunters. There was room for all and each profited from the other's special talents. The hunters provided the farmers with game and the farmers increased the food supplies of the hunters. The Phetla, Polane, Phuthi, Fokeng, Hoja, and Taung chiefdoms all have traditions of peaceful accommodation and frequent intermarriage with San. Such marriages were usually between male farmers and female hunters, and the children were brought up as members of the farming communities. In this way the farmers incorporated many of the members of the aboriginal hunting bands. Such marriages continued to take place in the nineteenth century, when BaSotho chiefs still made a point of taking aboriginal women as junior wives, thereby strengthening their claims to dominion over the land. Moshoeshoe himself did so.[1]

The farmers in turn were influenced by the hunters. San words were taken into the SeSotho vocabulary and the BaSotho adopted many of the San place-names. To this day the map of Lesotho and the Orange Free State is studded with click names. Also, according to one tradition, the BaSotho took over the San technique for circumcising boys.[2]

By the late eighteenth century, however, the population between the Vaal River and the Maloti mountains had increased to such an extent that farmers were competing with hunters for game and water supplies. Where conflicts occurred, the farmers eventually prevailed. Some San took refuge on the mesa-like mountains that rise above the high veld plateau; others withdrew to the Maloti and Drakensberg ranges in the south-east or to the arid country in the west.

The build-up of population also led to increased interaction among the farming peoples. In most parts of the Orange Free State and the Caledon valley BaSotho greatly outnumbered Nguni, with the result that the Nguni settlers

[1] On relations between the farmers and the San, see p. 13 n. 1, above and also Stow, 'Intrusion'.
[2] Guma, 'Circumcision', p. 241.

lost their independence and their distinctive culture. A typical example of this process was the family of Makoanyane, Moshoeshoe's initiation-mate, who were incorporated into Mokhachane's chiefdom. Other Nguni moved southwards, beyond the range of the burgeoning Koena, Khatla, and Taung clusters of chiefdoms, but they too became strongly influenced by SeSotho culture.

The people who became known as Phuthi were the most striking example of this process. After breaking away from a Zizi chiefdom in the Tugela valley in the seventeenth century, a small group of Nguni settled on the high veld alongside the Phuthing chiefdom (a member of the Khatla cluster) in the valley of the Elands River, where they remained for about fifty years. There they intermingled with the Phuthing, adopted the SeSotho style of dress, and began to use the *phuthi* (duiker) as their totem and to call themselves Phuthi. Early in the eighteenth century the Phuthi chief quarrelled with his Phuthing neighbour and moved away to the Caledon valley with his followers. Under intermittent pressure from the north, the Phuthi moved south-westwards and southwards in successive stages until by the end of the century they had settled in the valleys of the Maphutseng and the Makhaleng and were pushing out cattle-posts towards the Orange River in the Quthing area. During their migration from the Elands, the Phuthi had encountered numerous bands of hunters and absorbed many of their women. They had also mingled with Fokeng communities and adopted still more of the cultural traits of the BaSotho. Their language, for example, incorporated a large number of SeSotho words. In southern LeSotho they had also encountered the Phetla and Polane chiefdoms which, like themselves, were of Zizi origin. Eventually, these chiefdoms began to amalgamate. Mokuoane, the heir to the Phuthi chief, married Maili, a member of the Polane ruling lineage, and in 1795 a son, Moorosi, was born to them. Moorosi's destiny was to be closely linked with that of Moshoeshoe.[1]

---

[1] The traditions of the Phuthi lineages as reported by E & M, pp. 24–30, Macgregor, pp. 46–50, Stow, 'Intrusion', pp. 108–33, and Mosebi Damane,

To summarize our knowledge of the historical background of Moshoeshoe's world: for several generations before Moshoeshoe's birth Bantu-speaking farmers had been colonizing the grasslands of the plateau south of the Vaal river valley from the north and the east, at the expense of the indigenous hunters. Except in the far south-west, the settlers from the north were more numerous than those from the east. Most of the ruling lineages were of Transvaal origin and the predominant culture was derived from the Transvaal. Indeed in cultural terms Moshoeshoe's people formed the southern fringe of a continuum that extended backwards with only minor variations across most of the grasslands of the Transvaal, eastern Botswana, and western Swaziland. But there were no political institutions or trade networks to bind these SeSotho-speaking peoples together. They were divided among numerous independent chiefdoms, which were linked only by tenuous genealogical relationships, buttressed by nebulous myths of origin. In the Caledon valley at the southern end, in particular, miniscule chiefdoms were still constantly being spawned by fission from the old.

Fission was the structural accompaniment of expansion. The process had developed while land suitable for cultivation and stock-farming was available further south. But by Moshoeshoe's time the population had become dense in relation to the environment and the farmers' technology, and further expansion was blocked by the greatest mountain massif in southern Africa. Except where the mountains were dissected by the valleys of the upper Orange river system, this region was not suitable for cultivation.[1] Deprived of their traditional outlet, the BaSotho were running short of land. Overpopulation and overstocking were beginning to cause soil erosion in the Caledon valley.[2] Famines were

Morena Moorosi, Morija, n.d., are difficult to reconcile in detail; but the process seems to have been as described in the text.

[1] See the topographical map, p. 330; also P. Smit, *Lesotho: a Geographical Study*, Pretoria, 1967, and Lucas G. A. Smits, 'The Distribution of the Population in Lesotho and Some Implications for Economic Development', *Lesotho*, vii (1968), 19–35.

[2] Robert C. Germond, *Chronicles of Basutoland*, Morija, Lesotho, 1967, ch. 3, surveys the evidence in missionary writings, 1833 ff., and concludes

more frequent and more devastating. Allegations of witch-craft—a sure sign of social dislocation in pre-industrial societies—were numerous.[1] And clashes between chiefdoms were becoming more venomous than before.

4. *'Thou wilt be called to govern men'*

Moshoeshoe's great-great-grandfather Monaheng had been the first Koena chief to lead his followers into the Caledon valley from the north. After Monaheng's death in about 1700 his descendants had multiplied, prospered, and quarrelled. They quarrelled over women and cattle, they quarrelled over status, they quarrelled for power.[2]

In Moshoeshoe's youth the status of his father was ambiguous. (See Genealogical Table, p. 367.) For one thing it was well known that Mokhachane's father, Peete, was not the biological grandson of Monaheng, for there had been a scandal in the family. When Motloang, the third son of Monaheng, died he left a widow who was still of child-bearing age, but no surviving children. By custom the widow should have gone to live with Motloang's younger brother, Mokoteli, to raise up seed by him for the House of Motloang, but this she refused to do. Instead she went to live with a certain 'Mualle, who was a foreigner by birth and a man of no standing. An Nguni from across the mountains, he never even managed to speak SeSotho properly. People said he went *pete-pete* when he spoke, so they called his son Peete. But Motloang's widow soon tired of 'Mualle, and Peete was brought up by Mokoteli. In SeSotho custom Peete was the

---

(pp. 71–2) that soil erosion of the gully or donga type had begun in the Caledon valley by 1833 as a result of overstocking. But since the population was much denser in 1822, before the disasters of the *lifaqane*, than it was in 1833, it is probable that the erosion had started before the *lifaqane*.

[1] Hence the apprehensions of Mohlomi, p. 26, below.

[2] E & M, pp. 75–85, 90–105. Additional details in Nehemiah [Sekhonyana] Moshesh, 'A Little Light'; Azariel Sekese, *Leselinyana*, 1 and 15 Apr. 1892 and 15 Nov. 1905; Abram RaMatšeatsana, *Leselinyana*, 15 Apr. 1891; M. Nchakala, *Leselinyana*, 15 June 1891; Anon., *Leselinyana*, 5 Oct. 1911; Macgregor, pp. 9–19; Tlali Moshoeshoe, Litaba tsa Basutu (1858); Arbousset (2); and Nehemiah Mosheh to J. M. Orpen, 4 Dec. 1905, Ellenberger Collection.

legal son of Motloang. Nevertheless his descendants called themselves the people of Mokoteli.[1]

Peete himself was not a popular or successful man, nor was his elder son, Libe. Libe had a reputation for meanness, many of his children died, one after the other, and he was said to be bewitched.[2] But Peete's younger son, Libenyane (little Libe) or Mokhachane, was generous and prospered. He attracted followers, accumulated cattle, and became recognized as the leading member of the Mokoteli family. Nevertheless we have no firm evidence that Mokhachane controlled more than the single village of Menkhoaneng. Descendants of other sons of Monaheng lived on either side of the Caledon between Fothane (near modern Fouriesburg) in the north and Qiloane (the Thaba Bosiu area) in the south, and some of them had many more followers than Mokhachane. They included the Koena of Motloheloa, the second son of Monaheng, who ruled villages along the Maoa-Mafubela stream a few miles south of Menkhoaneng: and the Motloheloa claimed that the Mokoteli were their subordinates.[3]

With these antecedents, at the time of his marriage in about 1810 Moshoeshoe was merely the senior son of a village headman who had pretensions to independent status. The traditions concerning the beginning of Moshoeshoe's own career have come down to us in a very distorted form. We have to interpret them in the light of the circumstances in which they have been preserved and transmitted. They were first recorded in writing by French missionaries who had talked with Moshoeshoe and his followers after Moshoeshoe had already become a great chief and the missionaries had become dependent on his favour. The BaSotho informants had an interest in exalting the role of Moshoeshoe, and the missionaries, writing for publication in France, had an

---

[1] E & M, pp. 99–100; Nehemiah [Sekhonyana] Moshesh, 'A Little Light', p. 226. This is essentially the story that Moshoeshoe himself related to Arbousset in 1840 (Arbousset (2), pp. 74–5). Modern informants descended from Mokhachane (I. 1–17) do not dispute the story.

[2] E & M, loc. cit.; Arbousset (2), pp. 53–4, 74–5.

[3] E & M, pp. 99–105.

interest in presenting the traditions in ways which would attract financial support for their Society from the French public. Many years elapsed before BaSotho wrote about these events, and for many more years the only BaSotho who did so were the products of mission education, writing for publication in colonial and mission journals, and greatly influenced by the missionary version. Our problem is to interpret the traditions in the light of these factors.[1]

Fresh from his *lebollo* the young Moshoeshoe seems to have acted like any other vigorous son of a MoSotho village headman. Cattle-raiding was both a manly sport and a way of increasing one's family's wealth, and Moshoeshoe seems to have enjoyed it as much as anyone and to have been more successful than most of the young bloods of the area.[2] As we have seen, he chose the name Moshoeshoe to identify himself as a victorious raider. The traditions suggest that his initiation-mate Makoanyane was the instigator of many of the cattle-raids, but missionaries may have exaggerated the role of Makoanyane, because he became one of the first BaSotho converts to Christianity.[3]

During Moshoeshoe's youth the most influential MoSotho in the area was a man named Mohlomi, who lived on the other side of the Caledon river, about thirty-five miles west of Menkhoaneng. Mohlomi, the son of Monyane the sixth son of Monaheng, created a deep impression on his contemporaries and after his death he was venerated as the most heroic Koena ancestral spirit of his generation. His name was then invoked by supporters of Moshoeshoe to validate the new order he was creating after the calamities of the early 1820s; and in turn the Mohlomi tradition was given fresh twists by the French missionaries, who added miraculous events derived from statements made by one of

[1] Arbousset (1), pp. 270–95; T. Jousse, 'Moshesh', pp. 7–9; Nehemiah [Sekhonyana] Moshesh, 'A Little Light'; E & M, pp. 106–11.

[2] On the heroic tradition among the BaSotho see Finnegan, Guma, and Kunene.

[3] It is especially in Arbousset (1), pp. 286–93, 313–15, that the role of Makoanyane is stressed. Arbousset (1), pp. 286–7, and Nehemiah [Sekhonyana] Moshesh, 'A Little Light', p. 227, say Makoanyane was initiated with Moshoeshoe, which is the tradition I have followed; E & M, p. 109, says that Ntšekhe and his son Makoanyane joined Moshoeshoe later.

Mohlomi's widows after she had been converted to Christianity. In this form the tradition was first published at length by the missionary Thomas Arbousset in 1842 and it was further elaborated in the account published by D. F. Ellenberger in 1912. More recent published versions, by BaSotho as well as white authors, depend very greatly on Ellenberger's account.[1] I have not been able to discover any living oral traditions concerning Mohlomi that have not been deeply influenced by Ellenberger. As Dr. Guma says, Mohlomi is now 'largely regarded as a legendary figure. The historical fact that he once existed is being pushed into the background and emphasis laid on the miraculous events accruing around his name.'[2] It is therefore difficult to delineate Mohlomi's actual personality and achievements.

The core of the Mohlomi tradition, as developed by Arbousset and Ellenberger, is that when he was a boy undergoing initiation he had a vision one night in his *mophato* when God told him: 'Go, rule by love, and look on thy people as men and brothers.'[3] In later life he became a highly successful doctor, diviner, and rainmaker. He was also an indefatigable traveller. He went on foot to visit peoples as far away as the Tswana on the verge of the Kalahari Desert, the Venda near the Limpopo River, the Nguni near the Indian Ocean, and the Phuthi near the confluence between the Caledon and the Orange rivers. As he travelled, he advised his chiefly hosts to rule their subjects wisely, to care for the poor, to abstain from warfare, and not to punish people who had been accused of witchcraft. In return for his medical services he acquired great wealth in cattle and with these cattle he was able to marry an exceptional number of wives and thus to create reciprocal kinship ties with numerous chiefly families. He also provided *bohali* for many

---

[1] Arbousset (1), 272–85; Macgregor, pp. 13–14; Nehemiah [Sekhonyana] Moshesh, 'A Little Light', p. 227; Sekese, *Leselinyana*, 1 Apr. 1892, 26 June and 3 July 1913; E & M, pp. 85, 90–8, 106–9; Leoatle, ch. 1; Mopeli-Paulus, chs. 3 and 15; S. M. Guma, *Morena Mohlomi, 'Mora Monyane*, Pietermaritzburg, 1960.

[2] Guma, 'Traditional Literature', p. 15.

[3] E & M, p. 90, following Arbousset (1), p. 276.

of his *bahlanka* and allowed his unmarried followers access to the huts of his junior wives. Towards the end of his life he became pessimistic about the prospects of the BaSotho and on his death-bed, in about 1816, he predicted that disasters would befall them: 'After my death, a cloud of red dust will come out of the east and consume our tribes. The father will eat his children. I greet you all, and depart to where our fathers rest.'[1]

Arbousset and Ellenberger say that Moshoeshoe was taken by his grandfather, Peete, to see Mohlomi when he was visiting a village near Botha Bothe.[2] Mohlomi advised Moshoeshoe never to kill people accused of witchcraft, to extend his influence by marrying many wives, and to assist people in distress. Mohlomi is also said to have identified Moshoeshoe as his heir, even though he himself had many sons. According to Arbousset, Mohlomi told Moshoeshoe, 'Some day, in all probability, thou wilt be called to govern men. When thou shalt sit in judgment, let thy decisions be just. The law knows no one as a poor man.'[3] Ellenberger added further details, saying that Mohlomi gave Moshoeshoe remarkable tokens of his esteem, 'brushing his forehead against his own' as a sign of blessing, and presenting him with one of his own ear-rings, an ox, a shield, and a spear.[4] Modern BaSotho authors and informants repeat this version, with variations and embellishments.[5]

These accounts are obviously distorted, but they contain a core of historical truth. Mohlomi was evidently an exceptional man. Above all he seems to have been the only

---

[1] E & M, p. 97, following Arbousset (1), p. 282.

[2] The versions differ in detail on almost every point of the Mohlomi tradition. Nehemiah Moshesh (i.e. Sekhonyana son of Moshoeshoe) says Moshoeshoe was sent by his father, Mokhachane, to visit Mohlomi: 'A Little Light', p. 227.

[3] Arbousset (1), p. 208.

[4] E & M, p. 106.

[5] See, e.g., Leoatle, ch. 1. Guma, *Mohlomi*, and Mopeli-Paulus, op. cit., ch. 3, are the longest accounts, but they, too, are embellishments of Ellenberger's. Informant 18 says that Mohlomi was an effective paramount chief of the Koena of Monaheng, which was certainly not the case. He also considers that all the Koena knew that Mohlomi was by birth the senior chief of the House of Monaheng and that it was Mohlomi who convened the *lebollo* for Lepoqo's initiation, neither of which was so.

MoSotho of his generation who perceived that the BaSotho chiefdoms were heading towards a crisis as a result of their quarrelsomeness and their victimization of scapegoats (witches) for private and public misfortunes, though he may not have realized that the underlying problem was the increase in the population density. Later in his life Moshoeshoe spoke of Mohlomi with admiration[1] and when he was very old he told his son Molapo that Mohlomi had indeed given him good advice.[2] But Mohlomi was in no sense a paramount chief of the Koena of Monaheng and there is no reliable evidence that Moshoeshoe himself ever claimed that Mohlomi had designated him as his successor.

Nevertheless Mohlomi seems to have stimulated Moshoeshoe's ambition and encouraged him to behave humanely and rationally. After their meeting, we are told, Moshoeshoe began to play a more purposeful role in the affairs of the Mokoteli. On one occasion he is said to have persuaded his father to spare the life of a criminal who would otherwise have been put to death. On another, with Makoanyane he carried out a successful attack on the Motloheloa in their own principal village in the Maoa-Mafubelu valley and put an end to their pretensions to be overlords of the Mokoteli. Moshoeshoe also began to attract a personal following. For example he persuaded the Mokoteli to restore cattle they had seized from a Fokeng named Makara, who had a reputation as a doctor and diviner, with the result that Makara and his people became Moshoeshoe's devoted supporters.

Later, in about 1820, when he was about thirty-four years old, Moshoeshoe left Menkhoaneng to found his own village below Botha Bothe mountain. Besides his own growing family, his followers included a few senior men who had been councillors of his grandfather, Peete; several of his initiation-mates and their wives and children; the Nguni family of Ntšekhe, including Makoanyane; and Makara and his people. Soon after he settled at Botha Bothe the Fokeng of

---

[1] In 1840, Moshoeshoe described Mohlomi as 'a wise and gentle king'; Arbousset (2), p. 16.

[2] E & M, pp. 107–8.

Ntsukunyane, his mother's people, also looked to him for leadership. Thus, in characteristic SeSotho style, Moshoeshoe took the first steps towards founding his own chiefdom, which comprised members of his own lineage, his wife's lineage, and other followers of diverse *liboko*. He still regarded himself as his father's man; but, as the vigorous headman of a growing village eight miles from Menkhoaneng, he had considerable scope for initiative when the calamities which Mohlomi is said to have predicted struck the peoples of the Caledon valley.[1]

[1] E & M, pp. 106–11; Nehemiah [Sekhonyana] Moshesh, 'A Little Light', pp. 287–9; Anon., *Leselinyana*, 15 Apr. and 15 June 1891; Sekese, *Leselinyana*, 15 Apr. 1892; Mopeli-Paulus, ch. 4.

II

HE BUILDS A CHIEFDOM IN A
TIME OF TROUBLES

1. *The Cloud of Red Dust from the East*

DURING Moshoeshoe's youth dramatic events were taking place among the northern Nguni below the mountain escarpment.[1] There, as in the Caledon valley, until the later eighteenth century the political units were small, segmentary chiefdoms and the chiefs made political decisions in consultation with councillors and local headmen. There, too, there was a shortage of land by Moshoeshoe's day. In addition the northernmost Nguni chiefdoms were competing for control of the trade with Delagoa Bay, where the Portuguese had a base for exporting ivory and importing beads and brass ware. These tensions led to conflicts which resulted in structural changes. In the first phase able chiefs began to reverse the process of political fragmentation by creating loose confederations of chiefdoms with standing armies. Zwide built one such confederation on the northern side of the Mfolozi River and Dingiswayo built another on the southern side.

The second and final phase was dominated by Shaka. Born at about the same time as Moshoeshoe, Shaka was the illegitimate son of Senzangakhona, head of the small Zulu chiefdom, by a woman named Nandi. Ejected from Senzangakhona's homestead, Nandi moved with her child from village to village, quarrelling with her successive hosts. During his early manhood Shaka served in Dingiswayo's army, distinguishing himself as a courageous and resourceful warrior. After Senzangakhona died in about 1816, Dingiswayo assisted his protégé to become installed as chief of the Zulu in place of the legitimate heir. Two years later Dingiswayo himself was captured and killed by his old

---

[1] The sources for the origins of Shaka's Zulu kingdom are discussed by Leonard Thompson in 'The Zulu Kingdom', *OHSA* i. 334–64.

enemy, Zwide. Shaka then succeeded Dingiswayo as the most powerful chief on the southern side of the Mfolozi. Unlike Dingiswayo he welded his subjects into a centralized kingdom.

Building on Dingiswayo's innovations, Shaka conscripted his adult male subjects into his army. Each regiment consisted of all the men of one age group from all parts of the kingdom. Between campaigns Shaka stationed the regiments in stockaded garrison towns at strategic points. The men lived under Spartan discipline, segregated from women, and they were not allowed to marry until their regiment was demobilized, when they were about forty years old. This military organization promoted loyalty to the state and its ruler at the expense of the old loyalties to chiefs and kinship groups.

Shaka also revolutionized the methods and objectives of warfare. In addition to the traditional long spears which were thrown from a distance, he trained his warriors to kill their enemies with short stabbing spears in hand-to-hand combat; and in place of mere cattle-raids he waged wars of destruction and of conquest.

Soon after the death of Dingiswayo, Shaka brought his chiefdoms under his own control and then defeated Zwide and incorporated his subjects also. By 1821 he controlled nearly all the territory between the Pongola and the Tugela. Thereafter he sent his regiments further afield on annual expeditions, killing the local inhabitants and looting their cattle. They devastated the country between the Tugela and the Mzimvubu rivers and they attacked settlements still further south. They also pillaged on the high veld beyond the Drakensberg mountains.

Shaka overrode the traditional Nguni checks upon rulers. He made his own political and military decisions and he appointed and dismissed subordinates at his pleasure. He used his middle-aged female relatives to keep an eye on his military officers and on the members of the conquered chiefly lineages whom he permitted to administer the civilian population. If he suspected a subject of disloyalty he had him killed, usually without the semblance of a trial.

A military genius, Shaka refashioned northern Nguni society at a time when it was suffering from great internal strains and he created the most powerful military state that ever existed in pre-colonial south-eastern Africa. But the cost in human suffering was terrible. His regiments made life precarious for all the peoples in south-eastern Africa and he practised capricious and conspicuous violence upon his own subjects.

Shaka's praise name was Dlungwana (the Ferocious One). His praises began with a paean to the great conqueror:

Dlungwana son of Ndaba!
Dlungwana of the Mbelebele brigade,
Who raged among the large kraals,
So that until dawn the huts were being turned upside-down.
He who is famous as he sits, son of Menzi,
He who beats but is not beaten, unlike water,
Axe that surpasses other axes in sharpness . . .[1]

They were also an ode to a tyrant:

He who while devouring some devoured others
And as he devoured others devoured some more.
Painful stabber, they will exhort one another,
Those who are with the enemy and those who are at home . . .
You are a wild animal! A leopard! A lion!
You are a horned viper! An elephant . . .
King, you are wrong because you do not discriminate,
Because even those of your maternal uncle's family you kill . . .[2]

At the height of his power Shaka slept in a separately stockaded section of one of his regimental barracks, surrounded by women; but he acknowledged no child as his own and he murdered at least one child whose mother claimed it was his. Modern writers have variously classified Shaka as a great lover, as a latent homosexual, or as impotent.[3] When his mother died in 1827—some said it was he who ordered her to be killed[4]—he presided over a mass

[1] Trevor Cope, ed., *Izibongo: Zulu Praise Poems*, Oxford, 1968, p. 88.
[2] Ibid., pp. 96, 108, 110.
[3] E. A. Ritter, *Shaka Zulu*, London, 1955, pp. 201 ff.; Max Gluckman, The Rise of the Zulu Kingdom (unpublished paper); Morris, p. 54.
[4] Arbousset (1), p. 150. Arbousset's informant was a former personal servant of Shaka's successor, Dingane.

slaughter of hundreds of his subjects and decreed that none should have sexual intercourse for a year. In the following year he strained his army beyond the limits of endurance, first sending it on an arduous campaign to the south against the Bhaca and Mpondo chiefdoms and then, without respite, ordering it to the north against a band of Zwide's former subjects who had fled to the vicinity of Delagoa Bay. On 22 September 1828, while his army was beyond the Pongola River, two of his half-brothers and his personal servant killed Shaka in broad daylight. But there was no reversion to the earlier political system. One of his assassins, his half-brother Dingane, seized power and ruled the kingdom.

The wars of Zwide, Dingiswayo, and Shaka had profound repercussions throughout a large part of eastern Africa. Many of the survivors of disrupted northern Nguni communities fled southwards to take refuge among the southern Nguni chiefdoms, where they were known as Mfengu (homeless wanderers). Others fled northwards in organized bands, conquering and subjecting the chiefdoms in their paths and setting up a series of military states which eventually extended as far north as modern Tanzania.[1]

For the inhabitants of the high veld the effects were catastrophic. Matiwane, chief of the Ngwane (an Nguni people who lived around the sources of the Mfolozi), was attacked in turn by Dingiswayo and by Zwide. He fled westwards and fell upon another Nguni chiefdom, the Hlubi, who occupied the sources of the Tugela. Matiwane defeated the Hlubi and killed their chief. The Hlubi then split. Some fled southwards, becoming Mfengu. Others under Mpangazitha, a junior son of the deceased chief, crossed the mountain escarpment into LeSotho. This was in about 1821. For a while the Ngwane of Matiwane occupied the territory vacated by the Hlubi, but in about 1822 they too were displaced, when Shaka invaded the area and drove them across the mountains in the wake of Mpangazitha. Soon after that Mzilikazi, a minor chief who had formerly been a subject of Zwide, defied Shaka and fled with a few hundred followers to the Transvaal. These three refugee bands under Mpan-

[1] J. D. Omer-Cooper, *The Zulu Aftermath*, Evanston, 1966.

gazitha, Matiwane, and Mzilikazi invaded the high veld as conquerors equipped with the short, stabbing spear. They overwhelmed the chiefdoms in their paths, seized their cattle and grain, butchered their people, incorporated the survivors, and created military states on the Zulu model.[1]

The BaSotho who bore the first thrust of the invasions were the Tlokoa and the Sia.[2] For several generations these chiefdoms had occupied the valley of the Wilge River. Their territories were easily accessible from the upper Tugela valley because the escarpment is relatively low in that area. Their ruling families were closely connected. Both were branches of the Khatla lineage and they had frequently intermarried.

When the invasions began, Sekonyela was the recognized heir of his deceased father, the chief of the Tlokoa of Mokotleng, but he was still in his teens and had not yet assumed the chieftainship. The regent was his mother, 'MaNthatisi. For a woman to rule was unusual in SeSotho custom, but 'MaNthatisi had exceptional talents. She was also very loyal to her own patrilineage. A Sia by birth, she employed Sia councillors, she had Sekonyela brought up by her brother, and in about 1815 she had him initiated in a Sia *lebollo*.

The Sia and the Tlokoa had long been in contact with their Hlubi neighbours below the escarpment. They exchanged goods, they raided cattle from each other, and several

---

[1] Ibid. See also Omer-Cooper, 'Aspects of Political Change'; William F. Lye, 'The Sotho Wars in the Interior of South Africa, 1822–1837', University of California, Los Angeles, Ph.D. dissertation, 1969; and Thompson, 'The Difaqane and its Aftermath, 1822–1836', *OHSA* i. 391–405. The oral traditions that have been recorded (see following footnotes) differ in detail, especially in the chronology of these invasions of the high veld by Nguni bands.

[2] The main sources for the *lifaqane* wars on the high veld are E & M, pp. 124–7, 130–42, 154–6, 176–89; [Platje Mhlanga] An Aged Fingo, 'A Story of Native Wars', *Cape Monthly Magazine*, 2nd ser. xiv (Jan.–June 1877), 248–52; Moloja, 'The Story of the "Fetcani Horde" by one of themselves', *Cape Quarterly Review*, i (1882), 267–75; N. J. van Warmelo, *History of Matiwane and the Amangwane Tribe as told by Msebenzi to his kinsman Albert Hlongwane*, Union of South Africa, Department of Native Affairs, Ethnological Publications, vii (1938). Recent accounts are in Marion How, 'An Alibi for Mantatisi', *African Studies*, xiii (1954), 65–76; J. D. Omer-Cooper, *Zulu Aftermath*, ch. 6; William F. Lye, 'The Difaqane: the Mfecane in the Southern Sotho Area', *JAH* viii 1 (1967), 107–31, and 'The Sotho Wars'; and Leonard Thompson, *OHSA* i. 391–405.

Hlubi groups who broke away from their own chiefs settled among the Tlokoa and Sia. At the time of the Hlubi invasion their relations were strained. 'MaNthatisi had allowed a Hlubi named Motsholi, who was married to a sister of Mpangazitha, to settle in her country with his followers, but in about 1817 Sekonyela and his age-mates had invaded Motsholi's village, killed Motsholi, and hacked off his brass collar as a trophy. Consequently when Mpangazitha himself fled to the high veld in about 1821 he had no compunction in falling upon the Tlokoa and the Sia, seizing their grain and their cattle, and driving them away from their homes.[1] Then, when Matiwane appeared on the scene some months later, he fell with zest upon his old enemy Mpangazitha.

That was the beginning of the *lifaqane*,[2] the time of troubles for the BaSotho. For several years there was chaos as the BaSotho chiefdoms competed with the Nguni invaders and with one another for diminishing supplies of grain and cattle. Between about 1821 and 1824 three main communities of men, women, and children, led by 'MaNthatisi, Mpangazitha, and Matiwane devastated the settlements in the Caledon valley and the grasslands to the north, dispersing the inhabitants, colliding with one another, and losing and gaining adherents. 'MaNthatisi attacked settlements as far apart as Botha Bothe, Kurutlele (near modern Senekal), and the triangle between the Orange and the Caledon rivers, and then returned towards her starting-point. Mpangazitha and Matiwane did much the same, sweeping westwards towards the Orange–Caledon confluence and doubling back eastwards again.

[1] On the Tlokoa and the Sia in this period see E & M, pp. 38–51, Macgregor, pp. 27–37, and J. C. K. Makoro, *Histori ea Batlokoa*, Mazenod, Lesotho, n.d. Mosebi Damane (Informant 39), the MoSotho historian, who is of Sia descent, supplied me with valuable information; and Captain R. S. Webb provided me with a copy of a letter from Felix Sekonyela, dated 10 Mar. 1955, which clarified the chronology of these events, which is confused in E & M.

[2] *Faqane* (plural *lifaqane*) is the SeSotho version of the Nguni word *mfecane*, meaning a forced migration. *Lifaqane* has been used as a proper noun by Ellenberger and Macgregor (p. 117) and later writers (R. A. Paroz, *Southern Sotho–English Dictionary*, Morija, 1961, p. 71) to apply to these wars in LeSotho, and the word is used in that sense by BaSotho today (Leoatle etc.).

During 1824 two of those communities settled on and around flat-topped mesa-like mountains near the Caledon, which they selected for defence: 'MaNthatisi's at Marabeng and Joalaboholo (near modern Ficksburg) and Mpangazitha's twenty miles further south-west at Mabolela (between Ladybrand and Ficksburg). Matiwane occupied the land around Senyotong (near Teyateyaneng). But there was no peace among them. In about March 1825 the struggle between Matiwane and Mpangazitha reached a climax in a five days' battle on the right bank of the Caledon. Mpangazitha was killed and his followers fled or became servants of the Ngwane.[1]

By that time the isolated and conservative society into which Moshoeshoe had been born was utterly disrupted. Most of the livestock and the grain stores were destroyed; most of the fields ceased to be cultivated. Many chiefdoms lost their entire ruling families and vanished as organized communities. Virtually every MoSotho had been driven from his home and subjected to deprivation and suffering. In many places human bones littered the landscape for another decade. After they had disintegrated only the stone walls of abandoned cattle kraals and homesteads remained as evidence of the pre-*lifaqane* population.

Demoralized survivors wandered around singly or in small groups, contriving to live on game and veld plants. Thousands had fled: some to the north, where they caused further devastations in the modern Transvaal; others into the Maloti and Drakensberg mountains; others to the south-west where they obtained a footing in the Griqua chiefdoms of Andries Waterboer and Adam Kok, or took service with white farmers in the Cape Colony, or crossed the mountains and joined the southern Nguni chiefdoms. Thousands more had died—by the spear, from starvation, and even from cannibalism, which was the ultimate proof that a society had disintegrated and its moral norms had collapsed.[2]

[1] The preceding paragraphs are adapted from my account in *OHSA* i. 391–4.

[2] On cannibalism during the *lifaqane* see E & M, pp. 217–26, and Arbousset (1), pp. 52–8. BaSotho historians accept the account by E & M—e.g. Leoatle, ch. 6, and Mopeli-Paulus, ch. 8. Arbousset and Ellenberger contend that the

In 1840 RaKotsoane, who had been the leader of a large band of cannibals, told the missionary Arbousset what had happened:

Hunger . . . was the first cannibal, it devoured us: numerous as we were, without cattle, without grain, little game in the plain and this plain being occupied by our enemies, what was to become of us? Each one ate his dog, then the sandals he wore on his feet, then his old antelope kaross, finally his leather shield. . . . After six or eight days of suffering, our limbs seemed to grow bigger, the joints would swell, our heads would become drowsy, our bodies in general and particularly our necks would become numb; terrible dysentery forced everyone to leave the cave frequently; and outside a hyena would take you and drag you to her young. Those who were courageous enough to hunt, or gather were especially exposed to becoming prey of the ferocious beasts which in those days of general famine spied upon us and finding us very weak would feed on our limbs, in the fields as well as at home, like enraged animals. Then we started to rush upon people and to devour them.[1]

Another cannibal leader told Arbousset:

Many preferred to die of hunger; others were duped by the most intrepid ones, who would say to their friends when they arrived from the field, weakened by fatigue and famished: *Here is some rock rabbit meat, get some strength*; however, it was human flesh. Once they had tasted it, they found it was excellent. . . . Yet perhaps it was cursed, because after having eaten it for several days, many people died of dysentery caused by it. All the evil that happened in our country cannot be told. Rataba, one of our principal chiefs, deceived the people. If you went searching for roots with him he would jump on you, he would tear you to pieces; then he would carry the parts to a remote place in a forest to devour them in secret like the panthers do. At home, in your absence, he would seize upon your children, he would cut off an arm and would throw it on a fire, and would feast on it, while his wives boiled the rest of these victims in pots; and in the fields he took pride in the surname of Lerimo

---

BaSotho who became cannibals during the *lifaqane* were adopting a custom that had long been practised by the Venda of the Transvaal: Arbousset (1), pp. 278–80, E & M, pp. 94–5, 217–8. This is not true.

[1] Arbousset (2), pp. 20–1.

(pre-eminent cannibal) which he had given himself. Finally, this man did so much that we ate him in his turn.[1]

The missionary asked him what he felt about these atrocities. According to Arbousset the man replied: 'Our heart *gnawed* us from within; but we were getting used to that type of life, and habit soon replaced the horror we had felt before.'

During the 1840s the French missionaries recorded autobiographical statements by converts. One declared that when his people were scattered by Nguni invaders, his father was killed, his mother died of starvation, and he attached himself to other BaSotho who were soon eaten by cannibals. He then took to the mountains and lived there alone for a year.[3] A second said that after being driven from their home by Mpangazitha his parents were caught, cooked alive, and eaten by RaKotsoane's people. He himself then went mad and believed he was bewitched, but he became the *mohlanka* of a warm-hearted patron who cured him of his madness by placing an iron collar round his neck.[4] A third convert told his missionary that mothers had eaten their own children and he and his family had fled to take refuge among the white farmers in the Cape Colony.[5]

In 1877 the dictated memoirs of Mhlanga, a Hlubi survivor of the *lifaqane*, were published in the *Cape Monthly Magazine*. After the Hlubi had been defeated by the Ngwane, Mhlanga wandered on his own in the upper Caledon area:

I was wandering on a path. I saw a man who called to me to stop. He came to me and told me to sit down. He caught hold of my skin mantle. I left it in his hand and ran as fast as I could. He was a cannibal, and wished to kill me. Afterwards I met two children. . . . One was dead. The living one was eating the flesh of the dead one. I passed on. Next I saw a company of people digging plants. I was afraid of them and hid myself. When I was still going I saw a long stone wall, not very high. There were people sitting there cooking. I saw human heads on the ground. I took another way and escaped from these cannibals.

[1] Ibid., pp. 21–2.
[2] Ibid., p. 22.
[3] Casalis, 29 June 1840, *JME* xvi (1841), 1–11.
[4] Arbousset, 29 Dec. 1841, *JME* xvii (1842), 201–15.
[5] Rolland, 7 Mar. 1842, *JME* xvii (1842), 361–74.

I came to some people of Ngojo [Tlokoa]. They asked me who I was. I told them. It was night already. They took me to a hut, where I slept. To get warmth I slept in the fire circle, from which the fire had been taken. I found my father with the people of Ngojo. While I was there my father went one day to steal cattle. He returned with two.

From this village we went to another one. We saw on the way some Basutos in a cave under a rock. They asked us to stay with them, but we would not. We were afraid. We saw the skulls of many people beside this rock. . . . I then went to a village. The Amangwana [Ngwane] came there and destroyed the village. I was taken away by them. . . . We became servants. Tshaka [Shaka] sent an army to fight with Matiwana. We were defeated and the Amazulu went back again . . .[1]

2. *The Struggle for Survival: Botha Bothe*[2]

The first intimation that Moshoeshoe had of the dangers emanating from beyond the mountains was in about 1820, when Matiwane led a preliminary raid into LeSotho. After attacking several communities near the Elands River, Matiwane penetrated as far south as the village Moshoeshoe had recently founded below Botha Bothe mountain. Deprived of most of his livestock, Moshoeshoe retreated to his father's home at Menkhoaneng. There he was attacked by Letuka, son of Mabula, a Fokeng chief whom Matiwane had dislodged from his home near the escarpment. Letuka captured more of Moshoeshoe's livestock and two of his wives; but counter-attacking, Moshoeshoe broke up Letuka's band, regained his cattle, and freed the captives. He also took prisoners, including two of Letuka's wives whom he kept for himself.[3]

In dealing with these first invaders Moshoeshoe used diplomacy as well as force. Before Letuka attacked he tried to buy him off with a present of cattle; and when Matiwane had retired below the mountains to fall upon the Hlubi, he sent messengers after him with a gift of five head of cattle. When still greater disasters befell the BaSotho in 1822,

[1] Mhlanga, pp. 250-1.   [2] See pp. 334-5, Note 5, below.
[3] On Letuka, see *JME* xx (1845), 403-4; E & M, p. 147; and D. F. Ellenberger in *Leselinyana*, Sept. 1917.

Moshoeshoe's response was similar. From time to time he paid tribute to various chiefs, including Mpangazitha and Matiwane, in the hope of avoiding conflict, but whenever he was attacked he fought back fiercely. Sometimes his gifts bought him immunity. Mpangazitha left him alone on his sweep southwards and so did Matiwane. But several lesser men raided him. In retaliation Moshoeshoe overwhelmed Motake, a Fokeng who lived in the Maoa-Mafubelu valley, and also the Fokeng chief Sephella, stripping them of their cattle.

The first formidable band of BaSotho raiders to operate in the Menkhoaneng area was led by Shekeshe, a Sia chief whom Mpangazitha had displaced from his home. Shekeshe ruined the Koena chiefs Mpiti and Sekake and killed Sekake. Moshoeshoe then fell on Shekeshe and demolished his band, capturing many cattle and three young girls. Two of these he took as wives for himself and the third he handed over to his half-brother Mohale. The surviving members of Shekeshe's chiefdom transferred their allegiance to Moshoeshoe, who then returned to his village below Botha Bothe mountain.

By that time Moshoeshoe had sent messengers to Lethole, the Khoakhoa chief, whom Mpangazitha had driven southwards from his home near 'Makalane (modern Clarens). Moshoeshoe proposed that they should form an alliance to defend the upper Caledon valley. As in other BaSotho chiefdoms, there were men of Nguni origins among the Khoakhoa. Some of Lethole's Nguni planned to assassinate Moshoeshoe, but Lethole prevented them and came to an agreement with Moshoeshoe. Each would remain autonomous, but they would co-operate against aggressors and in so doing they would act under the leadership of Moshoeshoe. In accepting Moshoeshoe as the leading partner in their alliance Lethole was expressing unusual confidence in a man whose origins were relatively obscure and whose followers were fewer than his own.[1]

---

[1] To this day the Khoakhoa chief and councillors set great store by their alliance with Moshoeshoe, stressing that it was an alliance between equals: Informant 22.

Soon after the conclusion of this alliance 'MaNthatisi's Tlokoa band invaded the area and captured Lethole. Lethole was ransomed with cattle but then, without Moshoeshoe's knowledge, Lethole invited Sepheka, the leader of a Nguni band, to join him in an attack on 'MaNthatisi's brother. The attack was successful, but then Lethole quarrelled with Sepheka over the distribution of the booty and he was captured and killed by Sepheka's people. During the next few years the Khoakhoa suffered greatly at the hands of the Tlokoa and other ravaging bands. Nevertheless Moshoeshoe always regarded them as his allies. He brought up Lethole's son and heir, Matela, among his own people and in later years he profited from the Khoakhoa alliance.

Meanwhile the Tlokoa advanced towards Moshoeshoe at Botha Bothe. Moshoeshoe attacked them and drove them into their camp, destroying their cooking pots, so that the engagement became known as the Battle of the Pots. But the Tlokoa rallied and Moshoeshoe fled southwards again to his father's village at Menkhoaneng. The Tlokoa followed and drove Moshoeshoe and his father and their followers deep into the Maloti mountains, where they lived precariously for several months. They had no grain and few livestock and game was scarce, but they became experts in extracting the maximum food value from the indigenous plants.[1] Later, with the help of one of Mpangazitha's sons, they managed to drive the Tlokoa away. Moshoeshoe then occupied Botha Bothe mountain, while his father and brothers re-established themselves at Menkhoaneng.

Botha Bothe mountain is a typical mesa—a sandstone hill about 300 feet high. The summit—an area of about two square miles—contains some good pasture-land and a strong perennial spring. It is a formidable natural fortress, but there are several relatively easily negotiable passes through the cliff face and on the southern side there is a narrow neck joining the mountain to the main Maloti range.[2]

[1] Semion Feko, *Leselinyana*, 16 Nov. 1911, lists the food plants that the BaSotho ate in times of famine. See also A. Jacot Guillarmod, *Flora of Lesotho*, Lehre, 1971, pp. 408–58, for the uses BaSotho made of indigenous plants.

[2] On the Botha Bothe mountain see James Walton, 'Villages of the Paramount Chiefs of Basutoland: I. Butha Buthe', *Lesotho*, i (1959), 15–21. I have

At first Moshoeshoe occupied a vast cave, just below the summit on the southern side. Later he built his village on top of the mountain. His councillors opposed these decisions, for previously only the despised San hunters had lived in caves and on mountain tops.

Meanwhile the young Tlokoa chief Sekonyela was anxious to make a name for himself independently of his renowned mother, 'MaNthatisi. He decided to attack the Mokoteli again in the hope of gaining control of the upper Caledon valley. Becoming aware of Sekonyela's intentions, Moshoeshoe sent for his father and his brothers, who joined him on his mountain with their followers. Moshoeshoe thereby assumed the leadership of the Mokoteli. Mokhachane, who was in his sixties, was content to take second place to his energetic senior son, who had had the imagination to discern the defensive potential of the mountain and had been the first to occupy it. Moshoeshoe built his own village on the northern side, just above the most accessible pass, and his brothers, Makhabane and Posholi, and his half-brother Mohale defended the other passes. They improved the natural defences of the mountain by building stone walls across the passes and the *lingaka* doctored the fortress with protective medicines.

For three months Sekonyela besieged Botha Bothe mountain, assisted by Letlala, his mother's brother, and Nkhahle, the chief of the other main branch of the Tlokoa. They aimed to starve out the Mokoteli by destroying all the crops in the fields around the mountain and preventing herdsmen from coming down to water and pasture their livestock. As the Mokoteli began to run short of food and their cattle began to die, Moshoeshoe tried various ruses. At one stage an old woman attempted to frighten the enemy away with a magical scarecrow, but the Tlokoa were not misled. Moshoeshoe did get some relief by coming to an agreement with Nkhahle, who was stationed on the western side of the mountain. Nkhahle allowed Mokoteli herdsmen to come

also benefited from visiting the mountain with Mr. E. M. Sehalahala in 1964 and from information supplied by Mr. Dan Hogan, a Peace Corps volunteer, who was doing irrigation work on the mountain in 1968.

down from the mountain with their cattle and to water and pasture them out of sight of Sekonyela.

Moshoeshoe also looked round for an ally to create a diversion. First he sent a messenger to invite Matiwane to attack Sekonyela, but without effect. He then sent another messenger to Sepheka, the Nguni chief who had killed Lethole. Sepheka duly arrived with a large force and made a surprise night attack on Sekonyela, killing many Tlokoa. Moshoeshoe restrained his own men from intervening in the battle and next morning the Tlokoa managed to drive Sepheka away. But Sekonyela himself was running short of food as a result of his scorched-earth policy and, disheartened by his losses, he lifted the siege.[1]

By that time Moshoeshoe had decided to lead his followers to a new home. Having heard that there was land to the south that had not been so badly devastated by the wars and that it contained a mesa which would make an excellent fortress, he had sent his half-brother Mohale to inspect the area, providing him with an escort of twenty-six men because his route lay through cannibal country. Mohale had returned with the report that the mountain was indeed defensible. Accordingly, a few days after Sekonyela withdrew, the entire Mokoteli community—several hundred people—left Botha Bothe with their livestock and portable possessions. It was June or July 1824—mid-winter and bitterly cold. Already famished by the long siege, the Mokoteli toiled seventy miles on foot, through mountainous country infested by cannibals, spending three nights on the way. As they climbed the Lipetu pass on the second day, the old people, the pregnant women, and the young children who were straggling behind the main column were attacked by the cannibal band of RaKotsoane. A rescue party saved most of the women and children but the cannibals caught Peete, Moshoeshoe's grandfather, and ate him.

As soon as they reached their destination Moshoeshoe took occupation of the mountain that Mohale had reconnoitred. He placed men to guard the passes and he did what was necessary to protect his people from human enemies and

[1] See below, pp. 335–6, Note 6.

malignant spirits. Stones smeared with medicine from his *lenaka* were driven into the ground at the tops of the passes and on the sites he selected for his *lekhotla,* his cattle kraal, and his personal hut. He called the place Thaba Bosiu, Mountain by Night, because, it was said, he arrived there in the evening and this essential protective work occupied him until the night was far advanced. Later, to intimidate enemies, the news was spread that the name meant that at night-time the mountain became larger than life.[1]

Thaba Bosiu is a mesa in the valley of the Little Caledon River, about fifteen miles east of its junction with the Caledon. Unlike Botha Bothe, it is completely detached from all the neighbouring hills. It rises about 350 feet from the surrounding valley. The belt of cliffs that encircles the summit is between twenty and forty feet high, and all of the six fissures that pierce it are steep and narrow. The summit has an area of rather less than two square miles and includes some good pasture and several perennial springs. Thaba Bosiu is a stronger natural fortress than Botha Bothe, but its passes are not quite so difficult to assault as those at Marabeng, where Sekonyela established himself soon afterwards. Nevertheless Moshoeshoe chose more wisely than Sekonyela. Marabeng, on the right bank of the Caledon River, lay open to attack by invaders who swept across the plains from the north or who followed the course of the Caledon valley, whereas Thaba Bosiu lay concealed behind the Berea plateau among the foothills of the Maloti mountains. Moreover the Maloti provided more accessible places of refuge for Moshoeshoe's surplus livestock in the event of prolonged pressure by enemies.[2]

[1] On the migration to Thaba Bosiu see E & M, pp. 146–8; Nehemiah [Sekhonyana] Moshoeshoe to J. M. Orpen, 4 Dec. 1905, Ellenberger Papers; articles in *Leselinyana* by Sekese, 15 Sept. 1892 and 15 Dec. 1905, Nchakala, 1 July 1891, Mlapokaze, May 1903, and RaMatšeatsana, 1 May 1891; and Arbousset, 29 Dec. 1848, *JME* xxiv (1849), 189–90. Information also supplied by I. 39, Mosebi Damane.

[2] On Thaba Bosiu see G. Tylden, *A History of Thaba Bosiu, 'A Mountain at Night'*, Maseru, 1945; James Walton, 'Villages of the Paramount Chiefs of Basutoland: II. Thaba Bosiu, the Mountain Fortress of Chief Moshesh', *Lesotho*, ii (1960), 11–19; and David Ambrose, *Oxfam Guide to Thaba Bosiu*, Lesotho, 1968. I visited the mountain with Mr. E. M. Sehalahala and the

At the age of about thirty-eight Moshoeshoe had found his final home. He was to live there for forty-six years, presiding over the consolidation, expansion, and defence of his chiefdom; and when he died he was buried there.

3. *Thaba Bosiu: Matiwane's MoSotho*[1]

Moshoeshoe's migration to Thaba Bosiu was a move from the area dominated by the Tlokoa chiefdom of 'MaNthatisi and Sekonyela who, though fellow BaSotho, had shown themselves to be irreconcilable enemies, to the area controlled by the Ngwane of Matiwane with whom Moshoeshoe had established a cordial relationship, although they were Nguni. According to Msebenzi, who was an Ngwane, it was Matiwane who rescued Moshoeshoe from Sekonyela and placed him at Thaba Bosiu.[2] Certainly Moshoeshoe regarded himself as Matiwane's vassal at this stage and paid him tribute.

Matiwane was building a new composite kingdom in the Caledon valley in much the same way as Mzilikazi was doing in the Transvaal. After his long feud with the Hlubi came to an end with the defeat and death of Mpangazitha early in 1825, Matiwane gained control over most of the Hlubi survivors. Around Senyotong Matiwane dominated the Nguni and BaSotho peoples he had conquered. Beyond this core area he was trying to reduce his neighbours to the status of vassals. Moshoeshoe's Mokoteli, newly placed at Thaba Bosiu, served his purpose admirably because they protected his southern flank. Conversely, Moshoeshoe was able to consolidate his position at Thaba Bosiu sheltered by Matiwane from attacks from the north.

When Moshoeshoe arrived, the valley of the Little Caledon was occupied by BaSotho under None who, being of the

official guide, Mr. Dickson Rafotho (Informant 56), and his son in 1964 and 1968. See plan, p. 48 and Plates 18–23.

[1] The main accounts by BaSotho are those of Nehemiah [Sekhonyana] Moshoeshoe and Tlali Moshoeshoe, op. cit., and Sekese and other contributors to *Leselinyana*. Accounts by Nguni participants are those of Mhlanga, Moloja, and Msebenzi (see p. 33, n. 2, above). E & M is the major synthesis.

[2] Msebenzi, pp. 24–7.

lineage of Ntsane the oldest son of Monaheng, was a distant
and genealogically senior relative of Moshoeshoe. Driven
from his original home in northern LeSotho, None had
recently ousted the previous inhabitants from the Thaba
Bosiu area. Moshoeshoe tried to keep the peace but this
was too much to expect of his followers, who were famished
by the effects of the siege of Botha Bothe. Led by Moshoeshoe's brothers, Posholi and Makhabane, they cut sorghum
in None's fields. In retaliation None's people seized Mokoteli cattle. Attacks and counter-attacks continued until the
Mokoteli routed None's people and gained mastery over
the lands immediately around Thaba Bosiu.[1]

More important for the future were Moshoeshoe's rela-
tions with the male relatives of the deceased Mohlomi—the
Koena hero of the recent past. Mohlomi's brother, Makhe-
tha, had been driven southwards from his home in northern
LeSotho by Matiwane and had settled nine miles south-
south-east of Thaba Bosiu at Tloutle (modern Roma).
Makhetha resented the intrusion of the Mokoteli into his
vicinity. First he incited None to resist them; and then, when
None had been ousted, he and his sons harassed other
BaSotho who were turning to Moshoeshoe for protection.
At one stage Moshoeshoe attacked and captured Makhetha,
but then he released him, anxious not to antagonize the
family of Mohlomi.[2]

During the siege of Botha Bothe and his early years at
Thaba Bosiu, Moshoeshoe attracted new adherents. Some
were men of standing with followers and cattle. Such was
Mokakailane, who joined Moshoeshoe at Botha Bothe
having been ill treated by his brother Sekonyela, the
young Tlokoa chief.[3] Another was Khoabane, chief of the
Marabe section of the Koena. During the wars Khoabane
had occupied Marabeng mountain until he was ousted by
Sekonyela soon after Moshoeshoe settled at Thaba Bosiu.
Then, after being severely mauled by the Ngwane and by

[1] Nehemiah [Sekhonyana] Moshesh, 'A Little Light', pp. 228–30; Sekese,
Leselinyana, 15 Sept. 1892; RaMatšeatsana, *Leselinyana*, 1 May 1891.
[2] 'A Little Light', pp. 230–1.
[3] Ibid., p. 288.

Makhetha's people, Khoabane found sanctuary with Moshoeshoe, with his surviving followers and livestock.[1] There
was also Letele, a son of Mohlomi. Driven from Hlohloloane
mountain (modern Clocolan) by the Ngwane, he fled,
destitute, to Moshoeshoe, who treated him with respect,
made him a senior councillor, and provided him with
bohali for a wife.[2] Besides these leading figures, numerous
individuals and family groups of humble origins attached
themselves to the chief of the Mountain by Night. Some
were BaSotho whose chiefdoms had been wiped out in the
wars; others were Nguni, including Hlubi who joined
Moshoeshoe after the defeat of Mpangazitha.

One of Moshoeshoe's most distinguished new adherents
was Tšapi. Of Nguni origin, Tšapi was a diviner with a
reputation for exceptionally accurate predictions. When we
first hear of him he was attached to Sekonyela. Then,
according to tradition, during the siege of Botha Bothe he
got within earshot of Moshoeshoe and prophesied that in six
days' time new enemies would attack Sekonyela and oblige
him to lift the siege and that Moshoeshoe would then
migrate southwards to occupy another mountain and consolidate his chiefdom. Later, after Sepheka had arrived as
predicted and while the Mokoteli were on their way to
Thaba Bosiu, Tšapi is said to have visited Moshoeshoe and
made further predictions. On his new mountain, he told
Moshoeshoe, 'All the black races will be broken in by you.'
Not long afterwards Tšapi joined Moshoeshoe on Thaba
Bosiu and he stayed there until he died in 1871. Moshoeshoe
consulted him frequently, especially before embarking on
military expeditions. He became the most famous diviner
in LeSotho and was believed to be able to communicate
with the spirits of Moshoeshoe's ancestors and interpret their
wishes.[3]

So long as Moshoeshoe was a vassal of Matiwane, most of

[1] Ibid., pp. 230–1.
[2] Nehemiah [Sekhonyana] Moshoeshoe to J. M. Orpen, 15 Apr. 1905,
Ellenberger Papers.
[3] Nehemiah [Sekhonyana] Moshoeshoe to J. M. Orpen, 4 Dec. 1905,
Ellenberger Papers; Casalis (1), pp. 284–6. See Maeder's portrait of Tšapi,
Plate 9.

his followers lived on the top of Thaba Bosiu. The chief's village was built on flattish land towards the northern end of the mountain and its *lekhotla* was the focal point of the chiefdom. According to Sekhonyana, Moshoeshoe's son who was born in 1826, the village consisted of three divisions, corresponding to the households of Moshoeshoe's three senior wives. His junior wives (*lingoetsi*) had their separate huts but were attached to one of the three households and performed the roles of domestic servants and sleeping partners for Moshoeshoe and his favoured guests. They and the men of the village were under the control of officers who were placed in charge of each House. Makoanyane, Moshoeshoe's age-mate and military councillor, was in charge of the House of 'MaMohato; Thafeng, a Mokoteli, was responsible for 'MaNneko's House; and Letele, son of Mohlomi, controlled the House of 'MaSekhonyana.[1]

Moshoeshoe's village was within a quarter of a mile of the easiest access to the top of the mountain—the Khubelu or RaFutho pass—as well as the RaMaseli pass. The other passes were guarded by Mahao, 'MaMohato's eldest brother, who had married Moshoeshoe's sister 'MaTšoeunyane (Maebeng pass); Makhabane, Moshoeshoe's brother (RaEbe pass); and Mokhachane, the chief's father, who built his village on the south-west corner of the summit (Mokhachane's pass). Other villages were under Posholi (the chief's brother), Makara (his early Fokeng adherent), RaTšosane (a Koena of the Molibeli lineage), Khoabane (the Koena of Marabeng), and RaTseala (of Nguni origin). Though all these villages, except perhaps that of Makara, were on top of the mountain, during the day there was much activity in the valley below, where women cultivated the fields and herdboys pastured the livestock. It is not possible to determine the size of Moshoeshoe's chiefdom at this time. In 1905 Sekhonyana wrote that Moshoeshoe's own village had then

---

[1] Nehemiah [Sekhonyana] Moshoeshoe to J. M. Orpen, 4 Dec. 1905. Mosebi Damane, I. 39, points out that Sekhonyana, as the eldest son of Moshoeshoe's third wife, had an interest in stating that the first three wives had senior status. This was Nguni custom. In SeSotho custom there is no fixed number of senior wives and Moshoeshoe may have recognized as many as six at various times.

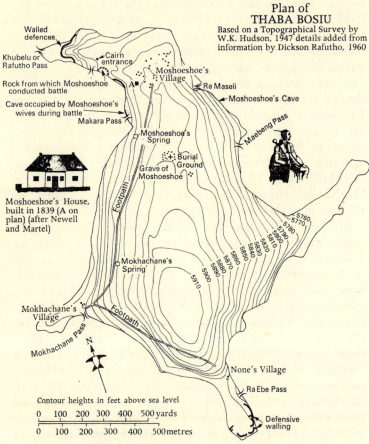

Plan of
THABA BOSIU
Based on a Topographical Survey by
W.K. Hudson, 1947 details added from
information by Dickson Rafutho, 1960

Walled defences

Khubelu or Rafutho Pass

Cairn entrance

Moshoeshoe's Village

Ra Maseli

Rock from which Moshoeshoe conducted battle

Moshoeshoe's Cave

Cave occupied by Moshoeshoe's wives during battle

Makara Pass

Maebeng Pass

Moshoeshoe's Spring

Burial Ground

Grave of Moshoeshoe

Moshoeshoe's House, built in 1839 (A on plan) (after Newell and Martel)

Footpath

5760
5770
5780
5790
5800
5810
5820
5830
5840
5850
5860
5870
5880
5890
5900
5910

Mokhachane's Spring

Mokhachane's Village

Footpath

Mokhachane Pass

N

None's Village

Ra Ebe Pass

Defensive walling

Contour heights in feet above sea level

0   100   200   300   400   500 yards

0   100   200   300   400   500 metres

Source : James Walton, 'Villages of the Paramount Chiefs of Basutoland :
II Thaba Bosiu, The Mountain Fortress of Chief Moshoeshoe,' *Lesotho*,
2 (1960), 17.

MAP 1. Plan of Thaba Bosiu

contained 3,000 fighting men, but that was probably too large an estimate.[1]

By 1828 Moshoeshoe's relations with the Ngwane were deteriorating. Although Moshoeshoe continued to pay Matiwane tribute and to treat him with great deference, some of Matiwane's councillors were jealous of the MoSotho's growing power and cattle-wealth and tried to persuade their chief to do away with him. According to one of Matiwane's followers, 'More than one of them said to Matiwane, "Chief, please have that mSuthu of yours killed", but he refused, saying, "As for me, I cannot kill a man who has done no harm." '[2] However, there were several occasions for friction, as when the Ngwane discovered that Moshoeshoe's people had made medicine from the body of an Ngwane who had been killed by Matiwane's executioners.[3] It was fortunate for Moshoeshoe that Matiwane did not bring his over-whelming military superiority to bear against him while the Ngwane were at the height of their power.

Moshoeshoe had probably never reconciled himself to the existence of Matiwane's kingdom in LeSotho on a permanent basis. During 1826, exasperated by Matiwane's onerous demands for tribute, he entered into negotiations with Shaka, sending him gifts that he knew would please him—feathers of ostriches, cranes, and finches for his warriors, and otter and jackal skins—and inciting him to attack Matiwane. This Shaka was not loath to do, for he had never abandoned the hope of avenging himself on Nguni leaders who had escaped from his control and set themselves up as independent rulers. Late in 1826 Shaka dispatched a powerful army to LeSotho.[4]

Early in 1827 the Zulu army crushed the Tlokoa of Nkhahle (who had separated from Sekonyela after a quarrel), the Fokeng of Tšehlo (whose survivors then joined Moshoeshoe at Thaba Bosiu), and several groups of Khoakhoa. Next it exterminated a community of Hlubi who had

---

[1] Sekhonyana, ibid.; I. 39. See also the plan of Thaba Bosiu, p. 48.
[2] Msebenzi, p. 26.
[3] Sekese, *Leselinyana*, 1 July 1892.
[4] E & M, pp. 171–2; Bryant, *Olden Times*, pp. 141–2.

occupied Hlohloloane after the death of Mpangazitha. Then,
crossing to the left bank of the Caledon near modern Maseru,
it ravaged much of the country as far as the Orange River
before retracing its footsteps. During these operations the
Zulu fought two major engagements against Matiwane, first
at Likhoele (near modern Mafeteng) where the Ngwane
broke and fled, and then, on their return journey, north of
Makulukameng (Platberg), where there was tremendous
slaughter on both sides. The Zulu invasion radically changed
the balance of power in LeSotho. Matiwane lost large
numbers of men and cattle, but the Tlokoa of 'MaNthatisi
and Sekonyela and the Mokoteli of Moshoeshoe, surviving
unscathed, emerged relatively stronger than before.[1]

Not long after the Zulu had returned home, Matiwane
heard that his territory was being invaded from the north.
After the death of Mpangazitha one of his sons had attached
himself to Mzilikazi for a while. Now the son was fleeing
southwards back towards LeSotho in a bid for freedom, hotly
pursued by Ndebele regiments. Matiwane sent his main
forces to meet the invaders, but they were defeated and the
Ndebele then ravaged the country around Hlohloloane and
captured many of Matiwane's cattle.[2]

By that time messengers of Matiwane had returned from a
visit to Moshoeshoe with the news that they had encountered representatives of Shaka on a friendly diplomatic
mission at Thaba Bosiu—a report that vindicated those
Ngwane councillors who had always distrusted Moshoeshoe.
Matiwane tried to calm them, presumably because he
realized it would be rash to provoke Moshoeshoe while his
northern flank was being threatened by the Ndebele. Nevertheless a regiment quickly set out to punish the insubordinate
MoSotho. According to Ngwane sources, Matiwane disapproved of this and even sent Moshoeshoe advance warning
of the expedition.[3]

The Ngwane regiment climbed the Berea mountain during

[1] Moloja, pp. 269–70; Sekese, *Leselinyana*, 1 Apr. and 1 June 1893; E & M,
pp. 176–8.

[2] Moloja, pp. 271–2.

[3] Msebenzi, pp. 38–41; Anon., *Leselinyana*, 19 June 1913.

the night in July 1827 and at dawn it debouched into the
Little Caledon valley, crossed the river, and made towards
the passes on the western and north-western sides of Thaba
Bosiu. Moshoeshoe left his women and children on top of his
mountain, where boulders and stones had been collected to
roll and hurl down on any enemies who penetrated the wall
defences that had been built across the passes. His men
confronted the Ngwane in the valley below. His own regiment, the *Matlama*, bore the brunt of the main attack at the
foot of the Khubelu pass. The first section to become
engaged was the *Mollo* (Fire) company commanded by
Mokolokolo, an enterprising Fokeng warrior who had been
attached to Moshoeshoe from his earliest days.[1] Greatly
outnumbered, the *Mollo* began to retreat, but relief came
when Moshoeshoe himself and the *Liqela* (Beggars) company reached the scene. The Ngwane were routed. During
the pursuit Makoanyane is said to have personally killed
ten Ngwane warriors. Thus Moshoeshoe survived the first
major attempt to storm Thaba Bosiu, and he threw off the
yoke of Matiwane.[2]

Meanwhile, after the Zulu had returned home, Matiwane
had sent an expedition southwards across the mountains
to explore the prospects of migrating to a place of greater
security from the relentless Shaka. It returned with a
glowing report on the fertility of the country of the southern
Nguni. Matiwane wanted to migrate without further delay,
but he met serious opposition. His brother Hawana accused
him of cowardice ('you must have eaten the lung of a sheep')
and although Matiwane then had Hawana killed, his
mother and other relatives continued to oppose the move,

---

[1] Informant 28, a descendant of Mokolokolo.

[2] Mlapokaze (who, as a young boy, witnessed the battle from the top of
Thaba Bosiu), *Leselinyana*, May 1903; Nehemiah [Sekhonyana] Moshesh, 'A
Little Light', pp. 231–2, and letter of 4 Dec. 1905; Sekese, *Leselinyana*, 1 May
and 1 July 1892; Arbousset (1), pp. 302–5; E & M, pp. 178–84. The only
surviving Ngwane account, Msebenzi, pp. 38–44, is substantially different.
It says that the Ngwane stormed the passes but were driven back by stones and
javelins thrown down on them from behind the walled defences. However,
Msebenzi himself was not present. Moshoeshoe's regiment, the *Matlama*,
consisted of three companies: the *Liqela* under Makoanyane, the *Mollo* under
Mokolokolo, and the *Linotsi* under RaTšiu (I. 39).

but by August 1827 their confidence in their prospects in LeSotho had been broken by the Ndebele invasion and Moshoeshoe's victory at Thaba Bosiu.[1] Matiwane and most of his followers then moved through southern LeSotho and across the mountains, to carve out a new territory for themselves at the expense of southern Nguni chiefdoms. In August 1828, however, they were crushed by a composite force of British regulars, colonial levies, and Nguni allies under the command of Colonel Somerset at a battle at Mbhlompo near the Mthatha River. Matiwane and a small band of loyal survivors then retraced their steps. As they passed near Thaba Bosiu, Moshoeshoe invited them to stay in LeSotho, but Matiwane preferred to return to the land of his birth, where it was not long before Dingane put him to death.[2]

4. *Thaba Bosiu: Expansion*

The defeat and withdrawal of Matiwane paved the way for the expansion of Moshoeshoe's chiefdom. Previously Moshoeshoe had been limited by the proximity of a neighbour who had vastly superior manpower and treated him as a mere vassal. Now he had become the most powerful and illustrious chief in LeSotho, south of the Tlokoa of 'MaNthatisi and Sekonyela at Joalaboholo and Marabeng.

During the six years following the departure of Matiwane, Moshoeshoe flourished and his fame spread throughout southern Africa. He expanded beyond his Thaba Bosiu fortress to establish control over more and more people and territory, encouraging his followers to resume their farming way of life that had been disrupted during the wars—to build permanent villages, to cultivate the land, and to breed cattle and sheep.

Before the fall of Matiwane, Moshoeshoe had allowed his half-brother Mohale to settle at Korokoro, ten miles

---

[1] Msebenzi, p. 30.
[2] Mhlanga, pp. 251–2; Moloja, pp. 270–7; Msebenzi, pp. 42–75.

south of Thaba Bosiu, and had begun to exert his authority over various groups of survivors of the *lifaqane*. Once Matiwane had left, expansion accelerated. Moshoeshoe offered neighbouring peoples the security of the Thaba Bosiu fortress in the event of further invasions. He lent *mafisa* cattle and sheep to those who were destitute. He also made his leadership attractive by allowing his subjects a great deal of latitude at the village level. This was particularly important for the clusters of Hlubi and Ngwane who had remained in LeSotho after the collapse of Matiwane's short-lived kingdom. He let them live in their own villages under their own headmen and retain their distinctive customs. All he insisted on was that they should co-operate with him against external enemies, bring their disputes with their neighbours to Thaba Bosiu for adjudication, and pay him the honours due to a great chief.

On one subject, however, Moshoeshoe was adamant. He did not tolerate cannibalism. One of the best-known anecdotes about Moshoeshoe concerns his handling of RaKotsoane, the Khatla chief who had lapsed into cannibalism during the wartime famine and had seized and devoured Moshoeshoe's grandfather, Peete, during the migration to Thaba Bosiu. The recorded versions of the story differ in detail but the essential features have the ring of authenticity. RaKotsoane was brought to Thaba Bosiu at a time when it was necessary to perform purification rituals in preparation for the initiation ceremonies for Moshoeshoe's eldest son, Letsie, and his age-mates. Moshoeshoe's councillors, including his father Mokhachane, were for killing the redoubtable cannibal, but Moshoeshoe replied that one does not destroy the tomb of one's ancestor. Instead he had the purification medicines rubbed into the bellies of RaKotsoane and his followers. He then sent them back to their homes with *mafisa* cattle and orders to abandon cannibalism.[1]

Thus Moshoeshoe inspired a moral as well as a material regeneration among the people whom the *lifaqane* had disrupted, scattered, and ultimately deposited in new combinations in southern LeSotho. Wherever his authority

[1] Sekese, *Leselinyana*, 15 June 1906; E & M, pp. 227–8; Leoatle, ch. 6.

extended, however tenuously, life became a little more secure and civility a little more pronounced.

Nevertheless he was aggressive where his material interests and those of his subjects were concerned. Cattle-wealth had always been the gauge of the success of a MoSotho chief. He needed cattle to distribute among his followers, to acquire wives and therefore servants, and to bind clients to him by *mafisa* loans. By the mid-1820s most of the livestock in LeSotho had been destroyed: it was dearth of cattle and grain that had led to cannibalism. Moshoeshoe therefore had strong incentives to obtain fresh supplies of cattle. The most vulnerable of the accessible sources were the herds of the southern Nguni chiefdoms, which had not been transformed into military states like the Zulu. These sources he located and exploited in co-operation with the Phuthi chief Mokuoane and his son Moorosi.

As has been explained, the Polane, the Phetla, and the Phuthi had been the first Bantu-speaking farming peoples to settle in southern LeSotho, and by 1822 Mokuoane was beginning to amalgamate them.[1] During the *lifaqane* they were severely mauled by a series of BaSotho invaders who had been dislodged from their homes further north. Some survivors fled to the Cape Colony where they became dependants of white farmers, others joined bands of San hunter-gatherers in the mountains of southern LeSotho. Mokuoane and Moorosi fled into the mountains and lived by raiding cattle from the southern Nguni until they, in turn, became the prey of BaSotho cannibals led by Motlejoa. In 1825 Moorosi overcame Motlejoa who fled northwards to Thaba Bosiu and Moshoeshoe sent his half-brother Mohale to investigate. Contrary to orders, Mohale attacked the Phuthi and returned to Thaba Bosiu with captured children and cattle. Mokuoane followed Mohale to Thaba Bosiu where, Moshoeshoe was to claim, the Phuthi chief formally submitted to his authority. Mokuoane then returned to his home area and, following Moshoeshoe's example, he settled on a mesa called Bolepeletsa, seventy

---

[1] See above, pp. 18–20.

miles south of Thaba Bosiu beyond the Orange River. During the next few years the leadership of the Phuthi gradually passed from the ageing Mokuoane to his son Moorosi.[1]

After Moshoeshoe had thrown off the yoke of Matiwane, he joined Moorosi in raiding the Thembu. In June 1828, at a time when the Thembu herds were weakly guarded because the men were attending a religious festival, Moshoeshoe and Moorosi seized a large number of cattle. They made another rich haul in December–January 1828–9. The booty from these two expeditions gave Moshoeshoe the means to attach many more people to him with *mafisa* cattle. However, his absence from Thaba Bosiu with most of his fighting men on the second raid nearly led to disaster.[2]

Moshoeshoe had tried to establish cordial relations with his old enemies, the Tlokoa. At the time of the second expedition against the Thembu, Moshoeshoe's senior son Letsie was being initiated with his age-mates in a *mophato* in the valley below Thaba Bosiu. According to an account written many years later by Sekese, who had been a child on Thaba Bosiu at the time, Moshoeshoe invited Sekonyela to join him on this expedition and, when he declined, he asked him to supervise Letsie's *mophato* in his absence and Sekonyela accepted. But the Tlokoa chief was not reconciled to the rise of Moshoeshoe and he seized the opportunity to attack Thaba Bosiu. Sekese says he was assisted by his brother Mokakailane, who had joined Moshoeshoe in 1824 but now betrayed him, informing Sekonyela that the Mokoteli chief's cattle were guarded by women only. Sekonyela launched a surprise attack at dawn. He burnt down Letsie's *mophato* and gained control of the summit of Thaba Bosiu, capturing the royal cattle and seizing 'MaMohato and other women. But Moshoeshoe's maternal uncle, RaTšiu, rallied the elderly men who, with the help of Letsie and his age-mates, routed the Tlokoa, freed their women, regained their cattle, and killed the spy, Mokakailane. Sekonyela and

[1] Sekese, *Leselinyana*, 1 Apr. 1905; Mosebi Damane, *Morena Moorosi*, ch. 1; E & M, pp. 159–64, 186–91.
[2] Damane, ch. 2; E & M, pp. 192–5.

Moshoeshoe would continue to be rivals for the leadership of the BaSotho for another quarter-century.[1]

The two BaSotho chiefs were not left to resolve their differences in isolation. Mzilikazi, the Ndebele leader, had created a military state on the Zulu model north of the Vaal River—a kingdom more powerful, more cohesive, and more enduring than Matiwane's.[2] From headquarters on the Aapies River north of modern Pretoria, his regiments preyed upon the Shona chiefdoms across the Limpopo, the Tswana chiefdoms to the west, and the BaSotho. In 1831 a strong Ndebele force campaigned in the south. After causing havoc among scattered groups of BaSotho who were trying to recuperate from the *lifaqane* between the Vaal and the Caledon, the Ndebele attacked Sekonyela's fortress of Marabeng, but, failing to storm its strong defences, passed on towards Thaba Bosiu. By the time they arrived Moshoeshoe had received warning of their approach. The Ndebele began to scale two of the passes, but the BaSotho hurled boulders, stones, and javelins down on them from behind their walled fortifications and eventually the enemy retired with heavy losses. According to tradition, as the Ndebele withdrew a MoSotho delivered some fat oxen to them, with the message: 'Moshesh salutes you. Supposing that hunger has brought you into this country, he sends you these cattle, that you may eat them on your way home.'[3] In later years Moshoeshoe was to take similar pains to save the face of another powerful but unsuccessful aggressor, a British Governor, General Sir George Cathcart. Mzilikazi did not launch another attack on the Caledon valley. His regiments could plunder more easily among the Shona north of the

[1] Sekese, *Leslinyana*, 15 July 1892 and 1 Apr. 1905; Damane, ch. 2; E & M, pp. 192–5.

[2] The major primary source on the history of the Ndebele of Mzilikazi is 'Mziki [A. A. Campbell], '*Mlimo: The Rise and Fall of the Matebele*, Pietermaritzburg, 1926, which is based on a tradition recited by Malida ka Mabuya. Excellent modern reconstructions are by William F. Lye, 'The Ndebele Kingdom South of the Limpopo River', *JAH* x (1969), 37–54, and 'The Sotho Wars', 1969, pp. 69–76 and 152–90.

[3] Casalis (1), p. 23. The Ndebele attack on Thaba Bosiu is also described in Arbousset (1), p. 312; Anon., *Leselinyana*, 1 Feb. 1906; E & M, pp. 203–11; and Bryant, *Olden Times*, pp. 431–2.

Limpopo. Moreover after 1831 he was hard pressed to defend his own territory against attacks by his old enemies, the Zulu, from the south-east and by new enemies, Coloured raiders, from the south-west.[1]

Since about 1825 Coloured raiders had also been making forays into the Caledon valley. Offshoots of the Griqua chiefdoms, they operated in small bands and were a menace because they possessed horses and fire-arms, which Moshoeshoe had never previously encountered.[2]

The Coloured raiders were encouraged and sometimes aided in their attacks on Moshoeshoe's outposts by relatives of the deceased Koena hero, Mohlomi. Mohlomi's brothers and sons had suffered greatly during the *lifaqane* and after Moshoeshoe moved to Thaba Bosiu he tried to help the survivors and to persuade them to accept his leadership. He treated Mohlomi's brother Makhetha with respect as the headman of a village; he made Letele, one of Mohlomi's sons, a councillor, and to another son, Mojakisane, he lent a substantial number of cattle on *mafisa*. Perhaps, too, it was at this stage that Moshoeshoe began to spread the story that Mohlomi had named him as his successor. But Moshoeshoe's brothers destroyed the prospects of a peaceful accommodation. Against his wishes, Posholi and Makhabane repeatedly raided Mojakisane's cattle and attacked Makhetha, with the result that Moshoeshoe lost the support of the senior surviving members of Mohlomi's family. By 1827 some were allying themselves with bands of San hunters[3] and with the Coloured raiders who were operating from bases east of Philippolis. These raiders repeatedly attacked Moshoeshoe's subjects in their villages, including Makhabane at Ntlokholo and Mohale at Korokoro. Sometimes they got clear away with BaSotho women, children, and cattle; at other times, BaSotho counter-attacked and regained their captives and their property.[4]

---

[1] Lye, 'The Sotho wars', pp. 162 ff.

[2] On the Griqua chiefdoms and the Coloured raiders see below, pp. 106–9.

[3] E & M, p. 197. This was a rare example of San hunter-gatherers fighting alongside Bantu-speaking farmers.

[4] 'A Little Light', pp. 232–3; Arbousset (1), pp. 310–12; Andrew Smith

By 1833 Makhetha had been killed, Letele had left Thaba
Bosiu to join Mojakisane, and Mojakisane had fled with his
followers and Moshoeshoe's *mafisa* cattle as far as Grahamstown in the Cape Colony. Nevertheless the Coloured raids
continued. Thaba Bosiu itself was invulnerable to them, but
Moshoeshoe could not defend the rest of his territory against
sudden attacks by horsemen with fire-arms. He had emerged
triumphant from the *lifaqane* wars, only to be threatened by
the first ripples of the waves of expansion coming from the
British Colony of the Cape of Good Hope.

5. *Rival BaSotho Chiefdoms*

In June 1833 LeSotho came for the first time under the
direct observation of literate people who left accounts which
have survived, when two French Protestant missionaries
and a lay assistant reached Thaba Bosiu from Cape Town
via Philippolis. From then onwards these men and their
successors wrote frequent and often detailed reports from
inside Moshoeshoe's territory to their headquarters in Paris.
Early in 1834 Wesleyan missionaries began to work on the
northern side of the Caledon.[1] In October 1834 Dr. Andrew
Smith travelled through LeSotho at the head of a large
official expedition from the Cape Colony, making copious
notes on his experiences.[2]

Here we describe Moshoeshoe and Sekonyela and their
chiefdoms in the 1830s, with the help of the writings of these
first literate observers. The effects of the alien impact upon
BaSotho society are the subjects of later chapters.

Moshoeshoe, who was about forty-seven years old when the
missionaries arrived, impressed his European visitors. The

Papers, vol. 10, pp. 146–7; Sekese, *Leselinyana*, 1 July 1892; E & M, pp. 196–9
and 212–16.

[1] The reports of the Wesleyan missionaries are in the archives of the WMS.
[2] Dr. Andrew Smith's most extensive records of his expedition are his unpublished journal and extensive field notes in the library of the South African
Museum, Cape Town (Andrew Smith Papers, vols. 10 and 12). *The Diary of
Dr. Andrew Smith, Director of the 'Expedition for Exploring Central Africa', 1834–6*,
ed. Percival R. Kirby, Van Riebeeck Society, Cape Town, 2 vols., 1939–40,
is briefer.

first recorded description we have of him was written by Thomas Arbousset on 29 June 1833:

Moshesh is a well-built man; he has a Roman head, an oval face, an aquiline nose, a little flat, a long chin, and a prominent forehead; his eye is lively, his speech animated, and his voice harsh. He is gracious in all his ways and his smile is benevolent. He is now in the prime of life and seems disposed to make every kind of sacrifice for the love of civilization, of which he is a great admirer.[1]

Later, in his memoirs, Arbousset's comrade Eugène Casalis recalled his first impressions of Moshoeshoe in an oft-quoted and somewhat romanticized passage:

The chief bent upon me a look at once majestic and benevolent. His profile, much more aquiline than that of the generality of his subjects, his well-developed forehead, the fulness and regularity of his features, his eyes, a little weary, as it seemed, but full of benevolence and softness, made a deep impression on me. I felt at once that I had to do with a superior man, trained to think, to command others, and above all himself. He appeared to be about forty-five years of age. The upper part of his body, entirely naked, was perfectly modelled, sufficiently fleshy, but without obesity. I admired the graceful lines of the shoulders and the fineness of his hand. He had allowed to fall carelessly round him, from his middle, a large mantle of panther skins as lissom as the finest cloth, and the folds of which covered his knees and his feet. For sole ornament he had bound round his forehead a string of glass beads, to which was fastened a tuft of feathers, which floated behind the neck. He wore on his right arm a bracelet of ivory—an emblem of power—and some copper rings on his wrists. After we had looked an instant at each other in silence, he rose and said, *Lumela lekhoa*, 'Welcome, white man!' and I replied by holding out my hand to him, which he took without hesitation.[2]

The Wesleyan missionary James Archbell described Moshoeshoe at his first meeting in June 1834 as 'a most intelligent and friendly man'.[3] Andrew Smith noted that when he was dressed in his traditional clothing he 'looked like a man and a chief while his gait and air showed he

---

[1] *JME* ix (1834), 53.
[2] Casalis (2), pp. 176–7. [3] Archbell, 17 Jan. 1834, SA/7, WMS.

felt himself both the one and the other'.[1] Later European visitors were unanimous in praising Moshoeshoe's fine physique and regal bearing. According to his son Tlali, Moshoeshoe as a child was less than the average height; but as a man he was evidently more than six feet tall.[2]

Unfortunately we do not have convincing portraits of Moshoeshoe in his prime. The illustration that purports to be a portrait as he was in 1833 was originally published in the first edition of Casalis's *Les Bassoutos* in 1859 and has frequently been republished.[3] It was engraved in a Parisian atelier and is somewhat idealized.[4] François Maeder, a French missionary assistant, made excellent portraits of several members of Moshoeshoe's family and entourage in 1844–5, but the effect of his drawing of Moshoeshoe is reduced by the western clothing the chief wore for the occasion. By the time Moshoeshoe was photographed in 1860 he was about seventy-four years old, but even then it is a man of great dignity who confronts the camera in his formal Victorian clothing.[5]

Thaba Bosiu was the capital and citadel of his chiefdom. Smith reckoned that 2,000 people lived on and around the mountain in 1834.[6] On the summit there were several dispersed clusters of huts and cattle kraals and two major villages—those of Moshoeshoe and his father Mokhachane. Moshoeshoe's village was by far the largest concentration of people in the chiefdom. According to Casalis,

The town of Moshesh . . . consisted of a mass of low huts,

[1] Andrew Smith Papers, vol. 10, p. 140.
[2] Tlali Moshoeshoe, Litaba tsa Mofuta oa Basuthu, Grey Collection, South African Public Library, Cape Town; T. J. Lucas, *Cape Life and Sport*, London, 1878, p. 245.
[3] Casalis, *Les Bassoutos*, Paris, 1859, p. 17.
[4] The portrait was engraved in the Parisian atelier of Delange in 1859. The engraver was probably provided with a sketch by Casalis (who had some artistic ability); and he certainly referred to the drawing which Maeder had made in 1845. See Plates 1 and 2. Notice, for example, the similarity of the ear-rings worn by Moshoeshoe in the two portraits. Communication from the Revd. Étienne Kruger, former Librarian of the Société des Missions Évangéliques de Paris (now the Service Protestant de Mission et de Relations Internationales, 102 Boulevard Arago, 75014 Paris), 7 May 1974.
[5] See *frontispiece*.
[6] Andrew Smith, *Diary*, i. 114.

around which people circulated by narrow lanes, encumbered with children and dogs. In the middle of the village was a vast space, where the cattle were penned during the night. It was divided into enclosures, whose stone walls, perfectly circular, showed a certain talent in construction. Contiguous to this was the court devoted to business and to public harangues.[1]

This was the home of Moshoeshoe, his wives, his children, his personal servants, and some of his councillors. By 1834 he had thirty or forty wives[2] and, according to Smith's estimate, about forty-eight children.[3] His first wife, 'Ma-Mohato, died that year, when their eldest son Letsie was an initiated youth aged about twenty-two.

Besides his wives there were numerous male dependants in Moshoeshoe's village—men who served him as herbalists, rainmakers, diviners, praise-singers, town criers, personal attendants, and herdsmen. Many of them were *bahlanka*—men who had no livestock except perhaps one or two sheep or cattle on *mafisa* loan. Such men could only marry if Moshoeshoe provided their *bohali*, which amounted to not less than ten head of cattle at that time (though parents of brides would often accept part of the *bohali* in sheep or goats). Moshoeshoe's senior wives were exempt from field work. His junior wives and the wives of his *bahlanka* weeded the fields in the valley below the mountain, and at harvest time he conscripted the services of freemen. The children of *bahlanka* inherited the status of their parents, since Moshoeshoe had provided the *bohali*. As Smith reported, 'Moschush [*sic*] speaks of his own children and then of the children of the oxen that is of the people for whom he has purchased wives. The latter also call him father.'[4]

Undoubtedly Moshoeshoe already controlled more personal dependants and more livestock—and thus more wealth and more labour service—than any chief in the Caledon valley had had at his disposal before the *lifaqane*. In SeSotho society there had always been propertyless men who had been obliged to become clients of men of substance, but

---

[1] Casalis (2), pp. 178–9.
[2] Ibid., p. 179.   [3] Andrew Smith Papers, vol. 12, p. 30.
[4] Ibid., p. 27. See also Chapter I, p. 12, above.

before 1820 they had been relatively few in number. By the 1830s, however, most men who had survived the wars had lost their cattle. Casalis wrote in 1837: 'With the exception of several individuals who succeeded in keeping their cattle in the recent wars, the people depend entirely on Moshesh and his sons for the means of subsistence.'[1] Two years later James Backhouse, a visiting English Quaker, wrote that during the wars

Moshesh obtained the assistance of such persons as had no cattle, and saved his, and the other people became dependent upon him for milk, which constitutes a principal article of their food. He afterwards lent them cows, but the increase was his; and his stock of milk-cows now amounted to about 20,000; they were dispersed through the numerous villages of his extensive and populous country.[2]

A radical social and economic change had taken place in SeSotho society. The *lifaqane* had drastically increased the proportion of propertyless men and promoted the concentration of wealth—and hence of clients—in the hands of a few successful men, among whom Moshoeshoe was pre-eminent.

Thaba Bosiu's renown as a citadel was established by the repulse of the formidable Ndebele army. Moshoeshoe saw to it that the stone walls defending the passes were kept in good repair. Supplies of boulders and stones were always available at strategic points commanding the passes and watchmen patrolled the perimeter of the mountain throughout the night. The MoSotho adopted neither the weaponry nor the military organization of Shaka. His military innovations were for defence. In response to the attacks that had been made on him during the *lifaqane* he had exploited the possibilities provided by the local terrain. But when his warriors went down from their mountain fortress to drive invaders away or to raid cattle, they used the traditional SeSotho knobkerrie (stick), long spear, battle-axe, and cowhide shield, rather than the short stabbing spear invented by

[1] 24 July 1837, *JME* xiii (1838), 5.
[2] James Backhouse, *A Narrative of a Visit to the Mauritius and South Africa*, London, 1844, p. 375.

Shaka; and they were loosely organized in fighting units under their territorial chiefs, rather than in professional, full-time regiments.[1] The nearest approach to a military specialist in Moshoeshoe's chiefdom was Makoanyane, who commanded the royal regiment under Moshoeshoe.

In the 1830s Moshoeshoe was to a great extent a personal ruler. He settled many petty disputes on the spot, reconciling the quarrelsome and imposing fines of cattle, sheep, or goats on offenders. When his anger was aroused he could terrify and sometimes even assault his subjects, but usually he was affable and tolerant of human foibles. On one occasion a missionary was astonished to see that he took an indulgent attitude towards a drunken warrior who abused him in scurrilous terms.[2] Moshoeshoe himself always abstained from strong beer (*joala*), wild hemp (*cannabis sativa*), and even tobacco, declaring 'If I were to drink, I should be talking folly before my people.'[3] In this, we are told, he was following the precedent that had been set by his grandfather, Peete, and maintained by his father, Mokhachane. He heard important cases in the *lekhotla* in the presence of councillors, among whom RaTšiu, his mother's brother, Makoanyane, his age-mate, and Khoabane, his first chiefly adherent, were the most prominent.[4] In a few cases before the arrival of the missionaries he sentenced murderers and adulterers to death, when they were bound and hurled over the sheerest part of the cliff on the eastern side of the mountain. After 1833 he scarcely ever imposed the death penalty.

On special occasions Moshoeshoe sent out messengers to summon his subjects to a *pitso*. Then all the circumcised men who acknowledged his authority came to Thaba Bosiu, carrying their weapons. A *pitso* served several important purposes. It was an instrument for communication—both

[1] Anthony Atmore and Peter Sanders, 'Sotho Arms and Ammunition in the Nineteenth Century', *JAH* xii (1971), 535–44. There are illustrations of a Hlubi warrior of Mpangazitha and a MoSotho warrior in Arbousset (1), pp. 227 and 291; and of a MoSotho warrior in Casalis (1), p. 62.

[2] Andrew Smith Papers, vol. 10, 147–8.

[3] Backhouse, *Narrative*, p. 372. Also Andrew Smith Papers, vol. 12, p. 15.

[4] Casalis (2), p. 184.

downwards from the government to the people and upwards from the people to the government. It was also a festival that promoted a consciousness of solidarity. Proceedings started with praise-singing and dancing. The royal praise-singer extolled the achievements of the king, warriors sang their own individual praises, acting out their parts as they did so, and all of them then joined in long, exhilarating war-dances, with Moshoeshoe himself a tireless and uninhibited performer. Then the official business was conducted. Chiefs and councillors made speeches and the crowd indicated their approval or disapproval. Commoners also took part in the debate, criticizing their seniors quite freely when they wished. Eventually, however, Moshoeshoe terminated proceedings by announcing his decision.[1]

The institutions of Moshoeshoe's growing kingdom were similar to those of the pre-*lifaqane* chiefdoms. One new factor was the enlargement of the political scale. In 1833 the missionaries estimated that Moshoeshoe had about 25,000 followers.[2] By 1838, according to Casalis, 12,000–15,000 subjects could be assembled at Thaba Bosiu within a single day.[3] Another novelty was the unprecedented wealth and prestige of Moshoeshoe. By 1833 he was recognized not merely as a *morena* (a chief) but as the *Morena e Moholo* (the Great Chief: the King).

Nevertheless European observers were wrong when, like Casalis, they concluded that his power was 'absolute'.[4] His councillors, his territorial chiefs, and his warriors were active participants in public affairs. The political system operated by discussion and consent rather than by violence and terror. Indeed Moshoeshoe's control over his subjects was too weak rather than too strong, as is apparent when one considers the kingdom from the territorial point of view.

By 1833, nine years after the migration from Botha Bothe, Thaba Bosiu was the centre of a flourishing sedentary popu-

---

[1] Andrew Smith Papers, vol. 10, pp. 143–8, describes the *pitso* at Thaba Bosiu on the occasion of his visit.
[2] Archbell, 17 Jan. 1834, SA/7, WMS.
[3] Casalis, Sept. 1838, *JME* xiv (1839), 90.
[4] Casalis, 24 July 1837, *JME* xiii (1838), 5.

lation. Numerous villages clustered on and around the neighbouring hills, and the valleys were filled with fields of
sorghum and maize. But this nuclear area extended no
more than about ten miles from the capital. Elsewhere in
the Caledon valley the process of rehabilitation from the
wars had hardly begun, except among the Tlokoa around
Marabeng. Over large stretches of fertile country the only
signs of humanity were skeletons and deserted homesteads
and cattle kraals. Moshoeshoe's brother Posholi lived about
twenty miles south-west of Thaba Bosiu, with a following of
young men who preferred the semi-nomadic and aggressive
life of the cattle-farmer and cattle-raider to the more settled
conditions around the capital. At Bolepeletsa, seventy miles
south of Thaba Bosiu, there was Moorosi, growing wealthy
like Moshoeshoe from his share of the booty they had seized
in their joint expeditions against the Thembu. Elsewhere
weaker BaSotho groups cowered on the tops of mountains,
owning no more than a few livestock and scarcely beginning
to resume cultivation. For them the wars were not yet over,
for they lived in constant dread of Coloured bandits. Moshoeshoe's influence extended across the devastated areas to
these communities: south-westwards towards the junction of
the Caledon and the Orange, westwards towards the sources
of the Modder River, and north-westwards towards the
Vet River sources; but his power over them was limited and
sporadic, for he was unable to protect them from their
enemies.

When the first French missionaries travelled to Thaba
Bosiu from Philippolis in June 1833, they kept well to the
north of the Caledon until they reached the vicinity of
Platberg. After leaving Philippolis they passed through
country teeming with game—antelopes, zebras, wilde-
beests, ostriches, and lions—but devoid of human inhabitants except a few San hunter-gatherers, until they reached
the sources of the Modder, where they saw their first BaSotho
village. Proceeding eastwards, they found about 500 BaSotho
living on the upper slopes of Thaba 'Nchu under Moseme,
and another 500 on Thaba Phatšoa. When they reached
the Platberg area (near modern Ladybrand), they met

groups of Hoja and also several hundred Nguni—survivors of the abortive kingdoms of Mpangazita and Matiwane.[1]

In October 1834 Andrew Smith approached Thaba Bosiu by a route on the southern or left bank of the Caledon. He failed to meet the people of Moorosi or Posholi and the first BaSotho he encountered were at Likhoele (near modern Mafeteng), where 'some thirty poor people lived in solitude and fed the few cattle they possessed upon the slopes of the mountain' for fear of plunderers.[2] In 1836, when the missionaries Arbousset and Daumas travelled through the plains north of the Caledon, once they were well clear of the valley they met a few scattered groups of Hoja and San, and for the rest nothing but deserted villages.[3]

North-eastwards from Thaba Bosiu Moshoeshoe's authority barely extended beyond the Berea plateau in 1833. He was cut off from the land of his birth and the entire upper Caledon valley and northern Maloti mountains by the chiefdom of the Tlokoa of Mokotleng, whose young ruler, Sekonyela, would be his principal MoSotho rival for another twenty years.

The chiefdom of the Tlokoa of Mokotleng was the most natural nucleus for the regeneration and reconstruction of SeSotho society after the chaos of the *lifaqane*. Before the wars began, the Tlokoa of Mokotleng had occupied the country around the Wilge river valley (modern Harrismith district) and had been considerably more populous than any of the Koena chiefdoms in the Caledon valley; and during

---

[1] Arbousset, 17 July 1833, *JME* ix (1834), pp. 33–52. In *JME* ix (1834), opposite p. 64, there is a map prepared by Casalis, based on his journey to Thaba Bosiu with Arbousset in June 1833, and his subsequent journey from Morija to Philippolis, showing the routes taken in those expeditions and the estimated limits of the country of the BaSotho. R. S. Webb, in a letter to Morena A. A. Moletsane, dated 3 May 1954, comments on this map and on the route taken by Arbousset and Casalis in June 1833: copy in LeSotho Archives, Maseru.

[2] Andrew Smith Papers, vol. 10, p. 105.

[3] Arbousset (1), which includes a map opposite p. 1. See also Captain William Cornwallis Harris, *The Wild Sports of Southern Africa*, Struik reprint of the 5th edition of 1852, Cape Town, 1963, with a map between pp. 353 and 354. Harris was an officer of the British army in India who spent his leave in 1836–7 on a hunting expedition in the modern Transvaal and Orange Free State. He did not cross to the southern side of the Caledon River.

the wars they had enhanced their reputation and maintained some cohesion under the leadership of the redoubtable 'MaNthatisi. In 1824 'MaNthatisi had settled on Joalabo-holo and her son Sekonyela on the neighbouring mesa of Marabeng (alias Khoro-e-betloa; now known as Sekonyela's mountain), on the right bank of the Caledon (near modern Ficksburg). Marabeng, where they concentrated in time of crisis, is the most formidable natural fortress in the entire region. It is crowned by a sheer cliff and the most accessible pass is commanded by heights on both sides, so that an enemy had to approach the summit in single file and defenders could subject him to a bombardment of stones and boulders from above. Today, though much of the summit is bare rock, it contains at least one strong spring and several acres of good pasturage. The present owner of the land considers that the mountain could carry 500 sheep for three months, or about 10,000 cattle for a week.[1]

Andrew Smith visited Marabeng on 7 November 1834 and noted in his journal:

Early in the forenoon we prepared to ascend the hill upon which was the residence of the chief [Sekonyela]. . . . At first it [the road] was of considerable breadth but near the narrow ravine along which it extended on approaching the summit of the hill, it became narrow and steep. Prior to the occupation of this hill by the Mantatees ['MaNthatisi's people] there was a free access to its summit by this ravine, but since their selection of it for a residence, the break in the perpendicular rocky wall, which like a belt encircles the hill towards its summit, has been obliterated by art. A stone wall of great thickness and not badly built has been carried across, from precipice to precipice, so as to complete what nature had left imperfect. In this wall a small passage, just sufficient to admit men and cattle, has been left, and during the night is secured by a strong wicker gate which thus makes it a perfect enclosure. Immediately inside the gate, upon the highest points of the hill from which the approach

---

[1] On 28 Aug. 1968, Mr. F. R. Duminy, owner of the farm North End which includes Marabeng, accompanied Mr. E. M. Sehalahala, Professor Brian Fagan, and myself on a tour of the mountain. Stone ruins were still to be found on the summit, and below the mountain on the northern side there were more extensive stone ruins of the village where Sekonyela lived later, in relatively peaceful times.

was to be commanded, piles of large stones were everywhere observed having been collected for the purpose of being hurled upon any who might venture to attack the citadel.[1]

It was 'MaNthatisi's policy, like Moshoeshoe's, to attract fresh adherents from the survivors of the shattered BaSotho and Nguni communities, to persuade them to resume cultivation, to build up their herds of cattle, and to extend her authority as far as possible. At the time of Smith's visit many of the small groups living between the upper Caledon and the Vaal regarded themselves as subjects of the Tlokoa, and in 1836 Thomas Arbousset found that the influence of the Tlokoa chiefdom extended about thirty miles north of Marabeng and also some distance to the south, across the Caledon. He estimated that between 1,300 and 1,400 people lived on the summit of Marabeng in peace time and that the total population of the chiefdom was about 14,000 BaSotho and between 2,000 and 3,000 Nguni.[2]

'MaNthatisi made an excellent impression on European visitors. Arbousset described her as 'a woman of great intelligence' with 'a sweet and agreeable expression' and 'a regular countenance and an elegant figure'. But Sekonyela made a bad impression. Arbousset found that he had 'a sullen and unsociable disposition' and that he inspired his own people 'with more of fear than of love'.[3] These statements are confirmed by oral traditions still current among the Tlokoa. Informants declare that Sekonyela was not an effective chief. He did not look people in the eye and perhaps he took too much *dagga* (wild hemp).[4]

Moreover by 1834 there was divided leadership. The old tensions between 'MaNthatisi's Sia favourites and the Tlokoa ruling patrilineage had become compounded with a generational cleavage. When Andrew Smith went on from Marabeng to visit 'MaNthatisi on Joalaboholo, he found that she 'was peculiarly reserved in his [Sekonyela's] presence' because 'she feared if she should seriously displease him he would kill her'. He explained:

It was only shortly before our arrival that he had risen into

[1] Andrew Smith Papers, vol. 10, p. 178.   [2] Arbousset (1), pp. 32–4.
[3] Ibid., p. 31.   [4] Informant 39, Mosebi Damane.

power the tribe having previously been managed by his mother since the death of his father, and such was the faith of most of its members in her judgment that they still insisted on her opinion being ascertained before any matter of importance was decided. The old woman, however, probably better acquainted with the disposition of her son than they were, was fearful of opposing him, and therefore the advantages which . . . might have been derived from her superior discretion . . . were not secured.[1]

Besides this cleavage at the centre the Tlokoa, with their record as ravagers during the *lifaqane* wars, were never very successful in inspiring confidence in other BaSotho and in Nguni communities. Moreover, although Marabeng itself was impregnable when efficiently defended, the greater part of the area which the Tlokoa sought to control was in the open plains to the north of the Caledon, which were very vulnerable to attack by Ndebele regiments and Coloured raiders.

By 1833 Moshoeshoe's chiefdom was surpassing Sekonyela's. He had more wealth and more followers. The basic reason was the difference in the calibre of the two leaders. Unlike his rival, Moshoeshoe was trusted and admired by his subjects and his allies, and respected by his enemies. Also, in selecting Thaba Bosiu as his citadel he had acquired the better-placed nuclear area.[2] Neither leader had solved the problem of dealing with the raiders from the south-west, but Moshoeshoe was the quicker to realize that the solution lay in obtaining his own supplies of horses and fire-arms. He would also respond more intelligently than Sekonyela to the new challenges and opportunities created by the arrival of white people.

[1] Andrew Smith Papers, vol. 10, pp. 184–5.
[2] In 'Sekonyela and Moshweshwe: Failure and Success in the Aftermath of the Difaqane', *JAH* x (1969), 439–55, Peter Sanders writes that he 'does not seek to refute the traditional estimates of the characters of the two chiefs', but that 'basically Sekonyela failed because, after 1829, he was poorer than Moshweshwe' (pp. 454–5). Why was Sekonyela poorer? He was less able.

III

THE KING AND HIS MISSIONARIES

1. *'My heart is white with joy'*[1]

EARLY in 1833 a Griqua hunter named Adam Krotz visited Moshoeshoe and told him there were white men of peace who were being helpful to the Griqua chiefs at Philippolis and Griqua Town. Moshoeshoe said that he too would like to have resident teachers (*baruti*) and he sent herdsmen after Krotz with 200 cattle so that he might get him 'at least one missionary'.[2] A band of Kora stole the cattle; but soon afterwards three Frenchmen reached Philippolis from Cape Town seeking a field for evangelization and Krotz was there to tell them about Moshoeshoe. Convinced that they had received a divine call the Frenchmen hastened to Thaba Bosiu. On 28 June 1833 the king, who was about forty-seven years old, welcomed them as the answer to his request.[3]

By this time Moshoeshoe had picked up scraps of information about what was happening to the south-west of LeSotho from various sources: from friendly Coloured hunters like Adam Krotz; from captured Kora raiders; from two European travellers who had visited him at Thaba Bosiu;[4] from BaSotho of various antecedents who had taken refuge with white farmers beyond the Orange River during the *lifaqane* wars and were now trickling back into the Caledon valley;[5] and from his own messengers whom he sent out to reconnoitre and make contact with the southern Nguni chiefs.[6]

---

[1] The contemporaneous first-hand evidence for this chapter comes exclusively from the European side. The main sources are the *JME* and the works by Thomas Arbousset and Eugène Casalis.

[2] Casalis (2), p. 138.

[3] Ibid., pp. 134–88.

[4] Arbousset (1), pp. 165–9.

[5] Lye, 'The Sotho Wars', ch. 6.

[6] We do not have precise information about the origins and development of Moshoeshoe's extensive diplomatic network.

He now realized that the Kora who were harassing him and limiting his capacity to pacify and control the lands beyond the immediate vicinity of Thaba Bosiu were merely the outer fringe of a diffuse social, political, and commercial network that extended all the way to the Cape of Good Hope, over 600 miles distant. He also perceived that within that network there were two main categories of people—white people (*MaKhooa*) and Coloured people (*BaKhothu*)—and that the former tended to dominate the latter. More dimly, he probably already had some inkling that there were two distinct categories of white people—Boers or Afrikaners (*MaBuru*) and British (*MaNyesemane*)—and that the latter controlled the government at the Cape of Good Hope which exercised varying degrees of influence and authority throughout the network. Moshoeshoe certainly knew that the southern Nguni chiefdoms had been in contact with white people for over half a century and that in 1812 and again in 1819 British soldiers, using fire-arms with devastating effects, had defeated the Xhosa and deprived them of land and cattle.[1] Finally, he was aware that since about 1825 Afrikaners were beginning to cross to the northern side of the Orange river in the wake of the Coloured frontiersmen and pasturing their large herds of cattle and flocks of sheep in the vicinity of Philippolis.[2]

The Kora and the Griqua were clearly the vanguard of more powerful forces. If Moshoeshoe and his chiefdom were to survive, he needed advisers to help him to understand and cope with the complexities of the wider world that was encroaching upon him. From Krotz he had learned that missionaries were a special class of white people who were performing that service for the Griqua chiefs, Andries Waterboer and Adam Kok.[3] If missionaries were doing that for the Griqua, why should they not do it for him?

Moshoeshoe was also anxious to harness the sources of white power. The social and political order into which he

[1] Monica Wilson, 'Co-operation and Conflict: the Eastern Cape Frontier', *OHSA* i, ch. 6; W. M. Macmillan, *Bantu, Boer, and Briton*, 2nd ed., Oxford, 1964.
[2] P. J. van der Merwe, *Die Noordwaartse Beweging van die Boere voor die Groot Trek*, The Hague, 1937. [3] Lye, 'The Sotho Wars', ch. 3.

had been initiated in his *lebollo* had been grievously disrupted. He continued faithfully to perform the sacrifices that he had been taught were necessary to placate the supernatural forces and he frequently consulted Tšapi, the best available diviner. But was it not conceivable that the traditional rituals were no longer sufficient? If the ancestors had been as influential as he had been taught to believe, would they have allowed the horrors of the *lifaqane*: the collapse of the old chiefdoms, the decimation of the population, and the widespread resort to cannibalism? If the medicines in his own *lenaka* were truly potent, would small groups of Kora be able to raid and humiliate him? Perhaps new remedies should be adopted now that he was confronted with phenomena that his ancestors had never encountered during their lifetimes. At least it was worth exploring what the *baruti* had to offer in the hope that he might be able to gain such power as they commanded.[1]

The three Frenchmen who greeted Moshoeshoe on 28 June 1833 were committed to the evangelization of a people of whose very existence they had been unaware when they left Europe. Thomas Arbousset, Eugène Casalis, and Constant Gosselin were all bachelors. The two ordained missionaries were still very young: Arbousset was twenty-three years old, Casalis a mere twenty. Members of old Huguenot families of the *petite bourgeoisie*, they had responded to the surge of missionary fervour that swept the French Protestant churches after the end of the Napoleonic Wars. Arbousset, a vigorous open-air man, was capable of enduring harsh conditions and destined to make his mark as an explorer as well as an evangelist, but it was the more scholarly and gentle Casalis who would establish greater empathy with Moshoeshoe. The third member of the party, Gosselin, was not ordained. Ten years older than Arbousset, a Catholic

---

[1] Moshoeshoe's profound interest in the teachings of the missionaries strongly suggests that the factors mentioned in this paragraph carried great weight with him. Claude Perrot's admirable work, *Les Sotho et les missionnaires européens au XIXe siècle* (Annales de l'Université d'Abidjan, 1970, Série F, Tome 2, Fascicule 1; Dijon, 1970), makes no reference to these special reasons why Moshoeshoe was, from the first, much more receptive to Christian teaching than other African rulers.

convert to Protestantism, and a mason by trade, Gosselin was an unpretentious man who always gave the impression that he was content with his subordinate status as a missionary aide.

The Paris Evangelical Missionary Society (Société des Missions Évangéliques de Paris) had been founded in 1822. The Society was supported by subscriptions from members of many Protestant churches in France and Switzerland, and controlled by a Committee which met in Paris. In 1829 the Committee decided to focus on southern Africa, acting on the advice of Dr. John Philip, the local Superintendent of the London Missionary Society, which had been working in the country since the turn of the century. By the 1820s the London Missionary Society had founded stations for the Griqua at Griqua Town and Philippolis and for the Tswana at Kuruman, as well as several stations in the Cape Colony. The first graduates of the Protestant seminary in Paris went to South Africa in 1829 and by 1831 Prosper Lemue, Samuel Rolland, and Jean-Pierre Pellissier were working among the Hurutshe in the Transvaal.

Arbousset and Casalis spent three years at the seminary in Paris under the supervision of the director, Henri Grandpierre. There they studied theology, Latin, Greek, and Hebrew, and literature, history, and science. They also attended lectures at the Sorbonne, the Museum of Natural History, and the Paris Geographical Society, and served as apprentices to a carpenter and a locksmith. This relatively rigorous training equipped them to master new languages and adapt to strange living conditions more effectually than their British contemporaries of the London and Wesleyan Missionary Societies. The first generation of French Protestant missionaries were also freer of racial pride than most of their contemporaries. But although they did not assume that culture was racially determined they did believe that nineteenth-century European culture was infinitely superior to anything African. As Arbousset wrote in 1832, he expected to be working in a country that was 'entirely strange to civilization'.[1] He and his fellows deemed it to be their duty

---

[1] Henri Clavier, *Thomas Arbousset*, Paris, 1965, pp. 89–92.

to civilize as well as to evangelize and their model of civilization was an idealized version of contemporary Europe.[1] Consequently, like other nineteenth-century European missionaries, the French Protestants would find it difficult to understand and impossible to respect customs that were radically different from their own—especially customs related to sex and marriage, like polygyny and bride-price. Moreover their background and training made them place great stress on the intellectual and individual approach to religion, and ignore or seriously underestimate the social, aesthetic, and psychological needs of Africans.

Initially, Arbousset, Casalis, and Gosselin had expected to join their colleagues beyond the Vaal River, but by the time they reached South Africa Mzilikazi's Ndebele had dispersed the Hurutshe and their missionaries had retreated. Consequently the three newcomers had no precise plans when they arrived at Philippolis and when they heard of Moshoeshoe's appeal it seemed to be the answer to their prayer. They hastened to Thaba Bosiu to assist a ruler who needed them, in the hope of converting him and through him an entire people.[2]

On the evening of 28 June 1833 Arbousset and Casalis explained themselves to Moshoeshoe in the presence of his councillors. In the words of Casalis:

Speaking in our turn, we said how greatly we had been moved by the description which had been given us of the misfortunes of the Basutos and of their present sad position. The observations we had ourselves made proved that these statements had not been exaggerated. We believed that we had for all those evils a sovereign remedy, the efficacy of which it would be difficult for the chief to understand at first, but which we earnestly besought him to try. All the misfortunes of men proceeded from their evil passions and from their ignorance. We were the messengers of a God of Peace, whose protection and love were

---

[1] On the civilizing mission see Clavier, pp. 93–5.

[2] Théophile Jousse, *La Mission Française Évangélique au sud de l'Afrique* Paris, 1889, vol. i, ch. 1; M. A. Boegner *et al.*, *Livre d'Or*, ch. 1; Jean Banquis, *Les Origines de la Société des Missions Évangéliques de Paris*, 2 vols., Paris, 1930–1; and the biographies of Arbousset (Clavier (1965); G. Gallienne, *Thomas Arbousset (1810–1877)*, Paris, 1931) and Casalis (H. Dieterlin, *Eugène Casalis (1812–1891)*, Paris, 1930).

assured us, and who was willing to protect and bless the Basutos also. If Moshesh and his people consented to place themselves with us under the care and protection of this God, we had the most perfect assurance that He would undertake to make the incursions of their enemies cease, and to create in the country a new order of belief and of manners which would secure tranquillity, order, and abundance. In order to prove to our new friends the firmness of our convictions on this subject, and the purity of our intentions, we offered to establish ourselves definitely in their midst, and to share their lot, whatever it might be.[1]

According to Casalis, Moshoeshoe replied as follows:

My heart is white with joy; your words are great and good. It is enough for me to see your clothing, your arms, and the rolling houses in which you travel, to understand how much intelligence and strength you have. You see our desolation. This country was full of inhabitants. Wars have devastated it. Multitudes have perished; others are refugees in foreign lands. I remain almost alone on this rock. I have been told that you can help us. You promise to do it. That is enough. It is all I want to know. Remain with us. You shall instruct us. We will do all you wish. The country is at your disposal.[2]

The mission had begun under the most promising circumstances.

2. '*The truths of the Gospel have conquered*'[3]

Moshoeshoe took the young Frenchmen under his personal protection. Within a week of their arrival he led them south-westwards from Thaba Bosiu to search for a site for their first mission station and when they said they were pleased with an uninhabited valley at the foot of the mountain Makhoarane, twenty-four miles away, he encouraged them to settle there. Moshoeshoe sent his senior sons, twenty-two-year-old Letsie and nineteen-year-old Molapo, with a number of their age-mates, under the supervision of

---

[1] Casalis (2), pp. 182–3.
[2] Ibid., pp. 183–4.
[3] Casalis (1), chs. 2–7, and (2), chs. 10–16; *JME* ix (1834), ff.; Jousse, vol. i, ch. 8.

their *malome* (mother's brother), Matete, with orders to help the missionaries settle down and listen to what they had to say.

The Frenchmen called their station Morija (after the biblical Moriah). Matete's young men provided them with fresh food and helped them build first a log cabin and then a stone house, and plant the seeds they had brought with them from France—wheat, fruit trees, and vegetables. The missionaries readily adapted to their new surroundings and they soon learnt enough SeSotho to be able to dispense with the services of the interpreter they had brought from Philippolis. They also kept in close touch with the king, making frequent visits to Thaba Bosiu.

In 1836 Casalis travelled to Cape Town where he married a young Scottish girl, Sarah Dyke, and in the following year the young couple founded a second station at the foot of Thaba Bosiu, leaving Arbousset in charge at Morija. During 1838 Gosselin completed building the Thaba Bosiu mission house and chapel, aided by BaSotho workmen supplied free of charge by Moshoeshoe. Four to five hundred people attended the Sunday services, and a hundred children and as many adults took lessons from Casalis during the week. On Sunday mornings Moshoeshoe himself came down from the mountain to church and at the end of the sermon he added his own comments for the edification of the congregation. Then he took dinner with Casalis and his wife at the mission house.

Moshoeshoe was an enthusiastic patron of his missionaries. He eulogized them in public, he encouraged his subjects to listen to them, and he gave serious consideration to all their advice. It was Eugène Casalis alone who established exceptional *rapport* with him. When Casalis returned from Cape Town with a wife the king was convinced that he had been sincere in declaring that he intended to make his home among the BaSotho and identify himself with them. Always fond of children, Moshoeshoe was fascinated by Casalis's daughter—the first white child to be born in LeSotho—and distraught when she was carried away by measles in 1839. The king spent hours on end with his missionary inquiring about the wider world, and the more he probed him the more he came to trust the man. When, twenty-two years after his arrival in LeSotho, Casalis eventually returned to Paris to become director of the seminary, Moshoeshoe paid him the greatest compliment he could possibly have expresseed: 'O Casalis, you are my teacher, my father, my mother. . . . *You are a true MoSotho*.'[1]

Casalis, for his part, was drawn to Moshoeshoe. Intellectually, he was intrigued by the king's curiosity; morally, he was impressed by his abstinence from strong drink and narcotics (though not from women); and he found that the king's political goals were largely compatible with his own vision of an independent, peaceful, civilized, and Christian African kingdom.

Moshoeshoe rapidly acquired a taste for the products of European civilization. 'There is no idea about civilization that we expound to him', wrote Arbousset enthusiastically in December 1835, 'that he does not understand; not one of our views on this or that subject of greater or lesser importance for him or his people that he does not approve; nothing in the interior of his house that he does not want to have like us.' Already, Arbousset added, he was amply provided with horses, saddles, European clothes, household utensils, and some colonial products and he understood the use of money as a means of exchange.[2] He always wore European clothes to receive visitors and when he left his mountain. If an African chief was staying with him, as was often the case, on Sunday morning he would fit him out from his wardrobe and bring him to church. In 1840 a visiting Wesleyan missionary reported that 'He was well dressed, a blue superfine surcoat, green military jacket and trousers with a cloth cap under which he wore a woolen [*sic*] cap of various colours; the only ornaments he wore were a number of long eardrops and two or three finger rings'.[3] By that time Moshoeshoe had employed a deserter from the

[1] Moshoeshoe to Directors, 18 Sept. 1855, *JME* xxxi (1856), 54. The italics are not in the original.

[2] Arbousset, 3 Dec. 1835, *JME* xi (1836), 144.

[3] Entry for 24 June 1840, Journal of W. Impey, 1838–1847. Papers lent by the Revd. L. Hewsen, WMS.

72nd Highlanders named D. F. Webber to build him a stone
house like his missionary's—though he continued to sleep
in his traditional hut.[1] He also bought wagons and planted
fruit trees, vegetables, and wheat. He was particularly
concerned to accumulate horses and fire-arms. During the
early 1830s he had captured some from Kora raiders and
began to experiment with them. As the French missionaries
approached Thaba Bosiu for the first time in June 1833,
they were met by a dozen horsemen, including Letsie and
Molapo, who were still 'entire novices in the art of riding',
and when they reached the top of the mountain they were
given a salute of musket-fire.[2] In 1839 James Backhouse, a
visiting English Quaker, found that the price of horses had
risen to ten guineas at Griqua Town because of 'the facility
with which they could be sold to a neighbouring Basuto
Chief'.[3] The trade in fire-arms is less easy to trace, because it
was frowned upon by white public opinion and not recorded
by the missionaries.

The introduction of these novelties by the king as well as
his missionaries set an example to his subjects. To see Moshoeshoe approach in European clothes at the head of a
cavalcade of armed horsemen must have impressed a
MoSotho villager.

Moshoeshoe himself became an expert marksman; but
according to Arbousset he was a poor rider—which probably
meant that Arbousset disapproved of his equestrian style
rather than his efficiency, for the BaSotho regarded him as an
excellent horseman.[4] He was immensely impressed by the
uses of literacy. Arbousset noted that one day during his
reconnaissance of northern LeSotho in 1840 his son Masopha
spent two hours helping him to spell, but the king, already
about fifty-three years of age, never managed to master the
skill.[5]

Moshoeshoe acquired imported goods in various ways.
Many of his clothes and household possessions were given

---

[1] Moshoeshoe to Sir George Napier, Governor, Cape Colony, 20 Apr.
1841, *BR* i. 40–1.
[2] Casalis (2), pp. 173–6.
[3] Backhouse, *Narrative*, p. 352.
[4] Arbousset (2), p. 90.   [5] Ibid., p. 116.

him by European visitors. Some goods he commissioned his missionaries to buy when they went on their shopping expeditions to Colesberg in the Cape Colony. Others he bought from traders who began to visit him soon after the missionaries arrived. Transactions were often by barter, Moshoeshoe giving cattle in return for his needs. Backhouse found that the going rate in Griqua Town in 1839 was six oxen for one horse.[1] From an early stage Moshoeshoe also used currency for some transactions. As early as 1834 he sold Dr. Andrew Smith some oxen for cash.[2] But the greater part of his wealth was always tied up in his vast holdings of cattle. 'Our coins are the cows', he said.[3] In 1839 Backhouse recorded that his milch-cows, including those held by his clients under the *mafisa* system, numbered 20,000.[4]

Casalis and his colleagues were optimistic about the success of their evangelizing and their civilizing of Moshoeshoe. The king was extraordinarily interested in their teaching. His public commentaries on their sermons, Arbousset admitted, often conveyed the essence of what they had been saying in ways that made it more intelligible to the rest of the congregation without distorting it.[5] Moreover Moshoeshoe became worried by a sense of guilt and concerned about his salvation. In 1837 Gosselin reported that Moshoeshoe publicly 'prayed Jehovah to forgive him his sins, to convert him, and give him a new heart, and he asked the same for his wives, his children, his mother and his people'.[6] He also repeatedly advised his people to accept the teachings of the missionaries. In 1842 he was telling former cannibals, 'It is the Gospel that is the source of the prosperity and the peace which you enjoy, and I am perfectly satisfied that any nation that does not enjoy the

---

[1] Backhouse, *Narrative*, p. 352.

[2] Andrew Smith Papers, vol. 10, p. 148. In December 1844 Arbousset reported that the Morija congregation had donated towards the cost of building a new church: £10. 5s. 7d. in cash, 66 head of cattle, 328 sheep and goats, and 4 muids of grain. He valued the cattle at 18s. a head, the sheep and goats at 3s. a head, and the corn at 12s. a muid. *JME* xx (1845), 175.

[3] Arbousset, 3 Dec. 1835, *JME* xi (1836), 144.

[4] Backhouse, *Narrative*, p. 375.

[5] Arbousset, 3 Dec. 1835, *JME* xi (1836), 144–5.

[6] Gosselin, 9 Apr. 1837, *JME* xiii (1838), 15.

instructions of religion is lost.'[1] And in the following year
Arbousset heard him tell his aged father, Mokhachane, that
'the truths of the Gospel have conquered'.[2] Nevertheless
Moshoeshoe did not himself become a Christian, for reasons
which will be explained later.

During these years articles on LeSotho began to appear
in Cape Town newspapers. Three were written by a trader
who claimed to have spent nine months at Thaba Bosiu
and to have dined with Moshoeshoe thirty or forty times.
He declared that one could travel through his country in
perfect safety and that civilization was making rapid strides.[3]
Two other articles were based on information supplied by
the French missionaries.[4] They extolled the king's interest
in modernization:

Moshesh is endowed with a mind naturally fond of improve-
ment. He seems to have felt that his Tribe was in a state of
barbarous ignorance, even before the contrast presented by
civilized nations had apprised him of the fact . . .

Not more than fifteen years ago, he had not as much as a
suspicion of the existence of white nations, and had never seen
either a gun or a horse; and at this present moment he is perhaps the Chief in South Africa who is possessed of the greatest
number of horses and fire-arms. He lives in a capacious and
comfortable house, built after the European style, employs
five wagons, his own property; and expends annually, at the
least, two hundred pounds sterling in the purchase of goods of
British manufacture. He is now particularly anxious to introduce
the cultivation of all European vegetables and fruit trees. He has
lately sent messengers to the Chiefs of Caffreland to propose a
plan by which the timber of their country may be made available
to the Basutoos.[5]

---

[1] Dyke, 1 Oct. 1842, *JME* xviii (1843), 366.

[2] Arbousset, 29 Dec. 1843, *JME* xix (1844), 251.

[3] A Subscriber, 'The Basuto Country', *Cape of Good Hope and Port Natal
Shipping and Mercantile Gazette*, 13 and 27 Dec. 1844, and 7 Feb. 1845.

[4] Anon., 'Moshesh, Chief of the Basutos', *South African Commercial Advertiser*,
1 Mar. 1843, and 'Additional Remarks on the Character of Moshesh, derived
from Personal Observation and from the Information of the Missionaries',
ibid., 4 Mar. 1843. The author was probably either Dr. John Philip, who
visited LeSotho in 1842, or Andrew Steedman, author of *Wanderings and
Adventures in the Interior of Southern Africa*, 2 vols., London, 1835, who also
visited LeSotho at about this time.

[5] 'Moshesh', *S.A.C.A.*, 1 Mar. 1843.

They also noted the humaneness of Moshoeshoe's rule:

Among the national benefits conferred by Moshesh on the Tribes of the Basutoos, the suppression of cannibalism should not be forgotten. That awful scourge took its rise during the wars that desolated the country from 1820 to 1830, and threatened to become a national habit when this Chief suppressed it effectually by judicious and firm measures.

He has also, by his example and interference, imparted to the Tribe a character of humanity and gentleness of manners, very remarkable. Robberies and murders are almost unheard of. Foreigners are everywhere respected and well received. Capital punishments have been done away with, and replaced by heavy fines.[1]

Finally, they remarked on the king's intelligence:

He has an active mind, and always appears to be thinking; his eyes, when there is anything to rouse him, flash with intelligence . . .

In conversation he delights, and discovers great versatility of mind, can suddenly adapt himself to those whom he addresses, and turn from one subject to another with a facility that is seldom seen, except in those who have been accustomed to move in good society. . . .

The most extraordinary feature of his intellectual character is his talent for generalization. While Mr. Casalis is reading to him any portion of ancient or of modern history, which he sometimes does at his request, his mind is always occupied with the philosophy of the subject, and striking his thigh with his right hand, and throwing himself back on the sofa of the Missionary, like a man who has found a new principle, or new proofs he had been hunting after in support of one in which he wishes to be more firmly established, he will sometimes express himself with feelings bordering on extacy. 'Casalis,' he will explain, 'I see men have been the same in all ages. Greeks and Romans, Frenchmen, Englishmen, and Basutoos have all one common nature.'[2]

3. '*A line of missionary establishments*'

By 1833 Moshoeshoe was beginning to extend his authority beyond his nuclear area round Thaba Bosiu. This process

[1] Ibid.   [2] 'Additional Remarks', *S.A.C.A.*, 4 Mar. 1843.

required great skill because the region was a complicated chess-board presenting the king with many problems as well as opportunities, and his own resources were limited. Expansion towards the south-east did not seem profitable, for the Maloti mountains were unsuited to agriculture. They were useful to have behind him as a sanctuary for his cattle should he be attacked by overwhelming forces, but they could not provide a viable permanent home for his people. In the opposite direction, to the north-west, lay the open plains of the South African high veld, desirable indeed, but vulnerable to attacks by Zulu and Ndebele impis and Coloured and white raiders. Moshoeshoe's preferred lines of expansion ran north-eastwards and south-westwards along the Caledon basin, between the high mountains and the open plains. But there were obstacles in both directions. To the north-east there was Sekonyela, the unpredictable but generally hostile Tlokoa chief, whose followers occupied most of the upper Caledon valley and cut Moshoeshoe off from the lands of his childhood and from the surviving remnants of his first allies, the Khoakhoa. To the south-west, on either side of the lower Caledon and in the triangle between the Caledon and the Orange, the country was partially occupied by scattered groups of survivors of the wars, some of whom acknowledged the leadership of kinsmen of the deceased hero, Mohlomi, while others were subjects of Moorosi, the Phuthi leader. But Moshoeshoe's prospects in that direction were impeded by the Coloured raiders who made life there insecure, and by the Griqua chiefdom centred on Philippolis, which had ambitions to expand eastwards towards Moshoeshoe.

It was the king's policy to destroy or pacify the raiders, to check the eastward expansion of the Griqua, and to extend his own authority up and down the Caledon basin by two complementary methods—incorporation and infiltration. He would incorporate the existing inhabitants into his own political system and he would have his own subordinates establish new villages further and further from Thaba Bosiu. To achieve these objectives he needed additional resources. Cattle he would continue to obtain by raids on the southern

Nguni chiefdoms, which had often proved profitable in the past. Horses and fire-arms he would acquire by capture from raiding parties, and as we have seen, by trade from white people. Such was Moshoeshoe's general strategy in the early 1830s.

This strategy was to be countered by newcomers to the Caledon basin. Several Griqua, Kora, and Tswana communities with their British missionaries settled at various places on the north-western side of the river; and white settlers entered the area in increasing numbers, especially after the Great Trek began in 1836. For the present we are concerned with the internal dynamics of Moshoeshoe's expansion programme. His confrontations with the newcomers are the subject of the next chapter.

In April 1835 Moshoeshoe led a large expedition of some 700 men, with nearly a hundred pack-oxen loaded with food supplies, south-eastwards across the Maloti mountains against the Thembu. This expedition was intended to yield a rich booty in cattle at a time when the southern Nguni were under attack by colonial forces from the Cape Colony, and also to give Letsie and Molapo an opportunity to prove their mettle as warriors, for they were restless at Morija and their father had recently narrowly prevented them from making an unauthorized attack on a Kora village. The Thembu expedition was a disaster. As Moshoeshoe was withdrawing he fell into an ambush, lost most of the live-stock he had captured, and sustained casualties. His full brother, Makhabane, was among those killed.[1] This was Moshoeshoe's last raid into Nguni country. From time to time he sent men against southern Nguni groups who, displaced from their homes by colonial forces, came to settle on land which he himself coveted in the lower Caledon basin;[2] but after the catastrophic 1835 expedition he relied mainly on peaceful methods of expansion.

This was in full accord with the wishes of his missionaries.

[1] Casalis, 20 May 1835, Josselin, Apr. 1835, and Arbousset, 3 Dec. 1835, *JME* xi (1836), 18–25, 40, 140–2; Azariel Sekese, *Leselinyana*, 15 Mar. 1893; History of Lesotho, 1833–1854, Ellenberger Papers, ch. 6.

[2] Annual Report for 1836, Daumas, 5 Dec. 1836, and Rolland, 28 Mar. 1837 *JME* xii (1837), 98–111, 133–41, 301–8.

They had deplored his decision to attack the Thembu and when he returned, chastened by his losses, they discouraged him from further aggression. Peaceful expansion was quite another matter. In this their interests coincided with the interests of the king. The extension of the authority of their patron involved the extension of their own influence, and provided the means were peaceful they could co-operate with a clear conscience. So Moshoeshoe and the Paris Evangelical Missionary Society became veritable partners in expansion.

Moshoeshoe had been acting politically when he led his first missionaries south-west from Thaba Bosiu and encouraged them to settle below Makhoarane, for that was the direction from which armed raiders had been coming to harass his people. These Coloured bands, with their colonial origins and contacts, were loath to attack mission stations or the protégés of missionaries, lest white traders should refuse to sell them arms and ammunition, or other white forces should retaliate. The mission station at Morija, with the adjacent villages of Letsie and Molapo, fulfilled the role that Moshoeshoe had in mind. It deterred Coloured raiders from directing further attacks against Moshoeshoe's people and constituted a major step in his expansion south-westwards. Soon afterwards Moshoeshoe's brother Posholi and his half-brother Mohale established new villages still further towards the south-west.[1]

Meanwhile Moshoeshoe was deriving other advantages from the cordial reception he had given his first missionaries. Pellissier and Rolland, members of the Paris Evangelical Mission Society, retreated south of the Vaal as a result of Mzilikazi's depredations and they naturally gravitated towards their more successful colleagues; and as new recruits graduated from the seminary, the Paris Committee sent them to strengthen the promising mission in LeSotho.

In 1833 Pellissier settled at Bethulie, near the northern bank of the Orange River four miles below its confluence with the Caledon, 135 miles south-west of Thaba Bosiu and

[1] Daumas, 20 May 1837, Arbousset, 12 Feb. 1839 and 29 Dec. 1841, *JME* xiii (1838), 41–51, xiv (1839), 300–7, xvii (1842), 210–15.

forty-five miles south-east of the Griqua settlement at Philippolis; and two years later Rolland founded another mission
station at Beersheba, forty miles nearer Thaba Bosiu, near
modern Smithfield. Both Bethulie and Beersheba soon became thriving mission stations and centres of African resettlement. Displaced groups of Tswana and Sotho origins
settled in and around them, with Tswana predominating
at Bethulie and BaSotho at Beersheba. Pellissier and the
headmen of the villages around Bethulie did not recognize
the temporal authority of Moshoeshoe, nor that of the
neighbouring Griqua regime at Phillipolis. On the other
hand Rolland acknowledged that Beersheba was subject to
Moshoeshoe. Thus Bethulie became a barrier to the eastward expansion of the Griqua, while Beersheba became an
advanced western outpost of Moshoeshoe's kingdom. Both
these stations performed further services for the king. The
wars having subsided, BaSotho refugees who had fled to the
Griqua states and to the Cape Colony were returning towards the land of their fathers. Many of them settled temporarily or permanently at Bethulie or Beersheba, where
they were able to regroup as organized sedentary farming
communities and were given opportunities to learn to read
and write in the mission schools. At Beersheba they were
also encouraged to think of themselves as subjects of Moshoeshoe.[1]

As new missionaries arrived from France they founded
stations at places agreed upon by the king and the mission.
In 1837 François Daumas founded a station at Mekoatleng,
thirty-two miles north-west of Thaba Bosiu, beyond the
Caledon.[2] This was a projection towards the Tlokoa chiefdom of Moshoeshoe's old enemy, Sekonyela. At the time

[1] On the early years at Bethulie see Pellissier's reports, *JME* x (1835),
50–4, 129–36, 290–1, xi (1836), 129–40, xii (1837), 225–35, 354–62, xiii (1838),
442–4, xv (1840), 321–38; also S. H. Pellissier, *Jean Pierre Pellissier van Bethulie*,
Pretoria, 1956. On Beersheba, see Rolland's reports, *JME* x (1835), 296–302,
xi (1836), 161–70, xii (1837), 16–25, 301–8, xiii (1838), 237–50, xiv (1839),
50–2, 173–7, xv (1840), 241–55; Daumas, *JME* xiii (1838), 41–51; and Frantz
Balfet, *Un Pionnier de la Mission du Lessouto: Samuel Rolland (1801–1873)*, Paris,
1914. See also Backhouse, *Narrative*, pp. 353–60.

[2] Arbousset, 20 Feb. 1837, and Daumas, 10 June 1838, *JME* xii (1837),
294–301, xiii (1838), 437–41.

this station was founded, the Mekoatleng area was occupied by a medley of small, impoverished African communities: Hoja and other SeSotho-speakers, Nguni survivors of the defunct chiefdoms of Mpangazitha and Matiwane, and a few Tswana. In the middle of 1838 they were joined by Moletsane, a Taung chief who had had a chequered career. Early in the *lifaqane* he had become a redoubtable leader of a military band and had had several collisions with the Rolong of Seleka, but then he had been overwhelmed by Mzilikazi, his following had been dispersed, and he had taken refuge for a while in Adam Kok's territory, before moving to Bethulie, then to Beersheba, and finally to the vicinity of Mekoatleng.[1] There he settled down to sedentary life, reunited most of the Taung survivors of the wars, and gradually incorporated the other inhabitants of the area into his chiefdom. He got on well with Daumas and was drawn into friendly relations with Moshoeshoe. This was partly because Moshoeshoe and Moletsane were served by members of the same missionary society and also because Moletsane's territory was wedged between the Tlokoa and his old enemies the Rolong, who were recouping their strength with the support of Wesleyan missionaries at Thaba 'Nchu.[2]

In February 1840 Moshoeshoe, accompanied by his sons Molapo and Masopha and the missionary Arbousset, made an extensive reconnaissance of northern LeSotho, keeping to the southern side of the upper Caledon and reaching nearly as far north as Mont-aux-Sources. He found that the valley of the Phuthiatsana (north of Teyateyaneng) was thinly occupied by survivors of the wars, of whom the most powerful was RaKotsoane, the erstwhile cannibal leader who had renounced cannibalism and recognized Moshoe-shoe, from whom he and his people had received many

---

[1] On Moletsane's Taung see Daumas, 12 Sept. 1838, 10 Nov. 1838, and 10 May 1839, *JME* xiv (1839), 129–38, 183–6, 412–14; 'Letter from Chief Molitsane to the Assistant Commissioners', 28 Jan. 1852, *BR* i 516–32; Azariel Sekese, *Leselinyana*, 15 July and 1 Aug. 1893; Ellenberger, *Leselinyana*, 7 Apr. 1915; E & M, pp. 165–9, 173–5; and J. C. Macgregor, *Traditions*, pp. 58–67.

[2] On the Wesleyan missionaries and the Rolong at Thaba 'Nchu see below, pp. 109–13.

sheep and cattle on *mafisa*. Beyond the Phuthiatsana they encountered several scattered communities—BaSotho, Nguni, and San. Sekonyela had placed kinsmen with followers on the left side of the Caledon opposite Marabeng (around Leribe), but they did not seem to be controlling the other inhabitants. In the Botha Bothe area they met Khoakhoa who recalled their alliance with Moshoeshoe and professed to look to him for protection.[1]

After that journey Moshoeshoe began systematically to expand to the north-east. First he placed his subordinate chief Khoabane with his followers eight miles north of Thaba Bosiu on the northern side of Berea mountain. Then in 1843 a newly arrived missionary, Pierre-Joseph Maitin, settled at Berea, alongside Khoabane. Moshoeshoe himself accompanied Maitin and other missionaries when they inspected the area. He approved the site and invited the headmen of the neighbouring villages to attend the foundation ceremony and instructed them to listen to the missionary.[2] In 1846 Moshoeshoe sent Molapo, his second son, and Lesaoana, who was the son of his deceased brother Makhabane and also the husband of his eldest daughter, with their age-mates and other followers, to settle in and beyond the Phuthiatsana valley. At first the missionaries tried to stop Molapo from leaving Morija, because they had educated and baptized him and they feared that the move would break his association with the church; but when they found that both Moshoeshoe and Molapo were adamant and that they wanted a mission station to be established near Molapo's new home, they acquiesced. As on previous occasions Moshoeshoe took part in the selection of the site for the new mission, which was named Cana. He formally donated it to the Society and he ordered Molapo's people to cut timber and thatching reeds and help the missionary, Daniel Keck, to build his home.[3]

Meanwhile in 1843 Christian Schrumpf had founded

[1] Arbousset (2).

[2] Maitin, 2 Jan. 1844 and 16 Feb. 1848, *JME* xix (1844), 369–76, xxiii (1848), 281–90.

[3] Arbousset, 9 Dec. 1846, 21 May 1847, and 30 Dec. 1847, *JME* xxii (1847) 202–11, 361–2, xxiii (1848), 214–15.

another mission station at Bethesda, about sixty miles south-south-west of Thaba Bosiu in the Maphutseng valley. By that time subjects of Moshoeshoe had occupied much of the territory between Thaba Bosiu and the Maphutseng, most of them recognizing as their immediate chiefs his brother Posholi, who lived at Thaba Tšoeu, or his half-brother Mohale, who lived near Mohale's Hoek. The Maphutseng valley was occupied by the Phuthi under Moorosi. From Moshoeshoe's point of view Moorosi was a subordinate chief, placed to defend the southern frontier of LeSotho from attacks by the southern Nguni; but Moorosi, who had built up a following of about 3,000 people in some thirty villages, regarded himself as an independent chief. In encouraging Schrumpf to settle at Bethesda Moshoeshoe calculated that he would be tightening his own hold over the Phuthi. Envoys of the king were present when the site of the mission was selected and in 1844 Moshoeshoe visited Bethesda and exhorted Moorosi and his people to attend the church services.[1]

By 1847, as we shall see, Moshoeshoe's south-western frontier was being infiltrated by white farmers and he was still finding it difficult to incorporate the kinsmen of Mohlomi into his political system. Consequently in that year, when the missionaries had the resources to establish new stations, he encouraged them to do so in that direction. Louis Cochet was located at Hebron, 76 miles from Thaba Bosiu, near modern Zastron, where Letele, Lebenya, and other relatives of Mohlomi were living; and Hamilton Dyke, Casalis's brother-in-law, was placed at Hermon, near modern Wepener, forty-four miles south-west of Thaba Bosiu.[2]

Thus by the end of 1847 the Paris Evangelical Missionary Society had nine stations in and near the Caledon valley, stretching from Bethulie and Bethesda in the south-west to Mekoatleng and Cana in the north-east. The missionaries

[1] Arbousset, 12 Feb. 1839, 29 Dec. 1841, and 28 June 1844, and Schrumpf, 25 May 1843, 11 Dec. 1843, 4 June 1844, and 13 Nov. 1844, *JME* xiv (1839), 300–7, xvii (1842), 210–15, xviii (1843), 441–8, xix (1844), 362–9, 451–64, xx (1845), 53–9, 210–23.

[2] Conference Report, 15 Feb. 1847, and Arbousset, 30 Mar. 1847, *JME* xxii (1847), 321–9, xxiii (1848), 4–13; Louis Cochet, Notes et souvenirs, SME.

and their families were a close-knit community, with a cultural as well as a spiritual sense of group identity. They visited each other frequently, they bought supplies for each other when they visited Colesberg or other market villages, and they met in annual conferences to co-ordinate their plans and prepare an annual report for the Committee in

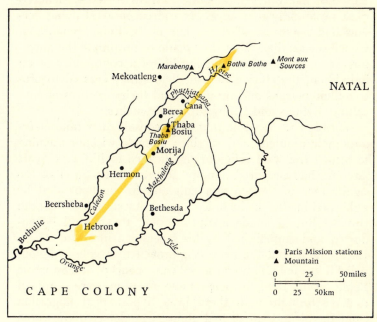

Map 2. Paris Missionary Society Stations in 1847

Paris. The corporate spirit of his missionaries was a boon to Moshoeshoe. Except for Pellissier, they all regarded themselves as living under his jurisdiction. They depended on him for protection and they were hopeful that eventually they would convert him and, through him, the BaSotho people. Moshoeshoe, in turn, had derived many advantages from his missionaries. In the eyes of his people they were the king's white men. They enhanced his prestige, they were helping him to understand the wider world that was impinging upon him, and they were loyal collaborators in the expansion and pacification of his kingdom.

4. *'Who will prepare food for me?'*

The Paris missionaries were confident that they were succeeding with Moshoeshoe in their evangelical as well as their civilizing mission, but their optimism was based on misconceptions about SeSotho religion and society. The BaSotho, like other small-scale African societies, believed most profoundly that ancestors and exceptional living persons had power to affect the fate of the living generation. Hence the sacrifices that they made to propitiate the ancestors at critical moments in the life of a community or an individual, the charms and medicines they created to protect their persons and property, and their practices of consulting diviners and killing supposed witches.

In 1834 Casalis wrote that 'they consult their rainmakers and their amulets, and sacrifice animals without seeming to attach the least religious significance to it'.[1] Five years later he had acquired a more accurate conception of the significance of the ancestor cult and in the book that he published in 1861 he included a good description of SeSotho rituals.[2] But he made an assumption, that would be endorsed and embellished by his successors, including D. F. Ellenberger, that the nearest approach to a valid religious belief that the BaSotho possessed was a concept of a Supreme Being (*molimo*) which their remote ancestors were supposed to have brought with them in a hypothetical migration from Egypt and which had almost completely disappeared during the intervening centuries.[3] Consequently, the missionaries equated *molimo* with the Christian God and denounced all other SeSotho beliefs and rituals as mere superstitions. Moreover many SeSotho customs seemed immoral to them, partly on theological grounds and also because they were radically different from their idealized version of nineteenth-century European culture—especially customs related to social stratification and to sex and marriage. Superstitions and evil customs were to be eradicated by inculcating a sense of sin and a fear of hell-fire.

[1] Casalis, 26 May 1834, *JME* x (1835), 43.
[2] Casalis, 5 Sept. 1839, *JME* xv (1840), 121–9; Casalis (1), pp. 237–99.
[3] Ibid, p. 254; E & M, pp. 237–40.

What is remarkable is that during the early years of their association so deeply did Moshoeshoe respect his missionaries, value their services, and give credence to their message that he yielded to many of their imperious demands. We can follow the missionary challenge and the king's response through a series of crises which the missionaries reported at length in their letters to their Society's Committee in Paris.

It was during the years 1839 to 1843 that the influence of Casalis reached it speak and Moshoeshoe made four substantial innovations that were inspired by his teaching. The first of these changes concerned burial rites.[1] When a MoSotho died it was customary to tie the corpse in the foetal posture, the chin resting on the knees; to sacrifice animals to enable the deceased to join the ancestral shades; and, if the deceased was a relative of a chief, to bury him in the wall of the cattle kraal. It was considered essential to perform these ceremonies in the appropriate manner, lest the shade of the deceased should torment his descendants. By 1839 Casalis realized that a change would be an important step towards liberating the BaSotho from fear of the dead. In June that year a converted woman died at Thaba Bosiu in the care of her brother, a catechumen, and Moshoeshoe allowed Casalis to bury her in the Christian manner in a plot of land he set aside near his village as a Christian cemetery. Several days later Casalis's own first-born child, a baby girl, died of measles and Arbousset conducted the burial service in the same cemetery in the presence of the king. Two days after that, 'MaNtsane, Moshoeshoe's senior surviving wife, threw herself to her death over a cliff face of Thaba Bosiu in a delirium brought on by measles. Her powerful Fokeng relatives, including RaTšiu, one of the king's senior councillors, prepared to bury her in the usual way. They broke down part of the wall of the cattle kraal alongside where Moshoeshoe's first wife, 'MaMohato, had been buried, they collected nearly a thousand cattle to parade in honour of the deceased, and they made ready for sacrifices. Moshoeshoe

[1] Casalis, 5 Sept. 1839, *JME* xv (1840), 121–9; Backhouse, *Narrative*, pp. 373–9; Casalis (1), pp. 87–91.

sent an urgent summons to Casalis, who climbed the mountain with James Backhouse and George Walker, visiting
English Quakers. They found the king arguing with the
crowd in favour of a Christian burial and he asked Casalis
to speak in his support. After a long debate, Moshoeshoe
had his way. 'MaNtsane was buried in the recumbent
position in the Christian cemetery. According to Backhouse,
Moshoeshoe said that 'he was not himself a converted man;
that he had long tried to resist the truths spoken by the
missionaries, but he was convinced, and he could no longer
stand against them', and he even told his old father, Mokhachane, that when he died he, too, would be buried in the
Christian manner.[1]

In 1840 Moshoeshoe repudiated another fundamental
custom: the initiation rites, in which adolescent BaSotho
were inculcated with traditional values. He ceased to convene initiation schools for his sons and the people of Thaba
Bosiu. In his annual report for that year Casalis wrote: 'The
rite of circumcision has been abolished by him for all his
family and for the people placed under his influence. He
declared himself very openly on the subject two months ago,
in instructing several pious individuals to snatch from those
immoral ceremonies one of his children who had been taken
there secretly.'[2] Long afterwards his successor Letsie informed
a Cape Colonial Commission that at least seven of his
father's sons were never initiated, including Majara (the
youngest son of 'MaMohato), Sekhonyana, Sofonia, and
Matsoso.[3]

Then in 1841 Moshoeshoe made a decision which, coming
on top of the others, gave grave concern to many of his
subjects.[4] Early that year Casalis baptized his senior surviving wife, 'MaSekhonyana (who was a Fokeng and a
cousin of his deceased first wife, 'MaMohato), and another
wife named 'MaMosebetsi. Having been taught by Casalis

[1] Backhouse, *Narrative*, p. 375.

[2] Casalis, 18 Nov. 1840, *JME* xvi (1841), 334; also Casalis, 5 June 1843,
JME xix (1844), 8.

[3] Cape of Good Hope, *Report and Evidence of Commission on Laws and Customs
of the Basutos*, 1873, p. 48, evidence of Letsie.

[4] Casalis, 20 May 1841, *JME* xvi (1841), 401–14.

to regard polygyny as a great sin, they asked Moshoeshoe for divorces. Moshoeshoe tried to persuade Casalis to drop the question of divorce but Casalis refused, making a strong appeal in Christian terms to the king's conscience. He drew up documents of separation and persuaded Moshoeshoe to place his mark on them. But, since women who had been rejected by their husbands were treated as little better than outcasts in SeSotho custom, Moshoeshoe felt a responsibility to these women. He let them keep their fields and their cattle, and he expected his menfolk to cultivate their fields as they did the fields of other royal women. To explain these decisions, he convened a *pitso* on the mountain. His converted councillor RaMatšeatsana was the only Christian present and it was he who told Casalis what happened. After the crowd had consumed the customary *joala* (strong beer) supplied by the king, Moshoeshoe spoke, saying,

My children *have fallen* into Christianity, two of my wives have fallen there also, what can I do? I feel that I myself am wavering and that soon I could fall there in my turn. Would to God that religion were a beverage! I would make you all drink it; but we have lacked missionaries. You still know nothing and hold me back, well aware that my body belongs to you and that a chief is the servant of his people. I announce to you that 'Ma-Sekhonyana and 'MaMosebetsi have left me. They are no longer my wives in the same way as in the past; however, their home is still under my control. When the sowing season comes, you will assemble as usual to cultivate the fields that I have assigned to them.

This statement met with strong opposition. A man who had the crowd with him gruffly interrupted the king:

No! It will not be so! We know of only one death that can separate wives from their husbands, it is the death that makes us descend to the grave. That death has already taken away the mother of Letsie and several of our other nurses; we have submitted to these blows that no shield can parry. But what is this new death, invented by the whites, that takes our wives away from us while they are still young and vigorous? We don't want it! Moshoeshoe, declare yourself frankly! Either 'MaSekhonyana and 'MaMosebetsi are still your wives, and we are ready to serve them as in the past, or they have ceased to be yours, and we no longer know them.

The crowd then turned on RaMatšeatsana, threatening to kill him as the councillor who had been the first to convert and had taken advantage of the King's confidence; and the *pitso* broke up in disorder.

Soon afterwards Moshoeshoe apologized to Casalis: 'We are still in darkness on many points, but I pray God to enlighten me and convert me; I hope that he will take pity on me, and then all will be well.'[1] In fact, Moshoeshoe did manage to care for the material interests of those former wives. They lived at the mission station below the mountain and continued to use the produce of the arable fields that had been assigned to them. Moreover the men cultivated their fields as in the past and in later years 'MaSekhonyana and 'MaMosebetsi were regarded as having remained wives of the king.[2]

Finally, in 1843 Moshoeshoe took a strong public stand against the killing of supposed witches. He had already made a practice of exposing the tricks of diviners who extracted presents from gullible people by making false claims. There are many stories about this. He would, for example, hide a necklace in the presence of a crowd and then summon the diviner and ridicule him for his failure to find the necklace.[3] In LeSotho, as in pre-industrial Europe, there was a deep-rooted fear of witchcraft.[4] It was believed that certain individuals possessed the innate power to inflict harm and even death on people, and many deaths that could not be attributed to known causes were deemed to have been the work of witches. In 1843 a woman named 'MaMothepane, who was a relative of Moshoeshoe and

[1] Casalis, 20 May 1841, *JME* xvi (1841), 409–10, 410–11, 414.

[2] Casalis, 5 June 1843, *JME* xix (1844), 8; Cape of Good Hope, *Report and Evidence of Commission on Laws and Customs of the Basutos*, 1873, p. 45, evidence of Letsie.

[3] Tlali Moshoeshoe, MS. 265a, Grey Collection, South African Public Libary, Cape Town; D. F. Ellenberger, *Leselinyana*, 31 Oct. and 12 Dec. 1912.

[4] For a review of recent works on witchcraft in Europe, see Lawrence Stone, 'The Disenchantment of the World', *The New York Review of Books*, xvii. 9 (Dec. 1971), 17–25.

perhaps a little mad, was dispossessed of a field by her immediate chief, Mojakisane, in south-western LeSotho. She cursed Mojakisane and soon afterwards he died— probably of typhus. The local people ill-treated her, sup- posing she was a witch, and Moshoeshoe gave her sanctuary at Thaba Bosiu. There, however, Moshoeshoe's wives were frightened of her and Mohale, Moshoeshoe's half-brother, encouraged them to intimidate her. Tempers rose. She shouted the terrible curse that their children would die and they themselves would become sterile. They then stoned her to death. Greatly shocked, Moshoeshoe convened a *pitso*, where he said:

In my infancy I received the name Lepoqo [dispute] because I was born at the moment when they were fighting in my father's village about a person accused of witchcraft. . . . I have never killed people except on the battle-field. This is the first time that the vultures have eaten anyone at my home. . . . When disease takes a child from me, do I go out to consult a diviner, to find out from him who has bewitched my family? You say there are diviners who know how to discover the sorcerers; these diviners deceive you. Pretend to be ill and show them a fine present, and you will see that they will not hesitate to identify the author of your sickness, even though you are quite well. . . . Hear me well today! Let no one ever have the audacity to come and tell me: 'I have been bewitched!' May that word never again be pronounced in my presence![1]

These four changes—the adoption of Christian burial customs, the cessation of initiation schools, the grant of divorces to baptized women, and the repudiation of the killing of witches—shook SeSotho society to the core. How- ever, two of the customs which the missionaries denounced even Moshoeshoe at the height of Casalis's influence would not abandon, because they were central to the structure of society and also to the power, the wealth, and the prestige of the king. These were the institutions of clientship and polygyny.

The traditional system of clientship was challenged by

---

[1] Casalis, 15 July 1843, *JME* xix (1844), 124–5.

Arbousset as early as 1835.[1] We only have Arbousset's
account of the incident, but it is very revealing:

On the first Sunday of October, having gone to preach at
Bosiu, I found Moschesch [*sic*] in his most distant hut in the
midst of a circle of his subjects. A young woman stood before
him, sad, silent, and yet resolute and assured. The chief spoke to
her in a rather excited way, and I heard him say to her two or
three times: 'You have done wrong.' I asked someone who the
woman was, and I was told: 'It is the wife of one of the Ba-
Tlauka [Bahlanka] of the King.' 'And what has she done?' I
continued. 'Her husband is dead, he has left a child, and she
wants to keep it, but Moschesch claims it.' I then listened more
carefully, and I heard the following debate. 'Mother of Maklobo,'
said the MoSotho king to the young woman, 'who is your mother?'
'So and so.' 'And your father?' 'Letsebele.' 'Who married you
to your man?' 'You, my Lord.' 'And to whom belongs the child
whom that man has given you?' 'To whom else but to me, because
you married me to my husband and not to my child,' replied
the poor woman, and the conversation ceased for a moment.

Soon afterwards, it started again. Moschesch, perceiving
that I was by his side, was embarrassed; he did not want me
to speak, because he knew well what my feeling would be
about this difference. But I believed it was my duty to speak,
raising my voice to make myself heard: 'You, woman, keep
silent,' I said to the MoSotho, 'and you, Moschesch, listen;
I too want to add a few words.' There was silence. 'Son of Mokhachane,' I then said to the chief, 'You have married this woman
to one of your BaTlauka [Bahlanka]?' 'Yes.' 'That's good.
And the MoTlauka [Mohlanka] is dead?' 'Yes.' 'According to
the law of the BaSotho,' I continued, 'this child should belong
to you?' 'Yes.' 'But this is a hard custom, very hard. According
to the law of the whites, when a husband dies, leaving children,
if the mother survives him, the children belong to her and she has
the right to enjoy them.' 'But that is not our custom.' 'I know
that, but your custom is very cruel. Indeed, who suffered the
pains of birth to bring this child into the world? Moschesch or
this woman? And who suckled it, and who took care of it?'
'Sir,' replied the king, 'it is I who nourished the mother *and* the
child *and* the father, with the milk of my cows.' 'That's very
good; you've acted like a good chief, you've shown yourself to
be their father. But now your MoTlauka is dead, your cows have

[1] Arbousset, 3 Dec. 1835, *JME* xi (1836), 147–53.

been returned to you, this woman has only her child left.'
'He's not hers, he belongs to me.' 'But once more, is he the son of
your womb?' Upon hearing that argument, the MoSotho king
began to laugh and I kept quiet.

However, the matter did not end there. Soon the dispute
started again, but I no longer took part. On both sides people
get hot and excited; one of the friends of the widow takes her
part and speaks rather lengthily in her favour, when suddenly
Moschesch violently throws a stone at him, hurls himself on him
across the crowd, batters his body and tries to kill him, which
he would have done except for some friends of the wretch who
pull him from his clutches and drag him outside; but their chief
follows them, and I am left alone with a son of the king, not
knowing what to do. He, frightened by the cries, says to me: 'Go,
sir, stop my father, he will kill that man.' I then work my way
through the crowd, I reach the chief. 'See, Moschesch, you the
king, the father of the BaSotho, see what you are doing.' At that
moment, the hapless man is taken away by his relatives; but the
chief still follows them armed with stones (for Moschesch, more
than any other person, does not know himself when he is in a
temper); then however he returns on his tracks, agitated, eyes
flaming, altogether beside himself. Unhappily he finds the young
widow who was fleeing. He throws her a severe look, and points
her to the entrance of the hut, then he seizes a stick to hit her.
The poor woman offers these few words as her sole defence: 'Calm
yourself, my father,' and she glides promptly into the hut,
where Moschesch strikes her twice in the back with the stick,
until finally I tear it from his hands, crying to him: 'Moschesch,
Moschesch, what are you doing?'[1]

This was a remarkable episode. Arbousset's account makes
it clear that he regarded Moshoeshoe's behaviour towards
the widow and her child as so degrading that it warranted his
public reprobation. But how would Moshoeshoe have described the affair? Less than three years previously he had
welcomed to his country this young foreigner and his two
companions. He had extended protection and hospitality
to them and he was listening attentively to their teaching.
Now this person, who was still a mere unmarried lad, twenty-
five years of age, was humiliating him, the king, in the
presence of his subjects for standing on his customary rights.

[1] Ibid., pp. 147–9.

As the missionaries became better acquainted with SeSotho society, they ceased to demand that he should do away with the clientship system, but polygyny was always a principal target of their reprobation. They told Moshoeshoe that they could never baptize him unless he separated from all his wives but one.[1] This he was not prepared to do. He was a sexually active man and he undoubtedly enjoyed sexual variety, but lust was by no means his reason for refusing to comply with the missionaries' demand. If it had been, it would not have been difficult for him to become a monogamist in form, while continuing to consort with other women. Moreover he was already about forty-seven years of age when the missionaries arrived and although he continued to take new wives and sire numerous offspring almost to the end of his life, sex was by no means his major driving force. When Casalis pressed him to cast off his junior wives, he asked: 'But in that case . . . who will prepare food for me and for the strangers who come to visit me?'[2] This question went to the heart of the matter. Wage labour was unavailable, for LeSotho had scarcely begun to be affected by a money economy; the system of clientage which Arbousset had attacked was not a source of sufficient female labour, because a patron was expected to find husbands for his female *bahlanka* who, once married, served their husbands. The only other legitimate status for a woman who served the king and his guests was that of wife to the king. Moshoeshoe had many guests. He was constantly visited by subordinate and allied chiefs and by ambassadors from other African rulers, who measured his power and prestige by the number of his wives as well as the number of his cattle. Casalis understood these things well.[3] But even he could not bring himself to consider the possibility of tolerating polygyny. In 1845 he wrote: 'Polygamy has its basis in interest as much as in sensuality. The woman acquired by means of several head of cattle is a faithful and inalienable servant. It is a qualified slavery, productive of a frightful excess of dissoluteness.'[4] Thus the matter of the king's wives

[1] Arbousset, *JME* xi (1836), 145.   [2] Ibid.   [3] Casalis (1), pp. 86–190.
[4] Casalis, 4 Mar. 1845, *JME* xx (1845), 283.

was an insurmountable obstacle to his conversion. To Casalis they represented 'a qualified slavery'. To Moshoeshoe they were a necessary attribute of his kingship.

5. *'Moshoeshoe is polluted'*

In their annual reports written in May 1848 the Paris missionaries looked back with some satisfaction on the results of fifteen years' work in LeSotho. They had created nine stations in territory under the jurisdiction of Moshoeshoe and his allies, Moletsane and Moorosi. They had baptized over 2,000 BaSotho, they were preparing another thousand for baptism, their Sunday services were attended by nearly 2,300, and over 600 pupils were attending schools run by the missionaries' wives at Morija, Thaba Bosiu, Mekoatleng, Cana, Bethesda, and Beersheba.[1]

The significance of these figures was greatly enhanced by the high standing of many of the converts. The Paris missionaries had had opportunities that were rarely granted in an independent African country. Most African rulers scarcely tolerated the presence of missionaries and used them exclusively for their own political purposes. The missionaries to the Zulu in the time of Shaka, Dingane, and Mpande made virtually no impact on African society; nor did the missionaries to the Ndebele under Mzilikazi and Lobengula. To listen to their teaching, they could only scrape together a few individuals who had been rejected by their own societies. In LeSotho, Moshoeshoe was the patron of the church. He sent his senior sons to Morija, he encouraged them and other relatives to convert, and, as we have seen, he introduced far-reaching innovations on missionary advice.

The conversion of people of standing began in 1839 and continued down to 1847. By that time many of the king's closest relatives had been baptized. They included Molapo and Masopha, his second and third sons by his senior wife,

[1] *JME* xxiii (1848), 370 (Bethesda), 376 (Morija), 381 (Thaba Bosiu), 403 (Berea), 407 (Mekoatleng), 411 (Beersheba), 418 (Cana), 421 (Hebron), and 427 (Hermon). The figures from the flourishing station Bethulie have not been included as Bethulie lay beyond the range of Moshoeshoe's political authority.

'MaMohato; Makhobalo, the surviving son of his second
wife; Sekhonyana, the only son of his third wife, and several
other sons. Libe, his father's elder brother, was baptized
in a great public ceremony. His half-brothers Mopeli,
Lelosa, and Tšiame were converted; so were his brother-in-
law Matete, his councillor RaMatšeatsana, and Makoanyane—his boyhood friend, initiation-mate, foremost warrior,
and military councillor. The missionaries also baptized
several of his women: Ntšebo, his half-sister; 'MaKoai and
'MaPefane, the mother and sister of 'MaMohato; and the
three most senior of his surviving wives—'MaSekhonyana,
'MaTlali, and 'MaMosebetsi.[1]

When Arbousset went to Cape Town in 1844, he took
with him for further education five Christian kinsmen of
the king—three sons, a half-brother, and a brother-in-law.
Their presence made a great impression in evangelical
quarters in the colonial capital and the visit was a triumph
for the Mission.[2]

Even so, Christianity had only a tenuous foothold in
LeSotho in 1848. It was strongest in the royal household,
but even there there was formidable opposition. Although
the missionaries tried very hard to gain the confidence of
key members of the older generation, they had very little
success. Libe, the king's uncle, was not baptized until he
was in his nineties and senile.[3] Mokhachane and Kholu, who
were regarded as destined soon to become powerful shades
because they were the parents of the king, were at the
centre of the resistance to Christianity in the royal family.

[1] *JME* xv (1840), 373 (RaMatšeatsana), xvi (1841), 135–44 (Molapo), 329
(Matete), 332–3 (Makoanyane, Masopha), 403 ('MaSekhonyana, 'MaMosebetsi), xvii (1842), 457 ('MaTlali), xix (1844), 4–5 (Mopeli, Makhobalo),
245 (Ntšebo), 379 (Sekhonyana), xx (1845), 101 ('MaPefane), 105 (Lelosa),
xxii (1847), 214–24 (Libe), xxiii (1848), 43 ('MaKoai), 281–7 (Khoabane). The
missionaries often referred to their converts by their baptismal names, e.g.
Abraham RaMatšeatsana, Jeremiah Molapo, Paul Matete, Joshua Makoanyane, David Masopha, Paul Mopeli, Stephen Makhobalo, Nehemiah Sekhonyana, Job Lelosa, Adam Libe, and Gideon Tšiame.

[2] Arbousset, 26 Sept. 1844, et seq. *JME* xx (1845) 128–41, xxi (1846) 43–51;
Albert Brutsch, 'The visit of Basotho chiefs to the Cape Colony in 1845',
Lesotho, viii (1969), 5–12. Arbousset's BaSotho companions on his Cape Town
trip were Masopha, Sekhonyana, Makhobalo, Mopeli, and Matete.

[3] Casalis, 8 Jan. 1847, *JME* xxii (1847), 214–24.

Mokhachane protested every time his son departed from
traditional ways and tried, unsuccessfully, to defy his son's
order suspending initiation ceremonies.[1] The best thing
the missionaries had bought to LeSotho, he told white
visitors, was sugar.[2] Moshoeshoe's mother was reputed to
encourage the king's young wives to use their physical
attractions to turn his thoughts away from monogamy.[3]
Kholu was by birth a member of the Fokeng clan, which had
great influence in Koena chiefdoms. Deemed to have been
the first BaSotho to have occupied the Caledon basin,
Fokeng took precedence over all others in initiation ceremonies. It was therefore significant that several of Kholu's
kinsmen, including her brother RaTšiu, who was Moshoeshoe's *malome* and a senior councillor, were equally opposed
to departures from custom.[4]

If the opposition in court circles had been confined to the
older generation, the missionaries might have had cause to
assume that it would only be a matter of time before their
teachings prevailed. But powerful men of the king's generation were as outspoken as any in their opposition to
Christianity. These included Moshoeshoe's brother, Posholi,
and his half-brother, Mohale, who were the leading territorial chiefs in southern LeSotho. The loyalty of these men
was essential to Moshoeshoe, if his kingdom was not to go
the same way as the Koena chiefdoms had done before the
lifaqane wars, when they had repeatedly split as a result
of secessions by members of the ruling lineages. Perhaps
Posholi and Mohale would have been less antagonistic to
Christianity if missionaries had been appointed to live
beside them, but that seems unlikely. Posholi was osten-
tatiously traditional in his way of life. The only times he
voluntarily went near a missionary was when he wanted a
tooth extracted, for he did admit that missionaries made
a better job of that than BaSotho doctors.[5] In 1844
Arbousset reported that 'Posholi frightens people who wish to

---

[1] Casalis, 4 Mar. 1845, *JME* xx (1845), 283-4.
[2] Jousse, 2 Mar. 1851, *JME* xxvi (1851), 249-50.
[3] Maeder, 1 July 1845, *JME* xxi (1846), 17.
[4] Casalis (1), p. 91.
[5] Arbousset, 28 June 1844, *JME* xix (1844), 452-3.

come to the prayers at Morija, telling them that they will lose their concubines and that since they are placed under his control he will chase them from their homes, or deprive them of their cattle, *if they convert before he does*.'[1] Mohale told Schrumpf that he did not want to hear anything about Christianity until a missionary had settled in his own territory.[2] Even among the next generation, Moshoeshoe's senior son and presumed heir was a constant disappointment to his missionary. Arbousset reported in 1843, ten years after Moshoeshoe had sent Letsie to live near him and listen to him, that 'Letsie, the principal chief of Morija, and all his village remain indifferent'.[3]

The influence of the missionaries was limited to a few localities in LeSotho. Each mission station was an island in an African ocean. A missionary could not possibly make regular visits to all the villages in his district, with the result that the masses of the people were relatively untouched. But each missionary did try his best to influence the chief to whom he had been assigned. The physical juxtaposition of Moshoeshoe's large village in a commanding position on the summit of Thaba Bosiu and Casalis's little mission station at its foot was symbolical of the relationship between a chief and his missionary. In most cases the lesser chiefs were less responsive to their missionaries than Moshoeshoe was to Casalis. At Morija Letsie paid little attention to Arbousset. At Cana Keck never exerted much influence over Molapo, even though he had been baptized before he migrated from Morija. At Bethesda Schrumpf's reports were a series of laments that Moorosi would have nothing to do with him. The exceptions were Daumas, whose relations with Moletsane at Mekoatleng paralleled Casalis's relations with Moshoeshoe, and Maitin, who baptized his chief, Khoabane, at Berea in 1847.

The *lingaka*—the herbalists, diviners, and rainmakers— did their best to foment resistance to the missionaries, for their prestige and livelihood were at stake. When measles

[1] Arbousset, 28 June 1844. *JME* xix, 453.
[2] Schrumpf, 29 May 1845, *JME* xx (1845), 461.
[3] Arbousset, 5 June 1843, *JME* xix (1844), 26.

swept LeSotho in 1839 and carried away many of the
children on Thaba Bosiu, Tšapi, Moshoeshoe's favourite
diviner, blamed the missionaries and tried to frighten the
king into withdrawing his patronage from them. One day
he painted one side of his body with white clay and smeared
the other with black carbon and, wearing no more than a
panther skin thrown across his shoulder, he climbed the
mountain. A crowd gathered round as he approached the
king's hut and shouted:

Son of Mokhachane, your grandfather Peete and the mother
of Letsie have appeared to me, I saw them this morning seated
before my door. I said, 'Tšapi, your eyes lie,' but to dissipate my
doubts Peete threw himself on me and almost crushed me under
his weight. I tried ineffectively to disengage myself from him, but
he agreed to move away only when he had given me a message for
you: 'The children of Thaba Bosiu die because Moshoeshoe is
polluted and because the school of the *Moruti* [missionary] and
the evening prayers offend the *Barimo* [ancestral shades].'[1]

Five years later Casalis reported that the missionaries were
being accused of eating human flesh in their communion
services.[2]

The strength of the opposition to reforms inspired by the
missionaries was demonstrated in the *pitso* Moshoeshoe convened to explain his divorce from 'MaSekhonyana and
'MaMosebetsi.[3] After that, when the missionaries strayed far
from their stations to preach in the villages they often met
with downright hostility. In December 1841, when Dyke
entered one village the chief decamped to the mountains and
most of the people who remained indulged in traditional
dancing (which the missionaries detested) rather than listen
to him, and at another village the chief remained in his
hut, carrying out a ritual sacrifice of a sheep.[4] In May 1842
Casalis reported that the villagers around Thaba Bosiu
regarded missionaries as sorcerers.[5] Converts were spurned

---

[1] Casalis, 15 Apr. 1839, *JME* xv (1840), 2–3. On Tšapi, see also Maeder,
1 July 1845, *JME* xxi (1846), 21–3; for Maeder's portrait, see Plate 9.
[2] Casalis, 21 Feb. 1843, *JME* xviii (1843), 368–9.
[3] See above, pp. 92–4; Casalis, 20 May 1841, *JME* xvi (1841), 409–11.
[4] Dyke, 2 Apr. 1842, *JME* xvii (1842), 454–5.
[5] Casalis, 20 May 1842, *JME* xviii (1843), 10–11.

by their old friends, as Makoanyane found when a former comrade in arms said that since the whites had come to the country, everything was upside down. 'The heart of Makoanyane is dead,' he was told: 'You have become a stranger to me.'[1]

By 1848 Moshoeshoe realized that Christianity had created a dangerous cleavage in his court and his country. His family was divided. His council was divided. Most of his territorial chiefs were resentful of the influence of the missionaries over him. The vast majority of the villagers were inclined to follow the *lingaka* in blaming them for their misfortunes. Moshoeshoe's reluctance to take the final plunge into Christianity was not due merely to his commitment to polygyny (important though that was). It might endanger his very kingship.

It is conceivable that if LeSotho had remained isolated from the rest of southern Africa for another generation, the Paris missionaries might have succeeded in their plan of converting the nation from the top downwards, though there were many obstacles in their path. As it was, LeSotho was under severe external pressure by 1848 and on 3 February that year an event occurred that was to have disruptive effects on the country and the mission: Sir Harry Smith, British High Commissioner for South Africa, proclaimed British sovereignty over all the territory between the Orange and the Vaal rivers, including LeSotho.

[1] Casalis, 21 Feb. 1843, *JME* xviii (1843), 369.

IV

BANTU, BOER, AND BRITON
IN THE CALEDON VALLEY

1. *The Settlers' Frontier Reaches LeSotho*

IN the 1820s Moshoeshoe had become a leader as an organizer of resistance to the invasion of his homeland by Africans. For the rest of his life he was primarily concerned with forces emanating from the wider world.

The projection of European power and influence into southern Africa had become a complex process since the Dutch East India Company established the first permanent European base in the Cape peninsula in 1652. By the end of the seventeenth century settlers from north-western Europe had occupied the land within about forty miles from Cape Town, where the rainfall is reliable. There they had created agricultural estates, using the labour of slaves imported from tropical Africa, Madagascar, and south and south-east Asia, and clients they incorporated from the indigenous peoples. The first white South Africans—the proto-Afrikaners—had already become the dominant caste in a racially stratified society.

After 1700 some settlers split away from the agricultural base in the south-western Cape and occupied the country northwards towards the Orange River and eastwards towards the Fish, living as near-subsistence, semi-nomadic pastoralists (*trekboers*). They spread out rapidly because the terrain was arid and suitable only for extensive pastoral farming and because their horses and fire-arms gave them a decisive advantage over the indigenous herding and hunting peoples (Khoi and San). As the trekboers advanced they incorporated some herders and hunters as clients, they killed others, and they pushed others off the land they had occupied.[1]

[1] On the Khoi and the San, commonly called 'Hottentots' and 'Bushmen' by Europeans, see Monica Wilson, 'The Hunters and Herders', *OHSA* i, ch. 2, and Richard Hall Elphick, 'The Cape Khoi and the First Phase of South

The Cape Colonial Government extended the boundary of the Colony from time to time and stationed a magistrate in the interior at Swellendam in 1746 and another at Graaff-Reinet in 1785, but the official boundary did not correspond with socio-political realities. During the first three-quarters of the eighteenth century trekboers became the most powerful element in the colonial population beyond the agricultural south-west, but towards the outer limits of their expansion there was always a frontier zone, on either side of the official boundary, where they had not yet established mastery and the colonial government had scarcely any influence.

A medley of peoples was propelled into the frontier zone from the heart of the colony: Khoi and San refugees, retreating to avoid being reduced to clientage; people of mixed descent who, too, were discriminated against if they did not withdraw; and pioneer trekboers. All of these peoples were influenced by the colonial society from which they had migrated as well as by the local physical and human environment. They owned, or aspired to own, horses and fire-arms; they controlled, or aspired to control, subordinates. They hunted, they bartered, they pastured their sheep and cattle, and they raided the indigenous inhabitants not only for livestock but also for children, whom they incorporated as clients. In the frontier zone, social and political groupings were weak, miniscule, and ephemeral, and anarchy was endemic because no authority was generally recognized as legitimate.[1]

While white settlers had been expanding relatively rapidly north-eastwards from the Cape of Good Hope, Bantu-speaking frontiersmen had been continuing their centuries-old movement in the opposite direction. During the eighteenth century the two frontiers were converging and southern Africa was becoming partitioned into two

African Race Relations', Ph.D. dissertation, Yale University, 1972. Elphick's work supersedes previous attempts to deal with the origins of the Khoi, their relations with the San, and their history to 1713.

[1] On the concept of a frontier zone, see Martin C. Legassick, 'The Griqua, the Sotho-Tswana, and the Missionaries, 1780–1840: The Politics of a Frontier Zone', Ph.D. dissertation, University of California, Los Angeles, 1970.

distinct types of society, colonial in the west and African in the east. During the second half of that century the eastern-most trekboers and the westernmost Nguni began to confront each other on the coastal side of the mountain escarp-ment in the vicinity of the Fish River. At first there was a military stalemate, Nguni numerical superiority being offset by white access to fire-arms, but in 1812 British regular troops began to tilt the balance in favour of the Whites. The Xhosa were driven back beyond the Fish in 1812 and beyond the Keiskamma in 1819. They fought again in 1834 and, as we shall see, in 1846 and 1850, and in 1857 in despera-tion they resorted to magic, but they were inexorably con-quered and the survivors retained control over only a small portion of the land that their ancestors had occupied west of the Kei River.[1]

Whites did not reach LeSotho until the 1830s. Before that, however, the high veld to the west of LeSotho, which the Whites called Trans-Orangia, had become a typical colonial frontier zone. Some of the indigenous San survived as auto-nomous bands of hunters, others were incorporated as clients by intruders from the colony. These intruders in-cluded groups of Khoi (*Kora*), whose ancestors had moved northwards in the seventeenth century to avoid Dutch control; people of mixed descent (*Griqua*) who had crossed the Orange River in about 1800; and other Coloured people who had left the Cape Colony more recently and still called themselves by their colonial name, Bastards. Until about 1825 white trekboers were few in the area—a mere trickle of colonial-based pioneers who periodically crossed the Orange River on hunting and bartering expeditions, or in search of seasonal pasturage for their sheep and cattle. By 1834, however, over a hundred trekboer families with their Coloured, Khoi, and San clients were permanently occu-pying large tracts of land in Trans-Orangia; and some trekboers were expanding eastwards into the better-watered and fertile lower Caledon valley.[2]

[1] W. M. Macmillan, *Bantu, Boer, and Briton*; Monica Wilson, 'Co-operation and Conflict: the Eastern Cape Frontier', *OHSA* i, ch. 6.

[2] Legassick, op. cit.; Lye, 'The Sotho Wars', ch. 3; P. J. van der Merwe, *Die Noordwaartse Beweging van die Boere voor die Groot Trek*, chs. 4, 7; *BR* ii. 424–38.

The most effective political entities in Trans-Orangia were two Griqua chiefdoms, one centred at Griqua Town, the other at Philippolis.[1] Both chiefdoms were supported by the London Missionary Society, which regarded them as civilizing and stabilizing agents and encouraged them to expand and incorporate the other inhabitants of the region. Nevertheless the Griqua political systems were weak and unstable. The leaders quarrelled, the other inhabitants resisted their claims to control them, and the trekboers had no respect for their authority. Nor were the Whites accustomed to obeying the laws of the distant Cape Government when they conflicted with their own interests. Many Whites bartered fire-arms and ammunition to the other inhabitants. Such transactions were illegal under the laws of the Cape Colony but, as the Governor realized, large quantities of gunpowder were being imported and most of it was finding its way to Trans-Orangia, 'where it is profusely supplied by sale, or barter, to the Bastards and Korannas, and other Native Tribes, in defiance of the severe penalties provided for this offence'.[2] In most cases trekboers accepted sheep and cattle in exchange for fire-arms, ammunition, and other goods, but in some cases they also took children for use as 'apprentices'.[3] There were even a few Whites who became leaders of pillaging bands. Thus the white infiltrators into Trans-Orangia accentuated the anarchic trends in the region, by disseminating fire-arms and ammunition indiscriminately, initiating new conflicts, and undermining the attempts of the Griqua chiefs to create viable political systems.

By 1834 these chronic disorders were backfiring into the Colony and in December of that year Governor D'Urban made a treaty with Andries Waterboer, the Christian chief of Griqua Town. Waterboer undertook to prevent violations of the colonial frontier, to assist the colonial authorities to recover stolen property and capture bandits, and to promote peace and civilization. In return he received a salary of

---

[1] Legassick, op. cit., and Lye, op. cit.

[2] Wade to Stanley, 14 Jan. 1834, C.O. 48/154, PRO.

[3] The evidence is overwhelming: e.g. Sass, 28 Sept. 1824, S.A. 9/2/c, LMS; Rolland, 28 Mar. 1837, *JME* xii (1837), 301–7; Arbousset (1), pp. 227–9, 252–3.

£100 a year and supplies of arms and ammunition. At the same time the Governor appointed the London missionary at Griqua Town his 'Confidential Agent'. This treaty had little effect. White people from the Colony continued to ignore Waterboer's authority and to sell arms and ammunition to all and sundry. Waterboer was not able to consolidate his regime, nor could he control the offshoot Griqua state at Philippolis, where Adam Kok III, succeeding to the chieftainship after ousting his elder brother in 1838, indulged in an expansionist drive to the east, claiming all the territory to the Caledon valley and nearly as far as Morija.[1]

Thus, while Moshoeshoe was extending his authority outwards from his base at Thaba Bosiu by placing kinsmen and subordinates at strategic points and exerting influence over neighbouring survivors of the wars, the forces that had been welling up in Trans-Orangia were spilling over into the Caledon basin. The first evidence Moshoeshoe had that the colonial frontier zone was closing in on him came in the mid-1820s, when mixed robber bands, operating from bases east of Philippolis, began to seize cattle and children from BaSotho villages. Then in 1833–4 12,000 people migrated to Moshoeshoe's immediate vicinity on the north-western side of the Caledon.

These newcomers had been living in the country northeast of the confluence of the Harts and the Vaal rivers, where the colonial frontier zone merged into the southern Tswana chiefdoms.[2] Most of the newcomers were Tswana who, like the BaSotho, had been battered by the wars. Others were Kora, Griqua, and Bastards. The newcomers migrated

[1] Legassick, chs. 10–11.

[2] The principal sources on the inhabitants of the Vaal–Harts area before their migration to LeSotho are the reports of the Wesleyan missionaries in WMS, and the following publications: William Shaw, *Memoirs of Mrs. Anne Hodgson*, London, 1836; Samuel Broadbent, *A Narrative of the First Introduction of Christianity among the Barolong Tribe of Bechuanas*, London, 1865; and John Edwards, *Reminiscences of the Early Life and Missionary Labours of the Revd. John Edwards*, 2nd ed., London, 1886. There is also much material in the Cape Colonial Government publication, *Evidence taken at Bloemhof before the Commission appointed to investigate the claims of the South African Republic, Captain N. Waterboer, Chief of West Griqualand, and certain other Native Chiefs to portions of the territory of the Vaal River now known as the Diamond-fields*, Cape Town, 1871 (cited below as *Bloemhof Blue-Book*).

largely because the Vaal–Harts area was too arid to support
them, whereas the Caledon region with an average of over
twenty inches of rain a year was relatively well watered.
They also had political reasons for migrating. In the Vaal–
Harts area they were caught between two fires: Mzilikazi's
Ndebele and Waterboer's Griqua. Many of them had taken
part in a disastrous expedition against Mzilikazi in 1831
and they feared reprisals; and Waterboer had recently
attacked them and was making it difficult for them to
obtain fire-arms and ammunition. Moreover, they were
encouraged to migrate by Wesleyan missionaries who had
been working in the Vaal–Harts area since the mid-1820s
and had become involved in territorial disputes with men of
the London Missionary Society who served Waterboer.[1]

In May 1833 Moroka (a young leader of the Rolong of
Seleka, a Tswana chiefdom), Barend Barends (a Griqua
leader), Jan Taaibosch (a Kora), Carolus Baatje (a Bastard),
and others made a reconnaissance towards the Caledon with
two Wesleyan missionaries. At Thaba 'Nchu they found
a MoSotho chief named Moseme living on top of the
mountain. Reporting to his headquarters in London, the
Wesleyan missionary Archbell said that Moseme and his
people had been made destitute by robbers from the west
and Moseme was most anxious for them to return with their
followers and settle below his mountain. 'Come to us as
soon as you can', Archbell quoted Moseme as saying. 'If
you do not come soon you will find none of us, for commandos are coming every day in search of our children. . . .
I have nobody left to cultivate the ground, and no cattle
left to eat the grass.'[2]

There followed a general exodus from the Vaal-Harts
lands and several new settlements were founded north-
west of the Caledon, each with its Wesleyan missionary:
at Thaba 'Nchu on the Modder River, 50 miles west-north-
west of Thaba Bosiu; at Platberg, 17 miles north-west of

---

[1] Archbell, 2 and 4 Sept. 1833, S.A. 5, WMS; *Bloemhof Blue-Book*, evidence
of Moroka, pp. 136–9, and Matlabi, pp. 261–5; Edwards, ch. 5; Legassick,
pp. 510–11.

[2] Archbell, 4 Sept. 1833, S.A. 5, WMS; also Edwards, ch. 5.

Thaba Bosiu (near modern Ladybrand); at Lesooane, 28 miles north-north-west of Thaba Bosiu (beyond Viervoet mountain); at Merumetšo, 43 miles north-north-west of Thaba Bosiu; and at Mpokoane, 36 miles north of Moshoe-shoe's stronghold (near modern Clocolan).

Thaba 'Nchu was far the most populous and prosperous of the new settlements. It was there that the Tswana migrants established themselves and they immediately began to cultivate the rich soil and reap good harvests of sorghum and maize. Thaba 'Nchu became a considerable township. It was divided into two main wards, one under Moroka, the other under Tawana, a member of another and more senior branch of the Rolong dynasty. By the end of 1834 the town had a population of about 7,000 people and another two or three thousand lived in neighbouring villages and cattle-posts. The numbers increased in later years, as a result of the incorporation of new settlers as well as natural increase. Moroka always had the larger following and in 1842 Tawana returned to the north-west, leaving Moroka the undisputed master of Thaba 'Nchu. From time to time Khoi and Coloured groups also settled near Thaba 'Nchu, and in 1840 there were four or five hundred Kora in the vicinity.[1]

Most of the migrants from the Vaal–Harts lands who regarded themselves as Bastards settled on the southern side of Platberg (Flat Mountain), a few miles north-west of the Caledon. They, too, cultivated the soil, growing wheat as well as maize; and they set up a form of government modelled on the institutions at Philippolis and Griqua Town, with an elective chieftainship—a system that gave rise to much friction. In 1839 500 Bastards were living at Platberg.

The settlement at Lesooane never amounted to much. Several Griqua families lived there intermittently for some years, but they did not give up their nomadic habits nor their taste for raiding. Within a decade most of them left the Caledon area to join Adam Kok or Waterboer, or to

[1] Reports of Wesleyan missionaries stationed at Thaba 'Nchu in S.A. 5, 7, and 12, WMS: Edwards, chs. 5 and 6; Andrew Smith Papers, vol. 10, pp. 239–43; Arbousset (1), pp. 229–30; Backhouse, *Narrative*, pp. 410–17; Journal of W. Impey, 1838–1847, WMS; Letter-Book of the Revd. J. Cameron, P.A. 11. 2, OFS; *Bloemhof Blue-Book*, pp. 136–9, 261–5.

return to the Vaal–Harts region. Barend Barends himself returned permanently to the north-west in 1838, after which his son-in-law, Pieter Davids, was the principal man among the few Griquas who remained in the Caledon valley.

Most of the Kora migrants, about a thousand strong, settled first at Mpokoane under the leadership of Jan Taaibosch, who had been baptized by the Wesleyans before he left the north-west. Jan Taaibosch was killed by a lion in 1836. Soon afterwards many of the Kora moved with their missionary seventeen miles westwards to Meru-metšo, on the northern slopes of the mountain that is still known as Korannaberg, where Gert Taaibosch became their leader. However, the Kora, like the Griqua, did not abandon their pastoral, nomadic, and raiding way of life and they became involved in serious fighting with their neighbours to the east—Sekonyela's Tlokoa.[1]

The Wesleyan missionaries soon made contact with Sekonyela, whose headquarters at Marabeng were only twenty-five miles east of Mpokoane. Sekonyela regarded Mpokoane as part of his territory. He permitted the Kora to settle there and he promptly asked the Wesleyans to provide him with a missionary, because he, like Moshoeshoe, was being raided from the west and 'others are getting teachers, but I have none'.[2] For a while, it seemed likely that the Wesleyans might perform the same role for Sekonyela that the Paris missionaries were performing for Moshoeshoe. In 1834 James Allison founded a new station, Mpharane, close to Marabeng. Soon afterwards Sekonyela came down from the mountain and built a village at its base, near the mission, and the Wesleyans founded another station with Sekonyela's brother, 'Mota, across the Caledon River in the Maloti foothills east of Botha Bothe. But Allison never managed to establish *rapport* with Sekonyela and friction arose between the Tlokoa and the Kora. Sekonyela's people raided cattle and horses from the Kora, and

---

[1] Reports of Wesleyan missionaries stationed at Platberg, Mpokoane, Lesooane, and Merumetšo in S.A. 3, 5, 7, and 12, WMS; Edwards, ch. 6; Andrew Smith Papers, vol. 10, pp. 153–9, 229–56; Arbousset (1), pp. 8–28; Backhouse, *Narrative*, pp. 383–94, 404–9; Letter-Book of the Revd. J. Cameron, OFS.   [2] Jenkins, 24 Dec. 1833, S.A. 5, WMS.

the Kora retaliated, using fire-arms and, on at least one occasion, fighting in co-operation with San who used their poisoned arrows with lethal effects. In 1840–1 the Kora devastated the Tlokoa village below Marabeng; Sekonyela fled to his brother in the Maloti; the Kora followed him and routed him again, and Sekonyela's chiefdom temporarily disintegrated. He himself, with a handful of followers, returned to the summit of Marabeng, after raiding the Wesleyan mission village at Mpokoane, but his people had dispersed. Some fled to the Maloti, others joined Moshoeshoe or Moroka, or took service with white farmers.

Sekonyela contrived to reassemble many of his people and re-establish a chiefdom of a sort, but he never fully recovered from the catastrophes of 1840–1.[1] The Wesleyan missionaries had little sympathy for him. Allison, who had founded the Mpharane mission and worked there for seven years, considered that the Tlokoa were the aggressors. The troubles arose, he wrote, from 'the systematic robbery practised by the Chief Sekonyela upon his neighbours', and his successor Francis Taylor said, 'His prevailing disposition is to plunder.'[2]

Moshoeshoe was not alarmed by the arrival of the newcomers from the Vaal–Harts lands. Since he himself had recently asked for missionaries and been pleased with the results, the presence of missionaries with the immigrant communities seemed to be a guarantee of their peaceful intentions towards him. Settling between Thaba 'Nchu and Mpokoane, they formed a protective screen between him and Mzilikazi's Ndebele and they also helped him blunt the attacks of the raiders from the west.

For several years the newcomers fulfilled Moshoeshoe's expectations. Raiders ceased to penetrate to the southeastern side of the Caledon; and in August 1836, when Mnyaluza, a southern Nguni chief, displaced from his home by the war on the eastern frontier of the Cape Colony in 1834–5, settled near Philippolis and began to raid subjects

[1] Reports of Wesleyan missionaries in S.A. 5, 7, and 12, WMS; Letter-Book of the Revd. J. Cameron, OFS.
[2] Allison, 16 July 1841, S.A. 5, WMS, and Taylor, 24 Aug. 1842, S.A. 12, WMS.

of Moshoeshoe at Beersheba and of Moroka at Thaba 'Nchu, Moshoeshoe and Moroka joined forces to destroy the Nguni settlement and drive the survivors away.[1] Moreover the Wesleyan missionaries treated Moshoeshoe with respect, giving him to understand that they acknowledged him and Sekonyela to be the paramount chiefs of LeSotho, including the areas occupied by the newcomers.[2]

By 1840, however, white emigrants from the Cape Colony had transformed the balance of power throughout south-eastern Africa. The trekboers who had been filtering into the Philippolis area since the mid-1820s constituted a gradual extension of the colonial frontier zone towards LeSotho. But in and after 1838 the settlers' frontier made a dramatic leap forward when organized parties with numerous wagons, large herds of cattle, and vast flocks of sheep crossed the Orange River. By the middle of 1837 about 5,000 had done so; by 1845 perhaps 14,000, roughly a fifth of the white population of the Cape Colony. These emigrants were later known as *voortrekkers*, their migration as the Great Trek.[3] Disillusioned by the policies of the Colonial Government, they were determined to cast off British rule, to deal with black and brown peoples in their accustomed way, and to carve out new homes for themselves in the areas that had been partially depopulated in the *lifaqane* wars. Both Mzilikazi and Dingane tried forcefully to prevent their intrusion, but Ndebele and Zulu weaponry and strategy were no match for those of the Whites. By the end of 1840 Mzilikazi had fled beyond the Limpopo, and Dingane was dead and had been succeeded by his half-brother Mpande, who came to power as an ally of the voortrekkers. Most of the emigrants then settled in Natal, where they set up a republican form of government, but others remained on the high veld on either side of the Vaal River.[4]

[1] Jenkins, 16 Sept. 1836, and Archbell, 1 Jan. 1837, S.A. 7, WMS; Daumas, 5 Dec. 1836, *JME* xii (1837), 133–41; D. F. Ellenberger, *Leselinyana*, 7 Aug. 1913. [2] But see below, pp. 126–30.

[3] The phrase 'the great Trek' was used as early as 1842 by Hendrick Hendricks, Secretary to Adam Kok III of Philippolis: 'Minutes of Private Conference . . .', Colesberg, 21 Dec. 1842, C.O. 48/234, PRO.

[4] On the Great Trek see C. F. J. Muller, 'The Period of the Great Trek,

The voortrekkers did not remain unchallenged for long. In 1835 a select committee of the British House of Commons had been making a critical review of the relationships between white settlers and native peoples in the British Empire; as a result of which in 1836, before parliament was aware that a large-scale organized emigration was taking place from the Cape Colony, it passed an Act, modelled on previous legislation applying to India, Australia, and British North America, providing that Cape Colonial courts could try British subjects for any crimes they committed against the indigenous inhabitants of South Africa as far north as latitude 25° south. Since the voortrekkers were British subjects, this made them theoretically liable to the colonial courts for their dealings with Africans.

For some years the colonial officials took no effective steps to control the voortrekkers. However, by the early 1840s they had second thoughts. Voortrekker embroilments with Africans, including an ill-judged raid to the south of Natal, led to anxiety lest the voortrekkers should cause such chaos among the Nguni peoples that the eastern frontier of the Cape Colony would become unstable. British officials were also influenced by the evangelical lobby, which denounced the voortrekkers' dealings with Africans on humanitarian grounds. They calculated that if Britain occupied Natal the voortrekkers would be kept under a tight rein, because they would have to depend on British trade routes for their supplies of arms and ammunition. Accordingly, a British military detachment occupied Port Natal (Durban) in 1842 and in the following year the republican legislature in Pietermaritzburg submitted and Natal became British territory. During the next few years most of the voortrekkers left Natal and spread out over the high veld, some to the south, others to the north of the Vaal River, occupying lands that had been effectively used by Sotho-Tswana peoples before 1822, but had then been devastated by the *lifaqane* wars. They claimed possession of the territory by

1834–1854', in Muller, ed., *Five Hundred Years: a history of South Africa*, Pretoria, 1969, pp. 122–56; *OHSA* i. 355–73 and 405–24; and E. A. Walker, *The Great Trek*, 4th ed., London, 1960.

virtue of their defeat of Mzilikazi and also, in some cases, by 'buying' land for livestock from Coloured and African people they found there.[1]

By 1843 the settlers' frontier had reached Moshoeshoe. All around him, except in the Maloti mountains in his rear, Whites were closing in upon the Caledon valley. In the west, trekboers were occupying land in the triangle between the lower Caledon and the Orange. In the north, voortrekkers were settling near Moroka's people and in the lands claimed by Sekonyela.

Fortunately for Moshoeshoe, the Whites were themselves dispersed and divided. Voortrekkers, determined on independence from Britain, did not see eye to eye with trekboers, who still recognized the authority of the Colonial Government; and voortrekkers were themselves grouped in rival factions, each with its own leader and its settlement area. Nevertheless the Whites were capable of presenting a united front against Africans. They were products of the same racially stratified colonial situation. Culturally they were indistinguishable, speaking the same Dutch dialect and recognizing the same Calvinist God. They were all stock-farmers, bent on appropriating the best springs and pastures and enlisting the services of black and brown clients as shepherds, cattleherds, and domestic servants. They lacked respect for African political authorities and resented European missionaries who supported those authorities. With their proven military capacity and their flow of fresh recruits and arms and ammunition supplies from the Cape Colony, white settlers had become a threat to the survival of every other political community on the high veld.

The black and brown communities were less united than the Whites. Culturally, Griqua and Bastards had far more in common with the white settlers than with Africans; and the Africans had only recently begun to recuperate from the *lifaqane* wars, during which they had been at each others' throats. Waterboer was not capable of offering effective

[1] J. S. Galbraith, *Reluctant Empire*, Berkeley, Calif., 1963; C. F. J. Muller, *Die Britse Owerheid en die Groot Trek*, 2nd ed., Johannesburg, 1963; *OHSA* i. 368–73.

resistance, for his followers were few and the territory he occupied was on the arid western fringe of the high veld grasslands; nor was Adam Kok, whose territory was already permeated by trekboers; nor Sekonyela, nor Moletsane, nor Moroka, whose exposed locations were fatal weaknesses. There was only Moshoeshoe. By 1842, in spite of his humble origins and the brevity of his career as an independent ruler, he had a concentrated following of between thirty and forty thousand people,[1] with a strong base in the foothills of the Maloti, whereas the total white population outside the Cape Colony numbered fewer than 10,000 people, widely dispersed between the Natal lowlands and the northern Transvaal. Moreover he was a popular leader and a natural diplomat with a clear grasp of politial realities. Moshoeshoe, therefore, became the organizer of the only serious resistance to white domination of the southern high veld.

But white settlers and the BaSotho were not shaping up for a conflict in a vacuum. Voortrekkers as well as trekboers were British subjects. Fire-arms and ammunition could only be obtained through the British commercial network. Therefore Britain held the key to the situation. It remained to be seen whether she would use it, and if so with what effect.

2. *'The Chief of the Basutos engages to be the faithful Friend and Ally of The Colony'*

By the late 1830s Moshoeshoe had a fairly clear picture of the dangers that confronted him. In response, his strategy was to amalgamate the diverse black and Coloured communities in the Caledon valley under his leadership, to keep white farmers as far away as possible, to accelerate a process of selective modernization with the help of his missionaries, and to offset settler power by diplomacy.

Trekboers were becoming a serious threat to Moshoeshoe's south-western flank. They were intimidating the inhabitants of the Paris mission station at Beersheba, his principal outpost in that direction; terrorizing the indigenous San

[1] Casalis, etc., to Lieutenant-Governor Hare, 30 May 1842, *BR* i. 43.

hunter-gatherers who still lived in the area; and occupying land in the triangle between the lower Caledon and the Orange, regardless of his protests.[1] In October 1839 twenty-five trekboers showed their utter disregard for his jurisdiction by invading LeSotho to seize and kill two Coloured men who had taken refuge in a village near Thaba Bosiu.[2]

Meanwhile, voortrekkers were threatening his northern flank. Their migration routes and early settlements were on the northern side of the Caledon—in the territory where villages whose headmen recognized Moshoeshoe were interspersed among the settlements of the recent immigrants from the north-west, and in the territory claimed by Sekonyela. Moroka, the Tswana chief at Thaba 'Nchu, became deeply involved. In 1836 his people warned the early voortrekkers that they would be foolish to settle near the Vaal River, because Mzilikazi, having been repeatedly attacked from that direction by Zulu impis and Griqua commandos, kept men posted to exterminate expeditions approaching from the south. When the voortrekkers ignored this advice and suffered the consequences, Moroka sent them pack-oxen to transport their goods southwards and he helped them to recuperate. For several months the voortrekker parties concentrated in the Modder valley near Thaba 'Nchu. Moroka also supplied men to join in their attacks on the Ndebele in 1837.[3] Nevertheless friction developed between the voortrekkers and Moroka. Influenced by his Wesleyan missionaries, Moroka favoured the British cause while the outcome of the British military expedition to Natal was still uncertain. When Jan Mocke, a voortrekker leader, discovered this by intercepting Wesleyan missionary correspondence, he tried to intimidate Moroka.[4]

Voortrekkers also gave Sekonyela rough treatment. In

---

[1] Moshoeshoe to Lieutenant-Governor Hare, 26 Nov. 1839, *BR* i. 36–7.

[2] Rolland to Lieutenant-Governor Hare, 28 Nov. 1839, *BR* i. 38–40.

[3] Archbell, 1 Jan., 1837, S.A. 7, WMS; statements by Moroka and other Rolong participants in these events in *Bloemhof Blue-Book*, pp. 137–46, 261–5.

[4] Commandant to Vermeulen, 18 Aug. 1842, C.O. 48/244, PRO; the Revd. W. Shaw to Secretary to Government, Grahamstown, 25 Oct. 1842, C.O. 48/224, PRO.; Declaration of Captain Maclawa, Modder River, 24 Sept. 1842, C.O. 48/234, PRO.

October 1837 his people made a daring cattle-raid against Dingane's southern outposts in Natal. Since some of the Tlokoa raiders rode horses, wielded fire-arms, and wore European clothes, Dingane assumed that it was voortrekkers who had stolen his cattle. Accordingly, when the voortrekker leader Piet Retief visited him later that month, Dingane was able to procrastinate by telling him to retrieve his cattle before he would entertain his request for land. Retief recrossed the Drakensberg with a commando and went straight to the Wesleyan mission station at the foot of Marabeng, because he knew that Sekonyela's people had been responsible for the raid. After sleeping at the mission, Retief sent for Sekonyela and, as one of his men later recalled: 'I had a pair of handcuffs in my bag; and, as Sekonyela was sitting on the ground, I ran up to him and said, "Look at these beautiful rings;" and thereupon I closed the handcuffs on his arms, saying, "That is the way we secure rogues in our country!"' Sekonyela was held hostage until his people had handed over the stolen cattle, which Retief returned to Dingane, and also a fine of fifty-three horses and thirty-three guns.[1] The news of this trick made a deep impression on Moshoeshoe.

During the brief respite while the majority of the voortrekkers were in Natal, Moshoeshoe decided to make his presence felt on the northern side of the Caledon. In January 1842 he organized a *letšolo* (hunting expedition) in the plains beyond Mekoatleng to demonstrate his military strength and assert his claim to territorial authority. The Paris missionary at Mekoatleng reported that when he passed through his station Moshoeshoe was at the head of several thousand men, of whom 500 were mounted and armed with guns, while the rest travelled on foot carrying their traditional weaponry.[2]

A year later, when voortrekkers were trying to whip up

---

[1] Daniel Bezuidenhout in John Bird, ed., *The Annals of Natal: 1495–1845*, 2 vols., Pietermaritzburg, 1888, i. 368–9. Other eyewitness accounts are in Sir George Cory, ed., *The Diary of the Revd. Francis Owen*, Cape Town, 1926, pp. 168–70, and Edwards, 10 Jan. 1838, S.A. 12, WMS. There are Tlokoa traditions that deny that Sekonyela's people were responsible for the raid on Dingane's outposts: I. 39.   [2] Daumas, *JME* xvii (1842), 321–2.

resistance to the British occupation of Natal, Moshoeshoe had his first personal dealings with one of their leaders. Andries Hendrik Potgieter visited him and tried to induce him to provide aid against the British, but he declined to do so.[1] On the contrary, the incident strengthened Moshoeshoe's resolve to pursue an opposite line of action.

Many years earlier Moshoeshoe had discerned the advantages of offsetting pressures from hostile neighbours by invoking the aid of distant powers as allies. In 1823 he had sought Zulu help against Sekonyela who was besieging him at Botha Bothe, and in 1826 he had incited Shaka to attack Matiwane who was threatening to subject him. Now, realizing that the conquerors of Mzilikazi and Dingane were becoming a serious threat, he turned to the Colonial Government for support. In his experience British officials and British policy and interests were more favourable to him than those of the white settlers. Andrew Smith had been a friendly visitor. The British had showed no signs of coveting his territory or ill-treating his people. Indeed, the Colonial Government had recently put an end to slavery and serfdom in the Colony and had refrained from exacting excessive reprisals from the Xhosa and Thembu after the frontier war of 1834–5. Settlers, on the other hand, were threatening the integrity of his kingdom.

Moshoeshoe derived most of his knowledge of the wider world from Casalis and his colleagues and he also depended on them as amanuenses for written communications with officials. By 1843 the Paris missionaries had reached the conclusion that their mission was being jeopardized by the infiltration of trekboers into the lands around Bethulie and Beersheba, the build-up of voortrekker power beyond the Caledon, and the deep-seated hostility of many of the settlers towards missionaries. They therefore looked to the only power that was available to protect them and the BaSotho with whose interests they were identified. Their patriotism as Frenchmen was not a deterrent, for France had no interests in southern Africa.

The decisive link between Moshoeshoe's missionaries and

[1] Captain Peter Davids to Captain Adam Kok, 13 Feb. 1843, *BR* i. 51–2.

the Colonial Government was Dr. John Philip, the South
African Superintendent of the London Missionary Society.[1]
Philip had been closely associated with the LeSotho mission
from the beginning. He had advised the Paris directors to
send their men to South Africa and he acted as their financial
agent in Cape Town. Because of his connections with the
evangelical lobby in England and his own immense energy,
he was able to exert considerable leverage on the Colonial
Government and he had close personal relations with
Governor Napier (1838–44). A champion of the interests of
the Khoi and Coloured people inside the Colony, he was
also a vehement critic of the dealings of white settlers with
Africans. Now, with the voortrekker breakthrough into the
interior, he hoped that Britain would annex the high veld
as well as Natal. Failing that, Britain should at least extend
to Adam Kok III and Moshoeshoe the treatment it had
accorded to Waterboer. The latter alternative was acceptable
to British policy-makers, who were searching for an economical way to stabilize the colonial frontier and appease
the evangelicals. Treaties with Kok and Moshoeshoe would
complete a semicircle of allied African states along the
borders of the Colony from Griqua Town to the Indian
Ocean. Thus Moshoeshoe's natural inclinations were given
form and substance by his missionaries, by Philip, and by
British officials.

On 25 November 1841 Moshoeshoe put out a feeler to the
colonial Governor in a dictated letter: 'It is always my
earnest desire', he said, 'to live in the most perfect harmony
with the Colony. I know very well that from there alone
proceed our safety and our welfare.'[2] Five months later
Casalis informed the Lieutenant-Governor of the Eastern
Province that Moshoeshoe 'is more and more convinced
that existence and independence are possible for his people
only under the protective aegis of the sovereign you
represent'.[3] This letter was accompanied by a document

---

[1] On Philip, see W. M. Macmillan, *Bantu, Boer, and Briton*, and *The Cape
Colour Question*, London, 1937.
[2] Moshoeshoe to Lieutenant-Governor Hare, 25 Nov. 1841, *BR* i. 42.
[3] Casalis to Lieutenant-Governor Hare, 30 May 1842, *BR* i. 42–3.

signed by all five Paris missionaries in the area, asserting
that Moshoeshoe's 'tribe' of thirty or forty thousand people
was progressing towards Christianity and Civilization under
the peaceful and enlightened leadership of Moshoeshoe, but
that it was being threatened by the emigrant farmers.[1]
Philip himself visited LeSotho in February 1842 and on his
return he informed the government—with some exaggera-
tion—that the power of Moshoeshoe was 'the only obstacle'
to the fulfilment of the voortrekkers' plan to exterminate all
the Africans on the high veld.[2] In September 1842 the
Government sent two Afrikaner officials from the Colesberg
district to try to prevent the trekboers from being seduced
from their allegiance to the Crown by the voortrekkers and
also to visit Moshoeshoe and Kok. Moshoeshoe handled
these colonial Afrikaners skilfully. He displayed the medal
which Andrew Smith had given him, applauded the wisdom of the Government in sending Afrikaner officials to
placate Afrikaner emigrants, and asked them to inform their
superiors that he wished Britain to extend its authority over
the entire area as far north as 25° south. In their report the
officials declared that Moshoeshoe was 'the most fit, sensible,
and stately heathen Chief we ever saw'.[3]

The Colonial Government then drafted treaties in consultation with Philip[4] and officials carried them to Philippolis
and Thaba Bosiu, where Kok and Moshoeshoe signed them
on 29 November and 13 December 1843.[5] Kok and Moshoeshoe each undertook to be 'the faithful Friend and Ally of

[1] Casalis, Rolland, Daumas, Pellissier, and Arbousset to Lieutenant-
Governor Hare, 30 May 1842, *BR* i. 43–4.

[2] Philip to Lieutenant-Governor Hare, 12 July 1842, *BR* i. 44–6.

[3] Field-Cornet G. D. Joubert and Commandant H. T. van der Walt to
Lieutenant-Governor Hare, C.O. 48–224, PRO; extracts from this report
in *BR*. i. 49–50. In one variant or another the word 'Afrikaner' was already in
occasional use, especially among those descendants of the seventeenth- and
eighteenth-century emigrants from Europe to South Africa who wished to
emphasise their dissociation from Europe: e.g. the Voortrekkers.

[4] For Philip's role, see Philip to Lieutenant-Governor Hare, 12 July 1842,
BR i. 44; Philip to Governor Napier, 25 Aug. 1842, *BR* i. 47; Montagu, Secre-
tary to Government, Cape Town, to Philip, 2 Sept. 1843, *BR* i. 52; Philip to
Montagu, 7 Sept. 1843, *BR* i. 52; and Napier to Hare, 8 Sept. 1843, *BR* i. 52–3.

[5] The Treaties are in C.O. 48/243, PRO; Moshoeshoe's treaty is also in *BR*
i. 55–6.

the Colony', to preserve order in his territory, to prevent the inhabitants from violating the peace of the colonial frontier, to hand over fugitive offenders to the colonial authorities, and 'to apprize the Colonial Authorities of any intended predatory or hostile attempt against the Colony which may come to his knowledge, and to cooperate cordially and in all good faith with the Colonial Government in preserving peace and extending civilization among the Native Tribes'. Kok was to receive an annual present of £100 and certain supplies of arms and ammunition, and Moshoeshoe was to receive £75 a year, 'either in money or in arms and ammunition as the Chief may desire'.

But that was not all. Whereas Kok's treaty did not define the extent of his territory, Moshoeshoe's treaty included a territorial clause of great importance. In the early 1840s there was a tangle of irreconcilable claims to jurisdiction over land and people on either side of the Caledon River. Moshoeshoe had become the most powerful chief; he had the most followers; his rule was the most popular; and he was beginning to see himself as the supreme chief over all the southern Sotho, Tswana, and Nguni survivors of the *lifaqane* throughout a vast but undefined area north of the Drakensberg mountains. But the extent of his power and influence was still limited. In migrating from Botha Bothe in 1824, he had yielded control over northern LeSotho to Sekonyela. In the south-west, in the triangle between the Orange and the lower Caledon, he had very few villages and trekboers were encroaching with their usual disregard for African authority. On the north-western side of the lower Caledon, his followers were contesting territory with the Tswana and Coloured immigrants who had migrated from the Vaal–Harts lands in 1833–4.

In 1841 Casalis, who knew Moshoeshoe's mind and shared his ambitions, had described his territorial claims in vague and relatively modest terms as extending 'from near the junction of the Caledon and the Orange Rivers to the country of the Mantatis [Tlokoa]'.[1] In July 1842, after he had visited Thaba Bosiu, Philip declared that Moshoeshoe

---

[1] Appendix by Casalis in Moshoeshoe to Governor Napier, 20 Apr. 1841, *BR* i. 41.

claimed all the country between the Orange and the Vaal east of a drift on the Modder River fifteen miles south-west of Thaba 'Nchu, but admitted that 'the exercise of his authority is limited to the country lying between the Orange River and the Caledon'.[1] Soon afterwards, Philip

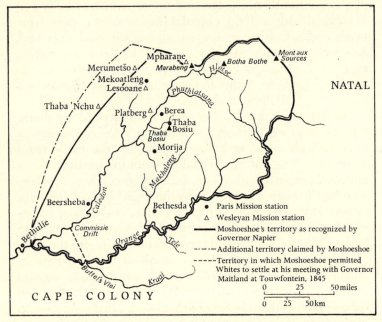

MAP 3. Moshoeshoe's Territory as recognized by Sir George Napier in 1843

himself drafted the territorial provisions that were incorporated in the treaty.[2] It defined Moshoeshoe's territory as including all the land between the Orange and the Caledon, with the addition of a strip from twenty-five to thirty miles wide on the north-western side of the Caledon, except near its source and at its junction with the Orange.[3] Britain

[1] Philip to Lieutenant-Governor Hare, 12 July 1842, *BR* i. 45.

[2] Philip to Montagu, Secretary to Government, Cape Town, 7 Sept. 1843, *BR* i. 52.

[3] 'The Territory of the Chief Moshesh is bounded from the west, from the junction of the Caledon with the Gariep [Orange] rivers to the sources of those Rivers near the Bouta Bouta, on the South by the Gariep River, from the junction aforesaid; and on the North by a line extending from about 25 to 30 miles North of the Caledon River, excepting near to its source and at its junction with

thereby recognized Moshoeshoe as the ruler of the land in the triangle between the lower Caledon and the Orange where few Africans had ever lived and trekboers were already penetrating; the land on the left bank of the upper Caledon which Sekonyela had wrested from Moshoeshoe and his Khoakhoa allies in 1824; and the lands on the right bank where BaSotho villages were interspersed with the settlements of the Coloured communities and their Wesleyan missionaries at Platberg, Lesooane, and Mpokoane.

The treaty as presented to Moshoeshoe left the status of Moroka's Rolong and Taaibosch's Kora ambiguous, because Thaba 'Nchu and Merumetšo are both almost exactly thirty miles from the Caledon River. Moshoeshoe tried to remove that ambiguity by informing the Colonial Government that he had signed the treaty in good faith that the territorial clause would be amended to make the boundary extend '10 or 12 miles' beyond the Wesleyan mission stations at Thaba 'Nchu and Merumetšo.[1]

Moshoeshoe had formed an alliance with a distant power, Great Britain, not only to promote his role as amalgamator of the BaSotho survivors of the *lifaqane* wars but also to resist the formidable pressures exerted by the expanding frontiers of white settlement. For the rest of his career he would regard this treaty as the charter of his territorial claims and of his relationship with the British Government. He would exercise all his diplomatic skills and, when necessary, fight with the utmost tenacity to translate the terms of his treaty into political realities.

3. '*Most willing to meet the wishes of Government*'

The conflicts in the Orange–Vaal region became more intense in the mid-1840s. As their numbers mounted by migration from Natal as well as the Cape Colony, voortrekkers penetrated deeper into Griqua and African territories

the Gariep where the Lands of Bethulie and the Territory of Sikonyela come close upon its Northern Bank.' C.O. 48/243, PRO. Also, with slightly different punctuation, in *BR* i. 55.

[1] Moshoeshoe to Civil Commissioner, Colesberg, 13 Dec. 1843, *BR* i. 56.

and, gaining confidence, they treated non-white authorities with increasing contempt; while African and Griqua chiefs clashed with one another as well as with Whites in a general scramble for territory, cattle, and fire-arms. European missionaries of different denominations tried to protect the people they worked among from settler pressures, but they themselves added fuel to the flames of discord among Africans and Griqua by espousing the conflicting claims of their respective chiefs. Colonial officials, already partly committed by the 1843 treaties, could not resist being sucked deeper and deeper into the cauldron.

As events unfolded, Moshoeshoe studied the region as a chess-board from his redoubt in the south-east, pushing subordinates out like pawns and knights and bishops to found new villages in contested areas, while conserving his larger pieces for the struggles that loomed ahead. Encouraging his followers to acquire their own horses and fire-arms, he himself established a powder-magazine at Thaba Bosiu. He also strove steadfastly to win and keep the confidence of British officials, convinced that his own interests and those of his people depended on the British alliance.

Two days after Moshoeshoe signed his treaty, William Shaw, General Superintendent of the Wesleyan Missions in South East Africa, who was visiting Platberg from his home in Grahamstown, wrote a letter to the colonial authorities protesting on behalf of his Society and the chiefs it served in the Caledon valley.[1] This was the beginning of a series of claims and counter-claims, each side trying to win the support of the Colonial Government. In European terms, was Moshoeshoe sovereign over the entire territory as defined in his treaty and amplified by him, with jurisdiction over all its inhabitants? Or were Moroka, Davids, Baatje, and Taaibosch, as well as Sekonyela, independent chiefs in independent territories?

Previously, the relations between the Wesleyan and the Paris missionaries had been correct, on occasion friendly, but never intimate. They had had a common interest in

---

[1] The Revd. W. Shaw to Acting Secretary to Government of the Eastern Province 15 Dec. 1843, *BR* i. 57-60.

opposing Afrikaner infiltration and in damping down conflicts among the communities in the Caledon valley. The
Wesleyans had often expressed admiration for Moshoeshoe
and, equally with the Paris missionaries, they had formed a
poor opinion of Sekonyela.[1] The two Societies had had a
tacit understanding that they should not encroach on each
other's established preserves, but they had never agreed on
the limits of their respective operations and there had been
resentment when one or other side had seemed to ignore the
understanding, as when Daumas founded his station at
Mekoatleng near Lesooane.[2]

Moshoeshoe's treaty precipitated an argument which
rapidly became acrimonious. Each Society aligned itself
with the chiefs it served and encouraged them to adopt
extreme positions. The advantage lay with the Paris mission
and Moshoeshoe. The treaty itself was a *fait accompli*, and
since Casalis was far the ablest diplomat of all the missionaries
concerned, Moshoeshoe was able to pursue an intelligent
and consistent course; whereas Moroka, Sekonyela, Taaibosch, and the Coloured chiefs suffered from the Wesleyan
practice of frequently transferring missionaries from one
station to another and, on occasion, from disputes among the
Wesleyan missionaries.

The Wesleyan missionaries were the prime movers of the
policies they espoused for themselves and their chiefs. The
relationship between Moshoeshoe and Casalis was a much
more egalitarian partnership between men who respected
one another, whose talents were complementary, and whose
political interests coincided. Casalis wrote and signed some
of the letters presenting the case for Moshoeshoe, referring
to the king in the third person. Other letters from Thaba
Bosiu purported to be composed by Moshoeshoe himself:
they were in Casalis's hand, but were written in the first
person and signed (marked X) by the king. The ideas,

[1] Typical of Wesleyan attitudes towards Moshoeshoe and Sekonyela before
1843 were those of W. Impey: Journal of W. Impey 1838–1847, Typescript of
Papers *re* S. Africa lent by the Revd. L. Hewsen, WMS; also J. Cameron, 23
July and 27 Aug. 1840, S.A. 12, WMS.
[2] Archbell, 23 Dec. 1834 and 9 July 1837, S.A. 7, and Edwards, 30 Mar.
1838, S.A. 12, WMS; Rolland, etc., n.d., *JME* xiii (1838), 21.

arguments, and facts set out in both classes of letters were the product of elaborate discussions between the king and his councillors. In African terms, Casalis was a royal councillor with special qualifications; in European terms, he was the secretary for foreign affairs. Since Moshoeshoe and Casalis were agreed about what the policy should be, theirs was an unusually fruitful co-operation between an intelligent but illiterate African ruler and a perceptive missionary who believed in his cause.[1]

According to the Wesleyans, Moroka, Davids, Baatje, and Taaibosch were leaders of independent communities. In 1833–4 they had settled on land which was 'entirely' or at least 'nearly' depopulated and Moshoeshoe had recognized their title to the land. Subsequently, they had never recognized Moshoeshoe's jurisdiction over them. Though they were not so numerous as Moshoeshoe's followers, they were 'more powerful', because they included Coloured people who possessed 1,500 horses and 2,000 muskets and were of 'superior intelligence' to Africans. The Government had erred in two respects: in making a treaty with Moshoeshoe without affording the same privileges to these other chiefs and to Sekonyela, and in attributing to Moshoeshoe rights over lands and persons north-west of the Caledon. To remedy these errors, the Government should make a similar treaty with the combined immigrant chiefs and another with Sekonyela, recognizing them as independent rulers north-west of the river.[2]

Where the Wesleyan case was the weakest was in its reference to Moshoeshoe's alleged recognition of the titles of the immigrant chiefs to the land. The Wesleyan missionaries were embarrassed about this. They knew that when the immigrants arrived in the area from the north-west in 1833–4 James Archbell, then their senior missionary, had drawn up a series of documents, full of long-winded legalistic

---

[1] Casalis to British Resident, 3 Feb. 1853, and statement by Dyke, n.d., *BR* ii. 19–20; H. Dieterlin, *Eugène Casalis (1812–1891)*, pp. 155–66.

[2] The Revd. W. Shaw to Acting Secretary to Government of the Eastern Province, 15 Dec. 1843, *BR* i. 57–60; the Revd. W. Shaw to Acting Secretary to Lieutenant-Governor, 18 Apr. 1844, *BR* i. 69–73; Letter-Book of the Revd. J. Cameron, P.A. 11. 2, OFS.

terminology, and that he might have persuaded Moshoeshoe and Sekonyela to put their marks to them. One document purported to show that on 7 December 1833 Moshoeshoe, described as 'Chief of the Bashutos', and Moseme, 'one of his subordinate Chiefs, resident at Thaba Nchu', sold outright and in perpetuity to Archbell and his colleagues, for the use of the Wesleyan mission, in return for 'Seven Young Oxen One Heifer Two Sheep & One Goat', an extensive territory centred on Thaba 'Nchu. According to another document, on 2 June 1834 Sekonyela 'Chief of the Manta-tees' [Tlokoa] sold to the same missionaries and Jan Captein [Taaibosch] for 'Eight Sheep Two Goats & Five Head of large Cattle' another extensive area around the Mpokoane mission. A third document states that on 17 July 1834 Moshoeshoe and Skonyela jointly sold to Archbell and a colleague, for eight cattle, thirty-four sheep, and five goats, a connecting tract of land around Platberg.[1] These docu-ments still exist, but their provenance is dubious. Moshoeshoe and Sekonyela could have had no means of comprehending the meaning of their tortuous jargon, even if an interpreter had contrived to find reasonably appropriate SeSotho terminology. Moreover, of course, neither Moshoeshoe nor Sekonyela had any customary right to dispose of territory. In 1840 James Cameron, a Wesleyan missionary who would later himself become an intemperate advocate of the Wes-leyan claims, had studied the documents and reached the conclusion that Moshoeshoe and Sekonyela had put their marks to blank sheets of paper, which Archbell had subse-quently filled in. By that time his former colleagues knew that Archbell was an unscrupulous man.[2] 'I see no hope

---

[1] The originals of these documents are in the archives of the Wesleyan mission station at Thaba 'Nchu. Copies are in P.A. 221. 1–2, OFS, and W. G. A. Mears, *Wesleyan Barolong Mission in Trans-Orangia 1821–1884*, [Cape Town] n.d., pp. 36–44, and *BR* i. 4–6 and iii. 97–8. There are commentaries in I. S. J. Venter, *Die Ruilkontrakte in 1833–34 aangegaan tussen Mosjesj en die Wesleyane* and *Die Sendingstasie Thaba 'Nchu 1833–1900*, Communications of the University of South Africa, C. 20 and C. 18, 1960.

[2] The relevant documents are in Philip Papers, vol. 3, folder 1, packet C, LMS, and S.A. 7 and S.A. 12, WMS. The climax of Archbell's disputes with his colleagues came early in 1839, when the 'Bechuana District Meeting' ordered a minute which Archbell had removed to be restored: Edwards,

for us,' wrote Cameron to the Revd. William Shaw (the General Superintendent of Wesleyan Missions in South East Africa), 'but to allow that Moshesh is still lord paramount of the soil and that we hold the lands under him for missionary purposes.'[1] Consequently, the Wesleyans did not deem it expedient to produce these documents in support of their claims.

In response to the Wesleyan challenges, Moshoeshoe and Casalis developed three main arguments. First, Moshoeshoe made a majestic claim to sovereignty over all the BaSotho and the entire disputed territory on historical grounds. Before 1818, he declared, the country in question, and much more, had been 'exclusively *known* and *owned*' by 'tribes' which 'went by the general name of Basutos, spoke one language, had the same habits and customs, intermarried, and considered each other as having had, at some remote period, one common origin'.[2] Then came the 'awful troubles' of the *lifaqane*, by the end of which Moshoeshoe had become recognized by all the BaSotho as their supreme chief:

Of all the aborigine Chiefs of the Basutos I was the only one who had succeeded in preserving his power and property. . . . All that remained in the land sought my protection and acknowledged my authority; thus I became entrusted, by the desire of the people, with the government of the whole Basuto country. The fugitives have returned by thousands from the Colony, and placed themselves and their country under my protection, and thus my title to rule Basutoland rests, first, on my being born Sovereign of a great portion of it, and secondly, on my having become the acknowledged Chief by the original proprietors of the remainder.[3]

Moshoeshoe's next claim was that when 'strangers' arrived from the north-west in 1833 he received them in accordance with the custom 'universally followed' by the Tswana and BaSotho.[4] He allotted them lands within his territory, where

25 Jan. 1839, S.A. 12, WMS. By that time Archbell had left the Wesleyan Missionary Society.

[1] Letter-Book of the Revd. J. Cameron, P.A. 11.2, OFS.
[2] Moshoeshoe to Secretary to Government, 15 May 1845, *BR* i. 82–3.
[3] Ibid., p. 84.
[4] Casalis to Civil Commissioner, Colesberg, 19 Mar. 1844, *BR* i. 66.

he allowed their chiefs to administer them but always under his own supreme authority. He could not have done more, because no chief could sell land to strangers, nor could a chief make a radical innovation without the approval of his subjects.[1] Finally, Moshoeshoe rebutted the Wesleyan contention that the newcomers had acquired independent rights by virtue of occupation, numbers, and power. Even when they had arrived in his territory, although the country appeared rather desolate, that was only because the people were hiding in fear of further attacks by Nguni and Coloured bands. BaSotho occupied sixty-nine villages north-west of the Caledon at that time, 'all under the Government of Moshesh'.[2] In 1845 Baatje, Davids, and Taaibosch had only one small village each and Moroka's Rolong were concentrated in and around the single town of Thaba 'Nchu,[3] whereas Moshoeshoe's BaSotho occupied at least 260 villages on the north-west side of the Caledon and another 440 villages on the south-east side, with a combined population of between 40,000 and 50,000 people.[4]

In these documents Moshoeshoe and Casalis had translated the ambiguities and complexities of a society in a state of flux into terms intelligible to European officials who were conditioned to the concept of political sovereignty over persons and territory. In so doing, they had distorted the facts about Moshoeshoe's ascriptive status in pre-*lifaqane* BaSotho society, his dealings with the immigrant chiefs and their missionaries, and the extent of his authority over land and people in the past as well as the present. But these distortions the Wesleyans could not easily refute, for none of them had the intimate *rapport* with their African or Coloured chiefs that Casalis had with Moshoeshoe, and all of them were relatively poorly informed about the history of the region and about the customs of its inhabitants. They could not even produce convincing evidence to rebut the assertions of Moshoeshoe and Casalis about the numbers

---

[1] Moshoeshoe to Secretary to Government, 15 May 1845, *BR* i. 85–6.
[2] Casalis to Civil Commissioner, Colesberg, 19 Mar. 1844, *BR* i. 65.
[3] Ibid., p. 67.
[4] Moshoeshoe to Secretary to Government, 15 May 1845, *BR* i. 84–5.

of BaSotho villages and people. The case presented by Moshoeshoe and Casalis was persuasive for the purpose in hand: convincing the colonial authorities. It was also an important ideological contribution to the incorporation of the diverse inhabitants of LeSotho into a single political community: a historical charter, legitimizing the King and the Nation and the bonds between them.

While the dispute over the status of the chiefs served by the Wesleyans dragged on, white settlers continued to penetrate the area, in defiance of a proclamation that Governor Napier had issued in 1842.[1] This movement was particularly formidable on Moshoeshoe's western flank. In some cases Moshoeshoe had allowed Whites to pasture their livestock there, under the impression that, like the main voortrekker parties, they would soon move on. In others, Whites 'bought' land from individuals who had no right to dispose of it. Casalis perceived the implications of this expansion. The missionary ideal of a civilized and christianized BaSotho nation, he wrote in a prophetic passage,

would be found to have been nothing but a dream, if this country fell into the power of the Dutch farmers. From that moment, the most favourable alternative for the BaSotho would be to escape poverty and destruction by entering into the service of the conquerors. Our congregations would then be dispersed, divided among isolated farms, and delivered to the mercy of ignorant and gross men who, for the most part, regard our efforts as an attempt to violate the rights of the so-called Christian nations.[2]

In October 1844 Moshoeshoe toured his western marches and circulated a notice declaring that all transactions in land and improvements, such as huts and cattle kraals, between the Caledon and the Orange rivers and within the boundaries of the Paris missions at Beersheba (whose inhabitants had formally accepted Moshoeshoe's authority) and Bethulie were unlawful and null and void.[3] But white penetration continued. In May 1845 Moshoeshoe informed

[1] 7 Sept. 1842, *BR* i. 48.
[2] Casalis, 5 June 1843, *JME* xix (1844), 3.
[3] Casalis to Lieutenant-Governor, 16 Oct. 1844; Moshoeshoe, 'Bekendmaking', 29 Oct. 1844, *BR* i. 80–1.

the colonial authorities that not less than 300 farmers were
within his territory:

> From their first appearance till now I have never ceased to
> warn them that I viewed them as mere passers by, and although
> I did not refuse them temporary hospitality, I could never allow
> them any right of property. . . . Notwithstanding my protesta-
> tions against it, many of the Emigrants have transferred their
> supposed rights to others without my knowledge or consent.[1]

In 1845 events in the Philippolis area obliged the colonial
officials to consider the implications of the alliances they
had made in 1843. Adam Kok's regime had never been
capable of restraining the individualistic Griqua from selling
and leasing land on a profligate scale to Whites in return
for livestock, brandy, fire-arms, ammunition, and other
consumer goods. Trekboers had already occupied a large proportion of the land by 1842. Then, after the British occupation of Port Natal, many ardent republican voortrekkers
returned to the high veld, participated in the scramble for
land, and incited the trekboers to join them in defying the
British authorities. The Griqua found themselves outnumbered and overpowered. Nevertheless, in February 1845
Adam Kok tried to exercise jurisdiction by arresting an
Afrikaner who was believed to have ill-treated two Griqua.
Voortrekkers then attempted to assume control of the terri-
tory, and would probably have done so if a British force had
not crossed the Orange River from Colesberg and scattered
them at Zwartkoppies, whereupon they retired to the
Winburg area, on Moshoeshoe's northern flank, leaving the
British officials to resolve the confusion around Philippolis.
Sir Peregrine Maitland, who had succeeded Napier as
Governor in 1844, had already begun to doubt the wisdom
of the 1843 treaties. Now he hastened to the scene to review
British relationships, not only with the Griqua and the trek-
boers in the Philippolis region, but with all the communities
on the high veld up to the limit of the Cape of Good Hope
Punishment Act along latitude 25° south.[2]

---

[1] Moshoeshoe to Secretary to Government, 15 May 1845, *BR* i. 86.
[2] John Franklin Midgley, 'The Orange River Sovereignty 1848–1854',
AYB 1949 (2), pp. 27–9; Galbraith, *Reluctant Empire*, pp. 205–9.

Maitland devised what he hoped would be an economical and efficient way of dealing with the chaotic conditions in the high veld. His great purpose, he told the Secretary of State, was 'to secure their lands and freedom to the numerous native tribes inhabiting the Country for hundreds of miles beyond the Colony to the North-East, against the encroachment and aggression of self-expatriated British subjects', who had 'contempt' for the 'Natives' and were indifferent to 'Native Rights and Native life'. He proposed to achieve this by making treaties with the principal chiefs, acknowledging their sovereignty, defining their boundaries, and dividing each of their territories into two parts: in one, which was to contain sufficient land for the present and future needs of their people, white farmers would be absolutely prohibited from occupying land; in the other, the chief would be allowed to lease land to white farmers. Each political community—black, brown, and white—would have complete control over its own internal affairs, but the Colonial Government would appoint a magistrate to settle disputes between Whites and others, exercising jurisdiction over British subjects under the Cape of Good Hope Punishment Act and over Africans and Griqua under the treaties to be made with their chiefs. The land rents paid by the Whites would be divided equally between the chiefs and the Government, and the magistrate would be empowered to call on the chiefs and on the white farmers to place armed men at his disposal when necessary.[1]

Maitland presented this plan to the Griqua chiefs, Kok and Waterboer, and the chiefs of the Caledon basin at a meeting at Touwfontein in Kok's territory on 30 June 1845. He told Moshoeshoe that he would not resolve his dispute with the chiefs served by the Wesleyans, and that he hoped Moshoeshoe would make some land available for lease by white farmers within the area that was not claimed by those chiefs. Moshoeshoe, who was accompanied by Casalis, had to weigh the value of the British alliance and the hope that the proposed magistrate would restrain the Whites, against

[1] Maitland to Glenelg, 1 Aug. 1845, C.O. 48/225, PRO; also, in part, *BR* i. 93–101.

the disadvantages of allowing some of the Orange–Caledon lands to pass irrevocably into white hands and failing to obtain recognition of his sovereignty over the country occupied by Moroka, Taaibosch, Davids, and Baatje. Without waiving his claim to sovereignty over the lands disputed with the Wesleyan-supported chiefs, he decided to accept the principles of the proposed treaty as outlined by Maitland; and he offered to allow Whites to lease land in the Orange–Caledon triangle extending about thirty miles eastwards from the junction of those rivers to Buffel's Vlei (Aliwal North) on the Orange and Commissie Drift on the Caledon. Moshoeshoe was also able to inform Maitland that the Taung chief, Moletsane, who was present and consented, wished the land he occupied around the Paris mission at Mekoatleng to be included in his territory.[1] Maitland persuaded Adam Kok to accept similar arrangements.

Whether Maitland's plan would actually 'secure their lands and freedom to the numerous native tribes' depended on the way in which it was applied. The first indications were ominous for Moshoeshoe and his people. Maitland sent a colonial Afrikaner official, Field-Commandant Gideon Joubert, whom Governor Napier had sent on a similar errand in 1842, with instructions to encourage his fellow-Afrikaners beyond the Orange River to co-operate, and to negotiate further with Moshoeshoe and Moletsane. By the time Joubert reached the Caledon basin he had spent a very difficult week among anti-British voortrekkers further north and he realized they would never submit to Maitland's scheme unless it was interpreted in their favour and nearly all their land claims were recognized. He then discovered that the Wesleyan missionaries' quarrel with the Paris missionaries could be turned to good account. If the Government made separate treaties with Moroka, Taaibosch, Baatje, and Davids, recognizing their independence from Moshoeshoe, they in turn would be willing to admit nearly all the white claims to land north-west of the Caledon,

---

[1] 'Minutes of Meeting at Touw Fontein: Terms of Treaty proposed by Governor Sir Peregrine Maitland to the Chief Moshesh', 30 June 1845, *BR* i. 88–91; Moshoeshoe to Maitland, 30 June 1845, ibid., pp. 91–2.

below Sekonyela's country. Joubert found that Moshoeshoe, on the other hand, after long consultations with Casalis and his BaSotho councillors, was adamant that Moroka and the other chiefs were his subordinates, and that he would not release more than a token addition to the land he had offered Maitland for white occupation in the Orange–Caledon triangle, by moving the southern point from Buffel's Vlei to the Kraai River.

In his confidential report Joubert recommended that the Government should make separate treaties with Moroka and the others and that, regardless of Moshoeshoe's stand, the line for white occupation should be moved further eastwards in the Orange–Caledon triangle. He declared that if the line was not changed, 289 white families on seventy-two farms would find themselves in the inalienable area and forced to move from land which they had been 'given' by Moshoeshoe. Joubert, who in 1842 had described Moshoeshoe as 'the most fit, sensible, and stately heathen Chief we ever saw', now asserted:

I expect that if it should so fall out that Mashoes becomes the only chief and the government enters into a treaty with him alone the government will not be able to rely upon his promises. He will be found to be a difficult and troublesome creature [schepsel]. His people considered apart from Marokka's, the Bastaarts, and the Coraners seem to be a poor defenceless lot. I have found no-one so upright and reasonable as Marocka and the boundary indicated by him is also reasonable.

Joubert had arrived at the principle of divide and rule: 'I also think that if Mashoes becomes chief over all and the others begin to become content with it he will become exalted and he will be a dangerous troublesome neighbour of the government's but if it remains under various chieftainships he will not easily become powerful.'[1]

Moshoeshoe and Casalis were disappointed by Joubert's manner and demands, but they hoped to offset any effort

[1] Report of Commandant Gideon D. Joubert, C.O. 2828 II, Cape Archives; transcription with English translation and commentary by R. S. Webb, LEC; English translation of part of the report (containing errors), *BR* i. 103–11. The word 'schepsel' used by Joubert is a derogatory term, applied to animals.

he may have made to discredit them. Moshoeshoe had made a good impression on Maitland at Touwfontein and this was reinforced by the presence of Arbousset in Cape Town with three of Moshoeshoe's sons,[1] with the result that, notwithstanding the contents of Joubert's report, Maitland informed the Secretary of State that

I know, from personal observation, that Moshesh himself, who has sent them [his sons], and contributed what he can to their maintenance, is a superior man, whose great and increasing influence over the neighbouring Native tribes, thus enlarged and strengthened by the education in European knowledge of these members of his family, is likely to prove very serviceable in preserving peace beyond the border . . .[2]

A month later, in October 1845, having received approval from London, Maitland appointed a British Resident to Trans-Orangia to inaugurate his scheme, instructing him on no account to intervene in disputes among blacks.[3] The first Resident resigned for personal reasons before achieving anything. His successor, Henry Douglas Warden, was to have decisive effects on Moshoeshoe and his people. Warden was born in London in 1800 and migrated to the Cape Colony in 1819. He had then served for twenty-five years in the Cape Corps, a Coloured regiment with white officers, before receiving this extremely difficult assignment.[4] His first task as British Resident was to complete a treaty with Adam Kok along the lines that Maitland had already negotiated. Then he went to Thaba Bosiu.

If Moshoeshoe was to profit from the British alliance, it was important to convince Warden that he was a co-operative and valuable ally. Accordingly, at this first meeting he confirmed that he would release for white occupation the land in the Orange–Caledon triangle below the line between the Kraai River and Commissie Drift, and he also agreed to Warden's proposal that he should meet the other

[1] See p. 100, above.
[2] Maitland to Stanley, 18 Sept. 1845, *BR* i. 111.
[3] Instructions to Captain Sutton, 27 Oct. 1845, *BR* i. 112–14.
[4] B. J. Barnard, ''n Lewensbeskrywing van Majoor Henry Douglas Warden', *AYB*, 1948 (1).

interested chiefs and try to resolve his differences with them.[1]
The meeting took place at Platberg on 10 March 1846.
Besides Moshoeshoe, Adam Kok, Moroka, Davids, Baatje,
Moletsane, Sekonyela, and a representative of Taaibosch
were all present, but they were not able to agree on their
respective statuses and boundaries. Instead, at Warden's
suggestion, they asked him to appoint a commission to
settle the matter, binding themselves to accept the commission's verdict and to keep the peace among themselves
in the interval.[2] But the commission was never appointed.
In March 1846 the eastern frontier of the Cape Colony
flared up in another bout of fighting, which engrossed the
attention of the Colonial Government and left Trans-
Orangia to its own resources.

The weakness in Maitland's scheme is that it placed an
intolerable burden on the shoulders of the British Resident.
In a frontier zone, where there is no consensus as to norms,
verbal and written agreements and moral suasion are of
little effect unless they are backed by superior physical
power. But the only standing force at Warden's disposal
was a single troop of the Cape Corps. For the rest, he had
to rely on the levies he could raise from among the very
communities he was meant to pacify. Consequently the
British presence did not diminish the anarchic trends
around Moshoeshoe. Among the Whites, republicans strove
to gain the upper hand over the colonially minded; among
the Blacks, cattle-raids and skirmishes marked the attempts
of each leader to consolidate his authority; Whites competed
with Blacks but each also sought allies across ethnic lines;
and a harassed and inexperienced Resident struggled from
crisis to crisis without resolving one of them.[3]

In this situation Moshoeshoe was concerned to expand and
consolidate his own strength and, at the same time, to
maintain the British alliance. He pursued his expansionist
policy vigorously on all fronts. In the north, he pushed his
son Molapo, his nephew Lesaoana, and his half-brother

---

[1] Warden to Maitland's Private Secretary, 8 Mar. 1846, *BR* i. 118–19.
[2] 'Application from Native Chiefs', 10 Mar. 1846, *BR* i. 119–20.
[3] Midgley, pp. 33–48.

Mopeli with their followers in among Sekonyela's people; in the north-west, his ally Moletsane and his subject Moseme disputed land and cattle with Moroka's people; and in the south-west his brother Posholi occupied Vechtkop, a mountain from which he could raid white farmers who persisted in occupying land east of the line between the Kraai River and Commissie Drift.[1]

The British alliance was important to Moshoeshoe because once the British had defeated the Xhosa again, as they seemed certain to do, they would be in a position to intervene decisively on the high veld. Therefore, when republican Afrikaners tried to get his support, he refused, and when Warden had scattered them with a mixed force at Winburg, he hastened to the scene and publicly proclaimed that the British could rely on him for help.[2] When Maitland was succeeded by a new Governor, Sir Henry Pottinger, in January 1847, with the significant additional title of High Commissioner 'for the settling and adjustment of the affairs of the territories in Southern Africa adjacent or contiguous to the Eastern and North-Eastern frontier' of the Cape Colony, Moshoeshoe made Casalis write him an updated version of his claims.[3] For the time being, Moshoeshoe and Casalis also gained the upper hand over Moroka and the Wesleyan missionaries in their contest for Warden's approval. In April 1847 Moshoeshoe visited Warden at his head-quarters in Bloemfontein with fresh evidence rebutting the Wesleyan claims and a few days later Warden reported to Cape Town that, while he was still not clear about the validity of the rival claims of Sekonyela and Moshoeshoe in the north, he was now convinced that Moshoeshoe had made his case for sovereignty over all the lands claimed by Moroka, Taaibosch, Davids, and Baatje, including territory extending almost to Bloemfontein.[4]

However, Moshoeshoe's success in gaining the approval of

[1] The Revd. J. Cameron to Warden, 26 July and 15 Aug. 1847, P.A. 11. 2, OFS; Arbousset, 9 Dec. 1846, *JME* xxii (1847), 202–5, and 30 Mar. 1847, *JME* xxiii (1848), 4–9.

[2] Warden to Maitland's Private Secretary, 29 June 1846, *BR* i. 124.

[3] Casalis to Pottinger, 14 Apr. 1847, *BR* i. 131–4.

[4] Warden to Pottinger's Secretary, 5 May 1847, *BR* i. 136.

Warden led to events that caused both of them to lose the confidence of Governor Pottinger. During the frontier war numerous groups of Nguni refugees from the scene of military operations fled northwards with livestock, including cattle they had seized from colonial farmers. Most of the refugees moved into the Witteberg mountains south of the Orange (the modern Herschel area), where Moshoeshoe's ally, the Phuthi chief Moorosi, had settled; but several hundred Thembu crossed the Orange above its confluence with the Caledon, where Moshoeshoe welcomed them as a useful accession to his black population. Early in the war Moshoeshoe led a military expedition to the Orange River and offered his services to the Colonial Government. Maitland replied that he did not need his support but that if he wished he could raid cattle from Nguni. Then in October 1847 Warden was ordered to investigate rumours that vast herds of stolen cattle were in the Witteberg. Instead of confining his response to an investigation, Warden impetuously raised a composite force of white farmers and BaSotho and crossed the Orange River into the Witteberg mountains; but the expedition was a disaster. He blundered into attacking friendly Thembu who had not been at war with the Colony and when the indignant Thembu counterattacked most of the Whites deserted and Warden lost nearly all the cattle he had seized. Pottinger reprimanded Warden for this 'totally unauthorized expedition' and blamed him for having been misled by 'the duplicity and perfidy of Moshesh and Morosi'.[1] Warden demurred. Moorosi, he agreed, was unreliable; but 'the Chief Moshesh I have ever found honest and straightforward, and most willing to meet the wishes of Government'.[2]

4. *'Peace is like the rain which makes the grass grow'*

In December 1847 Pottinger was succeeded by a new High Commissioner, Sir Harry Smith. Smith, who had served as a military officer on the eastern frontier under

---

[1] Pottinger's Secretary to Warden, 9 Oct. 1847, *BR* i. 148–50.
[2] Warden to Pottinger's Secretary, 27 Oct. 1847, *BR* i. 152–3.

D'Urban in the 1830s and later in India, was a self-confident, impulsive extrovert. He believed that he could solve the problems of southern Africa by the adroit use of his own powers of persuasion and a far-reaching extension of British authority. He rapidly advanced the frontier of the Cape Colony to the Orange River between Ramah and the Atlantic Ocean in the arid north-west. Then, winding up the war on the eastern frontier, he annexed the territory as far as the Kei River in the East and the Kraai in the north-east and, to dramatize the change, he convened the Xhosa chiefs, tore up their treaties, and humiliated them by making them kiss his feet. Next he crossed the Orange River and browbeat Adam Kok into surrendering rights which Maitland had recognized at Touwfontein. Kok lost his rents from lands leased to white farmers north of the Riet River and permitted white people to acquire permanent farms in the previously 'inalienable' area south of that river. Smith then summoned Moshoeshoe and the other Caledon valley chiefs to meet him at Winburg, the voortrekker village seventy miles north-west of Thaba Bosiu.[1]

Moshoeshoe rode to Winburg with Casalis and several of his sons and brothers, to receive a friendly rather than an overbearing reception. Smith gave him presents—two new saddles, a marquee tent, and a gold watch—and then, turning to business, explained his intentions. He proposed to proclaim British sovereignty over the entire area between the Orange and the Vaal. The Whites would be allowed to remain in occupation of the lands they already held, but they would be prevented from making new encroachments, and the Africans would continue to rule themselves according to their own laws and customs. Moshoeshoe raised the question of his disputes with Moroka and Sekonyela, but Smith brushed that aside. A commission would settle it if necessary.

'But for my part,' he added, 'I believe you are quite right, and I would beg of you not to be uneasy about it. In proclaiming the Sovereignty of the Queen, it is as much to protect Moshesh against his internal as his external enemies. Trust to me, and

[1] Galbraith, pp. 220–31; Midgley, pp. 50–9.

no one will dare to raise his hand against the Great Chief of the Basutos.' Then, raising his right hand about a foot above the desk, His Excellency added, 'Moshesh is like this;' then raising his left hand another foot above the right he said, 'but Her Majesty is as this.'[1]

Moshoeshoe did not object and he added his mark below Smith's signature on a written summary of the conference proceedings,[2] saying, 'his desire was that all should live together, that no limits should be made, and thus no one should say to him "this land is no longer yours;" what he required was that the Boers should be brought to order and governed'.[3]

A week later, after meeting several groups of Whites, Smith proclaimed the sovereignty of Queen Victoria over all the lands between the Orange and the Vaal, for the 'protection and preservation of the just and hereditary rights of all the Native Chiefs' and 'the rule and government of Her Majesty's subjects, their interests and welfare'.[4]

Moshoeshoe was still impressed by the advantages that might accrue from the British connection. Taking Smith's assurances at their face value, he had reason to believe that the British would restrain the Whites from encroaching further into the Caledon basin and that they would give him a free hand to complete the business of welding the African communities together into a single political entity. He would then be able to pass on to his successors a united LeSotho straddling the Caledon valley and protected by the British from aggression by white settlers.

Consequently, when the voortrekker leader Andries Pretorius organized resistance to the British, Moshoeshoe

---

[1] Casalis to Rolland, 14 Feb. 1848, *BR* iii. 101.
[2] *BR* i. 158–9.
[3] Casalis to Rolland, 14 Feb. 1848, *BR* iii. 101.
[4] *BR* i. 159–61. The official records of the Orange River Sovereignty, 1848–54, are in the OFS. Many of the relevant documents are published in *BR* i. and ii. British policy is ably dealt with in C. W. de Kiewiet, *British Colonial Policy and the South African Republics, 1848–1872*, London, 1929, as well as in the works previously cited by Galbraith and Muller. Midgley, op. cit., is a detailed history of the Sovereignty. F. A. van Jaarsveld, *Die Eenheidstrewe van die Republiekeinse Afrikaners: i. Pioniershartstogte (1836–1864)*, Johannesburg, 1951, deals with voortrekker politics on both sides of the Vaal.

opposed him. On 14 February 1848 Pretorius rode to LeSotho
where, meeting two sons of the king, he demanded to see
Moshoeshoe, 'to know why he made so strong a treaty with
the British Government'. Letsie and Sekhonyana told him
that if that was his business, Moshoeshoe would not see him.
Pretorius rode off in anger. 'Moshesh is no longer my friend,'
he said, 'I will have the great Chief Panda [Mpande, the
Zulu king] for my ally.'[1] Nevertheless Pretorius made further
attempts to get in touch with Moshoeshoe. He persuaded a
trekboer who knew him to try to arrange an interview, but
again Moshoeshoe declined.[2] He also wrote to the MoSotho
king, claiming that Afrikaners had saved him from his
enemies. But Moshoeshoe replied that the first Afrikaners
he had ever met—a trekboer hunting expedition in 1831—
had told him they were British subjects, and that he looked
on the British High Commissioner as 'the Protector and
Commander-in-Chief of all the whites in South Africa'.
Moshoeshoe also kept Warden and Smith informed of all
these pressures from Pretorius.[3] His predicament became
more serious in July when Pretorius, with nearly a thousand
followers, advanced on Bloemfontein. Warden asked Moshoeshoe to come to his assistance and he was about to do so when
he received a second message telling him to keep quiet.[4]
Pretorius then swept Warden and his little force of seventy
men across the Orange River and summoned Moshoeshoe
to meet him in Bloemfontein. But still Moshoeshoe refused,
and his gamble paid off. Smith made a rapid journey from
Cape Town with 700 men and three six-pounder guns.
When Smith crossed the Orange River, Pretorius's band
began to disintegrate and Smith scattered the remainder in
a sharp engagement at Boomplaats, forty miles north-east
of Philippolis (29 August 1848). Glowing with his triumph,
Smith applauded Moshoeshoe in his report to London: 'The

[1] Warden to Smith's Secretary, 24 Feb. 1848, *BR* i. 168.
[2] Midgley, p. 89.
[3] Pretorius to Moshoeshoe, 20 Apr. 1848, Moshoeshoe to Pretorius, 28 Apr.
1848, Moshoeshoe to Smith, 28 Apr. 1848, Moshoeshoe to Warden, 28 Apr.
1848, *BR* i. 169–71.
[4] Moshoeshoe to Smith, 15 Aug. 1848, *BR* i. 176, and note on this letter in
the Revd. H. M. Dyke MSS., LEC.

Chief Moshesh has been staunch in his allegiance and most peremptorily refused to see Pretorius, who used every effort to obtain an interview with him.'[1] Smith then proceeded to Winburg where he had further discussions with Moshoe-shoe and other chiefs. According to Moshoeshoe's missionary-interpreter, when the king tried to raise the land question, 'His Excellency appeared offended and declared he would hear of no limits, that all must live together, at which the Chief declared his satisfaction'.[2]

However, Moshoeshoe was destined to be disillusioned with the British. Smith had been given the South African appointment on the understanding that he would reduce British expenditures and in reporting the annexation he assured the British Colonial Secretary that the Orange River Sovereignty would not be a burden.[3] Consequently, after suppressing Pretorius's rebellion, he left behind him in the Sovereignty too weak an establishment to dominate the territory. Warden remained as Resident in charge of a few poorly paid magistrates and clerks and a military force of only about 250 men.[4] Warden and his magistrates were men of limited experience and narrow vision, conditioned to the racially stratified Cape Colonial situation. They were disposed to side with white farmers when their interests clashed with those of Africans, and with British missionaries when they differed from French. Moreover Smith himself was a man of his nation, his profession, and his times. In dealing with Moshoeshoe at Winburg he had not paused to reflect on the issues he had raised and later, when he had to make specific decisions, he was as partisan as his subordinates. Instead, therefore, of gaining protection from white farmers and liberty to complete the task of state-making on both sides of the Caledon River, Moshoeshoe was faced with intensified white pressures in the south-west and heightened opposition to incorporation by his black and brown neighbours in the north, aided and abetted by the British officials.

[1] Smith to Earl Grey, 23 Aug. 1848, *BR* i. 177.
[2] Minutes of Meeting at Winburg, 9 Sept. 1848, C.O. 48/287, PRO; extracts from these Minutes, *BR* i. 178; the quotation is from the comment by Dyke in the Dyke MSS., LEC.
[3] Galbraith, pp. 220–32.   [4] Midgley, pp. 142–3.

The king was obliged to move extremely warily. If he carried resistance too far, he risked concerted action by his white, brown, and black neighbours with British support. The fate of the Xhosa chiefdoms was a constant reminder that such a combination was possible and that, with their immense superiority in arms and ammunition, his enemies might overwhelm him and dismember his territory. He was not yet ready to take that risk. He needed more time to equip his men with horses and fire-arms and train them to use them effectively. On the other hand, if he gave his own people an impression of weakness, he risked losing control over them. His brothers and sons and their followers, lacking his own comprehensive overview of the distribution of power in southern Africa, might embark on a premature and disastrous conflict; or some of them might secede in the customary SeSotho manner and split the kingdom into autonomous sections which enemies would be able to conquer piecemeal. Moshoeshoe therefore resorted to a supple strategy. He encouraged his people to continue to penetrate the lands that were partially occupied by black, brown, and white neighbours who did not recognize his authority, with a view to incorporating as much territory as possible in his kingdom. He delayed committing himself to acquiescing in territorial demands by Sovereignty officials until it seemed essential, and then he appealed to Cape Town or London for redress and turned a blind eye to the activities of those of his followers who refused to submit. Meanwhile, he built up his military resources in preparation for the defensive warfare that might eventually be unavoidable.

Moshoeshoe came under pressure in the south-west and the north simultaneously. In the south-west, the British officials demanded further concessions. After Boomplaats, Richard Southey, Smith's private secretary, tried to persuade Moshoeshoe to meet him to discuss this question, but, lest he should be coerced into making a hasty decision without the opportunity of consulting his councillors and convening a *pitso*, Moshoeshoe sent sons and councillors to represent him and report back. Southey told them that he would advise Smith to promulgate a boundary running fifty miles further east than the existing Maitland line. Moshoeshoe rejected this demand and Casalis persuaded Smith not to insist on it.[1] Nevertheless in April 1849 Southey, back in Cape Town, sent very explicit instructions to Warden: 'Mr. Southey, by Sir H. Smith's desire, adds that no farmer is to be moved against his will, to make way for natives, from farms owned

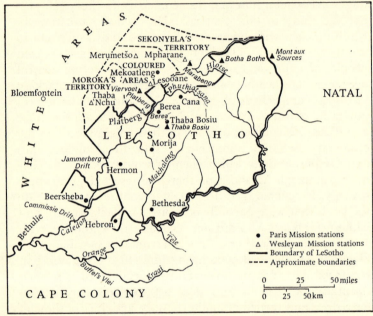

MAP 4. LeSotho and vicinity as divided by Major Warden in 1849

and occupied by him on 3rd February, 1848.'[2] The implication of this order was that the new boundary was to detach from LeSotho all the land which Warden, the local magistrate, and a few prominent farmers deemed to have been occupied by Whites at the time of the annexation, irrespective of the number of BaSotho who lived there before or after the operative date. The local officials did almost exactly as they were told. In an interview with Letsie, Moshoeshoe's eldest son, Warden insisted that Moshoeshoe's jurisdiction should

---

[1] Moshoeshoe to Rolland, 9 Dec. 1848, Southey to Moshoeshoe, 11 Dec. 1848, Casalis to Smith, 28 Dec. 1848, *BR* i. 209–14.

[2] Southey to Warden, 12 Apr. 1849, S.C. 3/1, OFS.

terminate about forty miles east of Maitland's line, except
for the Paris mission stations at Beersheba and Hebron and
corridors leading to them.[1] This plan would excise from
LeSotho over a hundred villages with several thousand
BaSotho inhabitants, including the village of Moshoeshoe's
brother Posholi at Vechtkop, in the interests of perhaps a
dozen white farmers.[2] On being asked by Warden if he
would consent to these limits, Letsie replied, 'Yes, as when
a dog consents to walk after him who drags it with a rope.'[3]

Moshoeshoe was urged by nearly all his kinsmen and councillors to reject this demand; but he decided to acquiesce,
while telling his missionaries to inform the High Commissioner
that 'he has signed it because of the intimidations employed
by the British Resident'.[4] These 'intimidations' referred particularly to the situation on Moshoeshoe's northern frontier.

There the officials had decided not only to lay down a
boundary between white and black areas, but also a series
of boundaries between the lands of the various black chiefs,
thereby negating Moshoeshoe's claim to paramountcy which
Napier had recognized and Maitland had left unresolved.
First they established a line between Moshoeshoe and his
old enemy, the Tlokoa chief Sekonyela.[5] But Moshoeshoe
was not to be deterred from trying to recover his ancestral
territory in the upper Caledon basin which Sekonyela had
seized from him fifteen years earlier, now that he had an
overwhelming numerical advantage. As Moshoeshoe's people
vied with Sekonyela's for control of land and livestock, their
neighbours became drawn into the quarrel—Moletsane's
Taung on the side of Moshoeshoe and Taaibosch's Kora and

[1] Warden to Moshoeshoe, 20 Sept. 1849, Warden to Smith, 20 Sept. 1849,
Moshoeshoe to Warden, 21 Sept. 1849, *BR* i. 279–84.

[2] Moshoeshoe to Warden, 1 Oct. 1849, *BR* i. 286–7; the note attached to this
letter in the Dyke MSS., evidently in the hand of Arbousset, gives the names of
ninety-eight villages cut off from LeSotho by Warden's line, LEC.

[3] Comment by Dyke on Arbousset to Warden, 21 Sept. 1849, *BR* i. 284–5,
Dyke MSS., LEC.

[4] Moshoeshoe to Warden, 1 Oct. 1849, *BR* i. 286–7; Arbousset, Dyke,
Maitin, and Lautré to Smith, 1 Oct. 1849, *BR* i. 287–90; the quotation is on
p. 287.

[5] 'Decision of the High Commissioner', 7 Dec. 1848, *BR* i. 208; Midgley,
pp. 202–10.

Moroka's Rolong on Sekonyela's side; and Warden committed himself more and more deeply until, against Smith's orders, he demanded that all parties should return captured livestock—a demand that led to endless recriminations, with each chief calling foul and applying to Warden for support as occasion arose.[1]

During 1849 the British Resident changed his mind about Moshoeshoe. If Warden had tried to carry out Smith's declared intention of achieving equity between black and white in the Sovereignty, he might have realized that the key to the situation lay in keeping faith with the MoSotho. Instead, under the influence of the white settlers and the Wesleyan missionaries, he informed Southey that 'Some decided steps must no doubt be taken to humble this tribe, or we shall not have quiet in the land. All the Chiefs have but one opinion towards Moshesh, and that is that he is becoming too rich and powerful to be longer a safe neighbour, and they are all anxious to join against him.'[2] Warden proceeded to organize a combination of chiefs. Each was to respect the lines laid down by the white officials and to join with him to discipline anyone who disturbed the peace. In form, this system was non-partisan; in fact, it was directed against Moshoeshoe. When Warden demanded that Moshoeshoe should accept his new boundary line in the southwest, he threatened that if he did not consent the British administration would side unequivocally with the Tlokoa in the north.[3] That was why Moshoeshoe acquiesced in the cession of south-western LeSotho to white farmers.

By that time the turmoil that followed the British annexation of the Orange River Sovereignty had caused a reaction against Christianity and hostility towards white people among the BaSotho. Christianity had won its early victories largely because the Paris missionaries had been the first Whites to settle in the country and their arrival had been followed by over a decade of peace and prosperity. The

[1] Midgley, pp. 219–27.

[2] Warden to Smith's Secretary, 5 Aug. 1849, *BR* i. 261.

[3] Warden to Moshoeshoe, 20 Sept. 1849, *BR* i. 279–80; J. J. Freeman Deputation 1849–1850, Box 2, AO 4/JJF2, LMS; D. F. Ellenberger, *Leselinyana*, 16 Oct. 1891, 13 Nov. 1893.

missionaries themselves had frequently claimed the credit for the new security and, with their dual stress on Christianity and Civilization, they had seemed to identify their religion with their race.[1] Consequently the collapse of security and the loss of land under pressures from white farmers and officials vindicated the traditionalists who had always been suspicious of Whites and rejected their religion. Whites in general seemed to be hypocrites: they professed a religion of peace while they stole the country.[2] The missionaries were widely assumed to be no better than other Whites, especially since they tried to restrain their congregations from participating in retaliatory cattle-raids. In October 1848 the missionaries instructed church members to disobey Moshoeshoe's command that every man in northern LeSotho should take part in a massive raid on the Tlokoa, and they then withheld communion from members who had done so and accepted their share of the booty.[3] This rash decision, which was made during the absence of Casalis, lost the missionaries much of the confidence they had gained since 1833. After 1848 they and their diminished congregations would find it difficult to live down the charge that Christianity was associated with cowardice and disloyalty.[4]

In or shortly before December 1848, Molapo, Moshoeshoe's second son and the missionaries' most important convert, abandoned Christianity.[5] A landslide followed. By 1852 all of the five royal kinsmen whom Arbousset had taken to Cape Town for education in 1844 had relapsed, and the only male relatives of the king who still practised Christianity were a half-brother, Lelosa, and a cousin named Taoana.[6] Moreover, as if to make amends for their previous

[1] e.g. Schrumpf, 25 Mar. 1847, reporting a speech by Casalis in the presence of Moshoeshoe, *JME* xxii (1847), 289–93.

[2] Maeder, 15 Feb. 1851, *JME* xxvi (1851), 176–85.

[3] Arbousset, 9 May 1849, *JME* xxiv (1849), 387–93; Dyke, 20 May 1849, ibid., pp. 430–2.

[4] Informant Mosebi Damane, I. 39.

[5] Arbousset, 29 Dec. 1848, *JME* xxiv (1849), 186–7.

[6] Casalis, 6 Apr. 1849, *JME* xxiv (1849), 305–7; Dyke, 22 Apr. 1850, *JME* xxv (1850), 368–75; Casalis, 14 Feb. 1851, *JME* xxvi (1851), 162–8; Casalis, Apr. 1852, *JME* xxvii (1852), 293–5.

aberrations, the relapsed royal converts were foremost in leading an exuberant revival of traditional customs and rituals and preparations for war. At the same time, a female diviner named Mantsopa was acquiring a reputation for being able to predict the occasion for victories, and in 1850–1 a revivalist movement initiated by the Xhosa prophet Mlanjeni swept through LeSotho. Mlanjeni's message was millennial: return to the old customs, obey the ancestors, sacrifice all yellow cattle, then Mlanjeni would place himself at the head of an army of true believers who would be immune from the effects of fire-arms and drive all the Whites beyond the seas. People throughout LeSotho greeted each other with the words: 'Molageni [Mlanjeni] is King!'[1]

Moshoeshoe could not ignore this reaction with its political as well as its racial and religious overtones. Although he continued to attend church services most Sundays, to see that his missionaries were not ill-treated, to talk to them in terms of their religion, and to consult them and use them as scribes, interpreters, and negotiators, he did not attempt to conceal his bitterness. He informed Arbousset that previously he had hoped that white people were different from Blacks, but he now knew that they, too, only looked after their own interests and trampled the rights of others underfoot.[2] Casalis he still trusted, but he told him he was disillusioned with the hopes he had built up. 'You are civilized', he said. 'You do not steal cattle, it is true: but you steal entire countries. And if you could, you would send our cattle to pasture in the clouds.'[3] There was no longer any talk of Moshoeshoe's conversion, nor of concessions to missionary ethics in his private or his public life. He took numerous new wives and he allowed none of them divorces. He convened initiation schools. He performed all the traditional sacrifices and purifications, especially before

---

[1] Schrumpf, 13 Feb. 1851, *JME* xxvi (1851), 168–76; Arbousset, Apr. 1851, *JME* xxvi (1851), 323–4; Perrot, *Les Sotho*, pp. 52–88, and 'Un Culte messianique chez les Sotho au milieu du xixᵉ siècle', *Archives de Sociologie des Religions*, xviii (July–Dec. 1964), 147–52. Molageni is the SeSotho form of the Xhosa name Mlanjeni.

[2] Arbousset, Apr. 1852, *JME* xxvii (1852), 284–5.

[3] Casalis, n.d., *JME* xxvii (1852), 3.

and after military expeditions. He consulted Mantsopa and he sent messengers to Mlanjeni.[1]

Nevertheless, the king kept a clear head. He had suffered too much at the hands of other Africans and derived too many benefits from his missionaries to become a racist. Moreover, his strong sense of realism showed him that to match Warden's inflexibility with recalcitrance, as his more impetuous councillors and kinsmen desired, might be heroic, but would be disastrous for his people.[2] If they were to survive as a national entity with a territory of their own, he would have to put up with the blunders of inept officials, for in the long run the best hope for the BaSotho still lay in an accommodation with the British Government. He therefore pursued essentially the same policy as he had before Warden had laid down the hated boundary lines, encouraging his subjects and allies to retain effective control over as much territory as possible, making sure that he made a net profit in cattle and especially in horses from the incessant raiding, but doing everything that was reasonable to avert a general conflict.

In February 1850 the Revd. James Freeman toured South Africa on behalf of the London Missionary Society, and when he reached Thaba Bosiu Moshoeshoe and Casalis seized the opportunity to appeal through him to London, over the heads of the British officials in South Africa. Freeman, convinced that Moshoeshoe had been grievously wronged, wrote to Earl Grey, the Secretary of State, declaring that the boundaries that Smith and Warden had imposed on him were 'essentially and radically unjust . . . cruel . . . impolitic . . . and unnecessary'.[3] Meanwhile, in the south-west Moshoeshoe's tough brother Posholi acted independently now that his land had been included in the white sector, raiding the herds of the white farmers and making life difficult for them. In the north Moshoeshoe's subject

---

[1] Schrumpf, 13 Feb. 1851, *JME* xxvi (1851), 174–5, and 24 Dec. 1851, *JME* xxvii (1852), 129–31.

[2] Casalis, 14 Feb. 1851, *JME* xxvi (1851), 162–8.

[3] Freeman to Grey, 20 Aug. 1850, J. J. Freeman, *A Tour in South Africa*, London, 1851, pp. 248–53; also J. J. Freeman Deputation 1849–50, Box 2, AO 4/JJF2, LMS.

Moseme held fast to land inside the area that Warden had allotted to Moroka, while his ally Moletsane remained rooted between the Tlokoa and the Kora and Rolong. Members of all these communities, as well as Moshoeshoe's kinsmen, were involved in frequent raids. Warden persisted in interposing himself in these disturbances, essaying the hopeless task of allocating blame and demanding compensation for each foray, and shifting more and more decisively from the role of impartial arbitrator to that of outright partisan. Moroka became a 'good' chief and Moshoeshoe the cause of all the troubles. By September 1850 Warden was holding Moshoeshoe responsible for the return of all the horses and cattle that Moroka claimed had been raided by Moseme's and Moletsane's followers, and threatening him with war: 'I should indeed be grieved', he wrote, 'to find you involved in a war with Government, the result [of which] would be the break-up of your people as a nation.'[1] Soon afterwards Warden informed the High Commissioner's secretary:

The Basuto people have within the last few years become exceeding rich in cattle and horses, and possess more firearms than all the other tribes in the Sovereignty put together. All this appears to have rendered them proud and insolent towards their neighbours. The time I imagine is not distant when it will be necessary to place the Basuto people under some restraint.[2]

Before Warden moved against Moshoeshoe, Smith's 'peace' had collapsed on the eastern frontier of the Cape Colony. Moshoeshoe, like others, had seen this coming and, far from conspiring with the Xhosa chiefs, as his white enemies were to allege, he warned Warden about it in advance.[3] Although Warden passed the message on to Smith, the High Commissioner remained optimistic about his frontier arrangements until Christmas Day 1850, when the Xhosa began their last and most sustained military challenge to British supremacy, inspired by the prophet Mlanjeni and aided by Coloured people, including members of the Cape Mounted Rifles, who had their own reasons

---

[1] Warden to Moshoeshoe, 24 Sept. 1850, *BR* i. 326.
[2] Warden to Smith's Secretary, 5 Oct. 1850, *BR* i. 338.
[3] Warden to Smith, 10 Nov. 1850, *BR* i. 349.

for being disillusioned with the Colonial Government.[1]
This war, which lasted into 1853, absorbed all the British
military forces in South Africa except for those already in
Natal and the Sovereignty, leaving Warden without any
prospect of reinforcements from the Cape Colony.

Nevertheless Warden persisted in his aggressive policy. In
the south he started by repeating his error of 1846, leading his
troops, augmented by white and Griqua levies and by
Posholi's people, who were attracted by the prospects of
booty, into a conflict with some Thembu who had settled
north of the Orange and Moorosi's Phuthi on the southern
side of that river.[2] He then directed his attention to the lower
Caledon valley, where he ordered an Englishman named
Bailie to organize some Mfengu refugees into an armed force
to drive the BaSotho inhabitants beyond the boundary
line, in spite of the fact that he had promised them continued
rights of occupation when he had imposed the line on Moshoeshoe in 1849. This plan was abortive. When Bailie led
his force against Posholi in August 1851, he was roundly
defeated, the Mfengu survivors were scattered, and Bailie
himself fled to the Cape Colony. By that time Warden himself had organized a joint expedition to humble Moshoeshoe
and his Taung allies in the north.[3]

In June 1851 Warden applied his long-considered plan
for a concerted attack on Moshoeshoe and Moletsane, informing the High Commissioner that 'nothing short of a
severe humbling of the Basuto and Bataung tribes will give
permanent peace to this extensive country'.[4] For this grand
enterprise he ordered levies from the other white, brown,
and black communities in the Sovereignty, expecting to
muster a force of 3,000 men. The response fell far short
of his expectation, for even the white population had lost

[1] Galbraith, pp. 245–51.
[2] Midgley, pp. 314–17.
[3] Schrumpf, 1 June 1851, *JME* xxvi (1851), 369–75; Cochet, 22 July 1851,
JME xxvi (1851), 460–8; Dyke, 18 July 1851, *JME* xxvii (1852), 4–13; Cochet, 29 Dec. 1851, *JME* xxvii (1852), 161–5. For an informed criticism of
Warden's actions by an Afrikaner observer, see Josias Hoffman (the later
President of the Orange Free State) to Hogge and Owen, 15 Jan. 1852, *BR*
i. 488–94.
[4] Warden to Smith's Secretary, 1 June 1851, *BR* i. 403.

confidence in his incessant interventions in African affairs. His total strength was less than 1,400 men—160 troops, 120 white farmers, 180 of Kok's Griqua, 70 of Taaibosch's Kora, and 800 of Moroka's Rolong.[1] Camping at Platberg, he ordered Moshoeshoe to meet him there; but mindful of the fact that in similar circumstances a Xhosa chief had been seized by British officers, the king accepted his councillors' advice to send two missionaries with one of his junior sons. On 25 June Warden sent Moshoeshoe an ultimatum: by 5 July he was to hand over 6,000 head of good cattle and 300 horses, representing compensation and fines for damages alleged to have been inflicted by Moshoeshoe and his allies on the other communities.[2] On 29 June Warden convened the allied chiefs and told them that the time had come 'for the weak nations to combine and show that they were strong [enough] to put down murder and robbery, even though it were the powerful chief Moshesh'.[3] At dawn the next day, before his ultimatum to Moshoeshoe had expired, he ordered his composite forces to attack Moletsane's Taung, who had occupied Viervoet mountain between Platberg and Mekoatleng. Covered by a six-pounder gun, they ascended the mountain and drove the Taung before them, capturing 3,000 cattle; but numerous BaSotho under Moshoeshoe's son Molapo and half-brother Mopeli then gained the summit and took the aggressors unawares, killing over 200 Africans—mainly Rolong who had drunk themselves into a stupor on captured Taung beer. Warden quickly retreated to Thaba 'Nchu with the survivors. His grand enterprise had collapsed, and with it his method of pacifying the Sovereignty.[4]

---

[1] Major Donovan, Cape Mounted Rifles, to Lt.-Col. Cloete, 4 July 1851, *BR* i. 420.   [2] Warden to Moshoeshoe, 25 June 1851, *BR* i. 413–14.

[3] 'Notes of a Meeting held in the Camp at Viervoet near Platberg, on the 29th June, 1851', *BR* i. 415–20.

[4] Major Donovan to Lt.-Col. Cloete, 4 July 1851, *BR* i. 420; Warden to Smith, 6 July 1851, ibid., pp. 421–2; Statement by Kolooi (a Taung participant), 5 July 1851, B.R. 1/4, OFS: Casalis, 8 July 1851, *JME* xxvii (1852), 14–22; Dyke, 18 July 1851, *JME* xxvii (1852), 4–13; Arbousset, 6 Aug. 1851, *JME* xxvi (1851), 409–20; Cameron, 9 Aug. 1851, S.A. 12, WMS; D. F. Ellenberger, *Leselinyana*, 6 Nov. 1913; Warden to Clerk (Warden's apologia), 20 Sept. 1853, *BR* ii. 65–9.

After the battle of Viervoet, British prestige slumped and the MoSotho king found himself courted by Whites of all shades of opinion from both sides of the Vaal River—ardent republicans like Pretorius, British loyalists, and even an adventurer named van der Colff who compounded the confusion by sending Moshoeshoe forged letters in the name of Pretorius and pillaging all and sundry at the head of a mixed group of bandits. Warden tried to re-establish control with the help of a contingent of Zulu with British officers supplied by the Governor of Natal, but their lack of discipline merely added fuel to the flames.[1]

Having tasted victory, the BaSotho were in a militant mood and even if Moshoeshoe had wished he could not have prevented his people from raiding their neighbours. Even so, he acted with his usual realism. He had no wish to give the British military machine a pretext for turning on him when it had overcome the Xhosa, as he realized it was certain to do. Therefore, although Moshoeshoe sent friendly messages to Sandile and Sarili, the leaders of the Xhosa resistance, and possibly also supplied them with gunpowder, he did not encourage his people to join them.[2] He also refused to enter into any combination with Afrikaners against Warden's demoralized regime in the Sovereignty; but he did ask his missionaries to appeal for redress to Warden's superiors.[3]

Earl Grey, the Colonial Secretary, was receptive to the missionaries' appeal. Freeman's letters and the outbreak of the frontier war had already raised serious doubts in Grey's mind about Smith's expansionism and Grey had sent two special representatives to South Africa—William S. Hogge and C. Mostyn Owen. Ostensibly, Hogge and Owen were assistants to the High Commissioner. In fact Grey desired

[1] Midgley, ch. 10; *BR* i. 422 ff.

[2] The British military officers engaged in the war against the Xhosa suspected Moshoeshoe of playing a significant role in the Xhosa resistance, but it seems probable that he did little more than keep in regular communication with the Xhosa chiefs by messengers. Smith to Warden, 17 June 1851, *BR* i. 411–12; Moshoeshoe to Smith, 13 Oct. 1851, *BR* i. 457; Smith to Moshoeshoe, 3 Nov. 1851, *BR* i. 466; Midgley, pp. 328–9, 384, 423, 454.

[3] 'Representation of the Missionaries of the Paris Society to the British Authorities', 8 July 1851, *BR* i. 422–7.

them to re-evaluate British policy in the territories Smith had annexed and he encouraged Hogge to write frank, informal letters as well as official reports.

The assistant commissioners went first to King William's Town where they found Smith fully occupied with directing the frontier campaign. Faced with more effective resistance from the Xhosa than he had expected, Smith was losing touch with reality—relying on incompetent military subordinates and creating in his imagination a vast conspiracy, comprising Afrikaner rebels and African chieftains, with Moshoeshoe in the centre.[1] Remaining on the Xhosa frontier himself, Smith sent Hogge and Owen to the Sovereignty with a free hand to do as they thought best there.

When they reached Bloemfontein in November 1851, they found the place full of rumours of BaSotho invasions and Afrikaner intrigues, but Hogge quickly perceived two cardinal features of the situation. In annexing the Sovereignty, Smith 'was either deceived, or deceived himself, in supposing that the majority of the white people here ever desired British authority to be extended over them'; and 'the principal cause of the subsequent troubles have [sic] been the incessant interference in the incessant quarrels of the native Tribes'.[2] Hogge and Owen decided that the first thing to do was to make a deal with Pretorius and his Transvaal voortrekkers, releasing them from their status as British subjects in return for an assurance that they would not interfere south of the Vaal River. This was done in a Convention signed near the Sand River on 17 January 1852. In this Convention, the assistant commissioners recognized that the Transvaalers had the right to rule themselves without British interference; disclaimed any alliances with African chiefs beyond the Vaal; and agreed that white people, but not Africans, would be allowed to obtain supplies of fire-arms and ammunition from the British colonies.[3]

The assistant commissioners then concentrated on the

---

[1] Smith to Grey, 20 Sept. and 16 Oct. 1851, Hogge to Grey, 16 Oct. 1851, Grey Papers, Durham University Library.

[2] Hogge to Grey, 19 Dec. 1851, Grey Papers.

[3] De Kiewiet, chs. 4–5; Galbraith, pp. 252–60; Midgley, chs. 10–11.

affairs of the Sovereignty, where they found that nearly everyone—Black, Brown, and White—was full of complaints against Warden. Moshoeshoe and Moletsane and their Paris missionaries made the best of their opportunity to vindicate themselves, sending the commissioners copies of their official correspondence with the Government and summaries of events since 1833.[1] Early in February, Moletsane and Moshoeshoe's brother Mopeli and sons Molapo and Masopha had discussions with the commissioners at Winburg.[2] Hogge and Owen then visited Thaba Bosiu, where Moshoeshoe agreed to return the cattle and horses that his people had stolen from Whites and to compensate Moroka for the cattle and horses he had lost while assisting Warden, though the numbers were not specified.[3] On 22 February Moshoeshoe had a further talk with Hogge near the Orange River. Hogge admitted that the Warden administration had been unfair to the BaSotho and the Taung. He assured Moshoeshoe that Warden would be dismissed and Bailie would be arrested; that the Sovereignty Government would stop interfering in African quarrels and imposing boundaries between Africans; and that, although a boundary would be enforced between black and white areas, the line would be moved westwards in the triangle between the Orange and the Caledon. However, Hogge insisted on the return of the cattle and horses to the Whites and the Rolong, as previously agreed.[4]

Hogge summed up what he had discovered in the Sovereignty in a long unofficial report to Earl Grey on 26 March.[5] When Warden decided to launch the campaign that led to his defeat at Viervoet, he had succumbed to lobbying by James Cameron, the Wesleyan missionary at Thaba 'Nchu:

[1] 'A Sketch of the Principal Events relative to the Government of the Basutos since 1833', *BR* i. 1–4, 499–532.
[2] 'Minutes of Meeting held at Winburg on the 7th of February, 1852, between Her Majesty's Assistant Commissioners, the Chief Molitsane, Paulus Moperi, and Molapo and David, sons of Chief Moshesh', *BR* i. 535–49.
[3] *BR* i. 549.
[4] Arbousset, 2 Mar. 1852, *JME* xxvii (1852), 201–10; extracts from this letter, *BR* iii. 82–4; D. F. Ellenberger, *Leselinyana*, 11 Dec. 1913.
[5] Hogge to Grey, 26 Mar. 1852, Grey Papers.

The two Missionaries [*sic*] societies, who reign over the natives of the Sovereignty—the French residing with Moshesh, Molitsane & co, and the Wesleyans on the side of Moroko—viewed each other with no feeling akin to Christian charity. Mr. Cameron led the latter with distinguished acrimony, Messrs. Casalis and Daumas the former with more politeness but less success. Major Warden's clerk was Mr. Cameron's brother-in-law, and these two working in couples gained complete influence over him and turned the scale against the French church militant. In all disputes Moroko & co were ever right, & Moshesh & co in the wrong, till at last Major Warden took up arms in defence of Moroko's injured innocence, & called out the Boers to assist him.

Both Warden and Smith had duped Moshoeshoe on the boundary question:

When Sir Harry Smith imposed the permanent authority of the Queen, and it was accepted by the natives, not a word was said about the definition of limits. On the contrary, they were told 'neither white or black should be removed from their present habitations' but that they should both drink out of the same fountain and live in peace. This Utopian scheme was simply impracticable, but the 'non-removal' which it pledged was not forgotten, and as in the boundary arrangement a most decided departure took place from this principle to the sole detriment of the coloured race, they have since not failed to complain of the injustice done them, and bring it forward as a reason for their acts of hostility.

Finally, Hogge reported that since Viervoet Moshoeshoe had acted with considerable restraint:

There is ample evidence that three Boers who have fled, and as yet escaped apprehension, urged that Chief [Moshoeshoe] to waylay Captain Parrish's party [the Zulu contingent] coming from Natal, and afterwards to attack Winburg. This he resolutely declined and other propositions of the same nature, in fact though feeling himself deeply aggrieved by Major Warden's policy towards him, and notwithstanding that his people have made some aggressions on the Territory which find much justification in the buccaneering inroads upon them carried out by the Bastards and others in our pay, he has on the whole shown much forbearance, and if he has found himself compelled when declared an enemy to the Queen to throw himself into the arms of the disaffected Boers, and enter into their plans, he has been moderate, when compared with them, and has abstained from carrying into effect all extreme measures urged upon him.

Nevertheless Hogge still believed that Britain should retain responsibility up to the Vaal River, in the hope that the newly independent Transvaal would drain off the anti-British Afrikaners, leaving a co-operative white population in the Sovereignty.

By the time Hogge wrote that letter Grey had left the Colonial Office as a result of a change of government in Britain and Smith had been replaced by General Sir George Cathcart, a more conventional military officer, as High Commissioner and Commander-in-Chief in South Africa. Soon afterwards Warden was dismissed from his office and Hogge himself died suddenly in Bloemfontein. Moshoeshoe was therefore faced with an almost entirely new hierarchy of British officials.[1]

While Cathcart was winding up the war against the Xhosa chiefdoms, Moshoeshoe and his people were deploying their strength, fortified by Hogge's assurances that the boundary would be changed in the south-west and that the British would no longer interfere in African affairs.[2] They raided livestock from white farmers in the triangle between the Orange and the Caledon; they put intense pressure on the hapless Moroka, whose power and prestige had slumped with those of his patron, Warden; and, provoked by injudicious raids by Sekonyela, Taaibosch, and Baatje, whose conduct was as erratic as ever, they carried out a massive attack on the Tlokoa in May 1852, capturing most of their livestock and destroying many of their outposts.[3] All these

[1] Sir John Pakington succeeded Earl Grey as Secretary of State for the Colonies when the Derby ministry replaced the Russell ministry in March 1852; Sir George Cathcart took over from Sir Harry Smith, whom Grey had recalled, as Governor of the Cape Colony and High Commissioner and Commander-in-Chief in South Africa in April; Hogge died in Bloemfontein in June; Henry Green succeeded Henry Warden as British Resident in the Orange River Sovereignty in July 1852. Earl Grey had ordered Smith to dismiss Warden as early as December 1851 and written the dispatch recalling Smith in January 1852.

[2] See above, p. 157.

[3] Arbousset, 15 June 1852, *JME* xxvii (1852), 361–6.

people made vociferous appeals to the British officials, the Whites and the Rolong insisting that Moshoeshoe and Moletsane had not carried out their undertaking to return their captured horses and cattle.[1] In September Owen advised Cathcart that unless the British Government was prepared to pay a considerable price the Sovereignty should be abandoned, 'so soon as this can be done with honour'.[2] Cathcart agreed. To rule the Sovereignty effectively, he warned London, would require a permanent garrison of 2,000 troops and a greatly increased civil establishment, which he knew the British Government would not provide. But he, too, raised the question of honour—the obsession of an imperial power which has over-extended itself: 'British authority having once been asserted, it could neither be retained nor abandoned with honour in the present unsatisfactory state of things.'[3] Cathcart decided to resolve this problem by making a military demonstration in the Sovereignty. He would 'define the equitable amount of compensation due by the chief Moshesh, and exact, and if necessary compel, prompt payment'. Presumably Moshoeshoe would submit without a fight; but if he resisted, Cathcart reported, there could be no doubt about the outcome.[4]

On 13 December 1852 Cathcart reached Platberg with 2,000 men, including detachments of cavalry and artillery with six-pounder guns and twelve-pounder howitzers. He summoned Moshoeshoe to meet him, but the king sent two of his sons, Masopha and Sekhonyana. Cathcart ordered them back to Thaba Bosiu with Owen, the assistant commissioner, who presented Moshoeshoe with an ultimatum demanding that he hand over 10,000 cattle and 1,000 horses within three days.[5] Overriding the objections of his kinsmen

---

[1] Warden to Owen, 17 June 1852, *BR* i. 567; Owen to Cathcart, 16 July 1852, *BR* i. 570–1; Moroka to Cathcart, n.d., *BR* i. 579–86; Moroka to Green, 27 Sept. 1852, *BR* i. 591–2; G. H. Meyer, J.P., and 45 other Winburg farmers to Cathcart, 5 Nov. 1852, *BR* i. 600–2.

[2] Owen to Cathcart, 18 Sept. 1852, *BR* i. 590.

[3] Cathcart to Colonial Secretary, 14 Nov. 1852, *BR* i. 607.

[4] Ibid., pp. 607–8.

[5] Cathcart to Moshoeshoe, 14 Dec. 1852, *BR* i. 616–18.

and councillors, the sixty-six-year-old king then crossed the swollen Caledon with Casalis and Dyke and a small escort. Cathcart said he hoped he met him in peace. 'I hope so, too,' replied Moshoeshoe, 'for peace is like the rain which makes the grass grow, while war is like the wind which dries it up.'[1] However, Cathcart reiterated his demands and, with no regard for Moshoeshoe's practical problems, he refused to allow him more than one extra day, brushing aside his explanation that he could not possibly persuade his people to surrender so much property in so short a time. Despite that, Moshoeshoe made a serious effort to comply. He announced a general levy (*sethaba-thaba*), contributing a large number of beasts from his own herds, and on 18 December he sent Cathcart 3,500 cattle with a message that more would follow. He was evidently expecting a reply to this message, for he took no steps to remove large herds of cattle from the Berea plateau, between the Caledon River and Thaba Bosiu.[2] Nevertheless Cathcart launched his attack without further warning.

The Commander-in-Chief's plan was to seize the cattle on the Berea plateau and then to impose terms on Moshoeshoe at Thaba Bosiu. At daylight on the 20th, leaving a guard in the base camp at Platberg, Cathcart crossed the Caledon with his striking force at a drift north-west of the Berea mission station and deployed in three columns. The cavalry, numbering 233 men, climbed the Berea mountain to the east of the mission and seized 4,000 cattle, but were then attacked by 700 BaSotho under Molapo and Moletsane and, instead of continuing southwards to the rendezvous with the other columns, they retreated northwards and recrossed the Caledon. An infantry column of 499 men climbed the mountain west of the mission and began to round up vast herds of cattle, but then lost most of them again as it crossed the Berea plateau, pursued by Molapo's horsemen, and descended on the southern side. On the plain about three miles west of Thaba Bosiu it joined Cathcart and

[1] 'Conference between Governor Sir George Cathcart and the Chief Moshesh', 15 Dec. 1852, *BR* i. 618–19.
[2] Mareka Nchakala, *Leselinyana*, 1 Sept. 1891.

350 cavalry and foot soldiers who had marched round the
western and southern base of Berea. Repeatedly attacked by
5,000 mounted BaSotho, armed with muskets, assagais, and
battle-axes, the combined British force withdrew two miles
westwards to occupy a village, where they formed a square
with the captured cattle kraaled in the centre. At dusk the
BaSotho closed in and managed to breach the kraal and
recapture 400 cattle, but they were then repulsed and the
shooting ended as darkness fell. In all, the British casualties
were 38 killed and 15 wounded. The officers reported that
they had inflicted far heavier casualties on the BaSotho.
In fact they had probably killed only 20 BaSotho fighting
men and wounded another 20, but they had also killed a
larger number of women and children in Khoabane's
village near the Berea mission station. The British had also
captured and held about 4,500 cattle and a few horses—
booty which, with those handed over on 18 December, fell
short of the 10,000 cattle and 1,000 horses Cathcart had
demanded.[1]

That night Moshoeshoe deliberated with his councillors
on Thaba Bosiu. Though they had won a partial victory,
they were awed by the discipline and fire-power of the British
troops. Already many BaSotho were preparing to retreat to
the mountains with their cattle; but that, Moshoeshoe
realized, would be a reversion to the worst days of the
lifaqane. The kingdom would disintegrate and the British
would have no further cause to restrain white farmers from
occupying the arable lowlands. The time had come for
diplomacy.[2]

[1] Eyewitness accounts: reports by Colonel A. J. Cloete, Lt.-Col. George
Napier, and Lt.-Col. William Eyre, 21 and 23 Dec. 1852, *BR* i. 620–7; account
by an anonymous British officer in General Sir Arthur Thurlow Cunynghame,
My Command in South Africa 1874–1878, London, 1879, pp. 85–9; accounts by
Paris missionaries Dyke, 28 Dec. 1852, *BR* i. 632–5, Casalis, 27 Dec. 1852,
BR iii. 84–9, Maitin, 28 Dec. 1852, *BR* iii. 89–92, and Casalis MS., Notes on
the Events of the War, n.d., LEC. Later accounts: Special Commissioner of the
Cape Argus [J. M. Orpen], *History of the Basutos of South Africa*, Cape Town, 1857,
pp. 97–102; J. M. Orpen, *Reminiscences of Life in South Africa*, Cape Town, 1964,
pp. 140–3; Azariel Sekese, *Leselinyana*, 15 Nov. 1892; D. F. Ellenberger, *Leselinyana*, 8 Jan. 1894; G. Tylden, *The Rise of the Basuto*, Cape Town, 1950, pp. 58–
62, with map on p. 56.
[2] Casalis, 27 Dec. 1852, *BR* iii. 88.

At midnight, in the presence of his missionary Casalis, Moshoeshoe dictated to his son Sekhonyana a letter to Cathcart:[1]

Thaba Bosigo, Midnight, 20th December, 1852.

Your Excellency,—This day you have fought against my people, and taken much cattle. As the object for which you have come is to have a compensation for Boers, I beg you will be satisfied with what you have taken. I entreat peace from you,— you have shown your power,—you have chastised,—let it be enough I pray you; and let me be no longer considered an enemy to the Queen. I will try all I can to keep my people in order in the future.

Your humble servant, Moshesh

Cathcart did not receive this remarkable missive till noon the following day. By that time he had retreated to the Caledon River, where his officers were urging him to bring up reinforcements from the Platberg camp and assault Thaba Bosiu. But Cathcart, in turn, had been astonished by the fighting qualities and numbers of the BaSotho. To resume the offensive, he realized, might be to embark on a guerilla war as long and as costly as the one he had recently concluded with the Xhosa. Moshoeshoe had provided him with exactly what he needed to save face. He therefore replied:[2]

Camp, Caledon River, 21st December, 1852.

Chief Moshesh,—I have received your letter. The words are those of a Great Chief, and of one who has the interests of his people at heart. . . . I have taken the fine by force, and I am satisfied. . . . I consider your past obligations fulfilled, and hope that you will take measures for preventing such abuses in future. In the meantime, as the Queen's Representative, I subscribe myself, Your Friend,

Geo. Cathcart, Governor.

Cathcart then returned with his troops to the Cape Colony, reporting to London that the expedition had resulted in 'the entire submission of the enlightened and powerful chief Moshesh', who would now be 'a valuable and willing ally'.

[1] *BR* i. 627.   [2] *BR* i. 627–8.

He explained that experience on the spot had revealed that
Moroka and Baatje were 'little better than men of straw,
set up by the Wesleyan missionaries to represent territorial
possessions held by that sect'. Sekonyela was the only other
chief of substance in the Caledon valley; but the Tlokoa
chief was 'scarcely able to resist the paramount influence of
the Chief Moshesh'.[1]

On receipt of these dispatches, the British Government,
stung by Cathcart's earlier assertion that contrary to Sir
Harry Smith's glib assurances it would be an expensive
business to rule the Sovereignty effectively, decided to
abandon the territory.[2] Sir George Clerk arrived in Bloemfontein in August as Special Commissioner to preside over
the withdrawal.

Cathcart's estimate of the relative strengths of the communities in the Caledon basin was accurate. Since Viervoet,
the groups who had migrated seventeen years earlier from
the Vaal–Harts country to the Caledon with their Wesleyan missionaries were in a parlous condition. People who
acknowledged Moshoeshoe as their king were in effective
occupation of the territory on both sides of the Caledon
River between the Tlokoa in the north-east and the Whites
in the south-west, except only for Thaba 'Nchu and Platberg. The brown communities and their Wesleyan missionaries had abandoned Mpokoane, Merumetšo, and Lesooane.
Moroka and Davids, who had fled from Thaba 'Nchu and
Platberg after Viervoet, were back again, but they were
impoverished. Moroka's following had declined from a peak
of over 10,000 to fewer than 5,000, and Davids's following,
which had never exceeded 1,000, had diminished in proportion.[3]

As for Sekonyela, since his setbacks in the early 1840s he
had rebuilt his strength to about 10,000 followers, but he
had done so by allying himself with the egregious Warden
and with his former persecutors, Taaibosch's Kora, who

---

[1] Cathcart to Colonial Secretary, 13 Jan. 1853, *BR* ii. 2–5 and 5–7.
[2] Newcastle, Colonial Secretary, to Cathcart, 14 Mar. 1853, *BR* ii. 38–9.
[3] Reports by Wesleyan missionaries Cameron, Giddy, and Ludorf in S.A.
12, WMS.

were still nomadic predators. With the collapse of Warden's grand alliance, Sekonyela's position had become precarious, but he had been unwilling or unable to restrain his people from persisting in raiding the villages of Moletsane and Moshoeshoe's kinsmen, Molapo and Mopeli.

In May 1852 Moshoeshoe had made a final attempt to establish a peaceful relationship with Sekonyela. After devastating his outposts and seizing vast herds of cattle, he had accepted Sekonyela's submission and refrained from attacking his stronghold, Marabeng.[1] But Sekonyela and Taaibosch resumed their raiding, in spite of the fact that the British officials had made it clear that they would no longer intervene in African disputes.[2] After the departure of Cathcart, Moshoeshoe's elated kinsmen clamoured for a final reckoning with their old enemies and in October 1853 the king decided to strike. He consulted Tšapi and Mantsopa, who predicted a great victory. He performed private sacrifices with his father Mokhachane, who was by then an enfeebled nonagenarian. He sent out spies to report on his enemies' dispositions. Then he led an army of between ten and twelve thousand men, recruited from all parts of the kingdom, towards Sekonyela's stronghold.[3] Before he announced his battle plan he addressed his warriors. According to Arbousset, who had it from a member of his congregation who took part in the expedition, the king said:

My companions in arms! This is the combat you have so long demanded of me. Men of Lesotho, yonder is the limit which Sekonyela formerly imposed on us in our own country. Behold the waters of the Phuthiatsana; quench your thirst in these waters which the son of Mokocho [i.e. Mokotjo, father of Sekonyela] ravished from us. God sees us from above and protects us. I have told the church, I have told the representative of the English Queen in this country that I was going to avenge the insults of the MoTlokoa. Had he not sworn his faith a year ago?

[1] Arbousset, 15 June 1852, *JME* xxvii (1852), 361–6.
[2] Dyke, 21 Oct. 1852, *JME* xxviii (1833), 21–7; Daumas, Feb. 1853, ibid., pp. 208–10; Casalis, 14 Mar. 1853, ibid., pp. 241–3.
[3] Arbousset, 8 Nov. 1853, *JME* xxix (1854), 161–73. This letter is wrongly dated 1854.

He has broken his word. Have I not spared his herds? He has taken mine. It is he who besieged us at Botha Bothe long ago. I wished to forgive him the ill he did us then; but he declines to accept my mercy. I wished the land to have two chiefs, like an ox with two horns. If it had only one, it would be deformed. Besides, listen, my grudge against the MoTlokoa is not a very big one; seize me Marabeng and the Kora, and you will have fought. Tomorrow, brothers, you will have reconquered for me this lofty rock, on which the MoTlokoa sits complacently; you will offer it to me for my own stool.[1]

Moshoeshoe then divided his army into three sections to surround the strongholds of Joalaboholo and Marabeng which the Tlokoa had occupied since 1824. He sent Posholi and Mohale round to the northern side and Moletsane and Mopeli to the western, while Letsie moved in from the south. The attack was a complete success. Taking their enemies unawares, the BaSotho first stormed Joalaboholo and then the previously impregnable Marabeng, where the victory was clinched when Masopha with a few men managed to scramble up an extremely difficult approach while Molapo and others assaulted the main pass. They killed Taaibosch and many of Sekonyela's kinsmen, including his senior son, and they swept up a vast booty, including nearly all the Tlokoa sheep and cattle and twenty-two Kora wagons found at the foot of Marabeng. Sekonyela himself escaped with a handful of followers and fled to the Special Commissioner for protection, but other survivors submitted to Moshoeshoe. The son of Mokhachane had finally conquered the man who had been his inveterate enemy for thirty-one years.[2]

While his people were celebrating their victory over the Tlokoa and assuming control over northern LeSotho, Moshoeshoe was facing up to the consequences of the British decision to withdraw from the Sovereignty. For the moment the white population were confused and in no position to threaten his kingdom, but the long-term implications of the

---

[1] Arbousset, 8 Nov. 1853, *JME* xxix (1854), 164–5.

[2] Ibid., pp. 161–73; Casalis, 4 Dec. 1853, ibid., pp. 41–2; Sekonyela's account, *BR* ii. 82–5; Clerk to Colonial Secretary, 3 Dec. 1853, ibid., pp. 76–8; Nchakala, *Leselinyana*, 1 Aug. 1891; Sekese, *Leselinyana*, 1 Dec. 1892; Ellenberger, *Leselinyana*, 31 Mar. 1914 and weekly to 26 May 1914.

British decision were ominous. Already the white Transvaalers were bullying the African communities in their
midst and making military expeditions against neighbouring
chiefdoms. In 1852 they attacked the Tswana chief Sechele,
whose *seboko* was the crocodile (Koena) and who was
therefore a putative relative of Moshoeshoe.[1] Judging from
that precedent, Moshoeshoe foresaw that once the Whites in
his own vicinity were freed from their British allegiance they
would be likely to covet the entire fertile Caledon valley.[2]
Full of forebodings, he therefore tried to retain the British
alliance and work out an agreement with the Special
Commissioner and his white neighbours before the British
withdrew.

Moshoeshoe's wish coincided, at least in part, with Clerk's
original intention. On his arrival in Bloemfontein in August,
Clerk told Owen, the Assistant Commissioner, to inform
Moshoeshoe that he trusted he would still consider himself
'the Friend of the Queen of England' and that he was
'most anxious that before he leaves the Sovereignty, the
long disputed boundary line between yourself and the Boers
should be settled'.[3] Moshoeshoe replied cordially but, mindful of his experiences with Warden, he said he reserved the
right to consider any specific arrangements that Clerk might
propose.[4] In December Moshoeshoe accepted an invitation
to Jammerberg Drift on the Caledon River (opposite modern
Wepener), where Clerk had arranged for him to discuss his
south-western boundary with a group of local farmers.
When Clerk found that they could not immediately reach
an agreement, he abruptly broke off the negotiations and
told Moshoeshoe that on the abandonment of the Sovereignty
his situation would revert to what it had been before the
British annexation.[5] Moshoeshoe construed this as meaning
that his 1843 treaty, as amended at Maitland's request in

---

[1] *OHSA* i. 435–42.
[2] Green to Cathcart, 30 Mar. 1853, *BR* ii. 43–5.
[3] Owen to Moshoeshoe, 23 Aug. 1853, *BR* ii. 59–60.
[4] Casalis to Clerk, 5 Sept. 1853, *BR* ii. 63.
[5] Clerk to Newcastle, 14 Jan. 1854, *BR* ii. 94–5 (a misleading report);
Deposition of J. G. Landman, 13 Sept. 1858, *BR* ii. 434; Orpen, *Reminiscences*,
pp. 170–6; Ellenberger, *Leselinyana*, 9 June 1914.

1845, would remain in force; but Clerk meant something quite different. The Special Commissioner had run into serious difficulties in his negotiations with the white population. The small group of British and European traders and land speculators who had settled in the Sovereignty were bitterly opposed to the British withdrawal, and most of the Afrikaners were loath to assume the responsibilities of self-government at a moment when the MoSotho king had emerged triumphant from the attacks by Warden and Cathcart. Clerk responded by manipulating the white population—cold-shouldering the 'loyalists' and encouraging the Afrikaners to produce leaders who were willing to treat with him for independence. He also appeased them by finding a pretext for cancelling Moshoeshoe's alliance.[1] When they asked him what had become of the king's treaty with Governor Napier, he replied: 'A war between two powers breaks all pre-existing treaties. The British Government having since the date of the Napier Treaty been at war with Moshesh, the Treaty is at an end.'[2] Then, without any further consultation with Moshoeshoe, he signed a Convention with them on 23 February 1854.

The Bloemfontein Convention released the inhabitants of the Sovereignty from their allegiance to the Crown and transferred the government to the white men who signed the document. It declared that the British Government had no alliances with any 'Native Chiefs or Tribes' north of the Orange River except Adam Kok, and that 'Her Majesty's Government has no wish, or intention, to enter hereafter into any treaties which may be injurious or prejudicial to the interests of the Orange River Government'. It also said that the new Government would be able to buy ammunition in British territories—a clause which could be read in conjunction with a provision in the Sand River Convention, prohibiting trade in ammunition with 'the native tribes . . . on both sides of the Vaal River'. Moreover, the document

[1] De Kiewiet, ch. 6; Galbraith, pp. 267–73; Midgley, chs. 15–18; Orpen, *Reminiscences*, chs. 36–41; Wm. W. Collins, *Free Statia: Reminiscences of a Lifetime in the Orange Free State*, Cape Town, 1965, chs. 3–4.
[2] 'Extracts from Minutes of a Meeting held at Bloemfontein on the 17th February, 1854', *BR* ii. 99; also *SAAR, OFS* i. 202, 204.

had a remarkable omission: it said nothing about a boundary between the new state and LeSotho.[1]

The day after he signed the Bloemfontein Convention, Clerk tried to reassure Moshoeshoe by informing him that a British consul would be stationed in the Cape Colony near the LeSotho border 'to promote good understanding and kindly sentiments',[2] but Moshoeshoe realized that this would be of little value and, in a desperate effort to lay a firmer foundation for peace, he rode to Bloemfontein with an escort of a hundred men, and a Paris missionary, Maitin, as interpreter.[3] On 10 March members of the provisional government of the new state entertained him and his sons Masopha, Majara, and Sekhonyana to dinner. Moshoeshoe addressed the gathering, stressing his hope that they would live in peace. 'I still confidently hope that the Land will be properly governed and peace maintained, if the rulers regulate their proceedings on principles of uprightness and truth, aiming at agreement among themselves and peace with their neighbours.'[4] On the same day, Clerk reluctantly granted him an interview, but merely indulged in generalities. When Moshoeshoe brought the discussion to the boundary question, the Commissioner replied that 'everything was settled, the farmers wanted peace'.[5] Clerk undertook to have another discussion with him on this question in the presence of the members of the provisional government, but he failed to do so. Instead, the next morning he curtly announced that he had no more time for business and, handing Maitin a letter recommending that Moshoeshoe and the new government should settle their land disputes by arbitration, he departed for Cape Town.

Moshoeshoe must have watched Clerk's cavalcade disappear with mixed feelings. For twenty years—ever since Dr.

---

[1] *SAAR*, *OFS* i. 216–20; also in G. W. Eybers, *Select Constitutional Documents illustrating South African History 1795–1910*, London, 1918, pp. 282–5.

[2] Clerk to Moshoeshoe, 24 Feb. 1854, *BR* ii. 100–1.

[3] Maitin, 15 May 1854, *JME* xxix (1854), 370–80 (extracts in *BR* iii. 93–6); Orpen, *Reminiscences*, pp. 181–91; Ellenberger, *Leselinyana*, 23 and 30 June 1914.

[4] *Friend of the Sovereignty*, 18 Mar. 1854, cited in *BR* ii. 105–7. According to Maitin this dinner took place the next day, after Clerk's departure.

[5] *BR* iii. 96.

Andrew Smith had visited him in 1834—he had based his foreign policy on achieving and maintaining a British alliance, to offset the increasing pressures from the white settlers. In spite of the failure of the British Government to provide sufficient funds to control the area, even after it had acquiesced in Harry Smith's impetuous annexation— a failure compounded by the bumbling inefficiency and partisan conduct of its agents, from Henry Warden to George Clerk—he had been a remarkably loyal ally.

Now, the departure of the officials and Clerk's unilateral repudiation of British treaty obligations left him face to face with white settlers, with no agreed boundary between them. Some time in the future, when the settlers had overcome their differences, increased in numbers, and made effective use of their preferential access to ammunition, they were likely to become a formidable threat to him or his successor. For the moment, however, Moshoeshoe was invincible: a king at the height of his power.

V

MOSHOESHOE'S LESOTHO

IN 1854 Moshoeshoe was about sixty-eight years old.[1] Until the 1820s he had known nothing of the wider world and the height of his ambition could have been to become no more than the chief of a few hundred villagers in the upper Caledon valley.[2] Now tens of thousands of Africans acknowledged him to be their *Morena e Moholo* (Great Chief) and hundreds of thousands more, from the Zambezi to the Fish, were inspired by his victories over successive invaders and his reputation for humane leadership. He had compelled British proconsuls and white settlers to treat him with respect. The first president elected by the citizens of the fledgling Orange Free State was Josias Hoffman, whom he had recently employed as a mason on Thaba Bosiu.[3] His name, simplified to 'Moshesh' by European ears, figured prominently in governors' dispatches and missionaries' reports to London and Paris. Writing to bid him farewell at the end of his term as High Commissioner for South Africa, Sir George Cathcart called him a 'great and enlightened chief' and subscribed himself 'your sincere friend'.[4]

This chapter analyses the kingdom that the son of Mokhachane had created and raised to the position of a major power in southern Africa.[5]

[1] The date of Moshoeshoe's birth is uncertain. See above, p. 1.

[2] See above, Chapter I.

[3] J. M. Orpen, *Reminiscences*, pp. 201–2; Hoffman to Commissioners Hogge and Owen, 15 Jan. 1852, *BR* i. 488–94.

[4] Cathcart to Moshoeshoe, 13 Mar. 1854, *BR* ii. 105.

[5] The published documents do not provide adequate evidence for an understanding of the political structure of Moshoeshoe's kingdom. The best account is in Casalis (1), ch. 12, but it leaves many questions unanswered. Consequently, this chapter is based largely on the testimonies of BaSotho informants whom I consulted in 1965, 1968, and 1972. Above all, I have profited from the co-operation of Mosebi Damane (I. 39), who has been most generous in responding to my many questions and sharing his knowledge.

1. *The People*

In 1854 the population of LeSotho was about 100,000.[1] The vast majority lived in the valleys of the Caledon and the upper Orange and their tributaries, below the 7,000-foot contour. The Maloti mountains were not yet the site of permanent villages, though herdboys were already beginning to establish seasonal cattle-posts up to perhaps 8,000 feet.[2]

This population was of diverse antecedents and cultures. The majority were BaSotho—but BaSotho who respected many different totems (*liboko*) and who had belonged to many different chiefdoms before the *lifaqane* wars. Among them, Moshoeshoe's own lineage was increasing rapidly at the expense of the others. This was partly because some men found it convenient to drop their original affiliations and had been accepted as Koena of Mokoteli;[3] but also because Moshoeshoe and his kinsmen had gained control over so large a proportion of the nation's cattle-wealth that they had been able to acquire numerous wives and sire a vast offspring.[4]

There were also large numbers of people of Nguni origin in LeSotho. From the earliest stages in the settlement of the region by Bantu-speaking peoples, Nguni had been strongly represented. The Phuthi chiefly lineage was of Nguni origin; Moshoeshoe's biological great grandfather in the patrilineal line was Nguni; and so was Makoanyane, his

[1] In 1847 H. M. Dyke estimated that 70,000 BaSotho, living in 670 villages within the boundaries of Napier's 1843 treaty, recognized Moshoeshoe as their great chief ('Carte du pays des Bassoutos', Paris, 1847, LEC; Frédoux, 13 Oct. 1852, *JME* xxviii (1853), 55–6). In 1848 Sir Harry Smith reported that, according to Casalis, Moshoeshoe had 80,000 subjects (*BR* i. 163–4). François Maeder estimated that Moshoeshoe's subjects—probably excluding the followers of his allies Moorosi, Moletsane, and Matela—numbered 80,000 in 1854 (*JME* xxx (1855), 43); Sir George Clerk put them at 60,000 (*BR* ii. 61). Casalis estimated that they numbered at least 150,000 in 1864 (*JME* xxxix (1864), 129). In 1869 J. H. Bowker, Governor's Agent, estimated that 125,000 people had 'looked upon Moshesh as their chief' in 1865 (BR V. 286).

[2] Robert C. Germond, *Chronicles of Basutoland*, ch. 37.

[3] Oral testimony, Informant 51 and others.

[4] On Moshoeshoe's wives, see above, Chapter I, pp. 7–8. His senior kinsmen also acquired numerous wives.

circumcision-mate, chief warrior, and closest friend.[1] Many more Nguni had settled in LeSotho during the *lifaqane*: followers of Mpangazitha who had survived his catastrophic defeat by Matiwane, followers of Matiwane who had remained in LeSotho after he had fled, and other fugitives from Shaka who had ridden out the *lifaqane* storms in the Maloti and then settled among the BaSotho.[2] Later, during each of the wars between the Cape Colony and the Xhosa and Thembu chiefdoms (1834–5, 1846–7, 1850–3), southern Nguni fugitives fled to Moorosi's country in the Orange valley or deeper into LeSotho.[3]

The third most numerous element in the population was San (whom white people called 'Bushmen'). Hunting bands had occupied the Caledon and Orange basins for centuries if not millennia and by the time of Moshoeshoe's childhood numerous San had been incorporated into BaSotho chiefdoms.[4] This process continued during and after the *lifaqane*. The Phuthi, in particular, were heavily mixed with San. Moorosi himself had San physical characteristics and one of his senior sons was called 'Boshimane'.[5] Moshoeshoe himself had several San wives.[6] However, in the late 1850s several bands of San continued to live in the Maloti and Drakensberg mountains, where some would survive as independent communities until the 1870s.[7]

Fourth, perhaps a thousand Kora and Griqua ('Coloured' people) were incorporated into LeSotho between 1820 and 1860—especially after Moshoeshoe had overwhelmed their little chiefdoms north of the Caledon at the time when he conquered the Tlokoa of Sekonyela in 1853. It is also probable that a few stray white men—British military

---

[1] See above, Chapter I, p. 8.

[2] Moloja, 'The Story of the "Fetcani Horde"', *Cape Quarterly Review*, i (1882), 267–75; Arbousset (1), chs. 6–9; Arbousset (2), *passim*.

[3] D. F. Ellenberger, History of the Basuto, 1833–1854, Ellenberger Papers, 7–29.   [4] See above, Chapter I, pp. 13, 16, 19.

[5] Testimony of Mosebi Damane, Informant, 39; Schrumpf, 13 Nov. 1844, *JME* xx (1845), 219.

[6] Maeder, n.d., *JME* xxvi (1851), 78.

[7] Sir Marshall Clarke, 'Unexplored Basutoland', *Proceedings of the Royal Geographical Society*, x (1888), 519; V. Ellenberger, *La Fin tragique des Bushmen*, Paris, 1953; Marion W. How, *The Mountain Bushmen of Basutoland*, Pretoria, 1970.

deserters and Afrikaner frontiersmen—were absorbed into the BaSotho nation.

The patterns of incorporation of alien elements varied considerably. The population of a typical BaSotho village had always been heterogeneous: it was still more so after the *lifaqane*. It included BaSotho of different *liboko* and people of Nguni and San parentage, who were sometimes servants (*bahlanka*) of the chief or headman. In such cases intermarriage took place and the children were brought up as BaSotho. At the other extreme there were villages and clusters of villages whose inhabitants remained Nguni in language, dress, and culture, with chiefs and headmen of Nguni lineages, but subject to the political authority of Moshoeshoe and his territorial chiefs or his allies. The main concentrations of unacculturated Nguni were in the upper Orange drainage system in the south, where several Nguni groups were allowed to settle by Moorosi after they had detached themselves from the Thembu and Xhosa chiefdoms during the frontier wars—for example, the Vundle under Tyhali, who did so in 1846–7.[1] Later, in about 1860, the Hlapo, of northern Nguni origin, settled in northern LeSotho near Botha Bothe.[2] Moshoeshoe and his territorial chiefs and allies made no attempt to interfere with the customs of these Nguni settlers. To this day the Vundle and the Hlapo are distinctively Nguni in language and custom and they keep much to themselves.

The mission communities also were culturally distinct from the rest of the BaSotho. Those Africans, about 2,000 in number, who lived on the mission stations at Morija, Thaba Bosiu, Berea, Cana, Bethesda, Beersheba, Hermon, Hebron, and Mekoatleng were subject to the jurisdiction of the French Protestant missionaries as well as to chiefly jurisdiction—a dual allegiance that created problems for both parties.[3]

[1] The southern Nguni communities in Lesotho are called Thembu, not Xhosa; but in Sesotho usage BaThepu (Thembu) is a generic term for all southern Nguni and most of the immigrants in Moshoeshoe's time were of Xhosa origin (Informant 39). On the Vundle, see below, pp. 336–7, Note 7.

[2] Testimony of the Chief of Makong, 'MaMazibuku Manizulu Mazibuku, I. 48; also A. Sekese, *Leselinyana*, 1 Dec. 1906, and J. C. Macgregor, *Traditions*, pp. 44–5.   [3] Chapter III above.

2. *The King and his Territorial Chiefs*

The kingdom of LeSotho was the product of the collapse of the old order of small, distinct chiefdoms and the extension of the authority of Moshoeshoe. But as people recovered from the *lifaqane*, centrifugal forces reappeared. Kinsmen of Moshoeshoe struck out on their own and chiefs of other lineages sought to regain their autonomy. LeSotho was therefore a somewhat fragile association of chiefs and their followers, maintained by external pressure, by a growing national spirit, and, above all, by the personality and political skill of Moshoeshoe.

The nexus of the kingdom was a complex and varying set of personal relationships—especially relationships between Moshoeshoe himself and his senior kinsmen and allies. In handling these relationships Moshoeshoe built on the methods he had learnt in his youth. By SeSotho custom subordinate status was marked by the performance of services. A subordinate attended on his chief (*morena*) when requested, to receive information and provide counsel. He brought his male followers with him to a public meeting (*pitso*) convened by his chief and to fight in his chief's wars. He sent working parties to cultivate his chief's lands (*letsema*), because their produce was consumed not only by the chief's family and personal dependants but also by all the men of the chiefdom at a *pitso* and in time of war. He allowed his followers to appeal to the chief's court (*lekhotla*) against his own decisions. He contributed cattle when required for general purposes (*sethaba-thaba*), such as the payment of compensation to neighbouring chiefs. He sent his young men to an initiation school (*lebollo*) convened by his chief. And, if a lion or a leopard was killed, ownership of the skin was his *morena*'s prerogative.[1]

In practice a man might fulfil some but not all of these services, in which case he was neither completely dependent nor completely independent. Indeed, like other pre-colonial Africans the BaSotho were accustomed to gradations of

---

[1] This paragraph, like those that precede and follow it, is based on the testimonies of many informants, notably I. 39, as well as on the contemporary documents.

authority and autonomy, and to ambiguities in the distribution of power.

The essence of Moshoeshoe's problem as a state-maker was how to build on these established institutions so as to hold his political community together while it was expanding greatly in scale. For this purpose, he used a system of 'placing' kinsmen at specific localities and delegating to them limited authority over the surrounding areas. He made sure that such kinsmen were accompanied by families of many different antecedents, so that each of his territorial chiefdoms included a cross-section of the population of LeSotho. Consequently, the revival of pre-*lifaqane* political allegiances was impeded by geographical dispersion. A placed chief, having built his principal village at the locality designated by Moshoeshoe, had the right to extend his authority over the surrounding country and its inhabitants, as Moshoeshoe had done from Thaba Bosiu in the 1820s and 1830s. He could exact the services due to a *morena* from his subjects while he in turn remained responsible for performing those services for Moshoeshoe.

The evidence is conflicting as to whether Moshoeshoe allotted a kinsman specific territorial limits when he placed him. In some cases he apparently did so: there is an eye-witness report that he did so for Molapo in 1847.[1] On the other hand no contemporary evidence has survived saying what the limits were of the territories he allotted to any of his kinsmen. A century later descendants of Moshoeshoe's territorial chiefs have different opinions. Some consider that the king established their boundaries, but they do not agree upon the locations of those boundaries. Others assert categorically that the king refrained from setting bounds to at least some of his territorial chiefdoms, but that when he placed a chief he expected him to expand as best he could, so that his territorial authority became commensurate with his skill in attracting followers and retaining their allegiance.[2]

[1] See below, p. 180.

[2] I. 3 (a descendant of Letsie) and I. 9 (a descendant of Molapo) consider that when Moshoeshoe placed a chief he gave him authority over a specified area and its population. I. 14 (a descendant of Lesaoana) categorically states that Moshoeshoe did not delimit the boundaries of the kinsmen he

By 1854, thirty years after Moshoeshoe had fled from
Botha Bothe to Thaba Bosiu with a few hundred followers,
LeSotho comprised three broad types of territory: a core
area around Thaba Bosiu which he ruled directly with the
help of Masopha, the third son of his First House; intermediate areas to the south-west and the north-east, where he

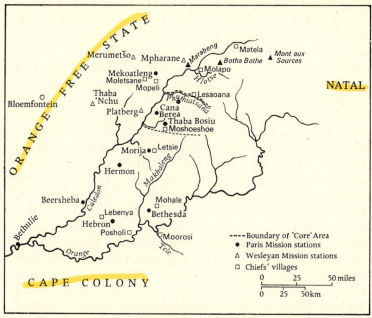

MAP 5. LeSotho in 1854

had placed Letsie and Molapo, the eldest sons of his First
House; and peripheral areas, where some of the territorial
chiefs were his kinsmen (his brother Posholi, his half-
brothers Mohale and Mopeli, and his nephew Lesaoana)
and others were the heads of lineages who had allied themselves with him as his junior partners (Moorosi the Phuthi
chief, Moletsane the Taung, and Matela the Khoakhoa).[1]

placed. Moshoeshoe almost certainly did establish boundaries between the core
area and the areas under Letsie and Molapo as described in the text, but he
very likely left the outer boundaries of Letsie and Molapo undefined, as well
as at least some of the limits of Mohale, Mopeli, and Lesaoana.

[1] See Table of Kinsmen of Moshoeshoe who were Territorial Chiefs in
1854, on p. 218.

But the actual situation was never as tidy and clear-cut as any such tripartite division might suggest.

Moshoeshoe's authority was greatest in the core area. The chiefs who lived there were his subordinates in the fullest sense: they performed for him all the services due to a *morena* without equivocation. From the capital—the still impregnable Thaba Bosiu[1]—the core area extended northwards to the Phuthiatsana River (which joins the Caledon north of Teyateyaneng) and southwards to a line running approximately east by south from the junction of the Caledon and the Little Caledon to include Ntlo-Kholo and the hills on the northern side of the Lehobosi stream (the modern Roma valley).[2]

Within this area the most important kinsmen of the king were Mokhachane, his father, and Masopha and Majara, his younger sons by 'MaMohato. Mokhachane lived in his separate village on Thaba Bosiu until he died, at a great age, in 1855, after which Moshoeshoe's mother, Kholu, went to live with her grandson and her granddaughter, Lesaoana and his wife, in northern LeSotho.[3] Majara was still in his twenties when he died in 1858. According to tradition, he died a violent death. A certain Kechane complained to Moshoeshoe that Majara was stealing his sheep and cattle and, after consulting his councillors, Moshoeshoe allowed Kechane to doctor his property and, in effect, to kill Majara. According to the missionaries, however, he died of typhus.[4] Majara left no children but after his death his wives were taken in leviratic marriage by Masopha, according to custom, to raise up seed for the House of Majara.[5]

---

[1] On Thaba Bosiu, see above, pp. 46–9.

[2] The southern limit of Moshoeshoe's core area, which became Masopha's district after the death of Moshoeshoe, has been obscured by the fact that in the 1890s Masopha was 'eaten up' by his nephew, Paramount Chief Lerotholi, and much of his land was given to Lerotholi's younger brother, Theko: Communication from Mosebi Damane, 8 Mar. 1973.

[3] Jousse, n.d., *JME* xxxi (1856), 324–5; Jousse, 14 Aug. 1857, *JME* xxxiii (1858), 56.

[4] Traditions concerning Majara were related by I. 6, 8, 12, and 39; Jousse to President Boshof, Orange Free State, 13 Dec. 1858, G.S. 1340, OFS.

[5] I. 12, the late Archbishop 'Mabathoana, Roman Catholic Archbishop of Lesotho, was of the House of Majara.

Of all Moshoeshoe's kinsmen, Masopha, his third son by 'MaMohato, most closely resembled him. About thirty-four years old in 1854, he was a courageous, intelligent, and generous man, greatly loved by his children, and fiercely loyal to his father. He had been educated by the missionaries and baptized in 1840 and four years later he was among the king's relatives whom Arbousset took to Cape Town for further education, but in 1848, at the time of the general reaction, he abandoned Christianity for ever, though he continued to keep on good terms with missionaries. During the 1840s, Moshoeshoe used him as the spearhead of expansion northwards into Sekonyela's country until 1847, when he recalled him to live near Thaba Bosiu. In 1853 he was the hero of the assault on Marabeng in which he led his men up a precipitous cliff and took the Tlokoa by surprise; soon afterwards Moshoeshoe sent him and his half-brother Makhobalo to found villages north-east of the Berea mission, towards the Phuthiatsana, where he remained until the second war with the Orange Free State in the mid-1860s.[1] Thereafter, during the king's declining years, Masopha was his right-hand man and the effective chief of the core area.

Within the core area the principal chief who was not of Moshoeshoe's lineage—the Koena of Mokoteli—was Khoabane, who lived near the Berea mission station. Khoabane was the chief of the Koena of Marabe. He had joined Moshoeshoe soon after Sekonyela had driven him from Marabeng in 1824. He was a mild man and, like all the other chiefs in the core area, a loyal subordinate of Moshoeshoe.[2]

Moshoeshoe's principal territorial chiefs in the intermediate areas were Letsie and Molapo, his eldest sons by 'MaMohato.

[1] Traditions concerning Masopha, who died in 1898, were narrated by I. 10 (Morosana, a son) and I. 11 ('MaMoorosi, a daughter), and also by I. 26, 39, 40, and 52. See also J. M. Mohapeloa, 'The Essential Masopha', *Lesotho*, v (1965–6), 7–17; Casalis, Apr. 1855, *JME* xxx (1855), 283–8; Maitin, 30 Nov. 1855, *JME* xxxi (1856), 106–9; Lautré, 30 July 1857, *JME* xxxiii (1858), 90–1; Maitin, 9 Dec. 1859, *JME* xxxv (1860), 128–9; and documents in *BR* (see index entry David Masupha in 1964 edition, vol. iii b).

[2] Khoabane was descended from Mokheseng, who was junior to Moshoeshoe's putative ancestor, Mokoteli (see below, p. 367): E & M, pp. 149–53; Casalis, 15 July 1843, *JME* xix (1844), 127–8; Maitin, 16 Feb. 1848, *JME* xxiii (1848), 281–90.

In 1833 Moshoeshoe had sent the two boys to found villages under Mount Makhoarane, with orders to assist the missionaries to establish their first mission station near by at Morija.[1] The brothers were never on good terms with one another. Tradition has it that they quarrelled over the possession of the skin of a lion they had killed.[2] In 1847 Moshoeshoe separated them and 'placed' them as territorial chiefs. Letsie remained at Makhoarane as his father's representative south of the Little Caledon and the hills north of the Lehobosi stream. Molapo migrated with his followers to Sebala-bala, on the southern bank of the Phuthiatsana River, twenty miles north-east of Thaba Bosiu where, Arbousset reported, Moshoeshoe convened a *pitso* at which 'he solemnly gave him the jurisdiction of the district of Cana [the name of the local mission station], of which he designated the boundaries'.[3] In 1854, after the final rout of the Tlokoa, Moshoeshoe moved Molapo twenty-five miles further north-east to Leribe, to consolidate control over the conquered territory beyond the Phuthiatsana.[4]

Molapo, who was about forty years old in 1854, was intelligent, energetic, and courageous, but somewhat unstable. In his youth he had fallen under the spell of the missionaries and acquired a taste for European products which he never lost, but after he left the church in 1848, disillusioned by the behaviour of British officials and Afrikaner farmers who professed to be Christians, he veered uncertainly between traditional and modern influences, and his life was clouded by the fact that his eldest son was quite mad.[5]

In 1854 Letsie was about forty-three years old. He was a well-built man, but had been blinded in one eye as a youth. As the heir apparent, he realized that it was in his interest

---

[1] See above, pp. 75–6.

[2] I. 39; Sekese, *Leselinyana*, 1 Oct. 1902. Tlali Moshoeshoe, Litaba tsa Basutu, Grey Collection, vol. 265c, South African Public Library.

[3] Arbousset, 30 Dec. 1847, *JME* xxiii (1848), 215.

[4] Arbousset, 9 Dec. 1846, *JME* xxii (1847), 202–5; Maitin, 7 Aug. 1854, *JME* xxx (1855), 11–12; Jousse, 14 Aug. 1857, *JME* xxxiii (1858), 57–8.

[5] On Molapo, I. 4–9 inclusive (descendants of Molapo) and 2, 39; Jousse, 14 Aug. 1857, *JME* xxxiii (1858), 57–60; reports of Coillard in *JME* 1858 ff.; and documents in *BR*.

to support his father's efforts to hold the kingdom together. But Letsie was never on intimate terms with his father. He lacked Moshoeshoe's intellectual gifts and he disapproved of Moshoeshoe's friendship with the French missionaries and his attempts to conciliate British officials. Moreover he had a reputation for cowardice which lost him the respect of many of his kinsmen.[1]

In all monarchical states the relationship between the king and his heir apparent is a crucial one, for an heir is a natural rallying-point for disaffected subjects. In LeSotho it was particularly delicate, because Moshoeshoe himself had set a precedent by creating the kingdom while his own father was still alive. Until the 1860s Moshoeshoe seems to have succeeded in keeping Letsie on a tight rein. He used Letsie's maternal uncle, Matete (whose loyalty was undoubted), and the French missionaries at Morija to keep an eye on him. The relationship was illustrated by events that took place in 1847. A man named Soula lived in the southern part of the kingdom, in Letsie's jurisdiction. He was the son of one of Matiwane's people who had invaded LeSotho during the *lifaqane* and remained behind when Matiwane fled. When Soula took a second wife there was a dispute over property. The relatives of his first wife threatened to take him to Letsie's *lekhotla*, but Soula denied that either Letsie or Moshoeshoe had any jurisdiction over him, an Nguni. Hearing this, Letsie had Soula forcibly brought to Makhoarane. There, Letsie's councillors, including Matete, advised Letsie to 'eat him up'—that is to say to confiscate his property, but not to kill him. Nevertheless, Letsie had Soula stoned to death. At that time the influence of the missionaries over Moshoeshoe was still great. Matete told Arbousset what had happened and Arbousset wrote to Casalis at the Thaba Bosiu mission station. Casalis consulted Moshoeshoe, who declared that Letsie seemed to have committed a judicial murder: only he, the king, had the right to impose capital punishment, and he rarely used it. On Moshoeshoe's instructions, Arbousset next summoned Letsie, his councillors,

[1] On Letsie, I. 1, 2, 3 (descendants of Letsie) and 38, 39; reports of Arbousset in *JME* 1833 ff.; and documents in *BR* (see Index).

and some visiting chiefs and conducted an inquiry into the facts of the case on the mission premises at Morija. The inquiry having gone against him, Letsie then convened a meeting of his councillors and subordinate chiefs, only to find that nobody approved of his action. Finally, on 19 July 1847, Moshoeshoe heard the case in his *lekhotla* at Thaba Bosiu. Letsie confessed that he had done wrong in ignoring his councillors' advice and in killing Soula, and Moshoeshoe concluded proceedings by publicly berating his son, calling him a 'Mokoni' (i.e. an Nguni) and a cannibal, and ordering him to mend his ways.[1]

Moshoeshoe also seems to have maintained substantial control over Molapo, until the strains of war separated them in 1865. In 1860, for instance, there was a contest of wills. Molapo had two sons of initiation age and there was a dispute about the control of the rites. The outcome was a compromise: the *bashemane* of Molapo's district were initiated in a separate *lebollo* near his village of Leribe, but they had first to go to Thaba Bosiu to fetch the ritual medicine from the king's supply.[2]

Soon after the migration to Thaba Bosiu in 1824, Moshoe-shoe's half-brother Mohale and full brother Posholi had begun to strike out on their own. After several moves Mohale made his headquarters at Kubake (near the later Mohale's Hoek), fifty-five miles south of the capital. As the eldest son of Mokhachane's Second House, he did not regard himself as a subordinate of Letsie, but he was loyal to Moshoeshoe and performed most of the services he demanded. After Mohale's death in 1861, however, Letsie gradually managed to exert authority over his sons.[3]

Posholi, on the other hand, was ambitious to establish an independent chiefdom in the old SeSotho manner. A head-strong man, wedded to the traditional way of life, he attracted

[1] We have only Arbousset's account of this episode: 21 Jan, 1848, *JME* xxiii (1848), 291–302.

[2] Coillard, 22 Feb. 1860, *JME* xxxv (1860), 211–13.

[3] On Mohale, I. 16, 17 (descendants), and 39; Arbousset, 29 Dec. 1841, *JME* xvii (1842), 212–13; Schrumpf, 25 May 1843, *JME* xviii (1843), 445; Jousse, 22 Aug. 1861, *JME* xxxvi (1861), 445–8; and documents in *BR* (see Index).

followers who, like himself, reacted instinctively to their immediate situation. He settled first at Thaba Tšoeu, but then moved further and further south-westwards until in about 1846 he established his village at Sisibe, near the north bank of the Orange River about ninety miles from Thaba Bosiu, in the area disputed by Whites. Regarding them as interlopers, he raided their cattle and tried to make life so unpleasant for them that they would abandon the area. In 1849 Warden's boundary line cut Posholi off from LeSotho and for the next three years he acted quite independently of Moshoeshoe, co-operating with Warden in driving some southern Nguni settlers out of the area in 1851, when he killed three of their chiefs and sold their captured children to Afrikaners for cattle. Later that year he was raided by a Thembu contingent operating under an Englishman, Bailie, and in 1852 Commissioner Hogge granted Moshoeshoe's request that Posholi should be recognized as his subject. Posholi then took part in the final BaSotho attack on Sekonyela, but he continued to live at Sisibe and to harry the local white farmers. Neither Letsie nor Moshoeshoe had much influence over Posholi. He convened his own initiation schools, he refused to provide men for *letsema* labour at Thaba Bosiu, he did not allow his followers to take their cases to Moshoeshoe's *lekhotla*, he contributed few if any livestock to Moshoeshoe's *sethaba-thaba* levies, and in time of war he would not concert his military actions with those of Moshoeshoe and his sons. Although Posholi did not have a large following, his restless behaviour was a source of embarrassment to Moshoeshoe by 1854. In later years it would be disastrous. And yet Posholi was by no means irrational. He was standing up for the rights of his people in the only way he knew and he doubtless regarded Moshoeshoe as foolish in trying to restrain him. Nor was he claiming absolute independence from Moshoeshoe. He recognized that his senior brother was in a limited sense his political superior, but he was not prepared to accept the slightest control by his nephew Letsie.[1]

[1] On Posholi, I. 1, 8, 9, 29, 39, 41, 51, 52, and 54; Arbousset, 28 June 1844,

West of Posholi several descendants of Mohlomi (the pre-*lifaqane* Koena hero) lived with small groups of followers in the vicinity of Qethoane or Koesberg and the French mission station Hebron (near modern Zastron). Major Warden's main 1849 boundary line passed well to the east of Qethoane but Warden had allotted a block of land around Hebron to Moshoeshoe and in theory connected it with the rest of LeSotho by a corridor. Moshoeshoe was anxious to keep control of this area and Cochet, the Hebron missionary, co-operated with him. One of the chiefs, Lebenya, grandson of Mohlomi, lived near the mission station and was loyal to Moshoeshoe, but the others, notably Letele and his son, were under constant pressure from white farmers and would eventually side with them in the hope of receiving rich rewards in captured BaSotho cattle.[1]

North-west of Qethoane a prosperous community of BaSotho lived around the French mission station Beersheba which, like Hebron, had been recognized by Warden as a BaSotho enclave in the white part of the Orange River Sovereignty. The BaSotho residents recognized the supremacy of Moshoeshoe, but he placed no territorial chief there and he relied on the missionary, Rolland, to look after his interests. By 1854 Beersheba was coveted and threatened by its white neighbours, who had built the town of Smithfield fifteen miles from the mission, and in times of crisis, as in 1858, Moshoeshoe ordered his people to evacuate the area and move eastwards into LeSotho.[2]

The southernmost BaSotho were Moorosi's Phuthi, the

JME xix (1844), 451–3; Dyke 18 July 1851, *JME* xxvii (1852), 4–13; Cochet, 29 Dec. 1851, *JME* xxvii (1852), 161–5; and documents in *BR* (see index entry Posuli), especially *BR* i. 237–8, 358–9, 403–4, 426, 481–2, 488–94, 542, 555–6, and ii. 177, 224, 235, 236, and 292.

[1] On Lebenya, Letele, etc., I. 20; Louis Cochet, Notes et souvenirs, SME; Cochet, Statement on the Hebron mission station, 28 Mar. 1868, LEC; Cochet, 22 July 1851, *JME* xxvi (1851), 460–8; Cochet, Apr. 1853, *JME* xxviii (1853), 339–41; Cochet, 20 Aug. 1858, *JME* xxxiii (1858), 406–13; D. F. Ellenberger, *Leselinyana*, 3 and 10 Oct. 1912; and documents in *BR* (see Index), especially *BR* ii. 236–9.

[2] On Beersheba before the war of 1858, see the annual reports of the missionary, Rolland: *JME* xxvii (1852), 321–5, *JME* xxviii (1853), 290–8, *JME* xxx (1855), 201–4, *JME* xxxi (1856), 332–8, *JME* xxxii (1857), 362–6.

descendants of the first Bantu-speaking settlers in LeSotho. Moshoeshoe had treated Moorosi's family as his subjects ever since 1825, when he had found Moorosi's father in parlous circumstances and given him assistance. Moorosi, who was about twenty years younger than Moshoeshoe, was prepared to treat Moshoeshoe as his superior, provided that he had local autonomy. In the 1840s Mohale had encroached into his territory and the missionary Schrumpf had founded the Bethesda mission near his great place in the Maphutseng valley (south of Mohale's Hoek). Feeling stifled, Moorosi had decided to migrate fifteen miles south-westwards across the Orange to Tulumaneng, near the junction of the Orange and the Telle (modern Palmietfontein). Schrumpf tried to stop this, regarding it as an attempt by Moorosi to escape from the Christian influence of the mission. Moshoeshoe tried to stop it also, but for political reasons. There was a show-down in 1847. Moshoeshoe rode to Bethesda with a cavalcade of sixty armed horsemen, including four sons and four missionaries, and convened a *pitso*. Moorosi and his followers were addressed sternly by Casalis, Arbousset, and Schrumpf, as well as Makoanyane and Moshoeshoe. 'When I received you, Moorosi', said the king, 'you were only a MoRoa [Bushman], you had scarcely a skin to cover your body. Today you lack nothing . . . . Why do you vomit the food I provide?'[1] Moshoeshoe concluded by ordering Moorosi to return to his Maphutseng home with all his followers. Temporarily awed, Moorosi feigned compliance. Within a year, however, he had completed the transfer of his people and his livestock to Tulumaneng, where he lived for the next two decades. There he consolidated a large chiefdom of diverse BaSotho, Nguni, and San elements in the manner of Moshoeshoe. Except for a brief period when he had been provoked by the rash invasion of his territory by forces from the Orange River Sovereignty and the Cape Colony in 1851, he restrained his people from raiding his white colonial neighbours further south. In 1857 a visiting colonial official was impressed by his physical appearance and his 'perfect self-possession, quickness, and good address in

[1] Schrumpf, 25 Mar. 1847, *JME* xxii (1847), 294–5.

conversation'.[1] He continued to perform services for Moshoeshoe, responding to summonses to Thaba Bosiu and contributing *sethaba-thaba* cattle. Moorosi was an excellent junior partner. He guarded Moshoeshoe's southern marches and established BaSotho control over the Quthing region south of the Orange.[2]

In northern LeSotho Moshoeshoe's most powerful kinsmen other than Molapo were his half-brother Mopeli and his nephew Lesaoana. Mopeli, as the head of the Third House of Mokhachane, was, like Mohale the head of the Second House, entitled by custom to a considerable degree of autonomy. In 1848 Moshoeshoe sent him and his followers from the Thaba Bosiu area to settle north-west of the Caledon near Platberg, to infiltrate the lands occupied by the Coloured communities and to check white expansion. As Moshoeshoe's deputy in the area he played a major part in the negotiations and conflicts with Major Warden and General Cathcart. After the fall of Marabeng he moved to Mabolela, thirteen miles north-east of modern Ladybrand, and supervised the resettlement of Sekonyela's country in conjunction with Molapo. Mopeli had visited Cape Town as a member of Arbousset's party in 1844 and, although he abandoned Christianity in the general reaction of the late 1840s, he continued to be influenced by his Christian education and he sent his senior son to school in Cape Town. Until 1853 he unequivocally recognized Moshoeshoe. In 1852, for example, he informed British commissioners that 'his cause is one with Moshesh, because he stands under him, and is not independent'.[3] Then, however, he considered he was not allotted his fair share of the cattle he had captured

---

[1] John Burnet, British Agent, Aliwal North, to the Secretary to the High Commissioner, 14 Feb. 1857, *BR* ii. 263.

[2] On Moorosi in this period, I. 9, 39, 46, 47, 53; Schrumpf, 25 May 1843, *JME* xviii (1843), 441–8; Schrumpf, 18 Jan. 1847, *JME* xxii (1847), 281–7; Schrumpf, 25 Mar. 1847, *JME* xxii (1847), 288–301; Schrumpf, annual report, 1851, *JME* xxvi (1851), 365–75; D. F. Ellenberger, *Leselinyana*, Jan. 1902; Azariel Sekese, *Leselinyana*, 1 Apr. 1905; Germond, *Chronicles*, pp. 329–40; and documents in *BR* (see index entry Morosi) especially i. 17, 137–8, 147–8, 152–3, 367, 612, and ii. xlvii–l, 31, 231–2, 235, 262–4, 349.

[3] Minutes of Meeting held at Winburg, 7 Feb. 1852, *BR*. i. 543.

from the Tlokoa, as is revealed in the praises he composed for himself:

When I had filled the clay pot with cow's blood
The owner of the cow [i.e. Molapo] got angry and took it away
He poured it into his own clay pot
.   .   .   .
When I have captured cattle, they are all taken from me.[1]

In 1854, therefore, Mopeli was feeling somewhat slighted by Moshoeshoe. Moreover, just as Posholi refused to submit to control by Letsie in the south, so in the north Mopeli regarded himself as wholly independent of Molapo.[2]

Lesaoana, who like Molapo was about forty years old in 1854, was the head of the family of Moshoeshoe's full brother Makhabane, who had been killed in the 1835 expedition against the Thembu.[3] His senior wife was his cousin Mathe, the only daughter of Moshoeshoe's First House. In 1845 Moshoeshoe placed Lesaoana at Mapoteng, twenty-five miles north-east of Thaba Bosiu. There he attracted many followers and he rapidly extended his authority over both sides of the upper Phuthiatsana. However, Mapoteng was only seven miles east of Sebala-bala, where Moshoeshoe placed Molapo in 1847, and although Moshoeshoe moved Molapo to Leribe after the fall of Marabeng, he moved Masopha towards Mapoteng at the same time, and Lesaoana felt hemmed in between them. Believing that as the senior member of the House of Makhabane he should have received better treatment than Letsie's younger brothers, in about 1861 Lesaoana migrated to 'Makalane in the Orange Free State, twenty miles north-east of Botha Bothe. There, the ageing Moshoeshoe would lose control of him and he would become the Posholi of the north: a cattle-raider and a

---

[1] I. 39, Mosebi Damane, citing Z. D. Mangoaela, *Lithoko tsa Marena a Basotho*, Morija, 1957, p. 30.
[2] On Mopeli, I. 9, 39; Dyke, 20 May 1849, *JME* xxiv (1849), 428–30; Maitin, 22 Apr. 1850, *JME* xxv (1850), 361–8; Mabille, 24 Jan. 1860, *JME* xxxv (1860), 292; Keck, 29 Jan. 1861, *JME* xxxvi (1861), 209; Daumas, 27 Dec. 1858, G.S. 1340, OFS; and documents in *BR*, especially *BR* i. 421, 535–49, ii. 163–4, 322–6.
[3] See above, p. 83.

major cause of the disasters that would befall LeSotho in the later 1860s.[1]

In defeating the Tlokoa in 1853, Moshoeshoe re-established regular contact with the Khoakhoa chiefdom in the far north-east. The Khoakhoa had become his allies in his Botha Bothe days, but had been separated from him by his migration to Thaba Bosiu.[2] However, Moshoeshoe had assumed responsibility for the young Khoakhoa chief, Matela. The missionaries had educated and converted him at Morija and in 1847 he had returned to the north. Making his headquarters at Qholaqhoe, twelve miles north-east of Botha Bothe, Matela gradually restored his chiefdom around the headwaters of the Caledon, east of Molapo. Neither Moshoeshoe nor Molapo interfered in his local affairs and his following was too small to play a significant part in events; but Matela and his descendants have taken pride in their claim to have been Moshoeshoe's first allies.[3]

Moshoeshoe's principal ally across the Caledon River to the north-west was Moletsane, the Taung chief who had settled near the French mission station Mekoatleng in 1838.[4] There he built up a considerable chiefdom of diverse elements—BaSotho and Nguni as well as Taung—in much the same style as Moshoeshoe. He had hoped to resume occupation of the ancestral Taung territory between the Sand and the Vaal rivers, but the white occupation of those lands and Major Warden's boundary lines had confined him to the area around Mekoatleng. More than once, Warden's

---

[1] On Lesaoana (also known as RaManella), I. 14 (a descendant) and 8, 15, 18, 35, 38; Arbousset, 30 Dec. 1847, *JME* xxiii (1848), 214; Jousse, 14 Aug. 1857, *JME* xxiii (1858), 54-7; Coillard, 22 Feb. 1860, *JME* xxxv (1860), 204-6; Sekese, *Leselinyana*, Feb. 1893; and documents in *BR*, especially i. 180 and iii. 175.

[2] See above, pp. 39-40.

[3] On Matela and his Khoakhoa chiefdom, I. 22 (the present chief, a descendant) and 35, 39; Casalis, 29 May 1845, *JME* xx (1845), 409; Arbousset, Annual Report for 1848, *JME* xxiii (1848), 374; Arbousset, 26 May 1854, *JME* xxix (1854), 445; Sekese, *Leselinyana*, 1 and 15 June 1893; Macgregor, *Traditions*, pp. 23-6; and *BR* ii. 56, 191-2, iii. 644. On these historical grounds, the Khoakhoa cheifs have resisted various attempts by descendants of Molapo to bring them under their jurisdiction and to this day the Khoakhoa chiefs have preserved their status as direct dependants of the King of LeSotho.

[4] See above, p. 86.

military combinations with his black and brown neighbours had caused him to flee across the Caledon. In 1854 he still possessed internal autonomy within his chiefdom, but he recognized Moshoeshoe as the senior partner in their alliance. For Moshoeshoe, he performed the important role of guardian of his north-western marches, in much the same way as Moorosi protected him on the southern side. Moletsane was about ten years younger than Moshoeshoe and he had an excellent understanding with his missionary, Daumas.[1]

Moshoeshoe had hoped to draw Sekonyela and Moroka into his orbit in the same way as Moletsane, for both of them, like Moletsane, had migrated from the lands of their birth to the vicinity of the Caledon valley as a result of the *lifaqane* wars. He did not succeed. Sekonyela, as we have seen, rebuffed all Moshoeshoe's attempts to come to a lasting agreement with him and he was overwhelmed in 1853.[2] After the fall of Marabeng Moshoeshoe incorporated most of the Tlokoa chief's former subjects into his kingdom. Many of them were quickly subjected by Molapo and Mopeli in northern LeSotho; others, after various migrations, settled in the Mokhotlong district many years later. Some of Moroka's kinsmen and councillors preferred an alliance with Moshoeshoe, but Moroka himself remained hostile and his Wesleyan missionaries reinforced that attitude, with the result that he and his people sided with the Whites when war came and the Thaba 'Nchu area was eventually incorporated in the Orange Free State.[3]

---

[1] On Moletsane, I. 29–32 (descendants); reports of Daumas, especially 15 Apr. 1844, *JME* xx (1845), 20–2, 22 Apr. 1850, xxv (1850), 375–80, June 1851, xxvi (1851), 445–52, and Feb. 1862, xxxvii (1862), 209–10; D. F. Ellenberger, *Leselinyana*, 10 June 1911, 7 May 1915; A. A. Moletsane, *Leselinyana*, 12 Aug. 1911; also documents in *BR* (index entry Molitsane), especially i. 84, 92, 103–4, 242–5, 516–32 and ii. 145–9, 322–5. He was baptized not long before he died, aged about 100, in 1885. According to his grandson, I. 29, he had thirty-three wives and more than 115 children: Morena Abraham Aaron Moletsane, *An Account of the Autobiographical Memoir*, Paarl, 1967, p. 1.

[2] See above, pp. 165–6.

[3] On Moroka, see above, pp. 110–11; also documents in *BR* (index entry Moroko) and in the WMS.

3. *Economic and Social Change*

During the mid-1850s LeSotho was prosperous. The people had built up their flocks of sheep and goats and their herds of cattle, which they still regarded as the most important form of wealth. They had also brought into cultivation much of the fertile land on both sides of the Caledon River and made LeSotho the granary of the southern high veld.[1]

The number of livestock and the production of grain varied sharply from season to season, depending on the rainfall, the incidence of hailstorms and locust plagues, and the political situation, but the trends were emphatically upwards. The density of population had not yet reached the limit for mixed farming, the soil was not exhausted, and the quality of husbandry was improving as a result of the importation of metal hoes and even a few ploughs and wagons, and the addition of wheat and potatoes to the customary crops, millet and maize.[2] As early as 1838, after several good seasons, Moshoeshoe had enough millet stored on Thaba Bosiu in the traditional large weatherproof baskets to last seven or eight years, and other chiefs had nearly as much; and Africans and Coloured people were travelling to LeSotho to obtain grain.[3] Whites who settled in the southern high veld also became largely dependent on Moshoeshoe's people for their grain supplies. Governor Cathcart found that 'his people grow almost all the corn that is used in the Sovereignty, where the burghers only rear cattle, which they

[1] There is need for an economic history of LeSotho based on intensive field work in oral history and a thorough examination of the documents: see a challenging review article by Edward Alpers, 'Re-thinking African Economic History: a contribution to the discussion of the roots of under-development', *Ufahamu*, Los Angeles, iii (3) (Winter 1973), 97–109. R. C. Germond's *Chronicles*, which consists mainly of translated extracts from the *JME*, is useful on agriculture and trade in the nineteenth century; see especially chs. 31 and 38.

[2] When the first census of Basutoland was taken in 1875, the average family possessed about 9 head of cattle, 1 horse, and 21 small stock, and there was about 1 plough to 10 families and 1 wagon to 100 families. In 1874, the grain exports of Basutoland averaged 4 bags per family. These figures are derived from Germond, p. 326, taking the number of families as one-fifth of the total population.

[3] Arbousset, 26 June 1838, *JME* xiv (1839), 60–1.

exchange for his grain'.[1] This would continue beyond the lifetime of Moshoeshoe.[2]

Since the 1830s traders had been visiting LeSotho from the Cape Colony with wagon-loads of merchandise. The volume of trade declined during the Sovereignty period, when political troubles had coincided with successive failures of the summer rains, but there was a rapid recovery in a series of good seasons after 1853. As in other parts of Africa where missionaries were the first white people to establish homes, trade followed the cross: the traders naturally gravitated towards the mission stations. During the mid-1850s several traders became semi-permanent residents and began to erect buildings at Beersheba, Mekoatleng, Thaba Bosiu, and, especially, Morija.

In 1854 Arbousset reported of Morija:

The trade in grain there is now considerable, stimulating the activity and increasing the affluence of the inhabitants. This trade is carried on by the farmers of the Orange Free State but, in addition, two speculators, one Dutch and the other English, have settled in the place with their families, and trade there in wheat, millet, cattle, and horses, the main resources of the inhabitants. A Boer, half wheelwright, half blacksmith; a brickmaker; and a tailor also live there.[3]

Four years later, according to Maeder, one of the half-dozen British traders at Morija had sold £3,700 worth of British merchandise during a fourteen-month period, including about 1,000 overcoats, 220 pairs of trousers, 220 jackets, 1,200 shirts, 200 hats, 350 saddles, 500 bridles, 500 pairs of stirrups, 7,300 knives, 8 ploughs, 1,500 hoes, 150 iron saucepans, and 6 wagons; and he had received in exchange about 2,000 head of cattle, 230 horses, some cattle hides,

---

[1] Cathcart, 13 Jan. 1853, *BR* ii. 8.

[2] The turning-point came in the 1880s, when the lands of Basutoland within its limited frontiers as defined in 1869 were becoming exhausted. Orange Free State farmers were beginning to turn to agriculture as well as stockfarming, and railways were beginning to bring imported grain to Kimberley and Bloemfontein: Germond, pp. 469–71. For an account of similar processes in other parts of southern Africa see Colin Bundy, 'Emergence and Decline of a South African Peasantry', *African Affairs*, lxxi (Oct. 1972), 369–88.

[3] Arbousset, 26 May 1854, *JME* xxix (1854), 447–8.

1,000 muids of wheat, some wool, and £50 in cash.[1] As these figures show, not much money was in circulation in LeSotho in the 1850s. Maeder noted that 'the use of money as the means of exchange has not yet been introduced into LeSotho; commerce is made by exchanging one object against another.'[2]

Moshoeshoe was by far the wealthiest man in the country. Using *letsema* labour, he controlled the produce of many acres of arable land in the valleys below Thaba Bosiu; but most of his wealth was in livestock, especially cattle. He accumulated livestock from gifts; from fines he imposed on persons found guilty of offences at cases tried in his *lekhotla*; from the marriage of his numerous daughters (*bohali*), for whom the rate was as high as thirty head of cattle, about three times the rate for commoners; and from cattle raids. When he himself led a raiding expedition, he kept a large proportion of the booty and distributed the balance among the other participants. When his territorial chiefs led raids, they were expected to send him a share of the booty and they often did so. Consequently Moshoeshoe's cattle-wealth had increased vastly during the previous thirty years. Even in 1852 and 1853, when he lost large numbers of cattle to General Cathcart, he probably made a net gain in personal cattle-wealth, if only as a result of the two great expeditions he led against Sekonyela and his allies.[3]

Only a small proportion of the king's livestock could be pastured in the vicinity of Thaba Bosiu. Of the rest, some were lent (*mafisa*) to men residing in various parts of the country and others were sent to cattle-posts far away from

[1] Maeder, 15 Jan. 1858, *JME* xxxiii (1858), 133. After an Orange Free State commando sacked Morija in the war of 1858, the same trader, J. Pullinger, claimed that the commando had destroyed his property to the value of £1,102, and that his goods had included: sugar, coffee, tea, jackets, cloaks, trousers, shoes, hats, shirts, blankets, shawls, buttons, needles, cooking utensils, table knives, clasp knives, nails, screws, brass wire, sickles, and stirrup irons (presumably for sale to BaSotho), and also 200 muids of wheat (value £200), 6 bales of merino wool (£90), 6 bales of coarse wool (£45), 15 oxen (£67. 1s. 2d.), and 100 brayed skins (£15) (presumably acquired from BaSotho): *SAAR, OFS* iii (1858), 458–9.

[2] Maeder, n.d., *JME* xxxi (1856), 207.

[3] Casalis (1), pp. 153–6; E. J. Rolland, 'Notes on the Political and Social Position of the Basuto Tribe', 30 Mar. 1868, BR IV. 128–30.

Thaba Bosiu under the charge of reliable followers. For example, after the final rout of the Tlokoa he sent Selebalo, one of his junior sons, to found a cattle-post at 'Mate, near his birthplace Menkhoaneng; and although 'Mate was within Molapo's region, Selebalo remained responsible directly to his father.[1] At about the same time he established cattle-posts at Tebetebeng south of the Cana mission station and Makhoarane east of Morija under two other junior sons, 'Mota and Ngakantsi, who likewise were directly subordinate to himself.[2]

In spite of the fact that Moshoeshoe, as *morena e moholo*, claimed to be the ultimate owner of all the cattle in LeSotho, most of the livestock was effectively controlled by others. Each territorial chief amassed livestock in much the same way as the king himself, and by the 1850s men like Letsie, Molapo, Moorosi, and Moletsane had large herds and flocks, though none of them matched Moshoeshoe's. Moreover village headmen and male heads of households at all levels in society possessed a few livestock, with the exception only of *bahlanka* (clients; servants) who used but did not own any livestock lent them by their patrons.

How many BaSotho were *bahlanka* in the 1850s cannot be determined. They can only have formed a small proportion of the total population. By no means all holders of *mafisa* were *bahlanka*: Moshoeshoe and other chiefs often lent *mafisa* to their friends and relatives as well as to their servants. Unfree retainers had never been numerous in LeSotho and although the proportion increased during the *lifaqane*, when many people lost all their property and were obliged to attach themselves to patrons, the process was reversed during the subsequent years of expansion, when some *bahlanka* came to be treated as freemen by their former patrons and others attached themselves as freemen to different chiefs and headmen.[3]

Women possessed few livestock; but since they were responsible for cultivating the arable lands it might have

---

[1] I. 13 (a descendant of Selebalo), I. 55 (a descendant of Lehau who had general responsibility for Moshoeshoe's cattle), and I. 39.

[2] I. 39.   [3] On *bahlanka*, see above, p. 8.

been expected that they would have controlled the disposition of grain, surplus to the needs of their households. However, this did not happen. The patriarchal tradition was still overwhelmingly strong in SeSotho society. Men had the major say in the administration of the property of their Houses, and, as Maeder's list shows, most of the manufactured clothing acquired by BaSotho was men's clothing.[1]

Consequently, the impact of trade tended to confirm rather than to change the distribution of wealth in LeSotho. Traders dealt with anyone who had property to dispose of, with the result that imported goods were distributed among the people in rough proportion to their control over grain and livestock. Moshoeshoe himself, benefiting from gifts as well as from trade, obtained by far the largest collection of European goods: household utensils, groceries, clothing, agricultural implements, wagons, fire-arms, and ammunition. He also employed white masons to erect stone buildings on Thaba Bosiu. Some of these acquisitions, including his European clothes and his stone house, he only used when he wished to impress Whites or visiting chiefs. Others, such as tea and sugar, hoes and saddles, he put to regular use. Several of his kinsmen and allies did nearly as well. But commoners, too, acquired a few imported goods, especially the Christians who were encouraged by the missionaries to wear European clothing.

It would not have been possible for Moshoeshoe to create a trade monopoly, even if he had attempted to do so. Nevertheless he did influence the flow of trade into and out of LeSotho in important respects, in the interests of national strength and security. Ever since he had experienced the devastating effects of the horses and fire-arms used by small bands of Coloured raiders in the late 1820s and early 1830s, he had encouraged his people to acquire them, and by the 1850s his example combined with white pressures had made every young MoSotho boy ambitious to own a horse and a gun.[2] Many of these were brought into the country by

---

[1] On the status of women in LeSotho, see Hugh Ashton, *The Basuto*, pp. 177–85.
[2] Casalis, 12 June 1851, *JME* xxvi (1851), 363.

BaSotho who had worked for white farmers in the Cape Colony or Trans-Orangia and had obtained them in lieu of wages. Others were plundered from neighbours during the incessant border disputes; and others were acquired by trade.

The horses were of Cape Colonial stock, which was predominantly of oriental origin with an infusion of English thoroughbreds. LeSotho proved to be relatively free of horse diseases. The animals flourished, adapted to the mountainous terrain, and developed into the hardy breed known by Whites as the 'Basuto pony'.[1] By the 1850s most men of military age owned a horse, though goods continued to be transported by pack-oxen. Moshoeshoe promoted this build-up not only by setting a personal example but also by being particularly sparing in handing over horses, as distinct from cattle, whenever he felt obliged to pay compensation for actual or alleged thefts.[2]

The arms trade was contrary to the accepted norms of white society in southern Africa and, by 1854, forbidden by the Sand River Convention and by colonial and republican laws.[3] Nevertheless there were always white farmers and traders who were glad to make a handsome profit from bartering arms and ammunition to Africans. In 1851 the Winburg magistrate reported 'The trade in gunpowder and firearms with the Natives is carried on within the Sovereignty to an extent almost incredible',[4] and although the trade declined thereafter it never completely dried up. The British officers involved in the Berea engagement in December 1852 estimated that the BaSotho forces included 'not less than six thousand well armed horsemen', as well as several thousand warriors on foot, and reported that the

[1] R. W. Thornton, *The Origin and History of the Basuto Pony*, Morija, 1936.
[2] For example, on the eve of the Berea engagement General Cathcart demanded 10,000 cattle and 1,000 horses, and Moshoeshoe delivered about 3,500 cattle and, apparently, no horses at all: G. Tylden, *Rise of the Basuto*, p. 59.
[3] On the arms trade, see Gavin White, 'Firearms in Africa: an Introduction', Shula Marks, 'Firearms in Southern Africa: a Survey', and Anthony Atmore and Peter Sanders, 'Sotho Arms and Ammunition in the Nineteenth Century', *JAH* xii (1971), 173–84, 517–30, and 535–44; also Tylden, pp. 36–7.
[4] Biddulph to Warden, 30 Mar. 1851, BR 1/4, OFS.

king had a 'great store of gunpowder' on Thaba Bosiu.[1] But whereas the BaSotho horses were sound, their fire-arms were not. They were a mixture of old military flintlock muskets of Napoleonic War vintage (which were being superseded in Europe by percussion-lock rifles) and cheap Birmingham trade muskets which were being manufactured in vast quantities for the African market. Moshoeshoe himself and some of his kinsmen were good marksmen when they had adequate equipment, but the BaSotho in general could not produce effective results with the fire-arms and ammunition at their disposal. Fire-arms were not a significant factor in Moshoeshoe's victories over the Tlokoa, nor in his rebuffs of the forces of Warden and Cathcart.[2] Indeed, his warriors went into battle wielding assagais and battle-axes as well as guns, and it was their traditional weapons that caused most damage to their enemies.[3]

Moshoeshoe never tried to imitate the Zulu military system. He did not create a standing army, nor did he establish national regiments based on age, nor did he institute rigorous methods of military training and discipline. As in the past, young BaSotho indulged in military games and in cattle-raiding exploits with their age-mates, if only against neighbouring villages. They also learned to manœuvre cattle by whistles, shouts, and strokes on the *lesiba* (a stringed instrument) for the purpose of confusing an enemy.[4] The introduction of horses gave them greater mobility but the military organization was extremely loose, for every man was a potential part-time warrior and provided his own horse and weapons.

The major military units were constituted on a territorial basis. When mobilized, the followers of a territorial chief formed a distinct unit under his command. These units were often subdivided according to age. The hard core of a chief's following consisted of his age-mates who had been initiated with him and thereby owed him exceptional loyalty,

---

[1] *BR* i. 629, 612; also *BR* ii. 3.   [2] *BR* ii. 83.
[3] Atmore and Sanders, *JAH* xii (1971), 538–41.
[4] Jousse, 14 Aug. 1857, *JME* xxxiii (1858), 57.

but as he grew older he formed additional sub-units of younger men and placed them under the command of a son or a commoner who had distinguished himself as a warrior. There was no standard terminology to distinguish the two levels of military organization. The word *mphi* (borrowed from the Zulu *impi*) was applied indiscriminately to units of different scales.

In this vital respect—direct military control—Moshoeshoe was scarcely more than first among equals. On Thaba Bosiu he possessed the largest store of ammunition in LeSotho; but at full strength his own *mphi*, the *Matlama* (Binders), included no more than the men who lived in the central part of the kingdom between the territories of Letsie and Molapo. It consisted of two divisions—the *Linotsi* (Bees) commanded by his age-mate Makoanyane and the *Mollo* (Fire) under Mokolokolo. Letsie, Molapo, Posholi, Mohale, Lesaoana, and Mopeli and the allied chiefs each controlled his own followers. Moreover, although Moshoeshoe claimed the power to dispose of all war booty, in practice a territorial chief was usually able to retain most of the livestock captured by his regiment.[1]

Concerted military action was therefore extremely difficult to achieve and sustain. A territorial chief and his councillors were able to conduct themselves according to their assessment of their personal and local interests as well as their degree of loyalty to the larger entity, LeSotho, and the king. Throughout the 1850s, as in the preceding decades, Moshoeshoe's political acumen and military talents constituted inspiring leadership and the pressures from black and white neighbours created bonds of common interest. Most of the territorial chiefs participated with their regiments in the expeditions against Sekonyela and the defensive actions against Warden and Cathcart. Co-operation was excellent in the two brief offensive operations against Sekonyela in 1852 and 1853 when, after holding councils of war with the territorial chiefs and their military councillors,

---

[1] I. 23, 38, 39; communication from Monica Wilson, 4 June 1973. Masopha, who lived in the central region of the kingdom, probably controlled his own regiment by 1854.

Moshoeshoe laid down the campaign strategies and each regiment played its prescribed role in the expectation of capturing valuable booty.[1] Co-operation was more haphazard when an enemy invaded LeSotho. Then, each chief was inclined to look to the defence of his own territory and livestock. Consequently the structural weaknesses in the military organization were liable to lead to the piecemeal disintegration of the kingdom in the event that a disciplined enemy equipped with modern weapons attacked LeSotho and sustained a prolonged war.

Although Moshoeshoe encouraged trade—especially trade in horses and fire-arms—he perceived that some of the activities of the traders had corrosive implications. He had accommodated to the presence of his missionaries because they performed exceptionally useful services, he admired them personally, they were of a different nation from his white adversaries, and they seemed to share his principal political objectives. In the 1850s, in spite of the general reaction against Christianity, he seems to have become reconciled to the idea that Christianity would ultimately prevail in LeSotho. 'Your teachings alone will survive', he told Casalis. 'It is only a question of time.'[2] The loyalties of the traders, on the other hand, lay elsewhere, for they were a projection of colonial society. Moreover, although many traders conducted themselves well in LeSotho, others set a bad example by purveying cheap alcoholic spirits which had a demoralizing effect on his people.[3] Still more ominous was the fact that traders were occupying land in LeSotho. Knowing how white farmers had first asked his permission to occupy land and later claimed to own it, Moshoeshoe had cause to fear that the trading stations would become bridgeheads for further dismemberment of his country.

To grapple with these problems Moshoeshoe introduced an innovation from the white world. Previously there had

---

[1] The fullest contemporary account of a BaSotho military expedition is Arbousset's description of the final defeat of the Tlokoa, based on information supplied by participants; 8 Nov. 1853, *JME* xxix (1854), 162–8.

[2] Editorial [Casalis], *JME* xxxii (1857), 3.

[3] Maeder, 15 Jan. 1858, *JME* xxxiii (1858), 133; Cameron, 12 Jan. 1852, SA/12, WMS.

been nothing precisely corresponding to statute law in
LeSotho. Custom carried immense authority and substantial
legal changes were usually made, step by step, by judicial
decisions in particular cases. Moshoeshoe was informed
about the legislative technique of European states and of
his white neighbours in the Orange Free State, who promulgated a written constitution and a series of laws soon after
they became independent. Moreover, he had at his disposal
printing presses owned by the French and British missions.[1]

First he dealt with the problem of trade alcohol. He was
dismayed that some white traders and farmers were bartering cheap brandy produced in the south-western Cape
Colony ('Cape smoke') and drunkenness was becoming
widespread among his people. He and his father had always
been complete abstainers. They did not drink even the
mildest form of SeSotho beer, though as a hospitable ruler
Moshoeshoe dispensed large quantities of strong beer (*joala*)
to his guests at Thaba Bosiu. On this point he fully agreed
with his missionaries, who were seriously concerned at the
spread of drunkenness.[2] Accordingly, after consulting his
councillors and his territorial chiefs he promulgated a law
against the introduction and sale of spirits. It was printed
in SeSotho by the Wesleyan mission press at Platberg and
in English by the government of the Orange Free State. It
read as follows:

Whereas the spirituous liquors of the whites were unknown to
former generations of our Tribe, *Matie* [Matsie, i.e. Nkopane,
father of Mohlomi] and *Motlomi* [Mohlomi] until *Bomonageng*
[BaMonaheng],—and our father *Mokachane*, now very advanced
in age, has never used any other drink than water and milk;
and whereas we deem that a good Chief and Judge cannot
claim to be competent to execute his duties, if he make use of
any thing of an intoxicating nature; and whereas spirituous
liquors create quarrelling and strife, and pave the way to the
destruction of society, (for surely the spirituous liquors of the
whites are nothing else than fire):

[1] The missionary Schuh was in charge of the printing press at Beersheba,
which completed the first printing of the entire New Testament in SeSotho in
1856: Schuh, Annual Report, *JME* xxxi (1856), 338–40.

[2] Maitin, 15 May 1854, *JME* xxix (1854), 372–3.

It is therefore made known to all, that the introduction and sale of said spirituous liquor within Basutoland is henceforth prohibited, and provided any person, whether white or coloured, contravene this order, the spirits shall be taken from him and poured out on the ground, without excuse or indemnification.

And this order shall be printed in the Basuto and Dutch languages, and posted up at the places of public meetings, and in the villages of the Basutos.

Given with the advice and concurrence of the great men of our Tribe, by us the Chief of the Basutos, at Thaba Bosigo, the 8th of November, 1854.

Moshesh, Chief.[1]

Five years later, Moshoeshoe dealt with the broader question of traders' rights in a remarkably prescient document:

I, Moshesh, write for any trader, whoever he may be, already in my land, and for any who may come to trade with the Basutos; my word is this:

Trade to me and my tribe is a good thing, I wish to promote it. Any trader who wishes to establish a shop, must first obtain permission from me. Should he build a house, I grant him no right to sell it.

Further, I do not grant him liberty to plough the fields, but only to plant a small vegetable garden.

The trader who fancies that the place he is sojourning in belongs to him, must dismiss the thought, if not, he is to quit; for there is no place belonging to the whites in my land, and I have granted no white man a place, either by word, or by writing.

Further, any trader who leaves a debt there from whence he comes, and he who contracts any whilst in my land, any such debt, if brought to me, I will enquire into, in our Court of Justice, that I may settle it; and the debt will be paid up in the manner the Basutos pay their debts. But the suer is to appear before me, and the debtor likewise, that justice may be done.

Further, the law that I issued on the 8th day of November, 1854, I renew this day, that people may be reminded of it, and conform themselves to it . . .

I am,

Mark X of Moshesh, Chief of the Basutos.[2]

Considering his background and his limited experience,

[1] *BR* ii. 133.   [2] *BR* ii. 536–7.

Moshoeshoe was most perceptive in grasping new opportunities for the welfare of his people, while laying down conditions that were essential for the survival of his kingdom in the face of white commercial expansion. He encouraged the diversification and increased production of grain with the use of imported ploughs; he influenced the inflow and outflow of goods by prohibiting or discouraging what he deemed undesirable and promoting what he considered beneficial; and he claimed absolute jurisdiction over white traders in his country and debarred them from acquiring ownership of land. He was in no position to foresee that the productivity of a still further truncated LeSotho would eventually decline to a point where a large proportion of his menfolk would be obliged to make up the shortfall by working for white people in the fertile lands of the northern Orange Free State, which in his day they had scarcely begun to cultivate, in diamond- and gold-fields which had not yet been discovered, and in manufacturing industries which had not yet been founded. Nor was he able to discern that the terms of trade and conditions of labour would be determined by forces beyond the control of his successors.

Moshoeshoe did not confine the legislative technique to problems created by white expansion. In 1855 he issued a law against a SeSotho practice of which he himself had never approved. It arose out of a case of murder which had been committed after a diviner had named the victim as the source of harm to the killer. Moshoeshoe himself had always been sceptical of the claims made by some diviners that they could identify evil-doers in this way and at a *pitso* in 1843 he had spoken out strongly against the killing of supposed witches.[1] The law that he promulgated on 27 August 1855 embodied his well-known and long-established policy. It was 'assented to by Letsie, by all my brothers, and by all men in the tribe, who spit on the lie of witchcraft, and cover its face with their spittle'. The crucial provision read: '*When anyone is killed in a case of witchcraft, the murderer will be most severely judged, and sentenced to death.*'[2]

[1] See above, pp. 94–5.
[2] *BR* ii. 152–3. These are the only three 'laws' of Moshoeshoe that have

4. *Maintaining the Kingdom*

The political community over which Moshoeshoe presided was many times larger than the chiefdom in which he had spent the first three decades of his life and served his political apprenticeship. Before the *lifaqane* a MoSotho chief could know every one of his followers personally and tour his entire chiefdom on foot in a day or two. Moshoeshoe could not possibly know all the hundred thousand people whom he regarded as his subjects and it took him several days to visit an outlying part of his kingdom on horseback.

He was constantly concerned with the problem of preventing a recurrence of the old process by which a chief's ambitious kinsmen and any other chiefs he might temporarily have subdued hived off with their followers to set up independent states. Posholi and Lesaoana were seizing their opportunities like any forceful kinsman of a pre-*lifaqane* chief, Molapo was manœuvring to secure a political inheritance independent of an elder brother whom he disliked, and Moorosi was striving to re-establish Phuthi autonomy so far as circumstances permitted.

A new problem that was emerging concerned the relations between chiefs and commoners. Generally, as in the past, a chief had an interest in his subjects' welfare because his power depended on the number of his followers and a dissatisfied man could always attach himself to a rival chief. Nevertheless there is evidence that the concentration of wealth and power in the hands of Moshoeshoe and his kinsmen was causing hardship and resentment. At a *pitso* in 1846, when Moshoeshoe announced a *sethaba-thaba* for a military expedition against an Nguni community in southern LeSotho, a commoner grumbled that he had never seen anyone profit but the chiefs;[1] and during a drought in 1859, a missionary noted that the chiefs were living as well as

survived. Others may have been issued: see Cape of Good Hope, *Report and Evidence of Commission on Native Laws and Customs of the Basutos*, Cape Town, 1873, evidence of Chief Letsie, George Tlali Moshesh, and Sofonia Moshesh (i.e. Letsie, Tlali, and Sofonia, sons of Moshoeshoe) and Chief Jobo (i.e. Lelosa, half-brother of Moshoeshoe).

[1] Arbousset, 18 July 1846, *JME* xxii (1847), 44–5.

ever while some of their subjects were starving.[1] The gap between chiefs and commoners was becoming more marked with the passage of time as some of Moshoeshoe's kinsmen, lacking his own sense of social responsibility, took advantage of their relationship with him.

Third, by the 1850s SeSotho society was permeated with new tensions generated by two decades of contact with the wider world. Missionaries were striking at the very roots of the traditional forms of social solidarity as well as the traditional religious beliefs and practices. Traders were ignoring the customary economic norms, according to which there was a fixed rate of exchange between one commodity and another (e.g. a cow and a sheep), in favour of the fluctuating values of the market economy. These pressures impinged most powerfully upon communities residing in the focal areas where chiefs, missionaries, and traders lived close together (as at Thaba Bosiu, Morija, Mekoatleng, and Beersheba), but they caused ripples of varying intensity throughout LeSotho. They were most effective among the younger generation. By the 1850s a wide gap had opened up between those whose value systems had been crystallized in a pre-*lifaqane lebollo* and others whose memories did not extend beyond the period when white missionaries, traders, and farmers were already present in or near LeSotho.[2] The world into which Moshoeshoe and his generation had been initiated was radically different from the only world experienced by his younger children and his grandchildren.

Moshoeshoe was determined to prevent the disintegration of his kingdom. In this, he was not merely pursuing personal wealth and power. Whereas in the old days political fragmentation had not been harmful to SeSotho society, in the conditions of the 1850s a disaffected chief who withdrew his allegiance would be likely to form an alliance with his white neighbours in the Orange Free State, as Letele would do in 1858, and once that process had begun there was

[1] Maeder, 5 Jan. 1859, *JME* xxxiv (1859), 128–9.
[2] Essays written by Tlali and Tsekelo, sons of Moshoeshoe, while at Zonnebloem school, Cape Town, in 1858: Grey Collection, vol. 265, South African Public Library, Cape Town.

no knowing where it would end. Events in the Transvaal, of which Moshoeshoe was well aware, already showed that when white farming communities made alliances with Africans they picked out the best land for themselves and reduced the chiefs and their followers to subject peoples.[1]

To counteract the centrifugal forces Moshoeshoe did not invent distinctively new institutions. As we have seen, he created no standing militia to enforce his will, nor did he monopolize imported resources.[2] Rather, he built on the institutions, customs, and norms he had known as a young man, adapting and stretching them to the uttermost to serve his purposes.

Moshoeshoe attracted and retained the services of able advisers.[3] His councillors (*matona*) resided at Thaba Bosiu and were his most intimate associates. Representing different interests and points of view, they kept him informed of the various currents of opinion and they were sufficiently talented to exert considerable influence over the territorial chiefs. The *matona* did not constitute an exclusive conciliar body, for Moshoeshoe always felt free to consult anyone he pleased. Nevertheless he valued the services of loyal men and was remarkably indulgent to them. He never seems to have dismissed an established *letona* and there is a tradition that he declined to punish a councillor who had been discovered sleeping with one of his royal wives.[4]

The longest surviving councillor of the previous generation was his mother's brother, RaTšiu, who as Moshoeshoe's

---

[1] Leonard Thompson in *OHSA* i. 435–42.

[2] Compare the hypotheses concerning state-making in pre-colonial Africa by Peter C. Lloyd, 'The Political Structure of African Kingdoms: an Exploratory Model', in M. Banton, ed., *Political Systems and the Distribution of Power*, London, 1965, 'The Political Development of West African Kingdoms', *JAH* ix (1968), 319–29, and *The Political Development of Yoruba Kingdoms in the Eighteenth and Nineteenth Centuries*, London, 1971; by Jack Goody, *Technology, Tradition, and the State in Africa*, London, 1971; and by Jan Vansina, 'A Comparison of African Kingdoms', *Africa*, xxxii (1962), 324–35. Note, however, that the early history of most kingdoms in tropical Africa is largely a matter of speculation, since the evidence is very tenuous, whereas in the case of LeSotho we have relatively rich evidence contemporary with the last thirty-seven years of the life of the founder king.

[3] Information on Moshoeshoe's *matona* was provided by I. 3, 4, 27, 28, 39, 51, 52, 55, and 56.　　　　　　　[4] The culprit was Makolokolo: I. 1 and 28.

maternal uncle (*malome*) had the customary right to deputize for the king when he was ill or absent from home. RaTšiu was a conservative—an advocate of strict adherence to custom. He lived to a very great age, for he was still alive in 1871.[1] But by 1854 the previous generation was dying out and most of Moshoeshoe's councillors were men of his own generation, whom he himself had selected. He chose them on the basis of their proven abilities, regardless of ascriptive status or ethnic background. Perhaps the most influential was Makoanyane, who was of northern Nguni origin. Moshoeshoe's boyhood friend and initiation-mate, he was described in contemporary documents as 'Joshua Nau, Chief Warrior of the Basutos' (1848) and 'Councillor and Generalissimo' (1862).[2] After RaTšiu, the man the king consulted most frequently on SeSotho custom was RaMatšeatsana, a member of the Hlakoana branch of the Koena, who had joined Moshoeshoe soon after he settled at Thaba Bosiu in 1824. Unlike RaTšiu, he became a Christian and Moshoeshoe also sought his advice on the handling of the missionaries and their converts.[3] Lelosa, a junior half-brother of the king, who lived at the foot of Thaba Bosiu, was another *letona*.[4] Traditions name two other men who may have been regarded as *matona* in the 1850s: Mokolokolo, a Fokeng, who seems to have served as a military adviser, second only to Makoanyane, and also as a composer of praise songs and an ambassador; and Lehau, who was of Nguni origin and was responsible for supervising the king's cattle and his arable lands.[5]

---

[1] On RaTšiu, see above, pp. 55, 101; Casalis, 5 Sept. 1839, *JME* xv (1840), 126; Casalis, 10 Nov. 1847, *JME* xxiii (1848), 121–2; C. D. Griffith, Governor's Agent, to High Commissioner, 18 Aug. 1871, BR VI. 232–53; Abraham RaMatšeatsana, *Leselinyana*, 15 Apr. 1891.

[2] On Makoanyane, see above, pp. 16 etc.; and documents in *BR* (index entry Joshua). The descriptions cited are in *BR* i. 176 and iii. 140.

[3] On RaMatšeatsana, see above, pp. 93–4; also RaMatšeatsana's own account, written in old age, *Leselinyana*, 15 Apr. and 1 May 1891. Informants 24 and 25 are his descendants.

[4] On Lelosa, 'Evidence of Chief Jobo [Lelosa]', *Report and Evidence of Commission on Native Laws and Customs of the Basutos*, Cape Town, 1873; and documents in *BR* (index entry Jobo Moshesh).

[5] On Mokolokolo, I. 28 (a descendant) and I. 1, 3; and above, p. 51; on Lehau, I. 55 (a descendant).

For many years after the arrival of the first missionaries in 1833, Moshoeshoe treated Casalis as a *letona* to advise him on his dealings with white people and to read and write his official correspondence. However, by the time of the British annexation in 1848 Moshoeshoe had had enough experience of diplomacy with Whites to assume fuller control over his foreign policy and thereafter he used missionary advice more sparingly. Furthermore Casalis left LeSotho in 1855 and although the king consulted other missionaries from time to time, he never confided in them so freely nor trusted them so fully as he had trusted Casalis.[1]

To dispense with the services of missionaries as interpreters and scribes was more difficult. Though Moshoeshoe never had time to learn to read and write, he had quickly become aware of the advantages of literacy and had encouraged his councillors and kinsmen to attend the mission schools. Several of his councillors did so and became Christians for a while: RaMatšeatsana was baptized in 1839, Makoan-yane in 1840, and Lelosa in 1844.[2] However, the mission schools in LeSotho did not bring their pupils to the stage where they could serve him as competent scribes and interpreters. For that, further education was necessary elsewhere, and the only BaSotho who acquired it were kinsmen of Moshoeshoe. Masopha, his third son of the First House, and Sekhonyana, his senior son of the Third House, and three other kinsmen had spent a year at school in Cape Town in 1844–5; two junior sons, Tlali and Tsekelo, attended Zonnebloem school in Cape Town in 1857–8; and in 1861 Moshoeshoe sent another junior son, Libopuoa, to St. Augustine's, the Church of England missionary training college in Canterbury.[3] However, on their return from Cape Town Masopha and most of his fellow scholars did not keep up their English and their reading and writing, and

---

[1] Arbousset left LeSotho in 1860.

[2] Missionary Conference Annual Report, 27 Apr. 1840, *JME* xv (1840), 373–4; Casalis, 7 Sept. 1844, *JME* xx (1845), 105.

[3] Albert Brutsch, 'The Visit of Basotho Chiefs to the Cape Colony in 1845', *Lesotho*, viii (1969), 5–12; David P. Ambrose, 'Jeremiah Libopuoa Moshoeshoe (1839–1863)', ibid., 24–9; and essays by Tlali and Tsekelo Moshoeshoe op. cit.

Libopuoa died in England in 1863; but Sekhonyana and, after 1858, Tlali and Tsekelo retained some linguistic and literary facility and Moshoeshoe used them as interpreters and scribes, though their skills were far from perfect.[1]

Moshoeshoe also tried to use his educated sons to counter-act the fissiparous tendencies of his territorial chiefs. For example, in 1858 he sent Sekhonyana south to restrain Posholi and convince the Orange Free State of his pacific intentions.[2] The result of his increasing use of western educated sons for political purposes was that as the king grew older commoners had less chance than previously of performing important functions. There was a tendency for both types of high office in LeSotho—*marena* (territorial chiefs) and *matona* (councillors)—to be monopolized by members of Moshoeshoe's own patrilineage.

The most respected diviners in LeSotho did not rank as *matona*, but their influence was immense and Moshoeshoe consulted them frequently, especially before he made major decisions. Tšapi was still respected in the 1850s, but the rising star was a remarkable woman prophet of Koena ancestry named Mantsopa, whose home was across the Caledon River near Platberg. She did not use the customary divining bones but was inspired by visions. She was famous for having predicted in considerable detail Moshoeshoe's victories over Warden, Cathcart, and Sekonyela, and in 1855 she was said to be announcing a long period of peace and harmony for the BaSotho.[3]

In a well-ordered pre-*lifaqane* chiefdom, a political decision was the end product of a prolonged series of discussions in

---

[1] J. M. Orpen to President Hoffman, 9 Jan. 1855, *BR* ii. 138; W. H. Cole-man and H. Olivier to President Boshof, 17 July 1856, ibid., p. 213.

[2] On Sekhonyana, see Nehemiah [Sekhonyana] Moshesh, 'A Little Light', *Cape Monthly Magazine*, 3rd ser., ii (1880), 221–33, 280–92; and documents in *BR* (index entry Nehemiah).

[3] On Tšapi, see above, pp. 46, 103, and Maitin, 30 Nov. 1855, *JME* xxxi (1856), 108. On Mantsopa, I. 18; Casalis (1), pp. 286–7; Arbousset, 8 Aug. 1855, *JME* xxxi (1856), 90; Daumas, 5 Feb. 1863, *JME* xxxviii (1863), 121–2; Jousse, n.d., *JME* xliii (1868), 449–50; and documents in *BR* (index entry Manchupa). Mantsopa was baptized by the French missionaries in 1868 (Jousse, loc. cit.).

which the chief, his councillors, and all the married men participated. An effective decision was one which embodied the consensus of the entire political community of adult men.[1] So far as practicable, Moshoeshoe applied the traditional methods to achieve the traditional objective.[2] When a decision had to be made on an important problem, he would first discuss it with those of his *matona* who were best informed about the subject—with RaTšiu and RaMatšeatsana if custom was involved, or with Makoanyane and perhaps Mokolokolo if it was a military matter. If it concerned relations with British officials or Afrikaners he would also consult a missionary, preferably Casalis, or a son, such as Masopha or Sekhonyana, who had had experience of white behaviour in Cape Town as well as at a mission station. The king would then convene a more formal but still private meeting of all his *matona*, at which he would explain the problem to them at great length and from every conceivable angle, and he would expect each *letona* to speak his mind, frankly and fully.

Next he would invite his territorial chiefs and other kinsmen and some of his village headmen to come to Thaba Bosiu with their own senior councillors and he would

[1] A good general account of decision-making in pre-colonial southern African chiefdoms, based mainly on the author's deep knowledge of the Tswana, is in I. Schapera, *Government and Politics in Tribal Societies*. See also a case study in decision-making in an Nguni chiefdom (the Mpondomise), David Hammond-Tooke, 'The "Other Side" of Frontier History: a Model of Cape Nguni Political Process', in Leonard Thompson, ed., *African Societies in Southern Africa*.

[2] This account of decision-making in Moshoeshoe's LeSotho is derived from documents written by white eye-witnesses (e.g. Casalis (1), pp. 233–6; Maeder, 1 July 1848, *JME* xxiii (1848), 442, 12 Nov. 1854, *JME* xxx (1855), 42, and n.d., *JME* xxxi (1856), 207), and the statements of modern BaSotho informants (I. 1–4, 8, 9, 27, 35, 37, 39, 51, and 52). Neither type of evidence is wholly convincing. White contemporaries were normally excluded from the most vital discussions, as was realized by Arbousset on 10 Sept. 1856, when he told his colleague Cochet, 'There is a great *pitso* today near Rachosane's—almost everyone goes on foot. The chiefs are prudent. They tell me nothing.' (LEC.) The statements of modern informants are affected by their experiences of institutions that have been profoundly modified by over a century of white over-rule and, in some cases, by their personal interests—as chiefs or commoners, or members of specific lineages or modern political organizations. Nevertheless, what follows in the text is probably an accurate account of what Moshoeshoe did when circumstance permitted.

expound the problem to them. Each chief would have the opportunity to consult his own councillors before he told Moshoeshoe what he thought should be done. This large council was known as the *lekhotla la mahosana* (council of princes). In February 1862 150 BaSotho attended such a council to discuss the relations between LeSotho and Great Britain, and on this occasion strangers were also present— ambassadors from Mpande, the Zulu king, and Faku, the chief of the Mpondo.[1]

Finally Moshoeshoe might convene a *pitso*. When summoned, every territorial chief who acknowledged Moshoeshoe as his *morena e moholo* was meant to proceed to Thaba Bosiu or another assigned place with all his male adult followers, fully armed, leaving behind only those who were necessary for purposes of defence. In practice, many thousands of men often attended.[2] Proceedings started as a festival: the king's servants provided ample supplies of *joala*, distinguished warriors sang their praise songs, and everyone indulged in war-dances. As late as 1862 Moshoeshoe himself was still showing 'surprising agility' in the singing and dancing.[3] After several hours of these activities, the people turned to business. In some cases Moshoeshoe and his *matona* explained why they had convened the *pitso* and announced the line of action they had decided to take. In others, Moshoeshoe used the *pitso* to sound out public opinion. A *letona* would introduce the subject and then there would be a general debate, in which any man had the right to speak and to make forthright criticisms of the authorities, even of the king himself, as had happened in 1841 when Moshoeshoe was strongly criticized for paying too much attention to the missionaries in the matter of his divorced wives.[4] Usually, however, the king, his *matona*, and his territorial chiefs were able to monopolize the debate and manage the meeting. Moshoeshoe himself invariably wound up the proceedings, tracing the history of the

[1] *BR* iii. 138–50.

[2] For example, a missionary estimated that between 3,000 and 4,000 men attended a *pitso* Moshoeshoe convened at Leribe, Molapo's village, in 1862: Coillard, n.d., *JME* xxxvii (1862), 408–9.

[3] Ibid.   [4] See above, pp. 92–4.

problem, refuting contrary opinions, and announcing his decision. 'When the assembly are satisfied,' wrote Casalis, 'they give vent to a sort of prolonged shout, dwelling upon the monosyllable: "*E!* . . . Yes! Yes!" Then each one jumps up and waves his shield, shouting with all his might, "*Pula! Pula!* (Rain! Rain!)" an invocation signifying we are satisfied, and only thinking of cultivating our ground.'[1] This response also indicated that the decision Moshoeshoe had proclaimed was not merely his personal decision, but the consensus of the entire nation (*sechaba*).

This elaborate process served many purposes. The *pitso*, in particular, was a socializing and nation-building institution. In the absence of a literary culture, it was a vital forum for political communication and education. It ensured that the great issues concerning the national interest were understood by every section of the male population. And it promoted concerted action, which was particularly important since Moshoeshoe and his *matona* had scarcely any means of exerting physical coercion over the territorial chiefs.

However, when making political decisions in Moshoeshoe's LeSotho it was not always expedient or even possible to go through all the stages which had been used in the pre-*lifaqane* world of small, isolated chiefdoms. For example, when he convened *lipitso* to honour missionaries—as in 1846 when he asked Arbousset and his Christian protégés to report on their experiences in Cape Town, in 1853 when he held a *pitso* to commemorate the twentieth anniversary of the foundation of the LeSotho mission, and in 1855 when he publicly took leave of Casalis on his departure for Paris— Moshoeshoe discreetly dispensed with the customary beer-drinking, praise-singing, and dancing out of respect for his guests.[2] Secondly—and this was much more significant— he was sometimes constrained to eliminate stages from the decision-making process, when white officials insisted that he should make commitments within a limited time and backed

---

[1] Casalis (1), p. 236.
[2] Arbousset, 20 May 1846, *JME* xxi (1846), 457–8; Casalis, 6 Aug. 1853, *JME* xxviii (1853), 401–12; Jousse, 10 Oct. 1855, *JME* xxxi (1856), 46–9.

up their demands with threats of physical violence, as when Cathcart ordered Moshoeshoe to deliver 10,000 cattle and 1,000 horses within three days.[1] Whites erred egregiously in assuming that Moshoeshoe was capable of committing his people to actions affecting their interests—such as paying compensation for the theft of stock or evacuating land claimed by white farmers—without full and prolonged consultation. Undertakings made without endorsement by the customary procedures lacked legitimacy in the eyes of the BaSotho and, consequently, were virtually unenforceable.

In addition to having the services of able and loyal councillors and holding frequent popular assemblies, Moshoeshoe used several other means to counteract the centrifugal forces in his kingdom. As the owner of vast wealth in sheep and cattle, he was able to bind people to him by judicious gifts, by lending livestock on *mafisa*, and by establishing cattle-posts under junior sons directly responsible to him within the regions of his territorial chiefs.[2] His wealth also enabled him to use marriage as a political instrument. He himself and his sons took wives from the families of dependent chiefs and allies, and his children and grandchildren made many cousin marriages which knit his family together under himself.[3] He also had considerable influence over Letsie and Molapo as a result of the fact that he had appointed their senior councillors from trusted members of his own age group when they first left Thaba Bosiu, and some of these men, like Matete, Letsie's *malome* and Moshoeshoe's brother-in-law, were always loyal to him.[4] Further, he 'adopted' several sons of allies and potential allies—bringing them to live at Thaba Bosiu for long periods in their youth, equipping them with cattle, horses, and guns, and providing the *bohali* for their marriages. He did this for Matela, the Khoakhoa chief, and Sefunelo, son of Moroka of Thaba

---

[1] Cathcart to Moshoeshoe, 14 Dec. 1852, *BR* i. 616–18.
[2] e.g. Selebalo: see above, p. 193.
[3] e.g. Mathe, Moshoeshoe's only daughter by 'MaMohato, his senior wife, married Lesaoana, the senior son of his full brother, Makhabane; and Masopha's first wife, 'MaTholoana, was the daughter of his uncle, Posholi. I. 11.
[4] I. 39.

'Nchu.[1] The French missionaries, too, remained a cohesive factor in spite of the withdrawal of most members of his family from church membership, because they shared his conviction that the welfare of the mission was linked with the integrity of the kingdom. Finally, Moshoeshoe was careful to satisfy the mass of his subjects whose ideas were still rooted in tradition, by fulfilling their ritual expectations. In October 1853, for example, before the army left Thaba Bosiu for the final attack on the Tlokoa stronghold of Marabeng, he consulted Tšapi and Mantsopa and visited his aged father, Mokhachane, to receive purification at his hands.[2] Moreover, after refraining for several years from convening initiation schools in response to missionary pressure he had resumed the practice by 1854, and the young BaSotho were being inculcated with respect for his authority in the *lebollo*.[3]

Nevertheless, in 1854 LeSotho had all the hallmarks of a first-generation kingdom, for its cohesion depended less on institutions than on the towering personality of its founder. Moshoeshoe possessed the charisma of a leader who had emerged in his people's darkest hour and steered them through unprecedented physical and moral disasters to a new plane of prosperity and self-confidence. Yet he remained a man of simple tastes. When he was not in the company of white people, he lived in traditional huts, wore traditional clothes, and ate traditional foods (supplemented by tea and sugar). He spent a great deal of his time with his *matona* in his *lekhotla*, listening to local gossip, hearing cases brought by the humblest of his subjects, and talking with visitors. He retained the common touch, never demanding obsequious behaviour from anyone, unlike his brother Posholi, who tried it and was laughed at for his pains.[4] His reputation for justice and clemency was proverbial. Every MoSotho was aware that he had an intense dislike for capital punishment and every MoSotho knew the story of how he had spared the life of the cannibal chief who had caught and devoured his grandfather, and had turned him into a loyal and law-

---

[1] I. 39.   [2] Arbousset, 8 Nov. 1853, *JME* xxix (1854), 163.
[3] See above, p. 3–5.   [4] I. 39.

abiding subject.[1] Indeed, he was widely known as 'a man who loved people'.[2]

He was also greatly respected. BaSotho were proud of the fact that their victories over a succession of black and white invaders had made Thaba Bosiu the centre of African diplomatic activity in southern Africa. Ambassadors frequently came to consult him from all the major chiefs—from Mzilikazi in the north to Sarili in the south, and from Sechele in the west to Mpande in the east.[3]

A mythology had grown up to legitimize the royal status of the man who had emerged from relative obscurity in a society where the hereditary principle was still universally respected. He was widely believed to have received the mantle of leadership from Mohlomi, the most venerated MoSotho of the previous generation,[4] and people made sacrifices to the shade of his grandfather and regarded his father and mother as having mystical powers while they were still alive.[5]

We have a glimpse of the aura of Moshoeshoe's leadership in Arbousset's account of a journey in southern LeSotho in 1852:

Everywhere on the way, people flocked from numerous villages towards Moshesh, to hail him and present him with sacred reeds. Others, the better to celebrate his passage, brought him cattle as presents. In everything, this African prince showed a tact that I greatly admire. His affability did not flag for an instant. Warmth, gaiety, nothing is lacking. He talks to everyone without distinction of age or rank. He even amuses

[1] See above, p. 53.

[2] A. Sekese, *Leselinyana*, 15 June 1906; I. 39. See also Tsekelo Moshoeshoe, Customs of a Ruler, in vol. 265d, Grey Collection, South African Public Library—an idealized description of a ruler derived from Tsekelo's knowledge of his father and written in 1858.

[3] The movements of messengers or ambassadors are difficult to trace in the contemporary documents. In 1854 Casalis made a general statement that every day a crowd of strangers came to Thaba Bosiu, 'delegates of all the tribes of Southern Africa': 6 June 1854, *JME* xxix (1854), 369. In 1860, Jousse reported specifically that ambassadors from Mzilikazi and Mpande were present in LeSotho: n.d., *JME* xxxvi (1861), 84–5.

[4] See above, pp. 24–7.

[5] Casalis, 6 Aug. 1853, *JME* xxviii (1853), 410–11; Jousse, 24 June 1854, *JME* xxix (1854), 412–15.

himself with the children as if he were one himself; and, still more astonishing, his memory is so good he seems to know the name and the history of each of his subjects. You can imagine that, with such qualities, he is popular amongst them.[1]

But charisma is not enough for effective leadership: skill is also necessary,[2] and this, too, Arbousset recognized that Moshoeshoe possessed in abundance:

The reputation of Moshesh as a good politician is well established in the country. This chief, in fact, possesses the principal qualities of the art: keen insight coupled with very sound judgment; much knowledge of men and of things; an open manner under which he cleverly conceals hidden thoughts; finally, a great degree of composure which does not preclude imagination. In negotiations he displays a tact which never fails him even with the whites, his superiors in other respects. Generally he appears humane and very conciliatory, strongly attached to his rights, but without a semblance of haughtiness. Whether it is a matter of principle or of habit, he is long in his speeches, vague, too often subject to digressions: one word that he lets fall here and there often reveals his true thought, and only the cleverest of his people grasp it.[3]

His greatest political talent was clear-headedness. Whether dealing with fellow BaSotho or with foreigners, he had a keen sense of reality—of his power and the limitations on his power, and of the potential consequences of the options that were open to him. Better, perhaps, than any other African leader who was confronted by the forces of European expansion in the nineteenth century, he managed to accommodate the intrusion of the modern world.[4] Some mission-

[1] Arbousset, 2 Mar. 1852, *JME* xxvii (1852), 208.
[2] See *Daedalus*, Summer 1968, *Philosophers and Kings: Studies in Leadership*, especially the article by Albert O. Hirschman, 'Underdevelopment, Obstacles to the Perception of Change, and Leadership', pp. 925–37, which distinguishes between charisma and skill.
[3] Arbousset, 6 Aug. 1851, *JME* xxvi (1851), 409. See a similar description of Moshoeshoe by Théophile Jousse, who succeeded Casalis at the mission station below Thaba Bosiu in 1855, in 'Moshesh, roi des Bassoutos', *Le Chrétien Évangélique: revue religieuse de la suisse romande*, 1867, pp. 67–8.
[4] For examples of studies of other African leaders confronted with similar problems, see Obaro Ikime, *Merchant Prince of the Niger Delta*, London, 1968; Yves Person, *Samori: Une Révolution dyula*, 2 vols., Dakar, 1968; Gerald L. Caplan, *The Elites of Barotseland, 1878–1969*, London, 1970.

aries perceived this, but expressed it in terms of their own cultural affiliations. For example, in 1852 Jean Frédoux, who had visited LeSotho from his mission station in Botswana, wrote:

This remarkable person is still today what he was some years ago. A civilized man on the [mission] station and on his mountain of the night still wearing his old costume; owning two good European-style houses and living right alongside in gloomy huts; today seated close to his missionary and tomorrow perhaps consulting some pagan prophet; going to listen to the teachings of the Gospel in church and maintaining a numerous seraglio at home,—Moshesh shows himself to be at the same time the man of the future and the man of the past.[1]

Of all his white contemporaries, it was perhaps Casalis who came closest to comprehending Moshoeshoe's political style:

It is a fact that this chief has rarely been understood by his subjects; that he has conducted himself on a host of occasions in a manner that seemed quite absurd to them at first, and that the successes he has obtained, the power and influence he enjoys, are the direct result of these anomalies.

For example, long before the arrival of missionaries in his country, he had based his political conduct entirely on the knowledge he had acquired of the human heart by attentive observation. From there, a system of temporisation and discretion, an invincible repugnance for extreme methods and causes, a great indulgence for the weaknesses of others and his own weaknesses; in many cases, the skilful use of generosity in the place of brute force.[2]

Writing in 1906, the MoSotho historian Azariel Sekese who had known Moshoeshoe characterized the distinctive qualities of his rule: he disposed even-handed justice: he did not retaliate against people like RaKotsoane the cannibal chief who had wronged him; he gave sanctuary and aid to refugees; and he was not too proud to pay tribute to other rulers, such as Shaka, for diplomatic advantage.[3]

---

[1] Frédoux, 13 Oct. 1852, *JME* xxviii (1853), 54.

[2] Editorial, *JME* xxxii (1857), 3–4.

[3] *Leselinyana*, 15 June 1906. On Sekese, the first significant MoSotho author, see Kunene, Daniel P., and Randal A. Kirsch, *The Beginnings of South African*

The quality of Moshoeshoe's achievement is highlighted when it is compared with that of Shaka. There is no reason to believe that there was any greater disposition to violence or despotism in the culture of the Nguni peoples than among the BaSotho.[1] Yet the Zulu and the MoSotho created two diametrically different types of states. Shaka's was militarized and predatory: Moshoeshoe's pacific and self-sufficient. Shaka ruled by fear: Moshoeshoe by consent. Shaka broke brutally with the past: Moshoeshoe built a bridge between the past and the future. The Zulu's career was cut short by assassination at the hands of his kinsmen: the MoSotho was to die peacefully of old age.[2]

Moshoeshoe had a robust constitution and before 1854 he had always enjoyed excellent health. Lautré, the medical missionary who had reached LeSotho a decade earlier, had only been called to attend the king twice: for a minor ailment in 1846 and to remove a tumour from near his right eye in 1848. In October 1854, however, Moshoeshoe fell seriously ill and although he made a complete recovery within a few weeks, it was clear that time was beginning to close in on the sixty-eight-year-old king.[3]

But his work was still incomplete. The state depended too much on his active leadership and not enough on durable, binding institutions. His trusted councillors were men of his own age group or older. His heir apparent possessed no more than average abilities and did not command the respect of his kinsmen, some of whom still cherished the old ambition of carving out their own independent chiefdoms.

Moshoeshoe had emerged as the leader of the southern Sotho during the 1820s, when their political system of small, autonomous, segmentary chiefdoms was smashed by the

[1] On the structure of Nguni society, see Monica Wilson in *OHSA* i. 116–30; also Hammond-Tooke, op. cit.

[2] On Shaka, see above, pp. 29–32.

[3] Lautré, 11 Jan. 1847, *JME* xxii (1847); Lautré, 10 June 1849, *JME* xxiv (1849), 469–70; Lautré, 6 Apr. 1855, *JME* xxx (1855), 345–6; Editorial (Casalis), *JME* xxxii (1857), 7.

Nguni invasions.[1] The system he then created was a reconstruction of the traditional order, with two innovations: the kingship itself as a new top tier, and the placement of his kinsmen as territorial chiefs over the heads of all other lineages (except in the outer marches). By the 1850s this system had become partially stabilized, because external pressures made it expedient for the territorial chiefs to accept it and also because he established a claim to legitimacy in traditional terms, for example by embellishing and appropriating the Mohlomi myth.

But Moshoeshoe was still a personal ruler. His territorial chiefs were related to him merely by personal loyalty, supplemented in most cases by kinship ties. These were fragile bonds in a society that was predisposed to fission and in which none of the territorial chiefs had Moshoeshoe's charisma or political skill. If LeSotho was to outlast his own lifetime, it was necessary to create a centralized army and a central administrative system with specialist officers, that is to say a bureaucracy.

The king was aware of the gravity of the problem and in later years he would frequently refer to the need for improving his system of government. Since there was nothing in SeSotho culture to help him to solve it, he had to look elsewhere. He had no means of knowing that there were kingdoms in tropical Africa—for example Asante, Benin, and Buganda—where rulers had created bureaucratic offices to offset the powers of their kinsmen and hereditary chiefs.[2] The Zulu model of a militaristic and predatory kingdom did not appeal to him. The European model, as described by his missionaries, seemed more appropriate.

[1] In Weber's terms, Moshoeshoe had been a 'charismatic leader' who had created a 'patrimonial kingdom' but he had failed to establish 'a rational system of administration with technically specialised officials': Max Weber, *The Theory of Social and Economic Organization*, New York, 1957. See also the discussion in Aristide Zolberg, *Creating Political Order*, Chicago, 1966, pp. 136–44; A. W. Southall's concept of the 'segmentary state' in *Alur Society*, Cambridge, 1956; and the discussion in Jack Goody, *Technology, Tradition, and the State in Africa*, pp. 9–11.

[2] We do not know precisely how the early rulers of African kingdoms like Asante, Benin, and Buganda took the first decisive steps from 'patrimonial kingdoms' towards 'bureaucratic states'.

He hoped that his mission-educated sons would become agents for modernization, but the education they received was not sufficiently rigorous or relevant and left them torn between the two worlds, ambitious to use their modern skills not as royal bureaucrats but as territorial chiefs.

Consequently, as Moshoeshoe began to age, his reconstructed traditional system tended to disintegrate into its component segments, the territorial chiefdoms. Since his white neighbours concurrently became stronger and more aggressive, the king was hard pressed to preserve his life's work during his final years.

Kinsmen of Moshoeshoe who were Territorial Chiefs in 1854

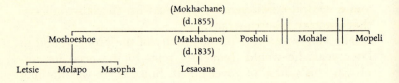

VI

MILITARY VICTORY,
DIPLOMATIC DEFEAT

1. *The Irrepressible Conflict*

CONFLICT was inherent in the situation the British administrators left behind them when they evacuated the
Orange River Sovereignty in 1854. Two communities were
competing for control of the Caledon valley and the grasslands stretching northwards to the Vaal: BaSotho whose
ancestors had occupied most of the area for several generations and Whites who had only begun to cross the Orange
River in the previous thirty years; BaSotho who were
engaged in agriculture as well as stock farming and Whites
who used land almost exclusively for pasture; BaSotho who
lived in compact villages and Whites who were dispersed in
family units, each 'occupying' a 'farm' of several thousand
acres. Moreover the Whites assumed that the boundary
which the British administration had proclaimed (but had
failed to enforce) between their territory and LeSotho was
still valid, while the BaSotho had reason to believe that it
had lapsed with British rule. Small wonder that the BaSotho
regarded the Whites as intruders and men like Posholi
expressed their resentment in the traditional way by raiding
cattle.

Initially, the white population of the new Orange Free
State was about one-eighth as numerous as the population
of LeSotho. According to a census taken in 1856, the Whites
numbered 12,859, of whom no more than 2,709 were men
capable of bearing arms, as against the hundred thousand
or so subjects of Moshoeshoe.[1] The Free State capital, Bloemfontein, was a mere village with only about seventy-five white
men.[2] The census also showed that the Whites employed
7,454 Coloured and African 'dienstboden' (house-servants

[1] *SAAR, OFS* ii, opposite p. 264. For estimates of the population of LeSotho,
see above, p. 172 n. 1.   [2] Wm. W. Collins, *Free Statia*, p. 85.

and herdsmen), but it did not enumerate the independent Coloured and African communities who were living within the presumed borders of the state, such as the Griqua of Kok and the Rolong of Moroka.

In spite of their numerical weakness, the Whites claimed much more land and owned many more livestock per person than their BaSotho neighbours. They were dispersed over a vast area between the Orange and the Vaal, holding titles that had been issued by the Sovereignty administration to eleven million acres. The 1856 census showed that they owned over 27,500 horses, 137,000 head of cattle, and 1,231,000 sheep and goats, a *per capita* average of about two horses, eleven head of cattle, and ninety-six small stock.[1] This was probably at least ten times as many horses, five times as many cattle, and twenty-five times as many small stock as the *per capita* average of Moshoeshoe's people.[2]

Soon after the British withdrawal the Whites laid institutional foundations for their state. In April 1854 an elected assembly sitting in Bloemfontein agreed upon a constitution which was subsequently amplified by laws and proclamations. The Orange Free State was a unitary republic, divided into five districts and sub-divided into thirty wards. The *burghers* consisted of the white inhabitants who had lived in the state for at least six months, and all male burghers who registered for military service could vote. They elected a unicameral legislature (Volksraad) and a president, who was assisted by an executive council consisting partly of officials and partly of Volksraad nominees. In each district there was a *landdrost*. He was appointed by the President subject to confirmation by the Volksraad and he had administrative and judicial duties. The voters also chose from among their numbers part-time military officers— field-commandants in each district and field-cornets in each ward. The President possessed war-marking and treaty-making powers, subject to the approval of the Volksraad, and

---

[1] *SAAR, OFS* ii, opposite p. 264.

[2] This is an extremely rough comparison. The BaSotho proportions are derived from the first census of Basutoland which was taken in 1875. At that time the BaSotho were prosperous and their *per capita* holdings of livestock were probably more numerous than in the 1850s. See above, p. 190 n. 2.

in time of war the military officers elected a commandant-general.[1]

These institutions would eventually gain legitimacy in the eyes of the burghers, but in its early years the Orange Free State was weak and unstable. The total revenue for 1856 was less than £18,000[2] and most of the officials were inexperienced and inefficient. Moreover the white population, small though it was, was ridden with factions. The small minority of British origin, who dominated trade and controlled the only newspaper, and some of whom had acquired claims to large tracts of land, maintained close connections with the Cape Colony and hoped to bring the state back into the British Empire. The burghers of Dutch descent had divided loyalties dating back to the 1830s, when trekboers had regarded themselves as colonial frontiersmen and voortrekkers had consciously rejected British authority. Some still looked southwards, like their British fellow-countrymen. Others were strongly imbued with the voortrekker spirit. Describing themselves variously as 'Afrikanders', 'Afferkaners', 'Afrikaansche Boeren', and 'Afrikaners',[3] they tried to prevent men of British origin from holding public office and they looked northwards to the still chaotic voortrekker communities beyond the Vaal River for ideological affinity, military aid, and political association.[4]

In spite of their differences on other questions, nearly all the Free State burghers had much the same attitude towards Africans. Like their settler contemporaries in North America and Australia, they fervently believed that, as Whites, they were superior to the indigenous peoples they encountered. As an Afrikaner historian has recently observed: 'In the Free State the Whites spoke continuously of the differences between "civilized nations and barbarians" and of "the natural differences of character, ways of thought,

---

[1] *SAAR, OFS* i. 194–201, 312–15, ii. 438–42; J. H. Malan, *Die Opkoms van 'n Republiek*, Bloemfontein, 1929; G. D. Scholtz, *Die Konstitutie en Staatsinstellings van die Oranje Vrijstaat*, Amsterdam, 1937; *OHSA* i. 429–30; M. C. E. van Schoor in C. F. J. Muller (ed.), *Five Hundred Years: a History of South Africa*, pp. 202–5.

[2] *SAAR, OFS* ii. 351–4.

[3] *SAAR, OFS* i. 43, 134, 152, 182, 257–8, 261.

[4] F. A. van Jaarsveld, *Die Eenheidstrewe van die Republiekeinse Afrikaners*.

and outlook that exist between a white people and a native tribe".'[1]

The passions that were aroused in the struggle between the Orange Free State and LeSotho were intensified by the atrocities committed by both sides. In previous generations colonial commandos had been accustomed to waging intermittent warfare against the bands of hunters and collectors whom they encountered as they expanded eastwards and northwards. They had shot down the men and women and seized the children as booty, training them to be domestic servants and herdsmen, and in many cases treating them extremely harshly.[2] The voortrekkers had done the same to the Africans they fought in Natal and on the high veld, and during the Sovereignty period Major Warden permitted and even encouraged the practice. In 1852 Moshoeshoe told Commissioner Hogge: 'We complain that children have been stolen from us by you, the Whites, and that they have been made slaves.'[3] Conditions did not improve during the early years of the Free State regime.[4] In 1858 Moshoeshoe reproached the President: 'The captains of your commando are no Christians, for I shall never believe that Christianity consists in carrying away women and children into captivity, in shooting down old and sick people.'[5] On the other hand, BaSotho were accustomed to dissecting corpses of enemies killed in battle and using the flesh and blood for ritual medicine, and when Free State commandos discovered the mutilated bodies of their fallen comrades they were horrified.[6] Thus, as the irrepressible conflict escalated, each

---

[1] H. J. van Aswegen, 'Die Verhouding tussen Blank en Nie-Blank in die Oranje Vrystaat, 1854–1902', D.Phil. dissertation, University of the Orange Free State, 1968, p. 31.

[2] W. M. Macmillan, *The Cape Colour Question*; J. S. Marais, *The Cape Coloured People*, London, 1939, and *Maynier and the First Boer Republic*, Cape Town, 1944.

[3] Sir George Grey, High Commissioner, to Secretary of State, 3 May 1856, *BR* ii. 187.

[4] Special Commissioner of the *Cape Argus* [J. M. Orpen], *History of the Basutos of South Africa*, pp. 139–43; J. M. Orpen, *Reminiscences*, chs. 55, 64–8; documents by J. M. Orpen in the Cory Collection, Rhodes University Library, notably CL 1189, 1193, and 1213; Sir George Cory, 'The Rise of South Africa', vi, *AYB*, Cape Town, 1940, pp. 142–57; *SAAR*, *OFS* ii. 11–13, 178–213, 317–18.

[5] Moshoeshoe to President Boshof, 16 May 1858, *BR* ii. 363–4.

[6] J. A. Roosema, Secretary to the O.F.S. War Council, to Landdrost,

side was appalled by the behaviour of the other. Free Staters were confirmed in their belief that BaSotho were savages: BaSotho found Free Staters deficient in *batho* (humanity).

For Moshoeshoe, Civilization, Christianity, and white people had ambiguous connotations. Ever since his first missionaries had arrived at Thaba Bosiu in 1833, he had admired their moral prescriptions and technical assets: their Bible, their wagons, their fire-arms, their capacity to read and write. He had set a personal example by acquiring European goods and going to church, he had sent many of his kinsmen to the mission schools, and he certainly desired that his people should become 'civilized' in the material sense. By 1854, however, missionary interference in the internal affairs of his kingdom, settler encroachments into his territory, the inconsistent and arrogant behaviour of British officials, and the peddling of alcoholic spirits by traders, had taught him to distinguish between the words and the deeds of white people. In addition, in failing to implement Napier's 1843 treaty, Warden and Smith had demonstrated that Whites themselves had no scruples against dishonouring documentary agreements when it suited their purpose. Now, with the British administration removed, Moshoeshoe had to deal directly with a government whose citizens claimed land that they could neither use nor defend effectively and that his own people needed and regarded as their birthright.

Moshoeshoe and his people had little fear of the Free State itself, or of the scattered and quarrelsome voortrekker groups beyond the Vaal. Indeed they rather despised the *MaBuru* (Boers). But the king knew from experience that Whites of all sorts were liable to co-operate with each other against Africans, and the fate of the Xhosa and Thembu chiefdoms was a constant reminder that he could not hope permanently to oppose the forces of white expansion. He therefore groped towards a policy that was a mixture of selective resistance and selective accommodation. He strove to isolate the Free Staters and Transvaalers from the British colonies, and to establish and maintain control over as much territory as possible. At the same time he sought to pave the way towards an agreement with the most powerful government that he knew—the government of the European country that dominated the trade routes, controlled the coastal colonies, and was capable of bringing overwhelming force to bear on the high veld—for the purpose of drawing it in to protect his people from conquest and disruption and to assist him to modernize his kingdom, without destroying the fabric of SeSotho society or undermining the authority of his monarchy.

2. *Prelude to War*

Somewhat surprisingly, Moshoeshoe was able to establish good relations with the first President of the Free State. Josias P. Hoffman, who presided over the provisional government and was elected President under the constitution in June 1854, was by no means a typical frontiersman. For one thing he was a cripple, as a result of an accident in Cape Town harbour in his youth. For another, he had unusual empathy with Moshoeshoe. In 1847, acknowledging that the country belonged to Moshoeshoe, he had asked his permission to settle on the bank of the Caledon at Jammerberg Drift (modern Wepener) and in 1852 he had written a long letter to the British Commissioners protesting that Warden had decreed an unjust boundary and had imposed it by a threat of force. Moreover, Moshoeshoe had employed him to build a house on Thaba Bosiu.[1]

In April 1854 Hoffman opened negotiations by sending a representative to Thaba Bosiu. The young man he selected for the task was Joseph M. Orpen, who was to play an important role in BaSotho affairs for many years. Born in Dublin of Anglo-Irish parents in 1828, Orpen had migrated to South Africa in 1846, taken part in military operations

---

[1] Hoffman to Assistant Commissioners, 15 Jan. 1852, *BR* i. 488–94; Hoffman to the British Resident, 20 July 1853, *BR* ii. 57; Orpen, *Reminiscences*, pp. 201–2.

against Moshoeshoe in the Sovereignty period, and then
been elected a member of the first Free State Volksraad.
After announcing his business, Orpen spent several days at
the Thaba Bosiu mission station while Moshoeshoe consulted
his people. The king then invited him to the *pitso* where,
after eliciting the information that Orpen still regarded
himself as a British subject, he declared 'The Queen has
not left us for ever', giving Orpen the impression that he
was trying to persuade his people that in spite of all that
had happened he intended to keep on good terms with the
British Government.[1]

The most pressing business Orpen had been instructed to
discuss with Moshoeshoe concerned Oetsi ('Witzie', 'Wietze'), a Kholokoe chief, who had been driven away from his
home in the Transvaal during the *lifaqane* and ultimately
settled around the sources of the Elands River in the Harrismith district of what became the Orange Free State. There
he had built up a following of about 2,000 people, who spread
over territory claimed by white farmers and harassed them.
Orpen reported that Moshoeshoe seemed co-operative and
Hoffman sent him back to Thaba Bosiu in May. Moshoeshoe
and Orpen then sent messengers asking Oetsi and other
chiefs and the landdrost and field-cornets of the Harrismith
district to meet them near Botha Bothe to resolve their
differences; and they themselves, accompanied by Moletsane
and about 160 BaSotho, rode north to Botha Bothe, only to
find that the white officials did not appear and the neighbouring farmers had abandoned the area. Nevertheless
Oetsi came to the rendezvous and Moshoeshoe told him to
mend his ways and offered him land south of the Caledon in
northern LeSotho if he would return the cattle he had stolen.
Moshoeshoe then returned home, while Orpen visited Oetsi
in his village but without getting satisfaction from him.[2]

Initially Orpen had held the derogatory views about the
BaSotho and their leader that were prevalent among the
Whites.[3] Now, however, Moshoeshoe had impressed him

---

[1] Orpen, *Reminiscences*, pp. 208–13.
[2] Ibid., pp. 214–18; report dated 13 June 1854, *SAAR*, *OFS* i. 321–8.
[3] Orpen, *Reminiscences*, pp. 209–10.

favourably and Casalis had shown him copies of Moshoe-shoe's correspondence with the British officials, which 'upset all my ideas about the history of the country'.[1] He therefore concluded his official report:

One owes a great debt of gratitude to the Chief Moshesh on account of his conduct in undertaking such a long and tiresome journey across a very mountainous region, and exposing himself to great inconveniences in his attempts to preserve peace and to obtain the solution to all conflicts. It is to be deplored that the boers did not come to meet him at the appointed time. Had they done so, Wietze would have been obliged to pay a fixed fine without any further trouble.[2]

Orpen also wrote a letter to the editor of the *Zuid Afrikaan*, a Cape Town newspaper, declaring optimistically that 'the most perfect understanding' existed between Moshoeshoe and the Free State Government: 'and, being treated by us as the paramount chief of the eastern tribes, *which he is by birthright*,[3] and deserves to be on account of his good qualities and enlightened policy, he keeps down the unruly minor chiefs, many of whom are ambitious and would wish for war'.[4]

In August 1854 Hoffman himself, accompanied by four field-cornets and two justices of the peace, spent four days at Thaba Bosiu, where they had long discussions with Moshoeshoe, his councillors, and his kinsmen including Letsie. The Free State officials found Moshoeshoe hospitable and co-operative. He undertook to put further pressure on Oetsi to cease his depredations and hand over stolen stock, promising not to allow him asylum in LeSotho before he had done so. He also agreed to order Moletsane and Mopeli to keep the peace and withdraw their followers from farms occupied by Whites in the north. In response to complaints of thefts in the south, he arranged that Letsie should participate with the Free Staters in an investigation on the spot. He even consented to Hoffman's proposal that the Volksraad

---

[1] Orpen, *Reminiscences*, p. 215. [2] *SAAR, OFS* i. 327.
[3] My italics: on this point, of course, Orpen was in error.
[4] Letter dated 29 June 1854, published 20 July 1854, cited in Orpen, *Reminiscences*, pp. 220–1.

should make a pass law, 'that no native shall be permitted to come into the Free State without a pass signed by a missionary', stating the person's name, how many cattle he had with him, and the farm to which he was going. Finally Moshoeshoe inquired whether the boundary he had proposed to the burghers and Sir George Clerk at the time of the British evacuation was acceptable. Hoffman said it was not and Moshoeshoe replied that they should settle it later.[1]

Hoffman pressed forward with his plan to resolve that vital problem by negotiation. Early in January 1855 he sent Orpen back to Thaba Bosiu to invite Moshoeshoe to go with his councillors and territorial chiefs to Bloemfontein in February, when the Volksraad was scheduled to meet. Moshoeshoe agreed. A few days later, however, Hoffman was obliged to ask him to postpone his visit.[2]

The Hoffman administration had never been supported by the more self-consciously Afrikaner citizens, some of whom were intriguing with Marthinus Wessel Pretorius, son of Andries Pretorius, the deceased voortrekker leader. The younger Pretorius, who had led the Transvaal delegation which had negotiated the Sand River Convention with the British Commissioners in 1852, aspired to combine all the white people north of the Orange River into a single republic, absolutely independent of Britain. Although he had not yet succeeded in uniting his own followers who lived in the Potchefstroom area with the other voortrekker groups in the Transvaal, he responded to approaches from the Free State.[3] In August 1854 he visited Bloemfontein in an abortive attempt to supplant Hoffman.[4] When the Volksraad met in February 1855, however, Hoffman's Free State opponents, who had come to regard him as too British in orientation and too soft on Moshoeshoe, found a pretext for ousting him.

As Hoffman was leaving Thaba Bosiu the previous August,

[1] All reports of these discussions come from the white side: *SAAR, OFS* i, 328–31; *BR* ii. 118–21, 123–6; Orpen, *Reminiscences*, pp. 267–71.
[2] *BR* ii. 136–8; Orpen, *Reminiscences*, pp. 266–7, 271–2, 283.
[3] Van Jaarsveld, pp. 147–52; *OHSA* i. 419–31.
[4] Orpen, *Reminiscences*, pp. 223–40.

Moshoeshoe had asked him to let him have a small keg of gunpowder to replace the powder that the BaSotho had expended in their salutes in honour of the Free State officials. The President had agreed, with the approval of the field-cornets who were with him, and in due course he sent Moshoeshoe a barrel of fifty pounds of powder.[1] When the Volksraad convened, Hoffman made no reference to the subject in his presidential speech, whereupon the Volksraad resolved that he had been guilty of High Crime ('Hooge Misdaad'), by a vote of fifteen to eleven. This fell short of the three-quarters majority required by the constitution for the removal of a president, but Hoffman's opponents occupied the fort that the British had built on the hill overlooking Bloemfontein and trained the cannon on the President's house. Hoffman then resigned.[2] His fall eliminated the one slight prospect that Moshoeshoe had of negotiating a comprehensive settlement with a Free State Government that understood his problems and respected his integrity.

The next in the long line of white officials Moshoeshoe had to deal with were Jacobus N. Boshof, Hoffman's successor, and Sir George Grey, who had arrived in Cape Town as British High Commissioner and Governor of the Cape Colony in December 1854. Boshof was known as the author of eloquent letters to British officials and Cape newspapers on behalf of the voortrekkers in Natal. An experienced administrator with thirty years' service in the eastern Cape, the Natal Republic, and, latterly, the Colony of Natal, he conceived his role to be to provide the Free State with a sound administrative legal system, to foster patriotism among the white population, and to steer the new state between the Scylla of voortrekker factionalism (which still prevailed in the Transvaal) and the Charybdis of British intervention (which had bedevilled the Sovereignty). His attitudes towards Africans were more typical of those of the majority of the Free State burghers than Hoffman's and, having had no previous contacts with Moshoeshoe, he

---

[1] Orpen, *Reminiscences*, pp. 267–71; *SAAR, OFS* i. 330.
[2] *SAAR, OFS* i. 85–93; Orpen, *Reminiscences*, pp. 288–97; Collins, pp. 73–6.

readily adopted the hostile views that prevailed among the burghers.[1]

Grey came to South Africa with a substantial gubernatorial record in Australia and New Zealand, where he had checked excesses by white settlers, taken an interest—exceptional among British officials in his day—in aboriginal languages and cultures, and striven to promote 'civilization' by providing schools and medical facilities and employing aborigines on public works for wages. But his approach was paternalistic and he believed in extending British control and undermining the powers of native chiefs. He tried to apply the same principles in southern Africa. As he got to grips with its complexities, he realized that the entire subcontinent was intimately interconnected, at least as far north as the Limpopo, and he gradually came to believe that it should be given coherence and order as a federation under the British Crown, with considerable powers devolved on local governments. But the time was not propitious for the fulfilment of this vision: most high veld Afrikaners were devoted to their newly established independence; his superiors in London had only recently committed themselves to eschewing British responsibilities north of the Orange River; and he himself had not thought through the problem of how to accommodate within his grand design the African polities, like Moshoeshoe's, which were still independent.[2]

Moshoeshoe sent cordial greetings to Grey when he assumed his duties in South Africa[3] and Hoffman, after being ousted from the presidency, warned Grey that the Free State was liable to precipitate a war, which would be foolish because the Free State was weak, and unnecessary because 'so long as Moshesh lives there will never be an occasion for such a war'.[4] Orpen, for his part, tried to make Boshof understand the complexities of the unresolved

---

[1] W. J. de Kock (ed.), *Dictionary of South African Biography*, i (Cape Town, 1968), 100–4.

[2] J. Rutherford, *Sir George Grey, 1812–1898*, London, 1961; W. P. Morrell, *British Colonial Policy in the Mid-Victorian Age*, Oxford, 1969.

[3] Casalis to Grey, 25 Jan. 1855, *BR* ii. 138–9.

[4] Hoffman to Grey, 27 Feb. 1855, *BR* ii. 139–41.

boundary dispute, drew his attention to a Volksraad resolution recommending that one of his 'first and principal
proceedings' as President should be 'to make an arrangement to fix the boundaries', and advised him to invite Grey
to arbitrate, knowing that Moshoeshoe would agree.[1] However, military officers in the Cape Colony, smarting under
Cathcart's retreat from Thaba Bosiu, prejudiced Grey
against the BaSotho, while Boshof determined to cast Grey
in the role of ally rather than impartial arbitrator.[2] The
stage was thus set for the new British and Free State office-
holders to put joint pressure on Moshoeshoe.

   In October 1855 Grey convened a meeting of Free State
and LeSotho representatives at Smithfield, the seat of the
landdrost in the southern sector of the frontier zone, where
white and black claims overlapped and where Posholi
(brother of Moshoeshoe), Sepeli (a son of Moorosi), and
Letele and Lebenya (descendants of Mohlomi) were harry-
ing the Whites by raiding their livestock. As Moshoeshoe
rode to Smithfield with his retinue of councillors and territorial chiefs he was unaware of what was in store, assuming
that his first meeting with the new officials would be an
occasion for courtesy and hospitality. Instead Boshof immediately launched into a tirade against 'wicked people' who
stole cattle, undeterred by Moshoeshoe's observation that
'I understood this to be a meeting of friendship'; and then
Grey himself addressed Moshoeshoe in terms both insulting
and intimidating: 'You have collected some barbarians,
and made a kind of nation. The question is whether you are
to succeed or fail. . . . It is impossible that a civilised nation
can allow a nation of thieves to remain on their boundary.
The President and I are ready to put them down.'[3] The next
morning, 6 October 1855, Grey summoned the king and his
leading men and insisted that they come to an understanding
with Boshof.[4] Anxious to avoid a breach with the High

---

[1] *SAAR, OFS* i. 103 (Volksraad resolution 20 Feb. 1855).

[2] Orpen, *Reminiscences*, pp. 313–14, 325–9; CL 1191, 1213, Rhodes University.

[3] Minutes of a Conference between the President of the Orange Free State
and the Chief Moshesh, in presence of His Excellency Sir George Grey, *BR*
ii. 154–9.   [4] Grey to Colonial Secretary, 17 Nov. 1855, *BR* ii. 165–6.

Commissioner, Moshoeshoe and his advisers then signed a document prepared by Boshof, with clauses endorsing the Free State pass regulations, prescribing procedures for the recovery of stolen stock, and prohibiting trespassing by subjects of Moshoeshoe on the 'farms' of Free State burghers or by Free State burghers on 'land in the territory of the Paramount Chief Moshesh'. But this Smithfield agreement said nothing about a boundary between LeSotho and the Free State. It left Whites and Blacks intermingled in the frontier zone and did not specify which government had authority there.[1]

After his ominous experience at Smithfield, Moshoeshoe tried to keep the peace, without abandoning his territorial claims. He explained his position to Boshof on 21 March 1856: his 'whole tribe' agreed with him that he had originally granted a few Whites the privilege of pasturing their livestock in his country, but not the right to treat the land as their private property; he had granted Maitland's request to release some of the territory in the triangle between the Orange and the lower Caledon for white settlement; he had then been coerced by Warden into putting his name to a document which robbed him of a vast area of land occupied by over a hundred BaSotho villages and only a few Whites, 'without the consent of my people'; and Clerk had later agreed that Warden's boundary was unfair and invalid. Moshoeshoe concluded: 'I do no wrong to the Whites, for we are reckoned by tens of thousands, and we have reserved to ourselves a mere skirt of land. The Boers are counted by thousands only, and they extend from the Orange River up to the Vaal River, and beyond it over a very very wide land.'[2] On secondary issues Moshoeshoe was extremely conciliatory, hoping to convince Grey—even if he could not satisfy Boshof—that he was pacific.

Boshof, on the other hand, left Smithfield with the feeling that war was inevitable and that he would be able to

---

[1] *BR* ii. 159–60. The BaSotho signatories were Moshoeshoe, Letsie, Sekhon-yana ('Nehemiah'), Masopha ('David'), Lelosa ('Yobo'), Makoanyane, and Makoai. On these events, see [J. M. Orpen], *History*, pp. 114–19.

[2] Moshoeshoe to Boshof, 21 Mar. 1856, *BR* ii. 176–8.

convince the High Commissioner that the BaSotho were the guilty party. On 7 April 1856 he told Grey: 'I feel assured that the real cause of a war between Moshesh and us will be the boundary question, of whatever other circumstance he may avail himself as a pretext. I shall endeavour as much as may be in my power to avert such an event, so far as may be at all consistent with my duty to protect the rights of the inhabitants and landowners of this State, who hold their titles from the British Authorities.'[1]

In April 1856 the Free State Government called up about 500 burghers to clear Oetsi and his people out of their rugged territory on the northern side of the Caledon near the Drakensberg escarpment. After an initial setback, when the commandos disbanded prematurely in defiance of their government, the operation was completed by the end of June under the command of Orpen, who was then land-drost of Harrismith and Winburg. The Kholokoe were scattered: some became clients of white farmers, others were absorbed by Moshoeshoe. They lost over 4,000 head of cattle, a third of which were retained by the Free State Government, the rest divided up among the members of the commandos, in much the same way as the BaSotho were accustomed to dealing with their booty. Moshoeshoe complied with Boshof's request to instruct Molapo and Moletsane to keep their people quiet, and Molapo even allowed Orpen to conduct a commando across the Caledon and search the northern Maloti mountains for Kholokoe fugitives who had taken refuge there with their cattle.[2]

As soon as Oetsi's stronghold was captured Boshof sent two envoys with a 'final appeal' to Moshoeshoe to hand over as many horses and cattle as Posholi and the sons of Mohlomi were alleged to have stolen before the Smithfield agreement, plus four times as many as they were alleged to

---

[1] Boshof to Grey, 7 Apr. 1856, *BR* ii. 180–1.

[2] Letters from Moshoeshoe, Molapo, Boshof, Commandant-General L. R. Botha, Landdrost J. M. Orpen, etc., Apr.–June 1856, *BR* ii. 180–92, 200–4, and *SAAR*, *OFS* ii. 361–91; O.F.S. Government Notice, 2 Aug. 1856, *SAAR*, *OFS* ii. 391–3; [J. M. Orpen], *History*, pp. 119–26; Collins, pp. 85–6; C.L. 1189, 1213, Rhodes University. Traditions concerning these events were narrated by Informants 5 and 36.

have stolen since that agreement, making a total of 782 horses and 567 head of cattle; failing which the Free State would 'take measures . . . to avenge the many injuries' committed by 'incorrigible robbers'. After consulting his councillors and such territorial chiefs as were available, Moshoeshoe told the envoys that he had not been able to stop people from harassing the farmers in the southern frontier zone and he dictated a reply to Boshof in which he undertook to convene a full meeting of his territorial chiefs. If they did not agree to punish the thieves and collect the demanded compensation, 'I will then consider them no longer subjects of mine, and leave them to you to punish in the same manner as you have done with Witsi [Oetsi].' In their report to the Volksraad the envoys explained that Moshoeshoe and Letsie seemed anxious to keep the peace, but that the young BaSotho were spoiling for a fight to establish control over all the territory as far as the Maitland line and they seemed likely to prevail.[1]

Moshoeshoe did convene a large *pitso* in September. What happened there we do not know, but there is evidence that the territorial chiefs and the people were in a belligerent mood and that Tšapi, Mantsopa, and other diviners were prophesying an overwhelming victory.[2] Moshoeshoe himself had deduced from the Smithfield discussions and the commando operations against Oetsi that the Free State Government was preparing to invade LeSotho. He shared his people's confidence in their capacity to defeat the Free State provided it was a straight fight between the two, but he was anxious lest the Free Staters should obtain assistance from outside—not so much from the north where the white Transvaalers were still quarrelling among themselves, but rather from the British colonies, since Grey had made a palpable threat of intervention during the discussions at Smithfield. Therefore, while encouraging the people in the frontier zone to keep control of as much land as possible,

---

[1] Boshof to Moshoeshoe, 27 June 1856, *BR* ii. 205–7; reply 12 July 1856, *BR* ii. 209–10; W. H. Coleman and H. Olivier to Boshof, 17 July 1856, *BR* ii. 211–16.

[2] Arbousset to Cochet, 10 Sept. 1856, LEC.

he did try to restrain them from lifting cattle from the white farmers.[1] In this he was not very successful; but he was determined that the Free State and not he should bear the responsibility for initiating hostilities, so that he could appeal to the moral instincts of Grey and the British Government and secure at least their benevolent neutrality.[2]

For several years Moshoeshoe had been in frequent communication with the African and Coloured chiefs throughout the subcontinent, as far north as Bulawayo. The intensity of this diplomatic activity was considerable. Moshoeshoe was concerned to know what was happening elsewhere and other chiefs were naturally anxious to have contact with the man who had successively defied Mzilikazi, Matiwane, Warden, and Cathcart. The substance of this activity cannot be determined with any precision. It was a verbal diplomacy with long and detailed messages conveyed by men of high status who knew their chiefs' minds and were selected for their physical endurance and the excellence of their memories.[3] In a curious private letter at this time Arbousset confided to a fellow missionary that when war broke out Moshoeshoe might receive assistance from Kok and Waterboer (the Griqua chiefs), Sandile (Xhosa), Moroka (the Rolong chief at Thaba 'Nchu), Mahura (the Tlhaping chief near the Vaal River), and Langalibalele (the Hlubi chief in Natal).[4] Moshoeshoe presumably did try to acquire brown and black allies—he would have been foolish not to—but the odds were against him. Concerted military action was not possible among chiefdoms which had a history of mutual hostility and were separated from one another by blocks of territory dominated by white settlers or by formidable natural barriers like the Maloti and Drakensberg mountains. Arbousset's pre-

[1] Schrumpf, 1 June 1857, *JME* xxxii (1857), 329, reports that Masopha co-operated with Free State farmers in capturing two BaSotho cattle-thieves.

[2] The argument in this paragraph is deduced from Moshoeshoe's many letters to Grey and Boshof in this period: *BR* ii and *SAAR, OFS* ii and iii.

[3] Maeder, n.d., *JME* xxxi (1856), 210. Modern informants stress the high status and remarkable endurance and memories of Moshoeshoe's messengers or ambassadors: e.g. I. 39.

[4] Arbousset to Cochet, 10 Sept. 1856, LEC.

dictions were subsequently proved wrong, for when war did come none of the chiefs he named sent any help to LeSotho.

Nevertheless Moshoeshoe's diplomacy aroused serious suspicions among white officials. Between June 1856 and March 1857 Sarili and other Xhosa chiefs ordered their people to kill all their cattle and refrain from planting crops, in the belief that such a demonstration of faith in the wishes of the ancestors, as revealed to a young girl in a vision, would result in the disappearance of the Whites and the return of the ancestral heroes from the dead with vast herds of beautiful cattle.[1] Officials in British Kaffraria intercepted messengers between Moshoeshoe and Sarili and jumped to the conclusion that Moshoeshoe was the centre of a vast anti-White conspiracy—in particular, that he had fomented the cattle killings to initiate a general war against white people throughout southern Africa.[2] Moshoeshoe denied the allegations,[3] which were almost certainly false. The cattle killings did not precipitate war, but mass starvation, and Moshoeshoe had no conceivable interest in fomenting them. He would have been acting completely out of character if he had encouraged a hundred thousand people to destroy their means of subsistence, for he was rational enough to know that it could only lead to tragedy and humane enough to deplore it.

Meanwhile the Free State was preparing for war, as Moshoeshoe realized. Boshof urged Grey to hasten the delivery of field guns he had ordered from England and to stop colonial traders from selling arms and ammunition to BaSotho.[4] In October 1856 the Volksraad debated the BaSotho problem behind closed doors. Initially members were not sure if a boundary existed between the Free State

---

[1] On the cattle killings, Monica Wilson in *OHSA* i. 256–60, and John Zarwan, 'The Xhosa Cattle Killings, 1856–1857', unpublished seminar paper, Yale University, 1973.

[2] These suspicions were set out most elaborately by John Maclean, Chief Commissioner of Kaffraria, to Grey, 20 Mar. 1857, *BR* ii. 269–77.

[3] Moshoeshoe to Grey, 12 Mar. 1857, *BR* ii. 268.

[4] Boshof to Colonial Secretary, Cape Town, 21 June 1856, *BR*. ii 204; Boshof to Grey, 16 Sept. 1856, *BR* ii. 239.

and LeSotho since the British had evacuated the Sovereignty, but eventually they unanimously resolved that the Warden line was a valid boundary, that a force of 800 burghers should be mobilized in the frontier zone, that Moshoeshoe should be sent an ultimatum, and that, failing a satisfactory response, Free State forces should invade LeSotho early in 1857.[1] Moshoeshoe kept negotiations open, eventually handing over more cattle than demanded but scarcely any horses, for, as he informed Grey, 'my people have no confidence that when they have given up their horses which are their strength, war will not be made upon them for the sake of their ground'.[2]

However, war was postponed for another year because the Free State became distracted by divisions among its citizens and an invasion by a white commando from the north. M. W. Pretorius had not regarded his failure to seize control of the Free State in 1854 as final. Although he still only represented one of three white factions in the Transvaal, he returned to Bloemfontein in February 1857 claiming to be the rightful ruler of the Free State and succeeded in alienating almost the entire Volksraad. As he left, discomfited, he threatened to return with an armed force. True to his word, he then fomented rebellion in the northern Free State and in April he came back across the Vaal River with a commando. However, Boshof confronted him with a larger force, bloodshed was avoided, and Pretorius signed a document acknowledging that the Free State was a separate, independent entity.[3]

The militant Transvaaler tried to involve Moshoeshoe in these events. In February the king was surprised to receive a message asking him to meet Pretorius in Bloemfontein. He sent a son, Ntsane, in his place, which made Boshof so incensed by his apparent connivance with a would-be usurper that he ill-treated the man.[4] Then in April Moshoe-

---

[1] Minutes of Volksraad secret sittings, 9 and 15 Oct. 1856, *SAAR*, *OFS* ii. 48–50, 57–8.

[2] Moshoeshoe to Grey, 12 Mar. 1857, *BR*. ii. 268.

[3] Van Jaarsveld, pp. 169–97; Collins, pp. 101–14.

[4] Moshoeshoe to Boshof, 3 Mar. 1857, G.S. 1340, OFS; Van Jaarsveld, pp. 170–1.

shoe received two emissaries from Pretorius, one of whom was Paul Kruger (later to be President of the South African Republic), who urged him to create a diversion in the southern Free State while the Transvaalers attacked in the north. Uncertain how this white quarrel would end, Moshoeshoe sent soft words to both Pretorius and Boshof, but refrained from taking advantage of the situation, and he wrote to Grey ironically deploring the quarrelsomeness of the Boers: 'Oh! my master, my heart is full of grief, when hearing that the Boers might shed blood.'[1] In the Colonial Office, London, some wag added the marginal note: 'Moshesh as peacemaker between the Dutchmen!!'[2]

3. *War and Peace: 1858*

The long-expected war broke out in March 1858. Although there were other points of friction further northeast, it arose primarily out of the situation in the lower Caledon valley, where black villages and white farms were interspersed between the boundary set by Maitland and claimed by Moshoeshoe, and the boundary set by Warden and claimed by the Free State. Early in 1857 Moshoeshoe sent his son Sekhonyana to establish a village in the disputed zone and control the local chiefs. For a while Sekhonyana's presence resulted in a decline in stock stealing, but by the beginning of 1858 Posholi, in particular, threw off all restraint and was occupying farms and damaging homesteads and orchards.[3]

When the Volksraad met on 1 February 1858, it received a request for help signed by a field-cornet and sixty-five other burghers in the disputed area.[4] Later that month J. Sauer, the landdrost of Smithfield, reported that, besides

---

[1] Moshoeshoe to Grey, 29 May 1857, *BR* ii. 282.

[2] Van Jaarsveld, p. 190.

[3] Notes et souvenirs du missionnaire L. J. Cochet, Cahiers 2, 1 Jan. 1857–20 Jan. 1862, SME. Cochet, who was stationed at Hebron in the disputed zone, was in regular contact with the local chiefs, especially Mohlomi's son Letele and grandson Lebenya. His manuscript is in the form of a journal which sheds light on the events leading to war.

[4] *SAAR, OFS* iii. 175–6.

refusing to remove his people from a white farm, Posholi was parading through his district with a body of armed warriors in the guise of a hunting expedition.[1] The response from Bloemfontein was slow and, initially, cautious. Burghers in other districts, where local problems included a serious drought and unresolved tensions with the Griqua in the western Free State, were loath to be conscripted for a war against a powerful African state which posed no immediate threat to themselves. Moreover the Free State Government was itself in the throes of a crisis. Boshof's firm handling of the Pretorius invasion had been followed by a backlash. Throughout February there was a political struggle inside and outside the Volksraad: Boshof resigned the presidency on 25 February and reluctantly consented to return to office four days later.[2]

While the Volksraad was in session Boshof ordered partial mobilization in the hope that a display of strength would make Moshoeshoe discipline the frontier chiefs. Failing that, Boshof intended to drive the Africans beyond Warden's line, but not to invade any of the territory that was indisputably part of LeSotho.[3] However, J. Sauer, landdrost of Smithfield, the senior official on the spot, became convinced that 'when we start with Posholi, we shall have to deal with the whole Basuto Nation'.[4] On 3 March, the Volksraad having completed its stormy session, Sauer, with two local field-cornets and two members of the Volksraad, held a meeting with Sekhonyana, Sofonia (another of Moshoeshoe's sons), Lebenya (a grandson of Mohlomi), and three of Posholi's men. According to Sauer's minutes of the meeting, Sekhonyana admitted that Posholi and Lebenya had 'disgraced themselves by robbing and harassing the Boers',[5] but Sekhonyana informed Boshof that nothing had been proved

---

[1] Sauer to Letsie, 11 Feb. 1858, *BR* ii. 289–90; Sauer to Sekhonyana [Nehemiah], 21 Feb. 1858, *BR* ii. 292–3.

[2] Minutes of the Volksraad session 1 Feb.–2 Mar. 1858, *SAAR*, *OFS* iii. 2–77.

[3] J. W. Spruijt, Government Secretary, Bloemfontein, to the Landdrosts of Caledon River, Winburg, and Harrismith, 18 Feb. 1858, *SAAR*, *OFS* iii. 197; Spruijt to Sauer, 26 Feb. 1858, *SAAR*, *OFS* iii. 205–6.

[4] Sauer to Spruijt, 26 Feb. 1858, *SAAR*, *OFS* iii. 210.

[5] *BR* ii. 302.

against them and no one had the right to remove people whom Moshoeshoe had placed. 'What can it be', he asked, 'but the country they want?'[1] A week later some of the Africans in the disputed zone, led by Letele, a son of Mohlomi, submitted to the Free State, receiving assurances that they could keep any cattle they raided from the BaSotho, while it became clear that Posholi, Lebenya, and others would remain loyal to Moshoeshoe.[2] A war council consisting of Boshof, Sauer, and several military officers and members of the Volksraad then decided that if Sekhonyana did not give satisfaction at a meeting arranged for the following day, the President should send Moshoeshoe an ultimatum with a time-limit, during which the Government would call up more burghers and complete its military preparations.[3] On 11 March, finding Sekhonyana evasive, Boshof handed him an ultimatum.[4] Within eight days Moshoeshoe was to declare in writing whether he would compel Posholi and Lebenya to leave the frontier zone, pay the compensation still outstanding for earlier thefts plus additional compensation for recent thefts and damages, and recognize the Warden line as the boundary between the Free State and LeSotho.[5] On 19 March, having received no reply, Boshof declared war.[6] By that time the Free State had mobilized about a thousand mounted men who, like the BaSotho, were organized on a territorial basis, under their field-cornets and commandants. They concentrated at two points, Smithfield in the south and Winburg in the north, with seven small field guns and trains of wagons to carry supplies and form defensive laagers. When war was declared, both columns moved towards LeSotho with the intention of fighting their way to Thaba Bosiu and dictating terms to Moshoeshoe.[7]

---

[1] Ibid., p. 307. Cochet, Notes et souvenirs, 4 Mar. 1858.
[2] *BR* ii. 310–11.   [3] Ibid., pp. 311–13.
[4] Ibid., pp. 313–18. Cochet, 15 Mar. 1858.
[5] Boshof to Moshoeshoe, 11 Mar. 1858, *BR* ii. 318–20.
[6] Ibid., pp. 326–8. Moshoeshoe did in fact reply to the ultimatum, reiterating his territorial claims and asking for arbitration by Grey, in a letter erroneously dated 22 Apr. 1858 and received by Boshof on 21 Mar.: *BR* ii. 329–30.
[7] On the 1858 war, besides Cochet's Notes et souvenirs, there are contemporary unpublished documents in the Orange Free State archives and the Paris and Wesleyan mission archives; published documents in *BR* ii, *SAAR*,

While these events unfolded Moshoeshoe remained at Thaba Bosiu. He gave Sekhonyana authority to negotiate till the last moment, but not to agree to sacrifice any territory. When war became inevitable, the king, his councillors, and his territorial chiefs put into effect a plan that must have been the outcome of many long deliberations. Herdboys took the bulk of the livestock deep into the Maloti mountains; the loyal BaSotho in the disputed zone withdrew towards Thaba Bosiu; and the chiefs prepared to contest the advance of the Free State forces but, if hard pressed, to retire gradually towards the capital, and when the commandos were sufficiently committed the younger chiefs would lead raiding parties deep into the Free State. If the burghers had confined themselves to clearing the disputed zone west of the Warden line, Moshoeshoe's strategy would have failed, for he made no serious attempt to hold that area.[1] As it was, the Free State invasion of LeSotho played straight into Moshoeshoe's hands. Diplomatically, he appeared in the best possible light as the victim of aggression; militarily, he made the optimum use of his rugged terrain, his loose military organization, and his numerical superiority of at least 10,000 mounted warriors over the 1,000 Free Staters.[2]

The northern Free State column advanced from Winburg to the drift that Cathcart had used to cross the Caledon (near modern Maseru), where it was attacked by the regiments of Molapo, Mopeli, and Moletsane between 12 and 14 April. Then, instead of proceeding direct to Thaba Bosiu, it moved down the right bank of the Caledon to Jammerberg Drift to await the arrival of the southern column. On 23 March the latter, aided by Letele's people, attacked and looted the loyal African villages and the French mission premises at Beersheba in the disputed zone,

OFS iii, and *JME* xxxiii (1858); a later account by a Free State participant in Collins, pp. 127–31; and summaries by Tylden (always at his best in describing military events), pp. 72–6, and Malan, pp. 350–6.

[1] 'Sekhonyana told Lebenya not to expect help from Lessouto': Cochet, 9 Mar. 1858.
[2] The Free State mobilized a total of about 1,500 men during the war, but not more than about 1,000 were present in the army at any one time.

which had already been evacuated by most of their African inhabitants.[1] Continuing eastwards the column destroyed the villages and fields of Posholi and Lebenya and then crossed the Caledon, losing fifteen men in a brush with Letsie's regiment near Mohale's Hoek before joining the northern column at Jammerberg Drift on 25 April. The combined force then moved on Morija, where it burnt Letsie's village and plundered the property of the missionaries and the traders, who, with the exception of the missionary aide Maeder, had fled into the mountains. Amongst other things it destroyed were Arbousset's papers, which included a great deal of information that would have been of value to historians.[2]

Meanwhile Moshoeshoe was calmly awaiting events on Thaba Bosiu. A Wesleyan missionary visited him there on about 12 April:

He received me kindly and politely, gave a long account of his political difficulties, and of the history of his tribe. I was much struck with the quiet and ease which seemed to prevail on the mountain. A number of men were sewing skins together to make karosses, women were about their domestic work, children were running about playing and one could scarcely think that a battle was about to be fought which might decide the fate of the reigning dynasty and of the country generally. The old chief himself seemed to be scarcely moved, at least he did not appear anxious.

Messengers then arrived with reports of the fighting at Cathcart's Drift:

On one messenger's reporting that the Boers' camp was surrounded by Basutos, and saying that Moshesh's son wished to know from his father whether they fall on the camp and destroy it, the old chief said No. . . . If the enemy persist in

---

[1] The destruction of the mission at Beersheba gave rise to a bitter controversy between the Paris Evangelical Missionary Society and the Free State Government: *BR* ii. 339–41, 443–68. On the background of Beersheba see above, pp. 85, 132, 147, 184, and also Frantz Balfet, *Un Pionnier . . . Samuel Rolland (1801–1873)*.

[2] The traders and missionaries claimed compensation for their losses at Morija. The Free State rejected their claims, but voted £100 to the Paris society for damage to its buildings. *SAAR, OFS* iii. 455–513; Arbousset, 22 June 1858, *JME* xxxiii (1858), 322 ff.

coming into my country my people must fight, but if the Dutch farmers wish to fall back and retire to their own land let them do so, without being pursued.[1]

On 6 May the Free State army formed a laager below Thaba Bosiu and beat off an attack, only to find itself facing the hitherto impregnable mountain, defended by several thousand warriors. By that time the burghers had heard that BaSotho raiding parties were causing havoc on their farms, seizing livestock and burning homesteads as they themslves had been doing to the BaSotho, and that in the western Free State 'Scheel Kobus', a Khoisan chieftain, and two Thlaping chiefs had also taken the opportunity to help themselves to their cattle. The morale of the Free State army had never been good. Now it collapsed dramatically. On 8 May, after some desultory firing at the mountain from two field pieces, during which one ball struck Moshoeshoe's European-style house, the invaders retreated to the Caledon, as Cathcart's British troops had done less than five years earlier. Then, after fierce arguments among the officers, the force disintegrated. The men rode back to their homes and families, leaving a crestfallen Boshof to deal with a victorious Moshoeshoe.[2]

Meanwhile Boshof, swallowing his pride, had appealed to Pretorius for help with which 'the head of the Barbarians shall be thrown down and there will be long years of peace for the emigrants'.[3] Pretorius responded, seeking to turn the Free Staters' distress to the realization of his ambition. He would assist on condition that the Free State merged its identity with the Transvaal.[4] He might have succeeded, for many Free Staters were anxious for such a union, had not Grey intervened.

[1] Richard Giddy, 9 Oct. 1858, Box labelled 'S.A. Kaffraria 1858–1864', WMS.

[2] Jousse, the Paris missionary stationed at Thaba Bosiu, was an eye-witness of the fighting around the mountain, 1 June 1858, *JME* xxxiii (1858), 361–3. Collins, pp. 130–1, gives an account of the quarrels that led to the disintegration of the Free State army.

[3] Boshof to M. W. Pretorius and S. P. Schoeman, 9 Apr. 1858, *SAAR, OFS* iii. 250–2.

[4] Van Jaarsveld, pp. 211–25.

Grey had watched every scene in the drama on the high veld with misgivings.[1] Even before the war began he had reached the conclusion that the Conventions had been a mistake. He realized that the British Government had itself been largely responsible for the anarchy in the frontier zone between the Free State and LeSotho, in abandoning the Sovereignty without an agreed boundary. He had also become better informed about Moshoeshoe and his people. He was lobbied by Orpen, who resigned his Free State appointment in disgust at the inability of the Government to stop its citizens from seizing San and African children and published a series of articles sympathetic to Moshoeshoe in the *Cape Argus*;[2] and Grey sent his own agent to LeSotho, who reported that the Free Staters 'avail themselves of the losses which they profess to have sustained to build up a plea for forcing back the Natives'—a verdict that was endorsed by a former landdrost of Smithfield.[3] Consequently when war broke out the High Commissioner proclaimed British neutrality; when the first reports indicated that the Free State seemed to be winning, he expressed annoyance that the Conventions permitted Whites to obtain arms and ammunition while denying them to Africans; and when the Free State army collapsed he foresaw dangerous repercussions along the frontiers of the British colonies. The whole performance led him to conclude that the division of the white South African communities into separate polities had destroyed their capacity to deal wisely or effectively with the Africans around them. The prospect that the two republics might unite seemed still more alarming. Such a state, he feared, would exert further pressures on Africans and might eventually become powerful enough to threaten

[1] C. W. de Kiewiet, *British Colonial Policy and the South African Republics, 1848–1872*, chs. 7–8.

[2] Also published in book form: Special Commissioner of the *Cape Argus*, *History of the Basutos of South Africa*, Cape Town, 1857. Orpen was known to be the author and when he tried to assist Sekhonyana in his negotiations with the Free State representatives on the eve of the war, Boshof placed him under arrest and had him expelled from the Free State: Boshof to Grey, 16 Mar. 1858, *BR* ii. 320–2.

[3] John Burnet to Grey, 15 Sept. 1856, *BR* ii. 236–9; J. H. Ford to Grey, 5 Nov. 1856, *BR* ii. 252–3.

the British colonies. For these reasons he offered to mediate between the warring parties if both would accept. He also informed the republics that, if they united, Britain would consider that the Conventions had ceased to operate.[1] The threat was effective. It turned the Transvaalers away from an action that might compromise their independence and their ammunition supplies, and it persuaded the confused and volatile Free Staters to place their fate in the hands of the High Commissioner.[2]

As for Moshoeshoe, he realized that his military advantage would prove ephemeral if it was not buttressed by a peace settlement endorsed by the one power that could determine the main course of events throughout southern Africa. When Boshof put out peace feelers, Moshoeshoe sent a withering reply on 16 May, denouncing the burghers' atrocities, especially the ravaging of the mission stations at Beersheba and Morija ('does their Christianity consist in destroying Christianity?'), and taunting them for their unwillingness to stand and fight;[3] but he responded favourably to Grey's offer to mediate and on 1 June he undertook to suspend military operations until the High Commissioner had arbitrated a peace settlement.[4]

Moshoeshoe found it much more difficult to secure a satisfactory peace than it had been to repulse the invaders. Although his warriors had overrun the eastern Free State and probably made a net gain in cattle and horses, his people were suffering severely. The Free State army had destroyed numerous villages with their grain reserves and standing crops. Large numbers of BaSotho women and children had fled from their homes. They were so short of food that they depended largely on wild plants, and there was an outbreak of typhus or typhoid.[5]

[1] Grey to Boshof and Grey to Moshoeshoe, 6 May 1858, *BR* ii. 358–60; Grey to Boshof, 3 June 1858, *SAAR, OFS* iii. 263–4; Grey to Colonial Secretary, 9 June 1858, *BR* ii. 395–6.

[2] Minutes of the Volksraad, 10 June 1858, *SAAR, OFS* iii. 87; Van Jaarsveld, pp. 225–34.

[3] Moshoeshoe to Boshof, 16 May 1858, *BR* ii. 362–5.

[4] Moshoeshoe to Grey, 28 May 1858, *BR* ii. 379–80; Articles of Agreement, 1 June 1858, *BR* ii. 382–3.

[5] Maitin, 14 July 1858, *JME* xxxiii (1858), 447–53; Daumas, 29 Sept. 1858,

We do not know what happened in the councils and general assemblies Moshoeshoe summoned at this time. His people certainly expected great things from his diplomacy, but Moshoeshoe lacked sound advice. His chiefs and councillors had a relatively narrow perspective and there was no Casalis among his missionaries. Moreover after the exhilaration of his military victory the king himself was feeling the weight of his seventy-two years. Instead of the diplomatic finesse that had previously been his hallmark, he became confused and unsure of himself as he prepared for yet another verbal bout with white officials.

Between the retreat of the Free State army and the arrival of Grey, Moshoeshoe sent him four letters, which were influenced and written by missionaries.[1] In the first (28 May), he complained that Britain allowed his enemies to obtain arms and ammunition while denying them to him. In the second (29 May), he said he was trying to restrain his warriors from following up their military advantage by razing white farms. In the third (dated 'June, 1858'), he rehearsed the history of his dealings with white people from the beginnings of settler infiltration into the Caledon valley, through his negotiations with the succession of British officials (Napier, Maitland, Smith, Warden, Hogge and Owen, Cathcart, Clerk) and Free State presidents (Hoffman, Boshof) to the war and the defeat of the Free State army. In the last (31 July), he summarized his main points and made a sweeping demand:

At first I did hope that the people so well received in my country should acknowledge my rightful sovereignty, and should live in peace with my own people, but instead of that they incessantly try to make encroachments upon me, and I [have] therefore been involved in severe wars. Now I say and all my people stand with me, since the land granted by me to the whites at the request of the representatives of the British Government and in exchange for its protection is a cause of perpetual wars between the whites and the blacks, I earnestly pray the British Government, by the medium of Your Excellency, to restore

JME xxxiv (1859), 1–4; Gosselin, 24 Dec. 1858, ibid., pp. 88–90; Jousse, 15 May 1859, ibid., pp. 321–6; Lautré, 7 Sept. 1859, ibid., pp. 461–6.

[1] *BR* ii. 379–80, 380–2, 384–8, 409–11.

unto his legitimate owner the country which was in my possession before the arrival of the whites in this country. In that great question we cannot acknowledge another Government but that of English, at the request of which tracts of land have been granted. When the British Government withdrew his protections from this part of the Orange River, the land should have been restored unto his legitimate sovereign.[1]

Boshof was bitterly disillusioned by the disintegration of the Free State army. On 20 May he informed a colonial magistrate: 'The boers, by their unaccountable sudden break up, have brought me in such a fix as I never yet was in all my life. They imagine that they have given Moshesh such a licking that he will keep quiet for many a day, poor fools. . . . After the conduct of our boers in this war I shall be indifferent, though I pity the State,—the English ought never to have given it up.'[2] Nevertheless the Free State made skilful preparations for Grey's arrival. In letters to Grey, the President tried to explain away his dealings with Pretorius and the sackings and lootings at Beersheba and Morija,[3] while the Volksraad appointed a commission to prepare a brief on the boundary question, and when Grey indicated that he himself intended to appoint an impartial commission, Boshof replied: 'I have every reason to believe that the Commission appointed by the Volksraad will be prepared to lay the proofs before Your Excellency in such a clear manner as to do away with the necessity for the appointment of a Commission of Enquiry as suggested by Your Excellency.'[4]

In the second half of August Grey crossed the Orange River and made brief visits to Bloemfontein and Thaba Bosiu, and Moshoeshoe agreed to attend a peace conference at Beersheba on 15 September.[5] Grey then hurried to King William's Town to arrange for the dispatch of troops to assist in the suppression of the Indian Mutiny and after

[1] *BR* ii. 410.

[2] Boshof to Resident Magistrate, Aliwal North, 20 May 1858, *BR* ii. 370-1.

[3] Boshof to Grey, 2, 10, and 16 June 1858, *BR* ii. 388-9, 396-7, 400-1.

[4] Boshof to Grey, 20 Aug. 1858, *BR* ii. 413-14.

[5] Minutes of Third Conference at Beersheba, 16 Sept. 1858, *SAAR*, *FS* iii. 358-9.

another exhausting journey he was at Beersheba in time for the conference. The Free State delegation was there, led by H. A. L. Hamelberg, a young Dutch lawyer who had recently settled in Bloemfontein; but Moshoeshoe was absent. He sent a brief letter of apology, saying 'I am very old and often troubled with headache, therefore I am not able to come to the meeting.'[1] In his place he sent his half-brother Lelosa and seven other men, none of whom had the standing of a territorial chief, and they declared that they were not authorized to make any definite commitments in the king's name. Grey was furious. Nevertheless he convened the conference, such as it was, and accepted the brief that had been prepared by the Free State Commission, including an *ex parte* summary of the causes of the war, a draft treaty endorsing the Warden line, and a number of depositions from early settlers who declared that when they first visited the Caledon valley in the 1820s and early 1830s the country south of Thaba Bosiu was populated only by scattered bands of hunters.[2]

Grey then travelled to Morija, where he had discussions with Moshoeshoe in the presence of Letsie and four missionaries. The High Commissioner persuaded Moshoeshoe to withdraw the sweeping and undefined territorial claims he had made in his letter of 31 July and instead to take the draft treaty submitted by the Free State delegates as a basis for discussion. On 23 September Moshoeshoe signed a document, consenting, amongst other things, to a boundary running through the disputed zone approximately midway between the Maitland line of 1846 and the Warden line of 1849, and gave Grey to understand that he was granting full powers to Lelosa and Makoai to complete the negotiations on his behalf.[3] Next, Grey rode to Aliwal North, where the Free State delegates submitted additional evidence in support of their claims and considered Moshoeshoe's counter-proposals. On 29 September a treaty was signed

[1] Moshoeshoe to Grey, 8 Sept. 1858, *BR* ii. 419–20.

[2] *BR* ii. 420–38; *SAAR, OFS* iii. 320–62. Cochet, Notes et souvenirs, 18 Sept. 1858.

[3] *SAAR, OFS* iii. 380–3. *BR* ii. 441 contains Moshoeshoe's covering letter to Grey, 23 Sept. 1858, but not his commentary on the Free State draft treaty.

there by the Free State delegates and Lelosa and Makoai.[1] After that Grey returned to the area in dispute and supervised the placing of beacons to mark the new boundary, in the presence of H. A. L. Hamelberg and T. W. Vowe of the Free State and Lelosa and Makoai.[2] The king made one last

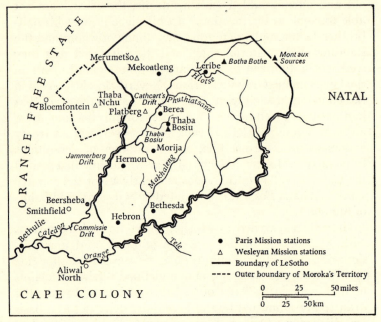

MAP 6. The boundary of LeSotho as arbitrated by Sir George Grey in 1858

effort to avoid a definite commitment. When Makoai arrived at Thaba Bosiu with copies of the treaty, he sent them back without his signature. However, John Burnet, Civil Commissioner of Aliwal North, whom Grey had used for previous missions to Thaba Bosiu, finally persuaded Moshoeshoe to place his mark and seal on the treaty on 15 October 1858.[3]

---

[1] *SAAR, OFS* iii. 330–3 (Minutes of meetings of the Free State Commissioners), 383–411 (Minutes of the peace conference at Aliwal North and related documents).

[2] *SAAR, OFS* iii. 411–19 (Report of the Free State Commissioners and related documents).

[3] Moshoeshoe to Grey, 15 Oct. 1858, *BR* ii. 485–6; John Burnet, 'Notes of Mr. Burnet's Mission to the Chief Moshesh . . .', 19 Oct. 1858, *BR* ii. 486–95.

The Treaty of Aliwal North stated that the northern boundary of LeSotho as far west as Jammerberg Drift on the Caledon was the one established by Warden in 1849, and it defined in detail a new western boundary between the Caledon and the Orange. This ran about midway between the Maitland and Warden lines and although it differed considerably from Moshoeshoe's counter-proposal of 23 September the net result of the differences was not very substantial. For the first time in Moshoeshoe's experience the treaty made territoriality correspond with allegiance. Whereas Warden's arrangements, made under the authority of Harry Smith's annexation proclamation, had allowed Africans on the white side of his line to continue to owe allegiance to Moshoeshoe, and vice versa, now all his subjects were to withdraw to the east of the boundary and all subjects of the Free State to the west within a reasonable time and without compensation. The large area around Beersheba previously occupied mainly by people who recognized Moshoeshoe became Free State territory, within which the Paris mission retained possession of a 6,000-acre mission reserve. Fugitive criminals were to be returned on request by both sides and BaSotho hunting parties were not to kill game in the Free State without government permission. There were several clauses laying down elaborate procedures for the recovery of stolen stock, culminating in the provision that if, after due warning, Moshoeshoe failed to punish chiefs whose followers had committed robberies, the Free State had the right to attack them without his interference. Finally Moshoeshoe undertook not to punish Letele and other Africans for having sided with the Free State in the war, though if they settled east of the new boundary they would owe allegiance to him.[1]

Grey revealed some of his thoughts as arbitrator early in October, while he was supervising the beaconing of the boundary, to Cochet, the Paris missionary at Hebron, which fell just inside LeSotho. Having himself made a

[1] The Treaty of Aliwal North, 29 Sept. 1858, *BR* ii. 475–9 and *SAAR, OFS* iii. 405–10; the description of the boundary, signed by Grey, n.d. (*c.* 5 Oct. 1858), *BR* ii. 482–4 and *SAAR, OFS* iii. 417–19.

series of long and arduous journeys, Grey was deeply angered
by Moshoeshoe's failure to keep his appointment at Beersheba. The evidence submitted by the Free State convinced
him that the lower Caledon valley had been occupied
exclusively by bands of hunters before 1819, that Whites
had then begun to enter it from the Cape Colony, and that
the BaSotho were interlopers. He also blamed the missionaries for encouraging Moshoeshoe to make exorbitant
claims and declared that if the BaSotho themselves were
not satisfied with the treaty it would be the missionaries'
fault. Cochet defended his colleagues, explaining that they
had very little influence over Moshoeshoe and that the
BaSotho themselves were solidly behind the king's claims.
He also tried to persuade the High Commissioner that the
rights and wrongs of the land dispute were not nearly so
clear-cut as the *ex parte* Free State evidence indicated. In
this Cochet was not successful, if only because Grey had
already made his decision; but by the time Grey completed
the marking of the boundary he was more friendly towards
Cochet and he was complaining that he had never seen a
'more unfair man' than Vowe, one of the Free State Commissioners.[1]

Moshoeshoe's diplomacy is more difficult to understand,
for none of the missionaries around him had his full confidence and all the surviving accounts are unsympathetic.[2]
His letter to Boshof of 16 May, with its denunciation of the
Free Staters for their unchristian and cowardly behaviour,
was scarcely recognizable as the work of the man who had
provided Mzilikazi and Cathcart with face-saving messages
after they had failed to defeat him. His territorial claims
of 31 July, apparently influenced by Arbousset, were too
sweeping to be realistic. His absence from Beersheba on
15 September, his refusal to give his envoys full powers, and
his final attempt to avoid signing the treaty—all these placed

---

[1] Cochet, Notes et souvenirs, 1–6 Oct. 1858.

[2] The missionaries who witnessed Moshoeshoe's counter-proposal at Morija
on 23 Sept. 1858 were H. M. Dyke (Hermon: Eugène Casalis's brother-in-
law), J. Maitin (Berea), T. Jousse (Thaba Bosiu), and J. D. M. Ludorf (Wesleyan, Thaba 'Nchu). Those present at Thaba Bosiu during Burnet's visit in
mid October were T. Jousse and Dr. P. Lautré (Thaba Bosiu).

him in a bad light with the man he had asked to arbitrate and the government from which he hoped to receive co-operation and protection in the future. Perhaps he was indeed ill during this period, as he claimed. At the very least he was in a state of severe depression.

Burnet's notes of his visit to Thaba Bosiu in mid October show that the old king was threshing around in his mind in genuine perplexity. He was deeply concerned that he had not been able to obtain more tangible advantages from his military victory. He suspected that the territorial changes Grey had made from those he had accepted in his counter-proposal on 23 September were substantial. He was worried about the effects of the clauses dealing with hunting and the recovery of stolen stock:

I know the Boers, they will not act up to the Treaty and trace the property stolen, but they will come afterwards, a long time, as they have always done, with a great demand upon me . . .

There is the same objection to the hunting clause. My people are hungry, and they are gone away in hundreds, men, women, and children, to kill game and get food, and how am I to keep this law at present? . . . they think God made the wild beasts for every one, for Whites and Blacks.[1]

Besides these specific objections, Moshoeshoe showed that he felt that once again he had been let down by a British official whom he had trusted to make a fair settlement of his disputes with his white neighbours: 'Yes! Sir George Grey is the fifth great man who has come here to make matters right between me and the Boers . . . and such arrangements have always ended by a piece of country being lost to my people.'[2]

Probably the most important factor influencing Moshoeshoe's diplomacy was that from the very beginning of the negotiations he foresaw that no peace settlement he was likely to obtain from Grey—who had insulted him at their previous meeting in October 1855—would possibly satisfy his chiefs and people. Grey's handling of the discussions at Morija confirmed his fears. It is significant that Letsie,

---

[1] *BR* ii. 492.   [2] Ibid., p. 490.

who had acquiesced in the arrangements made at Morija, found an excuse for absenting himself from Thaba Bosiu during Burnet's visit,[1] and that none of the other great chiefs was there.[2] Moshoeshoe's behaviour throughout these proceedings was a not very skilful effort by an ageing and perhaps sick ruler of a loosely structured kingdom to preserve his authority over his own people. He felt obliged to give the appearance of opposing at all stages a settlement that he knew from the first they would dislike.

[1] *BR* ii. 487.

[2] The BaSotho witnesses to Moshoeshoe's mark and seal on the treaty at Thaba Bosiu on 15 Oct. 1858 were Sofonia and 'Mota (junior sons of Moshoeshoe) and 'Yonker, sent by the Chief Mogale [Mohale]'. *BR* ii. 479.

VII

THE FINAL YEARS

1. *LeSotho in Turmoil*

AFTER 1858, when Moshoeshoe completed his seventy-second year, his physical and eventually his mental health deteriorated. On occasion he still gave white visitors the impression that he was younger than his years. In 1861 a newspaper reporter found him 'a hale, hearty man of 60 or 65 years old' and in the following year a missionary observed, 'One is always struck by the intelligence of Moshesh. When he talks all his features light up and his loquacity knows no bounds.' In December 1865, however, John Burnet, the magistrate of Aliwal North in the Cape Colony, who had made many journeys to Thaba Bosiu on behalf of successive High Commissioners, considered he was no longer capable of governing, his 'once vigorous mind partially gone'.[1] Perhaps that disastrous year did mark a turning-point, though he retained a tenuous hold on life into 1870.

The ageing Moshoeshoe had no illusions about the men he had to deal with and almost until the end he believed that the fate of his people rested exclusively on his own shoulders. Burnet reported in 1861: 'He has not the slightest confidence in anybody, British, Colonial, Free State, or Basuto, save only in himself. "I am Basutoland." '[2] However, he did not relapse into cynicism. He was, indeed, immensely proud of his achievements and was wont to deliver long harangues about the past, describing in animated detail how he had brought his people together and saved them from one danger after another. But he also looked to the future. He continued to hope that before he died he would have assured for his people peace, security,

[1] *Friend of the Free State*, 13 Dec. 1861, *BR* ii. 610; Coillard, n.d., *JME* xxxvii (1862), 408; John Burnet, Civil Commissioner, Aliwal North, to High Commissioner, 17 Dec. 1865, *BR* iii. 568.

[2] Burnet to High Commissioner, 29 July 1861, *BR* ii. 596.

and good government in a territory sufficient for their
needs; and in spite of feeling that he had been deceived by
successive British officials he clung to the belief that the
only means to that end was an arrangement with Great
Britain. If only he could penetrate the obstructions created
by the Queen's local representatives, she herself, he hoped,
would protect his people from their white neighbours,
allow them to preserve their customs, and help them to
stand on their own feet in the modern world by showing
him how to strengthen his political institutions. This was
the main thread in his diplomacy from 1858 onwards.

J. M. Orpen, the European with whom he had the greatest
empathy after Casalis's departure—Orpen had married the
daughter of Samuel Rolland, the Beersheba missionary—
reported in July 1863: 'Long before the war, and since it
too, I have often heard him express to his people his longing
and *expectation* that the day would come when they would
again be *safe* and *at peace* under Her Majesty's protection. . . .
Secondarily he hopes the connection would consolidate his
authority.'[1]

The phrase 'Indirect Rule' had not yet been invented,
but it was the essence of what Moshoeshoe had in mind.
It was a very tall order in 1863. The British Government
was still committed to a policy of non-intervention north
of the Orange River and, far from strengthening traditional
political systems, successive high commissioners were instructing white magistrates to undermine the powers of the
Xhosa and Thembu chiefs in British Kaffraria.[2] Moreover
Moshoeshoe's own subordinates did not fully understand
his reasoning and they were too jealous of one another to
co-operate effectively, with the result that they often
committed actions that endangered his plans.

Moshoeshoe's strategy was a realistic response to his
situation. He knew that his people lacked the power to
resist white expansion indefinitely. To attempt to do so

---

[1] Orpen to High Commissioner, 8 July 1863, *BR* iii. 220.
[2] Wodehouse to Newcastle, Secretary of State, 20 Aug. 1862, Wodehouse
Papers, Colonial Office: 'The more we can break down the power of the Chiefs
and raise up individual owners of property, each having something to lose in
case of war, the safer we shall be.'

would be suicidal. He was therefore constrained to select the best available option within the general framework of white power, and he did so by exploiting the divisions among the Whites and coming to terms with the British Government, which had no apparent interest in disrupting his nation, whereas his settler neighbours coveted his land and were reducing their subject peoples to serfdom.

Five more years would elapse, much blood would be shed, and Moshoeshoe himself would have sunk into senility before his strategy was, in some sense, fulfilled.

Moshoeshoe was justified in seeking advice for the strengthening of his monarchy, for a process of disintegration set in as his energy ebbed away during his final years. He continued to consult his well-tested councillors—RaTšiu, Makoanyane, RaMatšeatsana, and Lelosa (all of whom outlived him except Makoanyane who died in about 1863).[1] But these men, loyal though they were, were rooted in the old order. They had no constructive ideas for reforming the political institutions and were not much help in dealing with white officials who had a literary culture and whose languages were wholly different in structure and imagery from their own.

In earlier years Casalis had helped Moshoeshoe to bridge the two cultures and express his diplomatic intentions in correspondence in the English language. After Casalis returned to France in 1855 there was no adequate substitute. Théophile Jousse, his successor at the mission station below Thaba Bosiu, was a conscientious pastor who confined himself rather narrowly to his professional duties.[2] Mabille, who succeeded Arbousset at Morija in 1859 and became the dominant personality among the second generation of Paris missionaries, was a dedicated and efficient organizer, but strait-laced and culture-bound.[3] Moreover the missionaries

[1] The last reference I have found to Makoanyane is dated 18 Feb. 1862, when he is described as 'Joshua, a Councillor and Generalissimo', *BR* iii. 140.

[2] Jousse's personality is shown in his reports in the *JME* and his elaborate work, *La Mission Française Évangélique au sud de l'Afrique*, 2 vols., Paris, 1889.

[3] H. Dieterlin, *Adolphe Mabille (1836–1894)*, Paris, 1898; Edwin W. Smith, *The Mabilles of Basutoland*, London, 1939.

had been intimidated by the violent white attacks on Beersheba and Morija in 1858 and by Grey's insistence that they
exceeded their proper role if they gave Moshoeshoe political
advice, as distinct from writing literal translations of his
statements.[1]

In his later years Moshoeshoe often used western-educated
junior sons as councillors and scribes, but the results were
disappointing. In 1859 Sekhonyana crossed the mountains
and tried to create his own semi-autonomous chiefdom
around the headwaters of the Mzimvubu River. Tsekelo
was an opportunist. In 1860 he quarrelled with Masopha
and Letsie and fled to Aliwal North, to pour out vicious
stories against his half-brothers to Burnet, the colonial
magistrate; and soon afterwards he led a gang of white
toughs from Bloemfontein to Lelosa's village at the foot of
Thaba Bosiu, where they tried to spike a cannon that
Moshoeshoe had installed there. Though Moshoeshoe took
him back, he next emerged as a freebooter in the Posholi
manner.[2] Tlali was more stable and loyal, but the letters he
wrote without white assistance may have failed to convey
his father's precise meaning.[3] The documents that came
closest to fulfilling the king's intentions were probably those
penned by Orpen, who visited Thaba Bosiu occasionally.
But usually Moshoeshoe had to choose between the grudging
services of a timid missionary and the imperfect work of
a junior son, while on at least one occasion he resorted to
a semi-literate British trader whose performance was far
worse than Tlali's.[4] During a period of continuous white
pressure, the lack of an efficient secretary and a mature
consultant with knowledge of the wider world was a serious
handicap.

The king's authority over his territorial chiefs had always

---

[1] The Revd. S. Hofmeyr to Sir George Grey, 28 June 1860, *BR* ii. 563.

[2] Tsekelo Moshoeshoe to Sir George Grey, 21 Feb. 1861, *BR* ii. 578; Letsie
Moshoeshoe to President, O.F.S., 1 Dec. 1862, *BR* iii. 187–8; Burnet to Secretary to High Commissioner, 20 Feb. 1865, *BR* iii. 340.

[3] e.g. Moshoeshoe ('Written by George Moshesh') to President, O.F.S.,
18 Jan. 1862, *BR* iii. 122.

[4] Charles Ross ('Command and authorize by Moshesh') to Sir George
Grey, 13 Dec. 1859, *BR* ii. 542–4.

been a matter of personal influence rather than institutionalized power. His prestige remained immense to the end of his life and at critical moments he was often able decisively to affect the course of events. But his capacity to exert continuous supervision over the kingdom gradually declined, and with it the delicate equilibrium between the centre and the parts.

Letsie, who built his new village at Matsieng, five miles east of Morija, after his former home had been destroyed in the war of 1858, had a personal interest in holding the kingdom together. However, father and heir apparent never did achieve an effective relationship. With increasing years, Moshoeshoe's characteristic mildness became more pronounced and he was more loath than ever to discipline men like Posholi and Lesaoana, while Letsie would have preferred to use force against them when they acted irresponsibly. Letsie chafed under his father's tenacious control over major decisions and in August 1862 went so far as to inform the British authorities that he had resigned his chieftainship. That quarrel was patched up, but the king and his senior son remained at loggerheads. The father had little confidence in his heir: the heir, who completed his fiftieth year in 1862, felt humiliated at being treated, as he said, like a child.[1]

Nor did Letsie manage to improve his relations with his other kinsmen. His school-educated half-brothers—Sekhonyana, Tlali, and Tsekelo—disliked him intensely and despised him as an illiterate.[2] Molapo remained aloof and hostile at Leribe and was preparing to split the kingdom when his father died.[3]

The other territorial chiefs had similar ideas. In the south, Posholi was as uncontrollable as ever, Sekhonyana was striking out on his own, and Moorosi, who had played a

[1] John Austen, Superintendent, Wittebergen Native Reserve, to Burnet, 4 Jan. 1862 and 30 Aug. 1862, *BR* iii. 112–14 and 178; Burnet to Secretary to High Commissioner, 15 Sept. 1862, *BR* iii. 179–80; Commissioner van Soelen to Acting President, O.F.S., n.d. [1863], *BR* iii. 231–2.

[2] Nehemiah [Sekhonyana] Moshoeshoe to Sir George Grey, 3 Sept. 1860, *BR* ii. 569–72; George [Tlali] and Tsekelo Moshoeshoe to Sir George Grey, 3 Sept. 1860, *BR* ii. 572.

[3] Molapo Moshoeshoe to the Revd. Pearse, Natal, 12 Nov. 1861, *BR* iii. 110–11.

negligible part in the war of 1858, was also acting auto-nomously. In the north, Mopeli and Lesaoana regarded themselves as independent of Molapo and only tenuously subordinated to Moshoeshoe, while Moletsane, like Moorosi, hankered after full independence.

As Moshoeshoe's vitality flagged, there was an upsurge of lawlessness in LeSotho. Territorial chiefs followed the king's example and vied with each other in accumulating wives and cattle and the king's younger sons joined in the scramble for wealth and power, but none of them possessed his wisdom or his self-restraint. In spite of Moshoeshoe's life-long abstinence from liquor and his prohibition on the importation and sale of trade alcohol, Letsie, for example, was described by Burnet as 'a *drunken fool*'.[1] Burnet was an unsympathetic witness who often wrote severe things about Moshoeshoe also, but this particular charge had substance. Such abuses by the chiefs affected the general welfare. Wealth became more unevenly distributed and the quality of justice in the chiefs' courts deteriorated.[2]

So the kingdom that Moshoeshoe had created and held together in his prime by his immense energy, skill, and humaneness, rather than by durable political institutions, showed serious signs of fragmentation and decay. As early as 1861 Burnet predicted that 'should anything happen to old Moshesh the country would instantly be in a state of anarchy'.[3] And in 1864 Wodehouse, the High Commissioner, shrewdly observed: 'The fact is that all these Basuto chiefs are making arrangements and trying to acquire strength in anticipation of Moshesh's death, when each will try his luck.'[4]

After concluding the Treaty of Aliwal North, both Moshoe-shoe and the Free State Government respected the boundary which the High Commissioner had personally defined with beacons between the Caledon and the Orange. On the Free State side, the Government divided up most of the land

---

[1] Burnet to Secretary to High Commissioner, 1 Sept. 1862, *BR* iii. 178.

[2] Aimé Roche, *Clartés australes: Joseph Gérard, O.M.I. (1831–1914)*, Lyons, 1951, pp. 227–8.

[3] Burnet to Secretary to High Commissioner, 25 Feb. 1861, *BR* ii. 580.

[4] Wodehouse to Edmond Wodehouse, 7 Nov. 1864, Wodehouse Papers.

formerly occupied by Africans associated with the mission
stations at Bethulie and Beersheba into farms, but allowed
Letele and his son Koane (known to Whites as Jan Letele),
who had sided with the republic in the war, to remain with
their followers on the Free State side of the border; while
Posholi, Lebenya, and their people, who had fought for
Moshoeshoe, settled close by on the other side of the border.
Neither government was able to prevent its subjects from
resuming their old habits. Posholi raided Koane; and Koane,
boasting that as Mohlomi's grandson he was Moshoeshoe's
superior, developed a particularly lucrative form of cattle-
raiding into LeSotho, encouraged by Free State farmers and
colonial traders who supplied him with arms and ammunition and disposed of his surplus booty.[1] This was a festering
sore that bedevilled relationships between the two governments, but the effects were localized. Both governments
tried to restrain their turbulent subjects and, since Posholi's
attacks were usually directed at Africans rather than Whites,
these events on Moshoeshoe's western frontier did not in
themselves precipitate another round of general hostilities.[2]

Further south, beyond the Orange, the Tees River formed
the boundary between Moorosi's chiefdom and the Witteberg Reserve (modern Herschel District) of the Cape Colony.
Moorosi claimed more territory, extending as far as the
Kraai River, but the colonial authorities were unyielding.
Since 1853 many of the Tlokoa survivors of Moshoeshoe's
great victory at Marabeng (where he had routed his old
enemy Sekonyela) had taken refuge in the Witteberg Reserve, and Moorosi's people, sometimes aided by the mobile
Posholi, raided them from time to time. Nevertheless, the
Tees frontier was generally more peaceful than Grey's line
between the Orange and the Caledon.[3]

[1] Burnet to Secretary to High Commissioner, 20 Jan. 1862, *BR* iii. 123–4;
Friend of the Orange Free State, 20 Jan. 1862, *BR* iii. 124–6.
[2] Many relevant documents in *BR* ii and iii (index entries Letele, Jan;
and Posuli); also Louis Cochet, Notes et souvenirs, SME, and reports by Cochet
in *JME* xxxiv (1859), ff.
[3] Austen to Burnet, 10 Sept. 1859 and 5 Sept. 1863, *BR* iii. 106–7 and 235–
6; J. M. Orpen, *Principles of Native Government*, Cape Town, 1880, pp. 56–64;
Richard Giddy, 5 Aug. 1864, WMS.

Elsewhere, there were two directions in which the frontiers were still relatively open and there was scope for Ba-Sotho expansion. One was in the south-east, immediately below the Drakensberg escarpment, where the land around the headwaters of the Mzimvubu and its tributaries was only sparsely inhabited by hunter-gatherers. In 1844 Britain had recognized that the area belonged to Faku, the chief of the Mpondo, who lived further south near the Indian Ocean. Later, Moshoeshoe had made an agreement with Faku in terms of which he claimed to be Faku's superior, and in 1859 Sekonyana crossed the mountains with a few followers and founded villages in the vicinity of modern Matatiele. When his neighbours, the Mpondomisi, tried to eject him, Posholi and Masopha came to his aid. However, their expedition miscarried. In the following year, 1863, a more powerful community descended into the area from the high veld. These were the Coloured people (Griqua) of Adam Kok, about three thousand strong, who had sold out their land rights in the Orange Free State to the republican government and travelled with their wagons and livestock in voortrekker style through southern LeSotho and proceeded, with the approval of the High Commissioner, to found a new East Griqualand around 'Kokstad' to the east of Matatiele. Clashes followed and early in 1865 the Griqua drove Sekhonyana and his people back across the mountains. The BaSotho push to the south had failed.[1]

It is not certain how much significance Moshoeshoe attached to Sekhonyana's movements. He was not always on good terms with Sekhonyana and he told the colonial authorities that he had not approved of the Posholi–Masopha expedition. Probably he started by giving Sekhonyana a free hand to probe the situation below the mountains, intending to send more BaSotho there if the prospects seemed good and to use it as a place of refuge if the worst came to the worst in the Caledon valley; but on the arrival of Kok, with British approval, he deemed it expedient to disclaim further interest in the area.

[1] Documents in *BR* ii and iii (index entries Nehemiah [Sekhonyana]; and Kok, Adam); also Orpen, *Principles*, pp. 17–30.

The second direction of expansion was northwards, into the fertile high veld plains that the BaSotho regarded as theirs because they had been occupied by Sotho chief-doms before the *lifaqane* wars. Since 1853 Moshoeshoe's northern territorial chiefs had been engaged in peopling the lands they had conquered from Sekonyela and Taaibosch, whose northern limits Major Warden had roughly de-fined in 1849. The Treaty of Aliwal North (1858) in-cluded the statement that the northern boundary of LeSotho, down to Jammerberg Drift on the Caledon, 'is recognized to be that as defined by the late British Resident, Major Warden',[1] but Grey had not visited that area. In about 1860 Moshoeshoe's northern chiefs (Moletsane, Molapo, Mopeli, and Lesaoana) began to probe beyond the boundary and, finding that white farms were few and far between and their owners offered no resistance, they ex-panded more and more rapidly, receiving numerous addi-tions to their numbers from the heart of LeSotho, until they were building villages as far north as the Sand River.[2] In 1863 a Free State official reported: 'The Kaffirs [*sic*] are trekking into the Free State by hundreds every day, with waggons, etc. The farmers are all leaving their farms, being afraid of the Kaffirs.'[3] In the following year, after he had inspected the area, Wodehouse, the High Commissioner, wrote:

Between fifty and sixty of finer farms than I have ever seen anywhere have been gradually abandoned before the pressure of the Basutos all along the Border. There has been no resistance—not a Basuto [*sic*] suffered in any shape. They come quietly in parties of forty or fifty, build their huts, cultivate, and turn out their cattle exactly as they please. In most cases the owners have shortly fled away. In some cases they still hold on but make no resistance.

Wodehouse added: 'The Free State have up to this time done nothing to check them; as [President] Brand professes

---

[1] *BR* ii. 476.

[2] On northern expansion, there are many documents in *BR* ii and iii (index entries Molapo; Mopeli, Paulus; Lesaoana; and Moletsane); also in *JME* xxxiv (1859), ff. and in *SAAR*, *OFS* iii and iv.

[3] Sergeant A. Gordon to Commandant Every, 24 July 1863, *BR* iii. 225.

because the Line to which they were entitled had never been marked out by the Governor of the Cape.'[1]

How much control Moshoeshoe exercised over the course of events along his northern frontier in the early 1860s is difficult to determine. In moments of exasperation white officials—colonial as well as republican—regarded him as an evil genius with no moral scruples. In 1861 Burnet informed the High Commissioner: 'Moshesh, in spite of all my friend Orpen's bolstering up, will never be anything but a great humbug, an old liar and deceiver, without one particle of truth, faith, honesty, or sincerity.'[2] Moshoeshoe's behaviour in these years was, in fact, the resultant of the operation of extremely complex forces upon the mind of an ageing monarch who saw his life's work threatened with destruction. He believed most profoundly that his people were justified in establishing control over as much of their ancestral territory as possible, and he realized that if he went too far in restraining men like Posholi, Sekhonyana, and Lesaoana his monarchy might collapse altogether and LeSotho disintegrate into a number of separate and quarrelsome chiefdoms which would fall an easy prey, one after the other, to his white neighbours. He also perceived that, ironically, the more successful his chiefs were in extending the limits of LeSotho, the greater the likelihood that they would feel strong enough to reject his authority or the authority of his successor. Finally, he retained the conviction that it was essential to conciliate the British, as an insurance policy for the future. He undoubtedly encouraged his chiefs to expand to the north; but he tried to conceal the extent of his encouragement from white officials and to restrain his chiefs from actions that might inflame white opinion in the colonies as well as the republics and bring him into collision with the High Commissioner—such as shedding white blood or transgressing the boundary which Grey had personally demarcated between the Caledon and the Orange. He also resorted to numerous devices to refrain from incurring further definitive commitments that would limit

---

[1] Wodehouse to Edmond Wodehouse, 7 Nov. 1864, Wodehouse Papers.
[2] Burnet to High Commissioner, 29 July 1861, *BR* ii. 596.

his territory or reduce the power of his monarchy. With these objectives, Moshoeshoe inexorably became involved in a diplomacy that republican and colonial officials—and even his own territorial chiefs—often found devious.

2. *The Origins of the War of 1865*

Moshoeshoe was fortunate that for five years after the Treaty of Aliwal North his Free State neighbours were enfeebled by poor morale, internal discord, and weak government. Military defeat had revitalized the old issue of republican purity versus accommodation with Britain. Initially President Boshof and the colonial element persuaded a Volksraad majority to endorse Grey's proposal for a federation under the British Crown; but in 1859 London vetoed Grey's federation scheme, Boshof resigned, and the out-and-out republicans regained the upper hand, securing the election of M. W. Pretorius as President of the Orange Free State.

Pretorius, who was also President of a nearly united Transvaal, known as the South African Republic, with its capital at Pretoria, intended to use his dual offices to consummate the union of all the white communities north of the Orange River; but he soon lost the support of a section of the Transvaalers, who feared his policy would imperil their own independence, as Grey had threatened. The Pretoria Volksraad therefore made him choose between the two presidencies. He opted for Bloemfontein, but even so he could not refrain from encouraging his Transvaal supporters to rebel against the government in Pretoria. The Transvaal then relapsed into anarchy and Pretorius was an ineffective and frequently absentee president of the Orange Free State until 1863, when he resigned from Bloemfontein to concentrate on Transvaal affairs.

Then at last the Free State elected a President who, like Boshof but more successfully, applied himself to consolidating the territory as a separate republic, establishing good relations with his white neighbours to the south as well as the north, and dealing firmly with LeSotho. This was J. H.

Brand, son of the Speaker of the Cape House of Assembly
and himself an accomplished lawyer. The Free State's
period of weak leadership and divided loyalties was over,
and Brand swiftly mounted a diplomatic offensive against
Moshoeshoe, backed by a more united electorate and growing military strength.[1]

So long as the Free State was weak, Moshoeshoe's decline
did not have serious consequences. Frontier incidents frequently caused friction between the two governments and
there were several crises, but the Free State was in no
condition to wage war and Moshoeshoe had no desire to do
so. Generally, the king was careful to keep Free State
officials at arm's length, pleading his age and his health.
In February 1859, for example, he sent Tsekelo and other
junior kinsmen to attend a sitting of the Volksraad in Bloemfontein, with instructions to listen but to agree to nothing,
and in January 1860 he had Letsie represent him at a
conference with the Acting President to discuss the incessant raids and counter-raids across the Caledon–Orange
boundary.[2]

In May 1860, however, Moshoeshoe himself met Pretorius
at Wonderkop near modern Ladybrand. According to an
eye-witness, Moshoeshoe started by subjecting Pretorius to
'an oration of 3 hours continuance', which 'was followed
by several of his Chiefs in the same strain'. When Pretorius's
turn came, the king and his men applauded the President's
declaration that he was there 'to place you Moshesh,
Captains and people of the Basuto Nation, in my arms,
and there you shall all rest in security, lovingly'.[3] Next day
Moshoeshoe put his mark to a document concocted by the
President. To settle frontier disputes there was to be a mixed
court composed of a magistrate, two men appointed by

[1] F. A. van Jaarsveld, *Die Eenheidstrewe van die Republiekeinse Afrikaners*,
ch. 8; *OHSA* i. 431–5; M. C. E. van Schoor, 'Johannes Henricus Brand', in
W. J. de Kock (ed.), *Dictionary of South African Biography*, i. 110–17.

[2] Minutes of the OFS Volksraad, 16 Feb. 1859, *SAAR*, *OFS* iv. 19–22;
Minutes of Meeting between the Acting President of the O.F.S. and Representatives of the Chief Moshesh, 10 Jan. 1860, *BR* ii. 547–8.

[3] Account of a Conference between the President of the O.F.S. and the
Chief Moshesh, 30 Apr. 1860, *BR* ii. 560.

Pretorius, and two men appointed by Moshoeshoe. There was also to be a frontier police force of 220 men supplied by Moshoeshoe. Moreover, the document stated, 'The law shall be the same for all.'[1] The eye-witness account continued: 'The party then retired to partake of a dejeuner, during which several toasts were drunk' and Moshoeshoe's sons sang songs to the tune of 'God Save the Queen' and 'Home Sweet Home', after which 'Moshesh passed the night in Mr. Pretorius's tent, and the next morning he and Mr. Pretorius reviewed a portion of the Basuto army, numbering about 6,000 cavalry. Thereafter several salvos were fired by the Basutos. Moshesh danced like mad, and thus the conference broke up.'[2] All this was an elaborate charade. The mixed court was never established, the Ba-Sotho police force was never recruited, and genuine equality before the law for Blacks with Whites was the last thing Pretorius ever contemplated. Nor was Moshoeshoe duped by the theatrical atmosphere. From his African diplomatic network he was well aware that Pretorius was capable of brutality towards Africans.[3]

Early in 1862 a severe raid by Posholi across the Caledon–Orange boundary led to a major crisis. Expecting war, the farmers living near the border went into laager and traders left LeSotho, mindful of what had happened in 1858. However, Pretorius visited the area and when he discovered that Posholi's raid had been in retaliation for the forays of Koane, a Free State subject, aided and abetted by some of the frontier farmers, he reprimanded the farmers and took steps to control Koane.[4]

The situation in the north-east was more inflammatory. The Wonderkop agreement of May 1860 said nothing about the location of Moshoeshoe's northern boundary. At that stage Pretorius seems to have assumed that to leave it imprecise would be to the advantage of the Whites.[5] By 1861,

---

[1] Treaty between the O.F.S. and the Chief Moshesh, *BR* ii. 556: 'Die Wet zal gelijk wezen voor alle.'

[2] Account of a Conference, *BR* ii. 562.

[3] Memorandum by J. M. Orpen, 26 June 1861, *BR* ii. 590–1.

[4] Cochet, Notes et souvenirs, pp. 131–8; documents in *BR* iii. 115–37.

[5] Memorandum by J. M. Orpen, 26 June 1861, *BR* ii. 590–1.

however, it was apparent that the BaSotho were advancing and the Whites retreating. In April that year Pretorius and Moshoeshoe agreed on the location of a short section of the boundary, extending northwards from Jammerberg Drift (the eastern end of the line defined in detail by Grey) to the source of the Modder River, but that still left everything east of the Modder River in dispute.[1] Warden had roughly described the northern limits of the territories of Sekonyela and Taaibosch in 1849, but any beacons he may have placed there had vanished. In September 1861 the landdrost of Bloemfontein went to Thaba Bosiu to try to settle the question, but after convening a meeting of his councillors and territorial chiefs Moshoeshoe informed him that he did not recognize any boundary in the north. The BaSotho attitude was summed up by the comments of a chief who said: 'Is there any one here who was present on that line when beacons were placed in the time of Sikonyela and Gert Taaibosch? Are the Basutos the heirs of Sikonyela and Taaibosch that a limit should be imposed on them which they had not made themselves? We know the boundary line along which Sir George Grey placed beacons, but with regard to any other we know nothing about them.'[2]

Thereafter the chiefs accelerated their drive to the north and Moshoeshoe evaded every effort by the Free State to pin him down to a specific northern boundary. In March 1862 he was unyielding to a Volksraad commission that visited Thaba Bosiu.[3] In June, responding to a Free State invitation, he did send Mopeli and Tlali as his commissioners to observe the beaconing of a northern boundary, but the Free State Commissioners did not appear.[4] In March 1863 Free State officials placed beacons through the disputed zone in the presence of one of Moshoeshoe's junior sons, but the

---

[1] Meeting between the President of the O.F.S. and the Chief Moshesh, 12 Apr. 1861, and Proclamation by President Pretorius, 18 Apr. 1861, *BR* ii. 582–4.

[2] Account of an Interview between the Landdrost of Bloemfontein and the Chief Moshesh, 23 Sept. 1861, *BR* ii. 601.

[3] Report of the Commission sent by the Government of the O.F.S. to the Chief Moshesh, 21 Mar. 1862, *BR* iii. 153–8.

[4] Moshoeshoe to President, O.F.S., 19 June 1862, *BR* iii. 173.

king refused to recognize the boundary as beaconed.[1]
Three months later he informed a Free State delegation at
Morija: 'I *do* consent to a limit being made in the Winburg
and Harrismith districts. This answer has been agreed to
by my headmen at a meeting we had yesterday here at
Morija. Yes, we wish really that a limit be set down, but
we say, let it be convenient and agreeable to both nations.'[2]
J. J. Venter, who was Acting President after Pretorius resigned, was no more successful. In October 1863 Moshoeshoe
frightened him away from the disputed zone by confronting
him with a regiment of warriors.[3] Finally, in November,
Moshoeshoe attended a meeting at Platberg, but after a
brief discussion he went home and sent Venter a written
counter-proposal, claiming land which the Free State
declared would cut off 250 farms owned by white men who
held titles issued under British authority by the Sovereignty
administration.[4] That was how matters stood when Brand
assumed the presidency of the Free State in February 1864.

Meanwhile Moshoeshoe had been conducting a more constructive diplomacy with the British. In April 1859, in the
garbled letter written by the trader Charles Ross, he complained to Grey of 'the griefs and pains occasioned by the
encroachments and the cowardly and shameful wars by the
Boers!' and he asked for a British alliance and for educa-
tional, technical, and political aid:

And we hope to see soon established in our country industrial
Institution schools Hospital! and roads and even bridges in
prosperity! and many other branches of useful trades, so as to
raise our Rising children to that rank of a Nation! We hope also
of seeing men of better ability soon come to live with us, so as
to help us in this great work. We fell now the impossibility of
remaining any longer alone without a better system of Government and a new constitution, and also a right and just law. . . .[5]

[1] Minutes of a Meeting held at Morija, 28 May 1863, *BR* iii. 204–6.
[2] Moshoeshoe to Acting President, O.F.S., 29 May 1863, *BR* iii. 209.
[3] Austen to Burnet, 10 Oct. 1863, *BR* iii. 237.
[4] Moshoeshoe to Acting President, O.F.S., 25 Nov. 1863, *BR* iii. 239–40.
[5] Charles Ross (for Moshoeshoe) to Sir George Grey, 13 Dec. 1859, *BR*
ii. 543–4.

The High Commissioner was in no hurry to respond to this request, but when Queen Victoria's young second son, Prince Alfred, visited South Africa in 1860, Grey arranged for him to grant Moshoeshoe an interview at Aliwal North. The old king treated the Queen's son with deference he had never shown to any other white man and he handed him a written request:

My trust has always been in the Queen from the first, and I am the oldest of Her Majesty's servants and subjects in this country, and during all the governorship of the Queen's Ministers in this country, from Napier, Maitland, and H. Smith, down to Sir George Clerk, and in spite of everything that has happened to me, and in the midst of many troubles, I have been faithful in my allegiance to Her Majesty. My prayer to-day is that I may be restored to the same position among the Queen's servants that I first held, for I am become as the least of them. Let whatever fault I may have committed be to-day forgiven. You are the Queen's own Son, give me peace in her name.[1]

No action was taken on Moshoeshoe's pleas in Grey's time, but in his final report on LeSotho before he left South Africa in August 1861, Grey recommended that a special agent—and he suggested Orpen—should be sent to Thaba Bosiu to find out exactly what Moshoeshoe had in mind.[2]

Grey's successor was Sir Philip Wodehouse, aged 50, who had previously been Governor of British Guiana. Wodehouse was a realist with an independent mind and a strong will, and his judgement was less clouded by racial arrogance than that of the other British governors who served in South Africa. He has usually been regarded by white historians of South Africa as a 'bad governor', largely because he did not agree that white colonists should be given unqualified control over African and Coloured populations. For Moshoeshoe, however, he would eventually prove to be the type of Queen's representative he had been hoping to deal with ever since the 1830s.[3]

[1] Moshoeshoe to Prince Alfred, 18 Aug. 1860, *BR* ii. p. 568.

[2] Grey to Secretary of State, 14 Aug. 1861, *BR* ii. 597–8.

[3] J. J. Breitenbach, 'Sir Philip Edmond Wodehouse', in W. J. de Kock (ed.), *Dictionary of South African Biography*, i. 882–6; W. P. Morrell, *British Colonial Policy in the Mid-Victorian Age*, ch. 5.

In February 1862 Wodehouse sent Burnet and Orpen to explain to Moshoeshoe what British annexation would involve: 'neither he nor any of his subordinate chiefs could therafter be permitted to exercise unrestricted jurisdiction', for they would 'be required to submit to the jurisdiction of European Magistrates'.[1] During February, Orpen and Burnet spent nine days at Thaba Bosiu while Moshoeshoe and his councillors and territorial chiefs grappled with the implications of Wodehouse's letter.[2] Eventually, expressing their consensus, Moshoeshoe replied that ever since 1843 he had regarded himself as a British subject and a soldier of the Queen. He desired to have a sympathetic Agent stationed at Thaba Bosiu to provide regular contact with the British authorities and to advise him on political matters. He wished to be able to buy arms and ammunition. He would yield his right to inflict capital punishment (which he rarely used) and to make war without British consent. But he did not want British magistrates to be appointed, nor British laws to supersede SeSotho customs without the approval of his councillors and chiefs.

If the Government send Magistrates the Basutos will not understand. It will be like a stone which is too heavy for them to carry. What I desire is, that the Queen should send a man to live with me, who will be her ear and eye, and also her hand to work with me in political matters. . . . He should be a man who would be fully trusted by everybody, and he must know our ignorance and our ways. I fear to put my people under something which they cannot understand, they are like little children who must first be taught the A B C.[3]

In short, 'If I obtain an agent, I will be under the Queen as her subject, and my people will be her subjects also, but under me.'[4] Pressed to explain his attitude to his previous agreements with the British officials, Moshoeshoe placed a

[1] Instructions for the guidance of John Burnet and Joseph M. Orpen, 28 Jan. 1862, *BR* iii. 131.
[2] Minutes of Conferences, 11–21 Feb. 1862, and Report of the Commissioners, 22 Feb. 1862, *BR* iii. 138–51.
[3] Ibid., p. 143.
[4] Ibid., p. 144.

desk on the table in front of him, a letter on top of the desk, and a hat on the letter, and said

The table itself is the foundation of all, my original Napier treaty. The tablecloth is the minute of Sir Peregrine Maitland. The bottom of the desk is the minute of Smith, the upper part of the desk is what Sir George Clerk told me. The letter lying on the desk is that of Sir George Grey, in which he promises that my relations with Government will be recommended for consideration, and the hat upon the top is the arrangement I have now been proposing for the consideration of the Queen. . . . My connection with Government has been growing from the beginning. . . . Suppose the treaties are said to be dead, they are like grandparents in their graves, but their descendants are alive still.[1]

Wodehouse forwarded the report of Burnet and Orpen to London and asked permission to appoint a resident agent at Thaba Bosiu. The Colonial Secretary agreed, but Wodehouse did not carry on with the plan.[2] Pretorius, as President of the Orange Free State, travelled to Cape Town in the middle of 1862 to lobby the new High Commissioner, who had had no previous experience of southern Africa; and, as Wodehouse later admitted, 'The President . . . exhibited so much apprehension as to the selection of the agent, that I allowed the proposal to fall to the ground.'[3] No doubt Pretorius feared that Wodehouse would have appointed Orpen, who had known the Free State from within and, since the mid-1850s, had become dedicated to the BaSotho cause and regarded by the burghers as a dangerous enemy.[4] Pretorius also asked Wodehouse to supervise the beaconing of the northern boundary of LeSotho, which Grey had omitted to do, but Wodehouse, who had problems enough to keep him busy in the Cape Colony, declined to perform the task himself. Instead, he proposed to appoint a commission to mark the boundary if both parties agreed, but

[1] *BR* iii. 146.
[2] Wodehouse to Secretary of State, 19 Apr. 1862, *BR* iii. 163–4; F. Rogers, pp. Secretary of State, to Wodehouse, 5 June 1862, *BR* iii. 169.
[3] Wodehouse to Secretary of State, 13 Oct. 1865, *BR* iii. 494.
[4] Brand to Wodehouse, 5 Aug. 1864, *BR* iii. 290.

Moshoeshoe replied that he preferred to deal directly with the Free State.[1] Throughout 1863 there was no change in Moshoeshoe's relationships with the British authorities and, as we have seen, his people continued to exploit their neighbours' weakness by occupying land beyond Warden's boundary in the Winburg and Harrismith districts.

Moshoeshoe's respite from white pressure ended abruptly when J. H. Brand became President of the Orange Free State. On 5 February 1864, three days after he had taken his oath of office, Brand drew the High Commissioner's attention to Article 2 of the Treaty of Aliwal North, which stated that the High Commissioner, or commissioners appointed by him, would mark out the boundary between LeSotho and the Free State, and he asked Wodehouse to delimit the section that Grey had neglected to do.[2] Wodehouse replied that he would act as requested provided that Moshoeshoe agreed, and he sent Burnet to Thaba Bosiu to sound out the king.[3] Moshoeshoe was hesitant. Burnet explained that the treaty he had signed in 1858 clearly stated that Warden's line was his northern boundary. Moshoeshoe wished to obtain the confidence of the High Commissioner, but knew he would strain the allegiance of his northern chiefs if he was party to depriving them of the territory they had occupied during the last few years. With great difficulty Burnet managed to persuade him to sign a document consenting that Wodehouse should personally delimit the boundary. Then, reporting to Wodehouse, Burnet recommended that the Free State should be 'very accommodating . . . otherwise it is very doubtful whether Moshesh could clear his people out . . . without actual bloodshed'.[4] The Free State was not accommodating. The Volksraad had insisted that no modifications should be made in Warden's line without the approval of Free State commissioners and Brand himself took a lawyer's view of the

[1] Wodehouse to Moshoeshoe, 26 Aug. 1862, *BR* iii. 177–8; Wodehouse to Acting President, O.F.S., 21 Oct. 1862, *BR* iii. 184.
[2] Brand to Wodehouse, 5 Feb. 1864, *BR* iii. 250–2.
[3] Wodehouse to Brand, 12 Feb. 1864, *BR* iii. 253–4.
[4] Burnet to Wodehouse, 29 Feb. 1864, *BR* iii. 263.

matter: the treaty, and nothing but the treaty, must be enforced.[1]

Wodehouse travelled to Aliwal North in March 1864 intending to proceed with the marking of the boundary, but when he discovered how rigid the Free State attitude was he returned to Cape Town, telling Brand, 'I can anticipate no good result from my attempting to mediate with a Commission whose powers are thus restricted.'[2] The President, aware that the BaSotho were pressing forward as vigorously as ever into the Harrismith and Winburg districts, then convened a special session of the Volksraad, which passed a resolution reiterating the invitation to Wodehouse to intervene and authorizing him to 'make such modifications in the strict description of the line of Major Warden to the north of Jammerberg Drift . . . as His Excellency may consider just and reasonable and calculated to ensure the maintenance of peaceful relations'.[3]

In October 1864 Wodehouse did beacon off the disputed northern boundary. The memoranda submitted to him showed that the basic assumptions of the two parties were irreconcilable. The core of the Free State case was that in 1858 Moshoeshoe had given his written assent to the Warden line as his northern boundary, and in legal terms that case was completely watertight.[4] Moshoeshoe's claims rested on premises that placed natural rights, in terms of prior occupation and present needs, above treaty commitments. He submitted a list of names of chiefs and clans, and the regions they had formerly occupied, to show 'the true extent of Basutoland which has been taken away by the white men'. His memorandum concluded:

By the preceding list of deserted lands we explain and clearly maintain that this country belongs to us Blacks. We are now crowded together, and we ask why we should be further molested. Having taken so much country, are the white men not content? I point to the deserted Villages of the many Chiefs I have mentioned, and I ask if the ruined walls do not prove that those

[1] Brand to Wodehouse, 8 Mar. 1864, *BR* iii. 264–6.
[2] Wodehouse to Brand, 16 Mar. 1864, *BR* iii. 269.
[3] Minutes of O.F.S. Volksraad, 5 May 1864, *BR* iii. 280.
[4] Memorandum, n.d., *BR* iii. 299–303.

lands are theirs? If the day of equitable settlement has come, have these people not a right to be restored to their old habitations? All these Chiefs are now in my Country, and I say behold and judge between us.[1]

As a result of the report he had received from Burnet and Orpen, Wodehouse approached his task with considerable sympathy for Moshoeshoe and his people, but being rooted in a culture of written contractual obligations it was virtually inevitable that he should accept the premises and with them the conclusions of the Free State memorandum. After holding a conference with Moshoeshoe and others at Jammerberg Drift, he travelled north-eastwards through the disputed zone to near the headwaters of the Caledon River, accompanied by Burnet, by Free State commissioners, and by Tsekelo, Molapo, Mopeli, Moletsane, and Tlali, and he was shocked to observe that on the northern side of Warden's line several thousand BaSotho were occupying land that contained between fifty and sixty abandoned white homesteads.[2] Next, retracing his tracks, he beaconed off the boundary along Warden's line as accurately as he could. He then wrote to Moshoeshoe, explaining his actions and asking the king to 'give such directions as will lead to the speedy restoration to their lawful owners of the lands improperly appropriated, and effectually check all encroachments for the time to come'.[3] At the same time he urged Brand to 'allow the Chief full time for the removal of his people from the farms on which they are living'.[4] Wodehouse expressed his apprehensions of the consequences of his labours in a private letter to his son:

What the political results of my mission will be it is hard to say. I gave my Award at Aliwal and sent it to both parties. It is quite in favour of the Boers—and really could not be otherwise. The Line I have given does not give to the Free State one single farm which was not held under the authority of the British Government before the Free State came into existence, according to the admission of the Basutos themselves. . . .

[1] List of Refugee Chiefs in Basutoland, n.d., *BR* iii. 303–4.
[2] Daumas, Mekoatleng, 3 Nov. 1864, *JME* xl (1865), 14–19.
[3] Wodehouse to Moshoeshoe, 28 Oct. 1864, *BR* iii. 308.
[4] Wodehouse to Brand, 28 Oct. 1864, *BR* iii. 309.

Moshesh promised to abide by my decisions, and very possibly he and Letsie would be quite disposed to do so—but I doubt his power to compel Molapo and Paulus Moperi [Mopeli], the Chiefs immediately interested, to withdraw their people . . .

I can hardly bring myself to believe that the Free State will fairly screw themselves up for a fight . . .[1]

Early in November Moshoeshoe received Wodehouse's letter and another from Brand ordering him to remove his people from the Free State side of the line by the end of the month.[2] Missionaries reported that Moshoeshoe was 'desperately wounded'; 'the man was suffering and writhing'.[3] However, Orpen returned to LeSotho and urged Moshoeshoe and his subordinates to yield, holding out the hope that if they accepted Wodehouse's unpalatable decision the British Government might protect them from further Free State aggression. Letsie, who had no followers in the north, was relatively easily persuaded. Molapo and Mopeli, who had most to lose, were bitter:

I could see Moperi's lips quiver as he spoke about the narrow Lesuto that one could cross and recross in a day, and the wide open lands of the Boers which it would take weeks to pass over, and he said, 'What a destroyer without pity the white man is. Where are we to go? Where are we and our children to live?' And Molapo, while talking of his hastening to obey, broke out into a bitter laugh as he said, 'How am I to explain it to my people, that they are to leave their own villages where they were born?'[4]

After listening to Orpen—the only white man from whom he was willing to take such uncongenial advice—Moshoeshoe held a private meeting of his councillors and territorial chiefs, who agreed, some with extreme reluctance, to abide by the High Commissioner's verdict for the present, but only on condition that they would resist future Free State demands whenever that could be done without alienating the British authorities. Then, on 14 November, the king convened a great *pitso*, where the chiefs let off steam before

---

[1] Wodehouse to Edmond Wodehouse, 7 Nov. 1864, Wodehouse Papers.
[2] Brand to Wodehouse, 4 Nov. 1864, *BR* iii. 310–11.
[3] Orpen to Burnet, 14 Nov. 1864, *BR* iii. 313.   [4] Ibid.

publicly committing themselves to accepting Wodehouse's decision. According to Orpen, who had it from his MoSotho servant who was present:

Every Chief, till it came to the turn of Letsie, and then of Moshesh, spoke in favour of war. I believe, from my previous conversation with Molapo, that he had already come round, but that he did not dare to shew it, and spoke therefore with a view to his people's feelings.

The substance of the speeches was that the Boers were increasing in power, and that they would not remain satisfied with any line, but would endeavour eventually to take the whole country and reduce the Basutos to complete subjugation, as has been done over the Vaal River with the natives there and their country, that therefore the earliest opportunity to fight was the best. One said: Moshesh, the Boers are not asking, they are demanding, they are beginning to rule, if you wish to sell us as slaves to the Boers, please consent to their making war upon us and let us be beaten, and then we shall become obedient slaves, and they will be shooting us every day. Another said: We may consent to give in to-day, provided you also give now liberty that when a Boer next shoot a Mosuto we may at once rush into the Free State and commence the war. Will you allow that? And Moshesh not answering, they cried for war again, and every passionate speech in favour of war was loudly applauded.

Letsie said: God had been against them and it was useless to contend, they must give in on this occasion. Moshesh said: You speak of war, but are you ready for it, the Boers pay taxes and purchase food and weapons and are able to carry on a war, but what am I to feed my troops with? They cried: Tax us, take our cattle, sheep, anything, but don't let us be made slaves of the Boers. But Moshesh said, No, he would not enter into a war on the line question, which the Governor had already decided against them. They were in this *governed*, but some other cause might arise, and they must immediately remove the people, all in one day, instantly. And then each Chief gave in his adhesion with great respect and promising instant obedience.[1]

After that *pitso* Molapo and Mopeli ordered their followers to evacuate their villages on the northern side of the line and by the end of November a stream of refugees was passing southwards with livestock, corn supplies, and

[1] Orpen to Burnet, 25 Nov. 1864, *BR* iii. 316.

other movable property. Later, President Brand yielded
to repeated requests by Moshoeshoe and Molapo and
allowed men to return to reap their summer harvest until
the end of February 1865.[1] By that time the territory to
the north of the boundary was almost completely clear of
BaSotho and in March the High Commissioner congratu-
lated Moshoeshoe on 'the loyalty and wisdom' of 'your
conduct':

> At the time when I found myself under the necessity of com-
> municating to you my decision on the disputed boundary, I was
> perfectly sensible that the task of enforcing obedience to it on
> the part of the people of your tribe must be most unwelcome,
> and would require a great sacrifice of personal feelings on the
> part both of yourself and of the other Basuto chiefs, through
> whom your orders must be carried into effect. The result has
> been most creditable, and has given your people fresh claims on
> the friendship of the British Government . . .[2]

The king's diplomacy was bearing fruit. He had averted
the danger of a British alliance with his neighbour.

Meanwhile the local tensions did not in fact relax. Many
Free State burghers were longing to avenge their humiliation
of 1858 and President Brand was providing the firm leadership that had been lacking since Boshof resigned. Moreover he was underestimating the mood and the morale of the
BaSotho, for he assumed that they had evacuated the
northern side of the line because he had mobilized a commando, whereas it was the decision of the *pitso*, based on
quite different reasons, that had caused them to withdraw.[3]
On the BaSotho side, Moshoeshoe, Letsie, and Molapo
had no wish to precipitate a general war, but they were not
able to prevent others from giving expression to their pent-
up feelings. Posholi persisted in his rustling activities in the
south; Tsekelo helped himself to horses in the Winburg
district; and Mopeli's people seized and ill-treated three

---

[1] Letters from Moshoeshoe and Molapo to President Brand, 22 Nov. 1864
ff., G.S. 1340, OFS; Coillard, 5 Dec. 1864, *JME* xl (1865), 137–9; Volksraad
Minutes, 9–10 Feb. 1865, *BR* iii. 336–40.

[2] Wodehouse to Moshoeshoe, 13 Mar. 1865, *BR* iii. 343.

[3] Brand to Moshoeshoe, 25 Aug. 1865, *BR* iii. 446.

burghers.[1] The principal flash-point was in the far north-east, where Moshoeshoe's nephew and son-in-law Lesaoana occupied the mountainous country around the headwaters of the Caledon on both sides of Wodehouse's beacons. Lesaoana was a talented and intelligent man, but ambitious and foolhardy. There is no evidence that he attended the great *pitso* in November when the other chiefs more or less reluctantly agreed to evacuate the Free State, and, rather than doing so, he stood firm and raided white homesteads and cattle.[2]

In May 1865, having failed to persuade Moshoeshoe to discipline Lesaoana, Brand directed a commando to drive him out of Free State territory and ordered Moshoeshoe to stand aside.[3] Moshoeshoe was slow in replying and then he declined to say whether he would or would not assist his nephew.[4] In fact he did not help him, but Brand had decided to put an end to BaSotho infringements of Free State territory once and for all. After expelling Lesaoana, he issued a proclamation on 9 June rehearsing his charges and concluding:

Rise, then, burghers of the Orange Free State! To arms, in the name of God, for the defence of your rights and the protection of your homesteads and property, and for the suppression of the arrogance and violence of the Basutos! Be courageous and strong, and put your trust in the Righteous Judge who hears the prayer of faith.

And all ye fellow countrymen who are connected with us by ties of blood and friendship, flock to our banners and fight on our side.[5]

Moshoeshoe issued a counter-blast designed specially for consumption by the British authorities:

I make this proclamation in order to show that I am not wishing to fight with the Queen or any of her subjects, but only to protect my people from the aggression of the Free State

[1] Burnet to Secretary to High Commissioner, 20 Feb. and 22 May 1865, *BR* iii. 340, 351.
[2] On Lesaoana, A. Sekese, *Leselinyana*, 15 Jan. and 1 Feb. 1893, and many documents in *BR* iii and *JME*.
[3] Brand to Moshoeshoe, 18 May 1865, *BR* iii. 350–1.
[4] Moshoeshoe to Brand, 25 May 1865, *BR* iii. 351–2.
[5] Brand's War Proclamation, 9 June 1865, *BR* iii. 360.

Government, and I trust that my English neighbours will act as fairly towards me as I sincerely intend to act towards them, and that they will not assist the boers openly or secretly to crush me, for all persons know that my great sin is that I possess a good and fertile country.[1]

3. *Military Disasters*[2]

In the ensuing war about 5,000 burghers saw service at one time or another in the Free State commandos and about 20,000 warriors in the BaSotho regiments.[3] The Free State's fighting strength was increased by several hundred white volunteers from the British colonies, by a couple of thousand African allies (notably Moroka's Rolong from Thaba 'Nchu and several Tlokoa and Mfengu groups from Moorosi's country and the Witteberg Reserve), and, for a short time, by a commando from the South African Republic which declared war in August 1865.[4] On the other hand, although Moshoeshoe had been in contact with the Zulu king Mpande, his powerful son Cetshwayo, and several Transvaal chiefs on the eve of the war, he received no help from them or from any other African community.[5]

[1] Moshoeshoe's War Proclamation, n.d., *BR* iii. 362.

[2] Works on the war of 1865–6 include Wm. W. Collins, *Free Statia*, pp. 214–37; John George Fraser, *Episodes in My Life*, Cape Town, 1922, pp. 29–55, 415–18; J. J. G. Grobbelaar, 'Die Vrystaatse Republiek en Die Basoetoevraagstuk', *AYB*, 1939, ii; Sir Godfrey Lagden, *The Basutos*, 2 vols., London, 1909, ii. 339–99; Edwin W. Smith, *The Mabilles of Basutoland*, pp. 141–80; G. Tylden, *The Rise of the Basuto*, pp. 88–103; Jean van der Poel, 'Basutoland as a Factor in South African Politics (1858–1870)', *AYB*, 1941, i. 196–207; and twelve anonymous articles in *Leselinyana*, Oct. 1899–Mar. 1900.

[3] Collins, p. 268, says the Free State sent a total of '5,000 to 6,000 armed and able bodied men' on Commando during the war; Fraser, p. 417, says, 'the greatest number under arms at the same time ... did not exceed 2,500 men.' In 1864 Eugène Casalis estimated that the total population of LeSotho was at least 150,000 (*JME* xxxix (1864), 129); in 1869 J. H. Bowker, British Agent, estimated that on the eve of the war '125,000 people looked upon Moshesh as their Chief' (Bowker to Wodehouse, 27 Aug. 1869, BR V. 286); R. S. Webb, *Gazetteer for Basutoland*, Paarl, 1950, Part II, p. 50, cites an estimate of 175,000 as the total population of LeSotho in 1865.

[4] Proclamation by President Pretorius, South African Republic, 7 Aug. 1865, *BR* iii. 434.

[5] Moshoeshoe to Arbousset, n.d. [1860–1], *JME* xxxvi (1861), 84–5; Coillard, n.d., *JME* xxxvii (1862), 408–9; Report of Missionary Conference, 29 Apr. 1864, *JME* xxxix (1864), 287.

The Free State had a great advantage in *matériel*. Their basic weapon was still the double-barrelled muzzle-loading rifle, which they began to replace with the more effective Whitworth breech-loader in 1865,[1] whereas the BaSotho continued to use their traditional assagais and battle-axes plus a varied assortment of guns, mainly inferior smooth-bore muzzle-loaders. Both sides also had several field-pieces. The BaSotho had managed to smuggle in a few cannons and to cast others with the help of British military deserters, and the Free State had imported artillery from Britain, but their value was psychological rather than physical.[2]

After the first few months the crucial factor was the replenishment of arms and ammunition and here the Free State benefited from the Sand River and Bloemfontein Conventions, under which they were able to import British military equipment through normal trade channels via the Cape Colony, whereas once the fighting started very few traders were willing to defy the colonial laws and white public opinion to supply the BaSotho. Consequently, though Wodehouse proclaimed British neutrality,[3] the British role was by no means completely passive. However, the dependence of the Free State on the Cape Colony for arms and

---

[1] Fraser, p. 418.

[2] Tylden, pp. 91–2; Anthony Atmore and Peter Sanders, 'Sotho Arms and Ammunition in the Nineteenth Century', *JAH* xii (4) (1971), 535–45.

[3] Proclamation, 27 June 1865, *BR* iii. 370–1. Anthony Atmore, on pp. 283–4 of 'The Passing of Sotho Independence 1865–1870', in Leonard Thompson (ed.), *African Societies in Southern Africa*, says that the British prohibition of the sale of arms and ammunition to the BaSotho was 'based upon a legal fallacy, a fact of which Wodehouse was perfectly aware'. This was not so. In all his communications, including the two dispatches cited by Atmore, Wodehouse interpreted the Bloemfontein Convention of 1854, in conjunction with the Sand River Convention of 1852, as meaning that Britain was bound to supply both the republics with all the arms and ammunition they might desire to purchase and was obliged not to allow their sale to the BaSotho. Wodehouse regretted this, but I know of no evidence that he or anyone in the Colonial Office doubted this interpretation of the Conventions. Thus on 2 January 1866 Wodehouse explained to Cardwell, the Secretary of State, that 'Up to this time, and notwithstanding the professed desire of this Government to remain perfectly neutral, I have strictly observed these very unequal treaties, and while withholding supplies from the Basutos, have permitted the Free State to purchase all they needed' (*BR* iii. 582).

ammunition gave the British authorities a powerful diplomatic lever. Grey, the High Commissioner, had already used the threat to cut off the arms trade to prevent the amalgamation of the two republics. Wodehouse held it as a sword of Damocles over the Free State.

Both sides started the fresh round of warfare with shaky political and military systems. In their eleven years as an independent people the Free Staters had been torn by internal dissensions under a series of short-term presidents and acting presidents. In and after 1865 their elected Commandant-General, J. J. Fick, was still not able to create a cohesive army out of commandos recruited on a territorial basis and military discipline remained extremely lax.[1] At critical moments burghers disobeyed orders or simply deserted and went home, and the effective military strength of the Free State was always far short of the potential. However, President Brand was an energetic man in the prime of life. Staking his career on victory, he managed to sustain morale sufficiently well to prevent a recurrence of the débâcle of 1858.

Moshoeshoe remained at Thaba Bosiu throughout the war, outwardly calm and serene, but his intellectual as well as his physical powers were diminishing at the very time when his people needed firm, martial leadership. He could not prevent his more foolhardy kinsmen from committing irresponsible actions, nor did he have the will to discipline them when they had done so. Letsie and Molapo lost confidence in him and, consumed by their jealousy, they acted independently of each other. There was scarcely any central control over the BaSotho conduct of the war and the kingdom virtually disintegrated into separate chiefdoms, each pursuing its own interests and falling victim piecemeal to Free State commandos. Nevertheless, Moshoeshoe clung desperately to his diplomatic lifeline with the British authorities, sending them messages and letters complaining of Free State atrocities, denouncing the arms clauses of the Conventions, and insisting always that he was a loyal subject of the Queen.

[1] See, e.g., eye-witness accounts of the attempts to storm Thaba Bosiu in August 1865 in *BR* iii. 450–5, Collins, pp. 220–5, and Fraser, pp. 45–53.

At first the fighting followed much the same course as in 1858. The BaSotho sent their cattle and sheep into the mountains, and regiments under Posholi, Masopha, Molapo, and Lesaoana raided Free State territory. The main Free State army concentrated in the north and fought its way past Viervoet, across the Caledon River, and over the Berea mountain to the foot of Thaba Bosiu, where it was joined by a commando under Louis Wepener which had advanced from the south-west. In August the Free Staters made two attempts to assault Thaba Bosiu under cover of artillery fire. Either would have succeeded if the burghers had been disciplined, but both failed. In the second attack Louis Wepener led a party up the Rafutho pass on the north-west side of the mountain and was courageously trying to find a way round the walled fortification that blocked the top of the pass when he was shot dead, and soon afterwards the BaSotho charged down the mountainside and routed the Whites.[1] The Mountain by Night withstood its last attack in Moshoeshoe's lifetime and Brand joined the long succession of leaders whose men had failed to storm it: Matiwane, Sekonyela, Mzilikazi, Cathcart, and Boshof.

After surviving these perils Moshoeshoe assumed that the Free State army would dissolve again. He wrote to Brand suggesting that Wodehouse should mediate and he ordered several thousand head of his cattle to be sent down from the Maloti.[2] But then the resemblance to the events of 1858 came abruptly to an end. The Free State army invested Thaba Bosiu, a patrol spotted Moshoeshoe's cattle which had to be rushed on to the mountain where they created chaos until nearly all of them had died of thirst and hunger, and Brand rejected British mediation and stated his own conditions for peace.[3] Moshoeshoe was to become a Free State subject, evacuate Thaba Bosiu, and pay an indemnity of 40,000 head of cattle, 60,000 sheep, and 5,000 horses, and the greater part of LeSotho below the Maloti was to become Free State

[1] See sources cited in preceding note. Also Lagden, pp. 360–3, and Tylden, pp. 96–8.
[2] Moshoeshoe to Brand, 23 Aug. 1865, *BR* iii. 444.
[3] Brand to Moshoeshoe, 25 Aug. 1865, *BR* iii. 445–9.

territory. The old king played for time before he finally
rejected these terms[1] and meanwhile on 29 August he sent
his son Tlali to Aliwal North with an urgent appeal to
Wodehouse:

> After having run through all my country, killing women and
> children, burning all the villages and the corn they met with, I
> have sent to them for peace, but their conditions are so im-
> moderate, that I cannot comply with them . . .
>
> I consider myself subject to the British Government, and I
> hope your Excellency shall take interest in my cause, and come
> to establish peace as soon as possible, as I am determined the
> Government of the Free State will never have my country. I am
> therefore giving myself and my country up to Her Majesty's
> Government under certain conditions which we may agree
> upon between Your Excellency and me.[2]

Soon after the fighting began Wodehouse, as Governor
of the Cape Colony, tried to deter colonists from assisting
the Free State by issuing a neutrality proclamation, with
penalties for participating in the war.[3] As High Commissioner, he advised the Lieutenant-Governor of Natal to do
the same and informed the Secretary of State for the Colonies
that

> We also find ourselves much embarrassed in enforcing a policy
> of neutrality by the peculiar terms of the Conventions made at the
> establishment of the Free State and Transvaal Republics, by
> which we bound ourselves to supply them with all the arms and
> ammunition they might desire to purchase, and came under an
> obligation with the Transvaal not to allow the sale of either to the
> Native Tribes.[4]

By the time Wodehouse received Moshoeshoe's plea for
protection, however, Anglo-BaSotho relations had become
seriously strained as a result of the conduct of Moshoeshoe's
nephew, Lesaoana.

Lesaoana, as we have seen, had for several years been
acting as a virtually independent chief beyond Molapo's

---

[1] Moshoeshoe to Brand, 17 Sept. 1865, *BR* iii. 473.
[2] Moshoeshoe to Wodehouse, 29 Aug. 1865, *BR* iii. 458.
[3] Proclamation, 27 June 1865, *BR* iii. 370–1.
[4] Wodehouse to Secretary of State, 12 July 1865, *BR* iii. 394. See above,
p. 279 n. 3.

territory. There, north-east of the formidable Drakensberg escarpment, passage from the high veld to the coastal lowlands is relatively easy through Van Reenen's pass between Harrismith (Orange Free State) and Ladysmith (Natal). It was the natural route for travellers between Natal and both the republics. It was also an open frontier zone: white farmers owned land on both sides of the border and before the war Lesaoana himself had been in the habit of crossing into Natal to dispose of cattle he had captured in the Free State.

In May 1865, when he was driven out of the Free State, Lesaoana took refuge in Molapo's country, but he had already sent some of his livestock to an African reserve in Natal.[1] Towards the end of June, without the knowledge of Molapo or Moshoeshoe, he made a foray into Natal where he seized a rich booty from farmers who also owned land in the Free State; and on his way back, inside Free State territory near Harrismith, he attacked a party of Afrikaners who were returning from Natal to their homes in the Transvaal, killing five men, looting their property, destroying their wagons, and setting the women free after stripping off their clothes.[2]

Soon afterwards the Transvaal declared war on Moshoeshoe, and President Pretorius and Commandant-General Paul Kruger led a commando to the Free State. That, however, did not turn out to be of much consequence, for the Transvaalers saw very little action before they withdrew. What was catastrophic for Moshoeshoe's diplomacy was the reaction of the Natal Government and, through it, of the Imperial Government. Natal, which Britain had annexed in 1843, had been given a Legislative Council with an elective majority in 1856. Its white population of about 16,000 people consisted mainly of recent immigrants from Britain who were extremely conscious of their weakness *vis-à-vis* the

---

[1] Magistrate of Klip River County, Natal, to Secretary for Native Affairs, Natal, 29 May 1865, *BR* iii. 353.

[2] The raid by Lesaoana (alias RaManeella) gave rise to a massive documentation, *BR* iii. 372 ff. (index entry Lesaoana). See also discussions in *Leselinyana* by A. Sekese, 1 Feb. 1893 and 15 Jan. 1894, and in an anonymous article, 1 Jan. 1900.

far more numerous Africans in their midst, the independent Zulu kingdom to their north, and the Mpondo and other chiefdoms to their south.[1] Hitherto, except for the residents of the Ladysmith district, the Natal Whites had had few contacts with LeSotho and knew scarcely anything about it. Now, however, Lesaoana's raid caused an uproar.

The Natal Government immediately dispatched a force of colonial volunteers and British regulars to Van Reenen's Pass, asked Wodehouse to send additional troops from the Cape Colony, and, brushing aside Molapo's explanation that Lesaoana had acted in defiance of Moshoeshoe's orders to respect the colonial frontiers, demanded that Molapo and his father should return the stolen cattle, hand over Lesaoana, and pay for the costs of the military movements.[2] Finding that his father was not treating Natal's demands seriously and that his own territory was in danger of being overrun by Free State commandos, Molapo entered into secret negotiations with Natal. On 24 July he declared, 'It is my earnest desire to separate myself with my own proper people wholly and entirely from Basutoland, and to put myself fully and altogether under the protection and *control* of the Natal Government.'[3] Theophilus Shepstone, the ambitious Secretary for Native Affairs and the real force in the executive branch of the Natal Government, then planned a grandiose military adventure. A force of 20,000 Natal Africans under white officers should invade LeSotho, using Molapo's people as allies.[4] On 14 August Natal informed Wodehouse that its demands on Moshoeshoe totalled £35,000 – £20,000 to compensate the farmers for Lesaoana's thefts and the rest for military expenses.[5]

[1] *OHSA* i. 373–90.

[2] Lieut.-Gen. Sir Percy Douglas to Wodehouse, 1 July 1865, *BR* iii. 377–9; John Maclean, Lieut.-Gov. of Natal, to Wodehouse, 2 July 1865, *BR* iii. 379–81; Molapo to Resident Magistrate, Ladysmith, 5 July 1865, *BR* iii. 383; Shepstone, Secretary for Native Affairs, Natal, to Molapo, 11 July 1865, *BR* iii. 392–4. [3] Molapo to Shepstone, 24 July 1865, *BR* iii. 409.

[4] Shepstone to Colonial Secretary, Natal, 4 Aug. 1865, *BR* iii. 426–32. On Shepstone, see C. J. Uys, *In the Era of Shepstone*, Lovedale, 1933, and David Welsh, *The Roots of Segregation*, Cape Town, 1971.

[5] J. W. Thomas, Administrator, Natal, to Wodehouse, 14 Aug. 1865, *BR* iii. 440.

Meanwhile Wodehouse, who understood the affairs of
LeSotho far better than the Natal officials, was trying to
mitigate the effects of Lesaoana's raid. He asked for specific
facts about the raid, declined to send the requested military
reinforcements, and refused to allow Natal to invade LeSotho
with an African force or to deal separately with Molapo.[1]
An indignant and somewhat hysterical Natal legislature then
petitioned the Queen to be relieved of control by an 'absent
High Commissioner'.[2] However, the Secretary of State
repeatedly insisted that the colonies remain neutral in the
war between the Free State and LeSotho and expressed
confidence in Wodehouse's handling of the situation, including his judgement of 'the nature and amount of the repara-
tion which you will think it necessary to require of Moshesh'.[3]

Directly he heard of Lesaoana's raid, Wodehouse advised
Moshoeshoe to make full reparations to Natal and on
26 August, having received Natal's bill of costs, he wrote
a letter requesting Moshoeshoe to punish Lesaoana severely
and send Natal 10,000 head of cattle.[4] This letter was
delivered by William Reed, a clerk in Burnet's office at
Aliwal North, who spent the week of 15 to 22 September on
Thaba Bosiu.[5] Reed found between 1,500 and 1,800 people,
mostly men, on the mountain. They included Moshoeshoe's
councillors and kinsmen who normally lived in the central
part of the kingdom, such as Masopha (the senior active
warrior), Lelosa, and Tsekelo, and also five white traders
and military deserters. Reed experienced no shortage of food
on the mountain, but the place was rotten with the car-
casses of thousands of cattle and horses. Although the
commandos were maintaining a tight siege of Thaba
Bosiu, Moshoeshoe's people were living securely in the caves
in the cliffs that encircle the summit, and the Free State

---

[1] Wodehouse to Lieut.-Gov., Natal, 13 and 25 July 1865, *BR* iii. 395
and 410–12; Wodehouse to Administrator, Natal, 9 Aug. 1865, *BR* iii.
434–8.
[2] Petition of Natal Legislative Council, 23 Aug. 1865, *BR* iii. 443–4.
[3] Edward Cardwell, Secretary of State, to Wodehouse, 9 Sept. 1865, *BR*
iii. 468. Also Cardwell to Administrator, Natal, 26 Feb. 1866, *BR* iii. 626, in
which Cardwell rejected the petition of the Legislative Council.
[4] Wodehouse to Moshoeshoe, 26 Aug. 1865, *BR* iii. 456–7.
[5] Statement of William Reed, 30 Sept. 1865, *BR* iii. 481–6.

artillery was doing very little damage. Reed came to the conclusion that the BaSotho were getting the upper hand in the war. Moshoeshoe himself was in good spirits: 'Moshesh does not appear to be the least put about, he talks most of the night and sleeps till midday. He has his coffee and biscuit some 6 or 8 times a day, is perfectly cheerful and merry, and does not seem to fear anything.'[1] However, the king gave Reed to understand that he had no serious intention of satisfying Natal: 'From Moshesh's talk and his way of talking, I had great doubts as to the real meaning of his words. He never said, "the cattle have been restored," but "I have given orders that they shall be restored," implying how can you doubt that it has not been done. The impression from his manner was on my mind, "It has not been done." '[2]

Reed was correct in concluding that Moshoeshoe lacked the will or the power to satisfy Natal's claims, but he misjudged the military situation. The Free State lifted the siege of Thaba Bosiu on 25 September and there was a relative lull for some months. Then, beginning early in the new year, organized in four groups, the commandos systematically destroyed BaSotho villages with their grain supplies and standing crops and captured vast numbers of sheep and cattle, with the result that by March 1866 the BaSotho were facing starvation.

Meanwhile Wodehouse pursued a complex diplomacy. He continued to restrain Natal; he threatened to cut off Brand's ammunition supplies if he persisted in inciting the white and black inhabitants of the Cape Colony to break the law and join in the military operations with the lure of booty; and, while assuring the Colonial Secretary that he had no intention of annexing LeSotho, but merely of giving effect to the earlier plan of appointing a resident Agent to Thaba Bosiu, he instructed Burnet to proceed to LeSotho and impress on Moshoeshoe the absolute necessity of punish-

---

[1] *BR* iii. 484. Reed estimated that the dead cattle on Thaba Bosiu numbered 4,000 and that only 300 were still barely alive at the time of his visit: ibid., pp. 483–4. Later, the Paris missionaries estimated that 20,000 cattle and horses had died on the mountain: editorial, *JME* xli (1866), 1–4. On conditions on Thaba Bosiu during the siege, see also A. Sekese, *Leselinyana*, 15 Feb. 1893.
[2] *BR* iii. 486.

ing Lesaoana and sending 10,000 cattle to compensate Natal if his request for British protection was to be entertained.[1]

Burnet reached LeSotho on 1 November and remained there for six weeks. He quickly came to the conclusion that Moshoeshoe was in his dotage and the country was falling apart (6 November): 'Moshesh is done mentally. All is disorganization and jealousy among the greater Chiefs, who as well as the petties find the reins slipping from their hands. The great mass of the people are tired, worn out by the oppression and bad government of the Chiefs; and I am persuaded that the whole of Basutoland is ripe, rotten ripe for falling into the hands of the Queen's Government if a plan could be found.'[2] And again (9 December): 'Basutoland is in a bad state. Old Moshesh absolutely incapable, silly, and in fact imbecility itself. The only thing wanted is a leader to found a new order of things. Jealousy of each other causes both Letsie and Molapo to sit still and look calmly on at the misrule of the nation.'[3]

In particular, Burnet found that he could not persuade Moshoeshoe to give unequivocal orders for the punishment of Lesaoana and the collection and dispatch of the cattle to Natal, which were Wodehouse's preconditions for any form of British protection. The old king alienated both his senior sons by his apparent unwillingness to contribute any cattle from his own herds, and although Burnet persuaded him to sign a document ordering Molapo to punish Lesaoana, Burnet soon discovered that he had sent Molapo another message countermanding the order. Consequently Molapo

[1] Wodehouse to Acting Lieut.-Gov., Natal, 14 Oct. 1865, *BR* iii. 496–7; Wodehouse to Brand, 7 Nov. 1865, *BR* iii. 511–12; Wodehouse to Secretary of State, 13 Oct. 1865, *BR* iii. 493–4; Wodehouse to Burnet, 16 Oct. 1865, *BR* iii. 497–8; Wodehouse to Moshoeshoe, 17 Oct. 1865, *BR* iii. 498.

[2] Burnet to Wodehouse, 6 Nov. 1865, *BR* iii. 510.

[3] Burnet to Wodehouse, 9 Dec. 1865, *BR* iii. 549. Burnet probably exaggerated the extent of Moshoeshoe's imbecility. Nevertheless, he was certainly losing his grip by this time. Mabille, the Morija missionary, wrote on 30 Jan. 1866: 'Moshesh is now so aged, his faculties are so enfeebled, that he is no longer able to watch carefully over the interests of his people.' (Edwin W. Smith, p. 153.) Daumas, the Mekoatleng missionary, admired his courage during the siege and reported that he had decided to commit suicide by throwing himself over a cliff rather than fall into the hands of the Boers. (Daumas, 10 Nov. 1865, *JME* xli (1866), 47.)

resumed his efforts to negotiate directly with Natal, while Letsie independently sounded out Burnet for separate treatment. But although the BaSotho chiefs were disunited, Burnet reported that they were all agreed in wanting some form of protection from the Free State.[1]

On 17 December Burnet summarized his findings in a private letter to Wodehouse:

Moshesh's once vigorous mind partially gone, his judgment harassed and poisoned by these wretches [diviners and prophets], and no proper intelligence or confidence existing between him and his children on account of his jealousy of their interference with his authority coupled with their jealousy of each other as to the succession, it is not going too far to say that there is no Government in the country at present; and thus what prospect is there for the future?

After criticizing Moshoeshoe's kinsmen as incompetents, Burnet continued:

Should this apathetic compound of cowardice and disorganization on the part of the Basutos continue to exist, and should the Free State succeed in driving them into the mountains, and obtaining possession of all the more level Basuto country, the result will be a bloody period of savage retaliation, considering the bitter animosities between them. Should a peace be now patched up, because both sides are tired of war, a few years will produce fresh complications and another war.

Finally Burnet made a firm recommendation: 'If therefore it be the wish of the British Government to preserve Basutoland to the Basutos, and to civilize them, the only way seems to be to extend the Queen's authority over it, otherwise the Basutos will soon cease to exist as a tribe.'[2] Orpen had independently come to the same conclusion. He advised Wodehouse that the BaSotho were now willing to accept British control 'on any terms we please to dictate'.[3] On receipt of Burnet's report Wodehouse took the bull by the horns and proposed to the Colonial Secretary that

---

[1] Burnet's report on his mission, 12 Dec. 1865, *BR* iii. 553–66.
[2] Burnet to Wodehouse, 17 Dec. 1865, *BR* iii. 568–9.
[3] Wodehouse to Burnet, 3 Dec. 1865, *BR* iii. 538.

Britain should annex 'Basutoland' (13 January 1866).[1]
In a private letter accompanying his official dispatch, he
explained: 'Such a step really seems to offer the only
permanent prospect of tranquillity. The hatred existing
between them [the BaSotho] and the Boers is intense, and
neither party can keep the other quiet, while neither will
willingly quarrel with us, especially as we have complete
control over the supply of ammunition.'[2] The Colonial
Secretary refused (9 March 1866): 'The extension of British
rule in South Africa is a matter too serious in its bearings to
be entertained by Her Majesty's Government without some
overruling necessity, such as has not yet arisen, and cannot
be anticipated, I think, as likely to arise in the present
case.'[3]

By the time this refusal reached South Africa, the Ba-
Sotho had come to terms with the Free State. Moorosi submitted in November 1865, when he was recognized as chief
of the territory between the Orange River and the Cape
Colonial frontier on the Tees, provided he played no further
part in the war.[4] On 26 March 1866 Molapo and his
subordinate chiefs, who had lost thousands of sheep and
cattle to Free State and Transvaal commandos, signed the
Treaty of Mpharane (Imperani).[5] On 3 and 5 April Moshoeshoe, Letsie, Masopha, Posholi, and all the remaining
chiefs signed the Treaty of Thaba Bosiu.[6] Moshoeshoe
himself did not take part in the negotiations that led to that

[1] Wodehouse to Secretary of State, 13 Jan. 1866, *BR* iii. 596–8.
[2] Wodehouse to Cardwell, 15 Jan. 1866, Wodehouse Papers.
[3] Cardwell, Secretary of State, to Wodehouse, 9 Mar. 1866, *BR* iii. 632.
[4] Austen to Burnet, 3, 4, and 11 Nov. 1865, *BR* iii. 507, 508, and 515–16;
Commandant Wessels to Brand, 4 Nov. 1865, *BR* iii. 508–509; Austen to
Wessels, 5 Nov. 1865, *BR* iii. 509–10; Wessels to Austen, 5 Nov. 1865, *BR* iii.
510.
[5] *BR* iii. 643–4. Assessments of Molapo's behaviour differ. His descendants (Informants 4–9) claim that he was loyal to his father and his surrender
was a tactical decision agreed to in advance by Moshoeshoe. On the other
hand, the Paris missionaries had no doubt that Molapo had surrendered without his father's knowledge or consent: Daumas to Cochet, 27 Apr. 1868, LEC;
Jousse, 20 May 1868, *JME* xliii (1868), 294–8. A. Sekese, in *Leselinyana*,
1 Feb. 1894, asserted that as a result of the Treaty of Mpharane Molapo's
territory—the Leribe district—'belongs to Molapo and the Boers', not to 'the
sons of Mokoteli' (i.e. not to Letsie and his heirs).
[6] *BR* iii. 649–51.

agreement. A Free State doctor examined him and reported that he was not well enough to go down to the meeting-place. He sent Mopeli and Sekhonyana in his stead and signed the document later on the mountain.[1]

Under these treaties the BaSotho forfeited their occupation rights over about two-thirds of the arable land they had

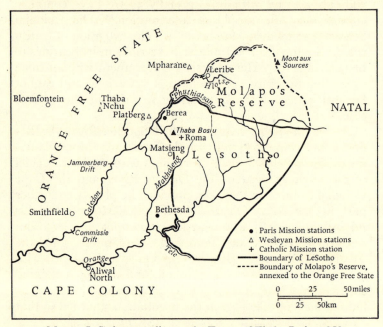

MAP 7. LeSotho according to the Treaty of Thaba Bosiu, 1866

held under the Convention of Aliwal North. They lost all their land on the right bank of the Caledon, and also their land between the Caledon and the Orange as far eastwards as a line passing three miles east of Letsie's village of Matsieng. Within the region left to them Molapo and his followers became Free State subjects, ruled by a commandant, in the territory north-east of the Phuthiatsana River. That left a truncated independent LeSotho, with a mere strip of arable land on either side of Thaba Bosiu and a frontage of only

[1] *Friend of the Free State*, 6 Apr. 1866, *BR* iii. 654–6; Anon., *Leselinyana*, 1 Mar. 1900.

twenty miles along the Caledon. The rest of LeSotho consisted of extremely rugged country, over 7,000 feet above sea-level except where broken by the steep valleys of the upper Orange and its tributaries—country which was inhabited only by bands of hunters and collectors and which the BaSotho regarded as useless to themselves except for cattle-posts.

4. *Diplomatic* Coup

As victory drew near a jubilant Orange Free State Volksraad began to make provision for the new order. On 7 February 1866 it decreed that the Paris missionaries were to be expelled from the conquered portions of LeSotho, on the grounds that they had meddled in politics and sympathized with the enemies of the state.[1] Next, on 26 February, it legislated for the disposal of the 'conquered territory'. The land along the new boundary was to be surveyed and divided into three lines of 3,000-acre farms, which were to be auctioned to white inhabitants of the Free State on condition that they occupied them. In this way the conquered territory was to be defended by a 'wall of flesh'.[2]

Later, after the submission of Molapo, the Volksraad devised regulations for its new subjects. Molapo's people were to pay an annual tax of ten shillings per hut and were liable to be conscripted for military service. They were not to leave their reserve without a pass signed by an official, subject to penalties of up to twenty-five lashes or three months' imprisonment with hard labour. No stranger was to be allowed into the reserve for more than twenty-four hours without permission. And, when parents requested it, the Commandant had the right to 'apprentice' their children to Free State burghers until they reached the age of majority.[3]

Finally, on 15 June, the Volksraad enacted a new and more stringent pass law for the inhabitants of what remained of independent LeSotho. No subject of Moshoeshoe was to

---

[1] Minutes of the Volksraad, 7 Feb. 1866, *BR* iii. 615.

[2] Collins, pp. 239–41; van Aswegen, p. 308.

[3] Ordinance for the government of Molapo and his people as subjects of the Orange Free State, *BR* iii. 696–9.

enter the Free State except to trade, to seek employment, or to deliver letters to officials. When he did so, a MoSotho was to carry a pass signed by his chief and he was not to travel in a party of more than four men, to bear weapons, or (unless he was a chief or a letter-carrier) to use a horse. Any white inhabitant of the Free State could arrest him for infringing these regulations and on conviction by a land-drost he would be sentenced to expulsion, or a fine of up to £10, or imprisonment with or without hard labour for up to three months, or compulsory service with a Free State inhabitant for not more than two years.[1]

The Free Staters duly expelled the Paris missionaries from all their stations outside the territory left to Moshoeshoe by the Treaty of Thaba Bosiu.[2] They also managed to keep Molapo and his followers submissive. However, they lacked the capacity to enforce the Occupation and Pass Laws in central and southern LeSotho. By 15 January 1867, when the purchasers of farms in the conquered territory were meant to take possession, only 116 farms had been auctioned. Moreover, few of these buyers ever occupied their land and most of those who did so were soon frightened off again. With their limited manpower it was one thing for the Free Staters to defeat the BaSotho in warfare, and quite another to control the territory they had 'conquered'.[3]

At a *pitso* on 31 March Moshoeshoe and the territorial chiefs of the central and southern regions (Letsie, Masopha, Posholi, etc.), shaken by the defection of Molapo, had decided to sign the Free State terms, harsh though they were, as a matter of convenience; but they never intended to evacuate their land. To them, the Treaty of Thaba Bosiu

---

[1] Pass Law for the subjects of the Chief Moshesh, *BR* iii. 705–6.

[2] T. D. Keck was allowed to remain at his station, Mabolela, north of the Caledon, on grounds of ill-health, and D. F. Ellenberger and C. Gosselin were undisturbed at Bethesda in the south. Of the two stations within the territory left to Moshoeshoe, one—Berea—was occupied by P. J. Maitin and L. S. Duvoisin, but the other—Thaba Bosiu—had been destroyed during the fighting and was not reoccupied till towards the end of 1866, when A. Mabille settled there pending the return of T. Jousse from leave in France. (Jousse, *La Mission Française Evangélique au sud de l'Afrique*, ii. 89–90.)

[3] Speech by President Brand at the opening of the Volksraad session, 8 May 1867, *BR* iii. 770–1; Collins, pp. 277–8; van Aswegen, pp. 308–10.

was 'The Peace of the Corn'.[1] Their ruse succeeded. During the months following the signing of the treaty many hungry, displaced BaSotho roamed around begging and pilfering, while others, whose villages has escaped the attention of the commandos, remained in occupation. Gradually, as they saw that the Whites were not able to stop them, they regained their confidence and those who had been dislodged built new villages or reoccupied old ones throughout most of the conquered territory. Early in 1867 they reaped a good harvest and put in another crop, while the chiefs had stone walls built to fortify the passes to the summits of several mesa-like mountains, selected for their strategic locations, notably Maboloka (south-east of modern Mafeteng, controlling the approaches from the south), Mathebe (dominating the wagon track from Mafeteng to Morija), and Qeme (a large plateau fourteen miles south-west of Thaba Bosiu), as well as Platberg and other mountains north of the Caledon. On top of each such mountain they laid in supplies of grain and of whatever ammunition they could lay their hands on.[2]

In February 1867 Ex-President Josias Hoffman, long since disillusioned by the policies of his successors, informed Burnet that 'the wretched plan of "the wall of flesh" ' was a failure. 'Without police or protection of any sort, the Boers fly from the goblins which they see from afar.' Hoffman also reported that the Free State was about to adopt 'the hellish plan of destroying, rooting out, and driving away the Basutos'.[3] He was correct. In March Brand called out the commandos again and instructed Commandant-General Fick to clear the BaSotho out of the conquered territory. So destructive were their sweeps that Letsie decided to make a formal submission in May, in the

---

[1] Journal of Father Joseph Gérard, 1864–1871, Archives of the Catholic Archdiocese, Maseru (typed copy), Apr. 1866: 'Moshesh and his children have signed and probably with a mental reservation. In any case there was no other way to save the harvest.' Also Jousse, ii. 89; Anon., *Leselinyana*, 1 Mar. 1900; and I. 39.

[2] Editorials, 8 Sept. 1866, 10 Jan. 1867, and 9 Mar. 1867 in *JME* xli (1866), 324 and xlii (1867), 2–7 and 81–3; H. M. Dyke and Dr. E. Casalis (son of Eugène Casalis), 3 Jan. 1867, ibid., 83–4. Also Anon., *Leselinyana*, 1 Apr. 1900.

[3] J. P. Hoffman to Burnet, 20 Feb. 1867, *BR* iii. 748–9.

name of all the southern chiefs. According to this treaty
they and their followers became Free State subjects, confined to only a small strip of arable land in southern LeSotho,
on conditions like those that Molapo had previously accepted
in the north.[1] Early in June Mopeli also submitted and the
Free State placed him and his followers north of Molapo
at Oetsi's Hoek.[2] But whereas Mopeli, like Molapo, ceased
to resist the Free State after he had signed his treaty, Letsie
refused to take orders from a commandant, and his followers
refused to budge from their homes. Moreover some of Moletsane's people were hanging on to their land north of the
Caledon and continuing to resist white attempts to take
occupation.

President Brand was exasperated by these developments
and when followers of Moletsane killed two white men he
sent Moshoeshoe another ultimatum. The old king signed
a defiant reply on 9 July:

I beg to know what is the cause of this year's war. Last year
it was through the wish to enlarge your country. This year it
seems that it is caused by your wish to exterminate the Basutos.
That wish has been the real cause of all the mischief of which
you have written . . .

Last year we made peace with you. I gave you 5,000 head of
cattle, but I have not given this country away, it belongs not to
me, as you know yourself very well that every country in the
world does belong to the people which dwells in it.

If I remove the Basutos, I have nowhere where I can establish
them. Although I do not like war and am afraid of its consequent
horrors, I cannot consent to buy the lives of my people with the
country belonging to them, where they were born, where their
forefathers were born likewise; besides I know of no country
where they could go . . .

Moshoeshoe concluded: 'Now I trust that you will consider
well all the matters spoken of in this letter, because I also
have been ordered by the Government of this country to
write as I have done.'[3]

[1] Reception of Letsie as a Free State subject, 22 May 1867, *BR* iii. 778–80.
[2] Reception of Paulus Mopeli and his followers as subjects of the Orange
Free State, 1 June 1867, *BR* iii. 783–4; Keck, 6 Sept. 1867, *JME* xliii
(1868), 8–10.   [3] Moshoeshoe to Brand, 9 July 1867, *BR* iii. 788–9.

Infuriated by the failure of Moshoeshoe and Letsie to fulfil their treaty commitments, Brand mobilized the commandos again. This time the Free Staters fought with the utmost ruthlessness, destroying villages and crops, seizing livestock, and showing no mercy to women or children.[1] The southern BaSotho resisted for a while, but the commandos, assisted as usual by their African allies (Rolong, Tlokoa, and Mfengu), gradually picked off their fortresses. Makoai's stronghold of Maboloka fell in September. In January Mathebe was captured and the redoubtable Posholi himself was killed. And on 22 February a commando temporarily gained control of the summit of Qeme, where it captured thousands of Letsie's cattle, sheep, and horses.[2]

By that time the commandos had wrecked many villages with their corn stores and standing crops, hundreds of people (mainly the very young and the very old) had died of starvation, and several thousand had fled into the Maloti mountains, to the reserves of Molapo and Mopeli, to Moorosi's country south of the Orange, to the Matatiele area south of the Drakensberg, or to Natal. Nevertheless, the bulk of the BaSotho survived and stayed in the vicinity of their homes. When a commando approached they fled to the nearest mesas where they found shelter in caves and subsisted on indigenous plants and insects if they had no cattle, but once the commando had passed through they returned and resumed cultivation. Once again the military situation was a stalemate. The Free State forces caused great havoc, but they could not exterminate their enemies nor could they permanently dislodge them. Regardless of the actions of their political leaders, the BaSotho clung to their land with peasant tenacity. In April 1867 a missionary noted, 'The Boers cannot be everywhere at the same time. While

[1] Brand to Members of the Volksraad, 16 July 1867, *BR* iii. 790–1; speech by Brand at the opening of the Volksraad session, 8 Aug. 1867, *BR* iii. 794–6; Jousse (for Moshoeshoe) to Burnet, 15 Oct. 1867, *BR* iii. 828.

[2] W. B. Fricke, Secretary of the Free State War Council, to Brand, 27 Sept. 1867, *BR* iii. 820–2; Commandant J. G. Pansegrouw to Brand, 31 Jan. and 23 Feb. 1868, *BR* iii. 851–3 and 877. Pansegrouw reported that he had captured 10,613 head of cattle, 8,000 sheep, and 1,500 horses on Qeme (p. 877).

they are devastating everything in one corner, the natives less than a league away are reaping and storing their harvest.'[1] It was the same a year later. The BaSotho resisted in their own way, 'yielding today only to return tomorrow, never allowing the invaders to settle or to build anything'.[2] Moreover, though he no longer controlled his territorial chiefs, Moshoeshoe himself remained unscathed on Thaba Bosiu, a symbol of national defiance.

The High Commissioner was dismayed by the effects of the war. It was exhausting the Free State's financial resources and exacerbating an economic depression in the colonies.[3] The flood of BaSotho refugees was causing turmoil in the eastern Cape and northern Natal.[4] There were rumours—not wholly unfounded—that Brand had hopes of following up his victories by expanding southwards from LeSotho through the independent Mpondo chiefdom to gain control of Port St. John's, and thereby free the republics from their dependence on the British colonies for their external trade.[5] Wodehouse was also moved by compassion for Moshoeshoe and his people, and he secretly provided money to help the BaSotho buy food.[6]

For a while Wodehouse's capacity to influence events in LeSotho was limited by increasingly restrictive instructions from London. Under Cardwell as Colonial Secretary he was prohibited from countenancing a British annexation of Basutoland (9 March 1866). Cardwell's successor, Lord Carnarvon, withdrew the long-standing permission to appoint a British agent to LeSotho, insisting that 'our connection with the tribe should for many reasons be strictly

---

[1] Duvoisin, 3 Apr. 1867, *JME* xlii (1867), 241–4.

[2] Editorial, 9 Mar. 1868, *JME* xliii (1868), 83. Robert C. Germond, *Chronicles*, includes several *JME* reports of BaSotho resistance to the Free State commandos, pp. 289–306.

[3] Fraser, p. 419.

[4] Austen to Burnet, 31 Aug. 1867, *BR* iii. 806–7; Burnet to Wodehouse, 16 Sept. 1867, *BR* iii. 813.

[5] Wodehouse to Secretary of State, 12 May 1866, *BR* iii. 687–9; Wodehouse to Cardwell, 15 Apr. 1866, Wodehouse Papers; Wodehouse to Edmond Wodehouse, 16 Apr. 1866, ibid.

[6] The Revd. H. M. Dyke, P.E.M.S., to Wodehouse, 10 June 1867, *BR* iii. 784–6, reporting on his distribution of 'the relief so generously granted by you for suffering Basutos'.

limited to a friendly mediation, such as can lead to no closer or entangling relationship' (25 July 1866).[1] Consequently, when the fighting broke out again in 1867, Wodehouse could only advise the king to come to 'an amicable arrangement' with the Free State.[2]

Moshoeshoe had other ideas. He clung doggedly to the hope that he might draw the British Government into the situation, and since he had failed to do so through Wodehouse and the Cape Colony he put out feelers to Natal. In July 1866, two months after signing the Treaty of Thaba Bosiu, he convened a *pitso*, as a result of which he sent Mopeli and Tsekelo to Pietermaritzburg to invite the Natal Government to annex LeSotho.[3] In May 1867 he made another approach to Natal, informing R. W. Keate, the new Lieutenant-Governor, that

I have not found as yet, with any of the Governors sent out by Her Majesty, any readiness to accede to my greatest and dearest wish, namely, that of being received, together with my people and my country, under the protection and the Government of Her Majesty. Still I hope that what has not been found feasible by Your Excellency's predecessors, may be done by Your Excellency.[4]

In September 1867, by which time his military situation was becoming desperate, Moshoeshoe sent yet another appeal to Natal.[5]

Theophilus Shepstone, who was always eager to promote the expansion of Natal and with it his own power and influence, welcomed Moshoeshoe's overtures. In September 1866 he reasoned:

. . . Basutoland has always been felt to be the centre of all native political agitation; it is centrally situated between the warlike

[1] Cardwell to Wodehouse, 9 Mar. 1866, *BR* iii. 632–3; Carnarvon to Wodehouse, 25 July 1866, *BR* iii. 716.

[2] Wodehouse to Moshoeshoe, 12 Apr. 1867, *BR* iii. 767.

[3] Moshoeshoe to Shepstone, 15 July 1866, *BR* iii. 713–14; Memorandum by Shepstone, 4 Sept. 1866, *BR* iii. 721–3; Shepstone to Colonial Secretary, Natal, 5 Sept. 1866, *BR* iii. 723–4.

[4] Moshoeshoe to Lieut.-Gov., Natal, 16 May 1867, *BR* iii. 777.

[5] Moshoeshoe to Lieut.-Gov., Natal, 16 Sept. 1867, *BR* iii. 812–13.

Cape frontier Kaffirs and the powerful Zulus on our northern border, and is the medium of all interchange of ideas on important political questions between those people; the control of Basutoland would therefore place in the hands of the [Natal] Government the key of all South African politics so far as natives are concerned ... with the Basuto under direct rule, as the population of Natal is, the interests of the British Government in South Africa would be immensely strengthened, and we should be in a position to dictate measures to all the neighbouring tribes, which might tend to their advancement and prosperity, and add greatly to the prospects of peace for the future.[1]

During 1867 white public opinion in Natal, which had previously been solidly behind the Free State, began to turn. F. Daumas, a Paris missionary whom the Free State had compelled to leave his station at Mekoatleng, moved to Pietermaritzburg, where he influenced people in favour of Moshoeshoe. D. D. Buchanan, a Pietermaritzburg lawyer, politician, and journalist, entered into communication with Moshoeshoe and espoused his cause.[2] Other Natal colonists seized on the idea of intervening on the high veld to acquire control of the trade route to the Transvaal or in the hope of obtaining grants of land. On 3 October the Legislative Council resolved

That the continued existence of hostile relations between the Basuto people and the Government of the Orange Free State is highly prejudicial to the interests of commerce; is inimical to the neighbouring British provinces; retards the progress of civilization amongst the native tribes of South-eastern Africa; and is rapidly demoralizing the white inhabitants, who are compelled by their position to take part in such hostilities.[3]

Lieutenant-Governor Keate forwarded Moshoeshoe's letters to London, with copies to Cape Town, and informed the

---

[1] Shepstone to Colonial Secretary, Natal, Sept. 1866, *BR* iii. 724. For Shepstone's plans for Basutoland, see also his memorandum, 4 Feb. 1868, *BR* iii. 858–61, and Lieut.-Gov. R. W. Keate to Wodehouse, 8 Feb. 1868, *BR* iii. 864–8.

[2] D. D. Buchanan to Wodehouse, 27 Mar. 1867, *BR* iii. 758–61.

[3] Extracts from Proceedings of the Legislative Council of Natal, 3 Oct. 1867, *BR* iii. 822.

king that the High Commissioner was the only official in South Africa who had authority to deal with his requests.[1]

Wodehouse welcomed Moshoeshoe's approaches to Natal and the clamour of the colonists for annexation in so far as they kept the BaSotho question before the British Government; but he considered that if LeSotho was to be annexed at all it should become a separate colony under the High Commissioner, or, failing that, a part of the Cape Colony rather than Natal. He did not share the widely accepted view that Shepstone's policies were beneficial to the African population. Moreover he did not trust the Natal colonists and officials, for he had discovered that they had deceived him by claiming that Lesaoana had seized many more cattle in his ill-fated raid than was actually the case.[2] Accordingly, on 3 May 1867 he informed the new Colonial Secretary, the Duke of Buckingham, that had it not been for the instructions he had received from his predecessors he would 'have advocated our receiving the Chief and his tribe as subjects of Her Majesty on well considered conditions', but not as part of Natal, for 'it is probable that Moshesh made his last overture to Natal only because he had entirely failed in his overtures to me.'[3] Likewise, commenting on Moshoeshoe's later approaches, Wodehouse told Buckingham that he stood by his remarks of 3 May.[4]

By the time these dispatches reached London the British decision-makers were inclined to respond to Moshoeshoe's appeals. Ever since Sir George Grey had denounced the Conventions the permanent officials in the Colonial Office had been half-persuaded by his arguments.[5] When news

---

[1] Keate to Moshoeshoe, 31 May 1867, *BR* iii. 781–2; Keate to Secretary of State, 4 June 1867, *Despatches from the Governor of the Cape of Good Hope and the Lieutenant-Governor of Natal on the subject of the Recognition of Moshesh, Chief of the Basutos, and of his Tribe, as British Subjects, Presented to both Houses of Parliament, July 1869, 23719*, pp. 104–6.

[2] John Ayliff, Treasurer, Natal, to Colonial Secretary, Natal, 20 Dec. 1865, *BR* iii. 574–5; Wodehouse to Acting Lieut.-Gov., Natal, 11 Jan. 1866, *BR* iii. 591–2.

[3] Wodehouse to Buckingham, Secretary of State, 3 May 1867, *BR* iii. 769.

[4] Wodehouse to Buckingham, Secretary of State, 17 Sept. 1869, *BR* iii. 813–14.

[5] C. W. de Kiewiet, *British Colonial Policy and the South African Republics*,

arrived of the outbreak of war in 1865, the Assistant Under-Secretary, T. F. Elliot, wrote a minute for circulation within the Office:

The war is the fruit of the wonderfully anomalous measures by which these Boers were created into an independent State. It will undoubtedly deserve mature consideration whether the Governor should not be encouraged to take advantage of any fair opening that the progress of events may afford, for once more bringing them within the control of the only responsible and civilized Government in South Africa.[1]

By 1867 the successes of the commandos had put an end to the prospect that the Free State burghers would voluntarily submit to the reimposition of British control, but they strengthened the arguments for accepting Moshoeshoe and his people. Moreover the expulsion of the Paris missionaries from LeSotho had inflamed evangelical opinion in Britain and on the European continent, and the Paris missionary society had sent a deputation, led by the well-informed and persuasive Casalis, to urge the British Government to intervene.[2]

The Duke of Buckingham, who succeeded Lord Carnarvon as Colonial Secretary in March 1867, and his Parliamentary Under-Secretary, C. B. Adderley, tilted the balance in favour of intervention, provided it could be managed without expense. In June 1867, Adderley wrote a minute: 'I should not object to Sir Philip Wodehouse's plan to put Basutoland in a "territory" state for a time. . . . But not one shilling should fall on the British taxpayer.'[3] In November 1867 the Cabinet reviewed the question in the light of the latest dispatches from South Africa and Buckingham persuaded his colleagues to authorize conditional inter-

p. 221; W. P. Morrell, *British Colonial Policy in the Mid-Victorian Age*, chs. 1 and 5.

[1] T. F. Elliot, Assistant Under-Secretary for the Colonies, Minute, 17 Aug. 1865, cited in Morrell, pp. 28–9.

[2] Directors of the Paris Evangelical Missionary Society to Secretary of State, 26 Apr. 1866, *BR* iii. 674–6; Casalis to Secretary of State, 13 Nov. 1866, *BR* iii. 734–6; Buckingham, Secretary of State, to Wodehouse, 9 Dec. 1867, *BR* iii. 834.

[3] C. B. Adderley, Parliamentary Under-Secretary for the Colonies, Minute 30 June 1867, cited in Morrell, p. 25.

vention.[1] On 9 December Buckingham instructed Wode-house 'to treat with the Chief Moshesh for the recognition of himself and of his tribe as British subjects'. The conditions were that 'Basutoland' was to be incorporated in Natal with the consent of the Natal Legislature (and thus without cost to Britain) and a boundary settlement with the Free State was to be 'an integral part of the arrangement'.[2]

These instructions gave Wodehouse a most onerous task. He had long since reached the conclusion that Britain should bring the BaSotho under its protection as a united people and with sufficient territory for their survival. But he had to deal with a LeSotho whose aged king had lost control of his territorial chiefs; an avaricious Free State that was determined not to be deprived of the fruits of victory; a covetous Natal that sought to control the BaSotho for reasons of prestige and economic gain; Cape Colonial politicians who had become involved in a series of quarrels with him as their Governor;[3] and superiors in London who would not tolerate the expenditure of British taxpayers' money for fresh adventures north of the Orange River.

Directly he received Buckingham's dispatch Wodehouse wrote to tell Moshoeshoe, Brand, and Keate that the British Government had granted the king's request that his people should become British subjects (13 January 1868).[4] Moshoeshoe replied (26 January): 'I have become old; therefore I am glad that my people should have been allowed to rest and to lie under the large folds of the flag of England before I am no more.' As to the details, he would gladly leave everything to the High Commissioner: 'It matters little to us to know to what Colony Basutoland is to be annexed, so long as we are under British protection and rule.'[5]

---

[1] Confidential Print for the Cabinet, 9 Nov. 1867, C.O. 879/2.

[2] Buckingham, Secretary of State, to Wodehouse, 9 Dec. 1867, *BR* iii. 834–6; also a private letter of the same date, Wodehouse Papers.

[3] Wodehouse, as Governor of a colony with representative but not responsible government during a period of economic depression, was in continual conflict with his parliament. The Cape Colony acquired responsible government in 1872, after he had left. See T. R. H. Davenport, 'The Move towards Responsible Government', *OHSA* i. 328–33.　　　　[4] *BR* iii. 839–41.

[5] Moshoeshoe to Wodehouse, 26 Jan. 1868, *BR* iii. 843.

But the agony of the BaSotho was not yet over. Brand
brushed aside all requests to suspend hostilities and pressed
home his military advantage. By March he believed he was
on the verge of crushing the last vestige of BaSotho resistance. 'For the miseries and suffering caused by this war,' he
informed Wodehouse on 3 March, 'the Basutos and their
Chief Moshesh are alone accountable.'[1] The war would
continue until Moshoeshoe had handed over Moletsane's
followers who had killed the two white men the previous
year. The treaties, Brand insisted, had left the BaSotho
with 'quite sufficient land'. In any case, he declared in a
revealing passage, 'The destitute can . . . always find employment in the Orange Free State'; those who had already
taken refuge there were 'contented and happy'.[2]

Meanwhile Wodehouse had been encouraging Moshoeshoe
to make his people resist further Free State encroachments.
Now, Brand's letter goaded him into action. He reminded
the Free State President that in 1858 Sir George Grey had
intervened at the Free State's request to save the republic
from devastation by the BaSotho. In 1864 he himself had
arbitrated the boundary favourably to the Free State but
Brand had ignored his recommendation to be moderate in
applying his award, and 'the consequence of the steps then
taken by the Free State has been this wretched and prolonged war'.[3] The present measures of the Free State, 'if
successful, must inevitably drive the population of Basutoland, in a state of beggary and destitution, into the Cape
Colony on the one side, and to the borders of Natal on the
other'. Such a policy, if persisted in, would be 'unfriendly'
towards the British Government. Consequently, Wodehouse
concluded, producing his trump card, 'I will peremptorily
prohibit' the passage of any further supplies of arms and
ammunition to the Free State.[4] Two days later, on 12 March
1868, he issued a proclamation declaring that Moshoeshoe
and his people were 'British subjects' and his territory
'British territory'.[5]

[1] Brand to Wodehouse, 3 Mar. 1868, *BR* iii. 886.   [2] Ibid., p. 887.
[3] Wodehouse to Brand, 10 Mar. 1868, *BR* iii. 891.
[4] Ibid., p. 892.   [5] Proclamation, 12 Mar. 1868, *BR* iii. 894.

Wodehouse promptly dispatched to Basutoland the entire Frontier Armed and Mounted Police, a Cape Colonial force, five hundred strong, instructing its commanding officer, Sir Walter Currie, to see that the fighting ceased. Currie reached Thaba Bosiu on 26 March and read the annexation proclamation 'to the great joy of old Moshesh and his tribe'. He found that in spite of all the operations of the commandos BaSotho continued to occupy the greater part of the territory Moshoeshoe had ceded in 1866 and that the new harvest was most promising. 'The fact is the disputed land is and has been all along occupied by the Basutos, nor is it possible for the Free State forces to get them out. . . . The crops throughout the country are really enormous.' But the BaSotho were very short of powder.[1] However, although Currie persuaded the Free State officers to suspend aggressive operations, their commandos remained on the LeSotho side of the 1864 line and the Volksraad insisted that the Treaty of Thaba Bosiu should be enforced.[2]

Wodehouse himself crossed the Orange in April. The Free State, incensed by his interference, adamantly refused to negotiate with him.[3] On 15 April he reached the valley below Thaba Bosiu where he was met by Moshoeshoe. In the words of a member of Wodehouse's staff: 'Moshesh was at this time very infirm and old. His hair was white and crimp, and his eyes were of that peculiar gray common amongst very old natives. His tall figure was much bent, and his limbs had a scanty covering of flesh on them.'[4] When they had reached the top of the mountain,

the Chief, surrounded by many circles of councillors and principal men of the tribe, had his say. He told them he was old—yes, very old. He had brought his people together. He had lived and seen enough. He asked his people to rely as he did on the friendship of the Governor 'Philippé Wodehousé.' He hoped they would regard the Governor as standing in his place, as he had lost all power to assist them now.[5]

[1] Sir Walter Currie to Wodehouse, 28 Mar. 1868, BR IV. 112–15.

[2] Wodehouse to Secretary of State, 9 Apr. 1868, *Despatches*, 23719, p. 44.

[3] Brand to Wodehouse, 8 Apr. 1868, ibid., pp. 51–3.

[4] G. St. V. C., 'A Page in Colonial History', *Cape Quarterly Review*, i (1882), 687.   [5] Ibid., p. 686.

When Wodehouse informed the gathering that Basutoland was to be incorporated in Natal, there were strong objections. Moshoeshoe himself, summing up his wishes in a letter dated 21 April, declared that he preferred that Basutoland should be 'a *native reserve* where natives alone should be allowed to dwell, and which would be dependent from the High Commissioner'.[1] Failing that, he would rather it became a part of the Cape Colony than Natal, because his commercial and diplomatic dealings had always been primarily with the Cape.

Wodehouse agreed with Moshoeshoe. He had a tense meeting with Keate and Shepstone, who had arrived expecting to incorporate Basutoland in Natal forthwith, and he concluded that Moshoeshoe's views were warranted and that they were shared by nearly all his chiefs. They had used Natal as a lever to draw Britain in, but they were alarmed at the prospect of being controlled by Shepstone and the Natal colonists once it became imminent. However, before Wodehouse reported to London he received a rap over the knuckles from the Secretary of State, on the grounds that he had exceeded his instructions in proclaiming the BaSotho to be British subjects without first negotiating a boundary settlement with the Free State and making sure that Natal was willing to incorporate Basutoland.[2]

The High Commissioner was sufficiently disconcerted by this rebuke to withdraw most of the colonial police force from Basutoland, leaving only a token detachment of 100 men under the command of J. H. Bowker. Nevertheless, he justified his conduct in official dispatches to Buckingham on 2 May;[3] and more freely on 9 May in a private letter to Sir George Barrow of the Colonial Office:

Shepstone . . . anticipated in his capacity of Secy for Native Affairs a great accession of dignity and power from this addition of the Basutos to those under his immediate control. He made quite sure of it and he came up here with Mr. Keate to take

[1] Moshoeshoe to Wodehouse, 21 Apr. 1868, *Despatches, 23719*, p. 57.
[2] Buckingham, Secretary of State, to Wodehouse, 26 Feb. 1868, ibid., pp. 87–8.
[3] Wodehouse to Buckingham, 2 May 1868, ibid., pp. 57–9.

possession, with a following of 70 Zulus, intended to be admiring spectators . . . it is very easy to understand that these Basutos, being in the greatest difficulties, believing themselves to be entangled with our claims for compensation for the raid into Natal, having made repeated fruitless applications to me, and being above all things desirous of our protection, suddenly hit on this notion of applying to Natal, trusting that if they were successful in their main object, they might subsequently modify the details. . . . The present expression of repugnance to the union is genuine and universal, and in my judgment sound and reasonable.

As to the official rebuke, Wodehouse defended himself vigorously and challenged his superiors to dismiss him if they could not give him their full support:

I have asked for and mean to ask for neither money nor assistance. If I be allowed to retain the rule of the Territory as High Commissioner, I will make arrangements which will secure peace and good government. But the matter is far too serious and too complicated to admit of half-measures. There must be full confidence in me or none. If I cannot be fully supported I must submit to becoming another of the many Governors that have been recalled from the Cape.[1]

Buckingham accepted Wodehouse's explanations and promised him the full support he demanded, on the understanding that Britain was not to provide financial or military assistance.[2] Nevertheless the outcome remained indeterminate.

The Free State sent a deputation to England to urge the British Government to disavow the annexation and repudiate Wodehouse. Buckingham gave the delegates a hearing, but told them that the annexation would not be rescinded and the Free State should settle the boundary question with the High Commissioner.[3] The crucial negotiations took place at Aliwal North in February 1869 between Wodehouse and commissioners appointed by the Volksraad. Moshoeshoe

---

[1] Wodehouse to Barrow, 9 May 1868, Wodehouse Papers.
[2] Buckingham to Wodehouse, 9 July 1868, *Despatches*, *23719*, pp. 89–90.
[3] Buckingham to Wodehouse, 24 Aug. 1868, Wodehouse Papers; Buckingham to Wodehouse, 9 Nov. 1868, *Despatches*, *23719*, pp. 92–3.

was not represented. Initially the Free State proposed the line of the Treaty of Thaba Bosiu and Wodehouse the 1864 line; but on 12 February they reached agreement, subject to ratification by the two governments.[1]

Basutoland's western boundary was to run from above Jammerberg Drift on the Caledon approximately south-eastwards to the junction of the Orange and the Cornet Spruit (the white name for the Makhaleng). The northern boundary was to be the Caledon River eastwards to the Phuthiatsana, the western limit of Molapo's reserve as annexed by the Free State in 1866. If Molapo made a written request to be released from his subjection to the Free State, the Volksraad was to grant his request, and the northern boundary of Basutoland would then extend further eastwards to the source of the Caledon.[2]

Compared with the Treaty of Thaba Bosiu line, the Ba-Sotho gained a considerable block of arable land in the west, including an additional frontage of forty miles along the Caledon. But compared with all earlier boundaries, the BaSotho came off extremely badly. They lost all their territory north of the Caledon and a considerable strip between the Caledon and the Orange. They were confined to a very small proportion of the arable lands that their ancestors had occupied before the *lifaqane* wars and far less than Governor Napier had recognized as coming under Moshoeshoe's sway in 1843 or Wodehouse himself had recognized in 1864.

From Aliwal North Wodehouse travelled to Basutoland to inform the people of the new boundary. On 22 February he addressed a great *pitso* at Korokoro, six miles south of Thaba Bosiu, near a camp where Bowker's small detachment of colonial police had constituted the only British presence in Basutoland during the previous ten months. The proceedings were reported in the *Friend*, a Bloemfontein

[1] Wodehouse to Granville, Secretary of State, 14 Apr. 1869, enclosing Minutes of Aliwal North Conference 4–12 Feb. 1869, *Further Despatches from the Lieutenant-Governor of Natal and the Governor of the Cape of Good Hope, on the Recognition of Moshesh, Chief of the Basutos, and of his Tribe, as British Subjects, Presented to both Houses of Parliament, 21 February, 1870, C.-18*, pp. 6–19.

[2] Ibid., pp. 17–19.

newspaper.[1] The reporter estimated that between two and three thousand men were present, including Letsie, Molapo, and Masopha (Moshoeshoe's surviving sons of his First House), Sekhonyana, Tlali, and Tsekelo (his educated junior sons), Moletsane (the Taung chief), and eight missionaries. The king himself was absent, 'old age and bodily infirmity having of late crept on him to such an extent as to render it physically impossible for him to descend from his rocky fortress, much less to travel to Korokoro'.[2] When Wodehouse's speech had been translated by a missionary, the only chief who objected, according to the *Friend*, was Moletsane, whose territory lay on the northern side of the Caledon. He claimed that 'the Governor had misled or deceived him, having previously promised him the restoration of his land'. Wodehouse replied that the only alternative would have been the collapse of his negotiations with the Free State, 'in which case the past miserable state of war, desolation, thieving, and murder would have continued indefinitely'.[3] He proposed to place Moletsane and his people in western Basutoland between the Caledon and the Orange. As for Molapo, he declared that 'he had never ceased to be the son of Moshesh' and that he had already applied to be relieved of his subjection to the Free State.[4] The *Friend* concluded that

The Chiefs, though feeling acutely the loss of so large a proportion of their beautiful country, admit that they are sick of war, and that but for the intervention of the British Government they would in all probability have ultimately lost the whole, they therefore pledge themselves to due submission to the behests of the High Commissioner. . . . The Basutos may be cramped for room, and feel themselves too much 'cooped up' in the mountains, but having now a well-defined boundary and British protection they have no further fear, if they behave themselves, that their lands will suffer further curtailment.[5]

The reporter added that he had found no signs of poverty in Basutoland: 'Horses and cattle in good condition, and

---

[1] *Friend of the Free State*, 25 Feb. 1869, BR V. 96–110.
[2] Ibid., p. 100.   [3] Ibid., pp. 102–3.
[4] Ibid., p. 104.   [5] Ibid., pp. 105–6.

immense tracts of land under cultivation, the Kaffir corn
[sorghum] and mealies growing most luxuriantly, meet the
eye in every direction.'[1]

From Korokoro, Wodehouse proceeded to Thaba Bosiu
to explain the settlement to Moshoeshoe. There is no eye-
witness account of the king's reaction, but according to a
missionary he inquired sarcastically: 'Is that peace?'[2]

Two white men then instigated an effort to obtain better
terms for the BaSotho. One was D. D. Buchanan, the Natal
lawyer who had been in touch with Moshoeshoe since
March 1867. Buchanan, assuming that Wodehouse had
deliberately deprived the BaSotho of their land, was probably encouraged to act by Theophilus Shepstone, who was
deeply disappointed that Basutoland had slipped from his
grasp. The other was the Paris missionary François Daumas,
who had founded the station at Mekoatleng in 1835 and
lived there, serving Moletsane and his Taung followers,
until the Free State expelled him and his family in 1866.
Daumas was embittered by a settlement that placed Mekoatleng and three other Paris stations in the Free State, where
the missionaries were not permitted to continue their work,
and necessitated the removal of Moletsane and his people
to western Basutoland.

Directly Buchanan heard of the terms of the draft Convention he wrote to Moshoeshoe, encouraging him to appeal
to the Queen if 'you and your people are disappointed and
dissatisfied with what is proposed to be done with your
country'.[3] On the advice of his sons Sekhonyana and
Tsekelo, and probably also of Molapo, Moshoeshoe agreed
to accept Buchanan's help. He replied (16 March 1869):

> I am dissatisfied,—I have been covered with shame,—and I
> feel great grief; for the hope I had has fallen to the ground,
> and the affairs have been settled in quite a different way to
> that which we have been led to expect. . . . I wish you to know
> that I had nothing to do in the transactions of Sir P. Wodehouse

[1] *Friend of the Free State*, 25 Feb. 1869, BR V. 109.
[2] Extract from a letter from the Revd. F. Daumas, 2 Nov. 1869, *Further Despatches*, C.-18, p. 69.
[3] Buchanan to Moshoeshoe, 27 Feb. 1869, ibid., p. 44.

and the Free State. I was never consulted. I am only left a small part of my country, which is overcrowded with people.[1]

Moshoeshoe then authorized Tsekelo to join Buchanan in Natal and travel with him to France and England where Daumas was already urging the British Government to insist on better terms.[2] There, developing their case in the form of a personal vendetta against the High Commissioner, they succeeded in stirring up opposition to the Convention. Eugène Casalis went to London to protest on behalf of the Directors of the Paris Evangelical Missionary Society; the Aborigines Protection Society supported them; and Charles Buxton and sixteen other Members of Parliament signed a memorial disputing Wodehouse's right 'to surrender any portion of Her Majesty's Dominions to a Foreign Power' and predicting that 'this cruel and unjust confiscation' of BaSotho territory would plunge the area into 'anarchy and bloodshed'. 'Your Memorialists, in conclusion, are utterly at a loss to explain the course taken by Sir Philip Wodehouse, and we earnestly trust that Her Majesty's Government will veto the Convention into which he has entered.'[3]

In the face of these criticisms, the British Government hesitated to ratify the Convention. However, Wodehouse instructed Bowker, his agent in Basutoland, to persuade the BaSotho chiefs and the Paris missionaries in Basutoland to repudiate Daumas, Tsekelo, and Buchanan.[4] Bowker was successful. Tlali wrote and Moshoeshoe put his mark to a letter declaring that 'Moshesh wishes now to certify that he has had nothing to do, whatever may be said, with Natal people or the Home Government, either by his son or by any one else who may say he has been sent by Moshesh.'[5] Letsie and Molapo also dissociated themselves from Tsekelo and the

---

[1] Moshoeshoe to Buchanan, 16 Mar. 1869, ibid., pp. 44–5.

[2] Moshoeshoe to Buchanan, 17 Mar. 1869, ibid., p. 45.

[3] Memorial to Granville, Secretary of State, n.d. [23 June 1869], ibid., p. 68.

[4] Wodehouse to Bowker, 13 Apr. 1869, BR V. 153–5; Bowker to Dr. Casalis, 31 Mar. 1869, LEC.

[5] George [Tlali] Moshoeshoe, etc., to Bowker, 13 Apr. 1869, *Further Despatches, C.-18*, p. 22.

local missionaries from Daumas.[1] Armed with these statements, Wodehouse was able to put up a cogent defence
of his actions. He reminded the Secretary of State that he
had been obliged to negotiate a boundary settlement with the
Free State without the backing of British arms. Buchanan
might 'attempt to induce Her Majesty's Government to
compel . . . the Government of the Free State to grant better
terms; but he does not appear to have any notion in what
way this compulsion is to be effected, beyond giving them
an order to do so'.

> I am sure your Lordship will not be disposed to take any such
> step, and to incur the risk of having to resort to force in support
> of a demand of very questionable propriety. I have never allowed
> myself to lose sight of the fact that forcible interference on our
> part would be regarded at home with great disfavour, and that
> conviction has naturally been one chief source of anxiety.[2]

Buchanan responded to Wodehouse's challenge by
threatening to 'lay waste the Free State'—presumably with
African contingents from Natal—but this proposal was
counter-productive.[3] Since the British Government never
had the slightest intention of using force against the Free
State, the only alternative it contemplated to ratifying the
draft Convention was disannexing Basutoland, which would
have left the BaSotho to cope with the Free State once again
without British intervention. This prospect alarmed Moshoeshoe who, in his last communication with the British
authorities, sent 'our Gracious Queen' a leopard skin
kaross as 'a token of my gratitude for the precious peace
we enjoy since we have been proclaimed British subjects'.[4]
Letsie and his councillors also reacted strongly:

[1] Dr. E. Casalis, for the Conference of the French Missionaries, to Bowker,
8 Apr. 1869, *Further Despatches, C.-18*, p. 23; Molapo to Wodehouse, 28 Apr.
1869, ibid., p. 25.

[2] Wodehouse to Granville, 30 Apr. 1869, ibid., pp. 20–2.

[3] Buchanan to Granville, 5 Nov. 1869, ibid., p. 47.

[4] Moshoeshoe to Wodehouse, 4 Nov. 1869, BR V. 365–6. Queen Victoria
accepted the kaross and Wodehouse was instructed to inform Moshoeshoe that
she would 'always feel an interest in the welfare of himself and his Tribe
under British protection'; but Moshoeshoe died without receiving the Queen's
message; Granville, Secretary of State, to Wodehouse, 22 Jan. 1870, *Further
Despatches, C.-18*, p. 41; Bowker to Wodehouse, 17 Mar. 1870, BR V. 452.

. . . I know nothing of the mission of Tsekelo to England. I am the eldest son of my father, and I have as much right to be believed when I declare that since the settlement made by His Excellency last year at Aliwal of all our difficulties with the Boers, I have always considered it as satisfactory as I could wish. . . . I declare this to be my opinion, the more emphatically so, that rumour is very active in this country, saying that England's protection may be withdrawn on account of Tsekelo's mission, as it may be found impossible to satisfy the claims set up by him. . . . [T]he only hope, where alone we could feel that we have a sure prospect of life and peace, is that the English Government should never forsake us, and specially not withdraw the protection at the present time.[1]

By the time Moshoeshoe's gift and Letsie's appeal reached London the British Government had decided to ratify the Convention, subject to the removal of a clause that would have provided compensation to the Free State for territory that the BaSotho had ceded in 1866 and was now to be included in Basutoland.[2] The Volksraad agreed to the deletion of the clause and on 24 December 1869 the Secretary of State sent Wodehouse the British Government's approval of the Convention as amended.[3]

5. *The Death of a King*

After the outbreak of war in 1865 the old king lost a great deal of his authority. Nearly all his senior kinsmen acted independently to promote their personal interests and their different perceptions of the common interest. Nevertheless Moshoeshoe remained far the most potent symbol of BaSotho unity and resistance to the Free State. Moreover, since

[1] Letsie to Granville, Secretary of State, 12 Oct. 1869, *Further Despatches, C.-18*, pp. 34–5.

[2] Granville to Wodehouse, 24 Sept. 1869, ibid., pp. 39–40.

[3] Brand to Wodehouse, 11 Nov. 1869, BR V. 378; Granville to Wodehouse, 24 Dec. 1869, *Further Despatches, C.-18*, p. 41. For the agitation against the ratification of the Convention without substantial changes in the boundary, see the correspondence between the Colonial Office and D. D. Buchanan, A. Kinnaird, M.P., Eugène Casalis (Director of the Paris Evangelical Missionary Society), F. W. Chesson (Secretary of the Aborigines Protection Society), and the Revd. F. Daumas in *Further Despatches, C.-18*, and *Further Despatches . . . presented to both Houses of Parliament, May, 1870, C.-99*; also Daumas to Cochet, 23 June 1869, LEC.

white officials continued to treat him as a responsible head of government, his kinsmen were obliged to seek his support for their diplomatic manœuvres. He was under continuous pressure to lend his name to their policies and, especially, to put his mark to documents and affix the seal which Governor Maitland had given him to authenticate his letters.[1]

It is not possible to determine precisely how much responsibility Moshoeshoe actually had for the messages and letters that were sent in his name in these final years, when he was handicapped by physical and mental deterioration as well as the lack of a reliable secretary and the intrigues of his kinsmen. Nevertheless there was a fundamental consistency in the manœuvres that were associated with his name. They were all aimed at the same basic objective that he had been pursuing ever since the 1830s: the preservation of as much unity, territory, and autonomy for his people as was possible in the face of the escalation of white power throughout southern Africa. Hence his acceptance of 'the peace of the corn'; his persistent appeals to British officials—in Pietermaritzburg when Cape Town seemed unresponsive; his initial encouragement of the Tsekelo–Daumas–Buchanan mission to Europe and his later dissociation from it. At all stages he managed to avoid becoming the puppet of those who would have had him surrender to the Free State. For example, early in 1868, when the situation seemed desperate after the death of Posholi and the storming of Qeme, a faction headed by Tlali tried to send a formal submission to Bloemfontein in the king's name, but he had taken the precaution of entrusting his seal to Jousse and Tsekelo persuaded the missionary not to release the seal for that purpose.[2]

During 1869 Moshoeshoe's elation at Wodehouse's annexation proclamation gave way to depression when he heard the terms of the boundary settlement that Wodehouse and Brand had agreed upon at Aliwal North, and his

---

[1] Maitland presented Moshoeshoe with a seal at their meeting at Touwfontein on 30 June 1845. It was inscribed: *Na Morena Oa Basuto: Ki Tiisitse* ('I, Chief of the BaSotho, have confirmed'). Editorial Notes, *Lesotho*, i (1959), 4.
[2] E. W. Smith, *Mabilles*, pp. 172–3.

depression deepened as it became evident that the terms would not be improved. This coincided with—and possibly precipitated—the onset of his final illness. In February he was too weak to attend Wodehouse's *pitso* at Korokoro. In March Tlali told Bowker that his father 'was in his second childhood and did not understand what was going on'. In August he became confined to his bed and from then onwards he ate very little food. But thanks to his robust constitution and healthy regimen he hung on to life for several more months, while his body slowly wasted away.[1]

While Moshoeshoe was nearing his end, Molapo applied to be relieved of his status as a Free State subject. He and his territory on the south side of the Caledon were formally incorporated in Basutoland in April 1870 (Leribe district).[2] Lesaoana, whose raiding proclivities had caused so much trouble, was settling down in his old home area in the Phuthiatsana valley.[3] Moletsane, the Taung chief, reluctantly migrated to western Basutoland (Mohales Hoek district) from the territory he had occupied since 1837 on the right bank of the Caledon.[4] Several of the descendants of Mohlomi, the hero of Moshoeshoe's youthful years, who had been living on the Free State side of the new boundary in the long-disputed southern frontier zone, moved inside Basutoland (Mohales Hoek and Mafeteng districts).[5] Further south Moorosi, the Phuthi chief, announced that 'he would follow in the footsteps of his master' and his territory beyond the Orange became part of Basutoland in 1872 (Quthing district).[6]

[1] Editorial, *JME* xliv (1869), 408–9; *Friend*, 25 Feb. 1869, BR V. 100; Bowker to Wodehouse, 28 Mar. 1869, BR V. 134; Mareka Nchakala, *Leselinyana*, 1 Nov. 1891.

[2] Molapo to Wodehouse, 24 Jan. 1869, BR V. 50; Extract from Secret Minutes of the O.F.S. Volksraad, 13 May 1869, BR V. 196; Minutes of Proceedings re Molapo's Transfer to Basutoland, 11 Apr. 1870, BR V. 459–60.

[3] Informants 14, 15.

[4] Bowker to Wodehouse, 16 May and 18 Oct. 1869, BR V. 200–2 and 352.

[5] Bowker to Wodehouse, 20 and 27 Aug. and 12 Nov. 1869, BR V. 280–1, 285–8, and 379–82.

[6] Austen to Colonel C. D. Griffith, Governor's Agent, Basutoland, 29 Feb. 1872, BR VI. 417–21.

Bowker estimated that whereas 125,000 people had regarded themselves as subjects of Moshoeshoe before the wars began in 1865, less than half that number were inside Basutoland (including Molapo's country) in 1869.[1] It is

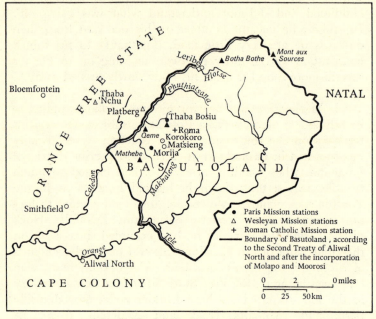

MAP 8. The British Colony of Basutoland

true that several thousand had died of starvation or been killed by Free State commandos during the wars, and several thousand survivors remained outside the boundaries of Basutoland after the wars were over. Moshoeshoe's son Sekhonyana, who had always been ambitious to establish an independent chiefdom, returned below the Drakensberg to settle near Adam Kok's Griqua, where his territory was annexed by the Cape Colony in 1879; and Moshoeshoe's half-brother Mopeli stayed at Witzieshoek as a subject of the Free State. In addition to Sekhonyana and Mopeli and their followers, many people who had at one time or another

[1] Bowker to Wodehouse, 27 Aug. 1869, BR V. 286-7.

acknowledged Moshoeshoe as their king remained dispersed in the Free State, Natal, and the Cape Colony as clients of white farmers, and in 1869 young men were beginning to be attracted to the newly discovered diamond diggings near the confluence of the Vaal and the Harts rivers.[1] Nevertheless Bowker's estimate of the population of Basutoland was too low. When a rough census was taken in 1875, it was calculated to be 127,707.[2] The majority of the people who had recognized Moshoeshoe as their king when his power was at its height in the 1850s resided inside Basutoland after its annexation.

In January 1870 Moshoeshoe roused himself to perform his last official duty. He convened a meeting of chiefs and head men on Thaba Bosiu and abdicated in favour of Letsie.[3] He thus transferred to his eldest son the paramountcy over a large proportion of the BaSotho who had survived the ordeals of the previous half-century. But the boundary defined at Aliwal North restricted Letsie's authority to a fraction of their ancestral territory. Moreover British over-rule was still an unknown quantity. Bowker was conducting a holding operation until the British and Colonial governments had decided who was to be responsible for Basutoland and how the territory should be administered.[4] It remained to be seen whether Moshoeshoe's hopes would be realized: whether British over-rule would not only prevent further encroachments by white settlers but also promote economic development and strengthen the political system.[5]

At the January meeting Moshoeshoe also announced that when Letsie died he should be succeeded by Motsoene, whose mother was Senate (the only child of Letsie's first wife) and whose father was Josepha (the eldest son of Molapo's

---

[1] Sekhonyana to Wodehouse, 20 Apr. 1868, BR IV. 216–18; Jousse to Currie, 5 Apr. 1868, BR IV. 195.

[2] R. S. Webb, *Gazetteer for Basutoland*, Part II, p. 50.

[3] *Leselinyana*, Feb. and Mar. 1870.

[4] Kimberley, Secretary of State, to High Commissioner Sir Henry Barkly (Wodehouse's successor), 17 Oct. 1870, describing Basutoland as 'a district in the position of an inchoate Crown Colony, waiting for annexation to one of its neighbours'.

[5] See above, pp. 267, 269–70.

first wife).[1] By this device Moshoeshoe presumably intended to heal the cleavage in SeSotho society caused by the rivalry between Letsie and Molapo. But his attempt to nominate Letsie's successor would be ignored. It was in conflict with custom, for there was no precedent for a chief prescribing such a remote succession, and claims to succession were customarily transmitted exclusively by males, so that when there was no son in a chief's First House the eldest son of the Second House had the strongest claim. It was also impolitic. Josepha was notoriously insane and Motsoene was only an infant, whereas Lerotholi, the eldest son of Letsie's Second House, was about thirty-three years old and had already proved himself as a leader of men.[2]

As Moshoeshoe's life flickered out, the population in the villages on Thaba Bosiu declined. Many younger people moved away from their enfeebled monarch to attach themselves to Letsie and other territorial chiefs. But his last days were not free of tension. His sons were jostling for the inheritance of his property—especially his cattle which, though decimated by his calamitous losses in 1866, were still numerous enough to cause jealousy. In addition, religious factions were competing for his spiritual allegiance. These two pressures were connected. Members of his junior Houses were in danger of losing their inheritance if the Paris missionaries had their way, for the missionaries regarded all the wives Moshoeshoe had married since Casalis and Arbousset arrived in 1833 as mere concubines, and their children as illegitimate.[3]

[1] Cochet, Notes et souvenirs, 20 Jan. 1870; *Leselinyana*, Feb. 1870.
[2] The position was further complicated by the fact that Moshoeshoe had previously made another arrangement: Senate was deemed to be a man and was 'married' to Lesaoana's daughter Maneella, and Lerotholi cohabited with Maneella to raise up seed for Senate. In due course Letsie was succeeded by Lerotholi, and Lerotholi was succeeded by his eldest son by Senate—Letsie II. This gave rise to further disputes in later generations, when Goliath, son of Letsie II's elder sister, Letsabisa, claimed to be Paramount Chief; in fact, the succession then went to Letsie II's younger brother, Griffith, and his descendants. Informant 16, Goliath Malebanye Potsane Mohale; and Informant 17, Bolokoe Malebanye Potsane Mohale. See G. I. Jones, 'Chiefly Succession in Basutoland', in Jack Goody (ed.), *Succession to High Office*, Cambridge, 1966, pp. 57–82, especially pp. 60 and 70–1.
[3] Mareka Nchakala, *Leselinyana*, 15 Oct. and 1 Nov. 1891.

Since the late 1840s Moshoeshoe had performed the traditional SeSotho rituals he had been taught to respect in his youth. He had convened initiation schools for his younger sons and their age-mates and under the stress of warfare he had resorted to every conceivable method of invoking magic to overcome his enemies. In August 1865 the daughter of a missionary observed, 'Moshesh has found out a way of defeating the Boers, not by force but by sorcery. He is told that he must merely remain on Thaba Bosiu and that a swarm of bees will destroy the Boers. These bees will be made with smoke and will return to the house in which they were made at night. That shows how superstitious Moshesh still is, and what influence the magicians have on the minds of the Basutos.'[1] In December the same year Burnet reported, 'At the present time not only Moshesh, but Molapo and Letsie, are to a great extent under the influence of witch-doctors and prophets. There are actually about half a dozen of them on Thaba Bosigo alone, whose dreams, charms, and revelations guide everything.'[2] Diviners and prophets continued to influence the venerable king as he neared his end.

The Paris missionaries were also active. By the end of 1869 they had reoccupied all their stations within the new boundaries of Basutoland, and two years later, when they compiled statistics for the first time since the wars, they claimed 3,261 adult church members.[3] They made two significant converts towards the end of Moshoeshoe's life: Mantsopa, the renowned prophet, and Moletsane, the Taung chief.[4] But they were not able to regain the ground they had lost among Moshoeshoe's kinsmen. The strategy of converting the BaSotho nation from the top had failed.[5]

After Jousse returned from leave in France in the second half of 1867, he resumed his efforts to convert the king, but he lacked the capacity to reach out across the cultural gap.

---

[1] Miss E. Maeder to Cochet, 18 Aug. 1865, LEC.
[2] Burnet to Wodehouse, 17 Dec. 1865, *BR* iii. 568.
[3] Annual Report of Missionary Conference, 1871, *JME* xlvi (1871), 212.
[4] Coillard, 16 Sept. 1869, *JME* xlv (1870), 11–18; Germond, 6 May 1870, ibid., pp. 287–8.
[5] Claude H. Perrot, *Les Sotho et les missionnaires Européens au XIXe siècle*, ch. 4.

Jousse found it difficult to communicate with him except in formal theological terms, or to judge him by norms other than his own. So priggish was he that he believed that the octogenarian king's physical decline was caused by his having sexual relations with the young wives he had married during the previous few years.[1]

Since 1862 the French Protestants had had competition from Catholic fellow countrymen.[2] Bishop Allard and Father Joseph Gérard of the Oblates of Mary Immaculate had obtained permission from Moshoeshoe to found a mission at Tloutle, later known as Roma, in a valley about seven miles south-east of Thaba Bosiu. They and their colleagues conducted a vigorous propaganda against the Protestants as well as the *lingaka*; and they, too, struggled hard to win the soul of the king. They assured Moshoeshoe that Protestantism could not possibly be the true religion of Christ, because it had been founded 1,500 years after his death, and they likened the hierarchical structure of the Catholic Church to that of Moshoeshoe's kingdom.[3] The Catholics adopted a less rigid attitude than the Protestants towards SeSotho customs, permitting *bohali* (the transfer of marriage cattle), which the Protestants had always condemned, provided that the bride was not compelled to marry a man against her will;[4] and their vestments, their incense, their images, their music, and their pageantry appealed to the sensuous side of Moshoeshoe which the Protestants neglected.[5] Moshoeshoe was particularly intrigued when a group of nuns arrived to strengthen the Catholic mission in May 1865, and during the critical months when the Protestant station below Thaba Bosiu lay ruined and deserted the nuns provided a refuge for several of his wives and children, and prepared food

[1] Cochet, Notes et souvenirs, 14 Dec. 1869.

[2] Journal of Father Joseph Gérard, 1864–1871; and Missions 1862–1868, also in the Archives of the Catholic Archdiocese, Maseru (being an English translation of parts of the short-lived journal, *Mission*, of which I have not been able to locate a copy); *Annales de l'Association de la Sainte-Famille*; Aimé Roche, O.M.I., *Clartés australes: Joseph Gérard, O.M.I. (1831–1914)*.

[3] Bishop Allard to Superior-General, O.M.I., 26 Mar. 1862, Missions 1862–1868, pp. 51–2; Gérard, 5 Feb. 1865 and 15 Dec. 1867.

[4] Gérard, Jan. 1866.

[5] Gérard, 15 Oct. 1865 and Jan. 1866; *Annales*, iii (4), 705–6, 736–7.

for Gérard to take to him.[1] The Catholics made their first converts in 1865 and in 1868 Moshoeshoe attended the baptism of an aged village headman on Thaba Bosiu.[2]

Moshoeshoe had welcomed the Catholic missionaries because he was impressed by their assurances that their converts would be loyal subjects and that they would teach them useful skills. He was disappointed in the Protestant converts, he told Bishop Allard, because they were not 'more respectful of other people's property' and 'more loyal and faithful'.[3] Besides, he was fascinated by the doctrinal rivalry. In November 1863 he informed the congregation at Tloutle: 'Though I am still only a pagan, I am a Christian in my heart. It is true that there is still some darkness as far as we are concerned when it is a question of discerning among the Christian religions which is the true one. However, I do not doubt that if you come to listen to these missionaries and take the trouble to examine the question, you will manage to discover which is the true religion of Jesus Christ.'[4]

The rivalry between the Christian missions grew extremely acrimonious. The Protestants regarded the Catholics as interlopers: the Catholics believed themselves to be saving the BaSotho from heresy. 'The Holy Virgin will break the head of all these heresies', wrote Gérard in his journal in January 1867.[5] In October that year, when Protestant missionaries arrived on top of the mountain while he was with Moshoeshoe, Gérard 'got a glacial handshake, as cold as in Siberia' and Jousse rebuked him for coming 'to work in my field'.[6] By that time the contest was spreading into SeSotho society around Tloutle. People were calling themselves BaFora (French) and BaRoma (Romans) and adherents of the one faction were interfering with the religious services of the other.[7]

---

[1] *Annales*, iii–v (1866–70); Roche, pp. 200–1.

[2] Gérard, 22 Oct. 1868.

[3] Bishop Allard to Superior-General, O.M.I., 26 Apr. 1862; Missions 1862–1868, p. 58. [4] Roche, p. 154.

[5] Gérard, Jan. 1867. [6] Gérard, 8 Oct. 1867.

[7] Gérard, 4 Feb. 1870. Cf. the situation in Buganda in 1892, when competition between British Protestant and French Catholic missionaries promoted

As Moshoeshoe neared his end, both missions intensified their efforts to convert him. Success would be a divine response to their prayers for the soul of a man they greatly admired and they sincerely believed that his eternal destiny depended on his conversion. Each mission also realized that success with the king would give an immense fillip to its ministry among his people.

Two distinct versions of what happened were recorded by those involved. The Protestant version is to be found in accounts by Jousse, the Thaba Bosiu missionary, and Adèle Mabille, the wife of the missionary at Morija. Mrs. Mabille was the daughter of Eugène Casalis, Moshoeshoe's first and most trusted European friend. She was born in 1840 in the mission house below Thaba Bosiu and Moshoeshoe had known her since she was a baby. According to her, she and her husband made an unsuccessful attempt to convert the king early in January 1870. Moshoeshoe hid his face while Mabille conducted a service by his bedside and afterwards he told Adèle he was afraid of her. When she suggested he ask God to have mercy on him, 'a sinner', he retorted angrily: 'You bad child, who said I was a sinner? I too shall go to heaven.' But as the Mabilles were leaving, Councillor RaTšiu told them that the king was 'under the influence of the Spirit—but he is in fear of men, in fear of the people'.[1] Soon afterwards, however, Jousse made a breakthrough. Previously Moshoeshoe had insisted that 'beyond a certain age one can learn new things, but one does not re-make one's heart', but at the end of January he was deeply affected when Jousse read from the fourteenth chapter of the Gospel of St. John, and added, 'Son of Mokhachane, a throne is prepared for you in heaven; believe in Jesus, the Saviour of the world, and you will be saved.' That night Moshoeshoe sent a messenger to ask Jousse to write and inform Casalis and Arbousset that he had become 'a believer'.[2] Next day

civil warfare between factions calling themselves Fransa and Ingleza: D. A. Low, *Buganda in Modern History*, Berkeley, Calif., 1971, pp. 13–54.

[1] E. W. Smith, *Mabilles*, pp. 183–4; also Adèle Mabille, *Leselinyana*, 21 Sept. 1911.

[2] Jousse, n.d. [Jan. or Feb. 1870], *JME* xlv (1870), 122–3.

other missionaries hurried to Thaba Bosiu and confirmed that Moshoeshoe's conversion was sincere. He told Adèle Mabille that he had become an age-mate of her three-month-old son, because 'when you told me of the birth of that child, I also was coming to birth. It is only now that I am beginning to be a man.'[1]

The Catholic version of Moshoeshoe's last days is derived from a journal kept by Father Gérard. On 26 January he noted that Moshoeshoe had been impressed by his explanation of the necessity of belonging to the Catholic Church.[2] But the Fathers were at a disadvantage, because the men and women who controlled access to the dying king were unsympathetic to their cause. On one occasion Fathers were denied entry to Moshoeshoe's hut on the grounds that he was too ill to see them; then, after Jousse had been admitted, they were allowed in for a while, but only in Jousse's presence.[3] The Catholics then adopted the tactic of visiting Moshoeshoe at night and in bad weather, when the guards were lax, but hearing of this the Protestants 'redoubled their efforts to surround him'.[4] On 4 February Moshoeshoe assured Gérard that he had told Jousse he was too ill to decide anything. 'I have two eyes, that is to say, the one looks at the BaRuti Fora, the other, the BaRoma.'[5] Finally, on 11 March Gérard recorded:

For the last fifteen days, I have redoubled the visits to Moshoeshoe. Always the same thing. On his side, a great weakness to declare himself for the true religion. A good reception, however, on his part. But, who does not see that he is not converted, wishing to satisfy both the Catholics and the Protestants? However, if he has a preference, it seems that it would be for us. . . . We struggle, so to say, with the Protestants who bar the passage right to his bedside. He had not had the strength to declare himself.[6]

Meanwhile, according to a MoSotho who became a Protestant convert, Moshoeshoe had been informing his kinsmen of his decision to be baptized by the Protestants

[1] E. W. Smith, *Mabilles*, p. 184.   [2] Gérard, 26 Jan. 1870.
[3] Ibid.   [4] Gérard, 4 Feb. 1870.   [5] Ibid.
[6] Gérard, 11 Mar. 1870.

and trying to control the disposal of his property. During February he summoned his sons to Thaba Bosiu to tell them, one by one, that he was going to be baptized. There was considerable dismay. Molapo made his meaning clear by holding traditional dances with the customary *joala*-drinking directly he left Thaba Bosiu.[1] Sons who had been born after 1833 were aghast at the implication that they would be deprived of their inheritance. Some time in February Moshoeshoe had his cattle gathered together and managed to stumble through his village and inspect them for the last time; and early in March he told Letsie he would inherit all his cattle, except those he had already assigned to the Houses of his junior wives and the *bohali* cattle each House received for the marriage of its daughters.[2]

Molapo's Protestant missionary, François Coillard, seems to have understood what was happening:

The baptism of such a chief as Moshesh could not be done in a corner. The missionaries would unquestionably have been accused of taking advantage of his weakness. He himself wished it to be public, that he might declare himself before all his people, and also (the crucial test) publicly put away the wives he had taken since the missionaries came into the country. . . . Already, the day after he had declared himself to M. Jousse, he had had the formal papers of release made out for them, but his sons, to whom each one represented so many head of cattle, opposed vehemently all his efforts to make suitable provision for them, and the complications thus arising were the real reason for the delay in his baptism.[3]

The Protestants published a notice in the March number of their monthly magazine, saying that Moshoeshoe would be baptized at the time of their annual missionary conference which was scheduled to take place at Thaba Bosiu on 20 March.[4] Early in March, when he was sinking into a coma, the date was advanced to the 13th and messages were sent

---

[1] Mareka Nchakala, *Leselinyana*, 15 Oct. 1891.

[2] Mareka Nchakala, *Leselinyana*, 1 Nov. 1891.

[3] Coillard to the Revd. J. Smith, Mar. 1870, in C. W. Mackintosh, *Coillard of the Zambesi*, London, 1907, p. 193.

[4] *Leselinyana*, Mar. 1870.

to all the Protestant mission stations urging people to attend the great festival.[1]

On the morning of Friday 11 March members of the Protestant congregations were already wending their way to Thaba Bosiu. Father Gérard, who went there himself to see what happened, found groups of Protestants were coming from all parts of Basutoland to be present at the baptism of the king.[2] But they were too late. At nine o'clock that morning Moshoeshoe died, as he had lived, in two worlds.[3]

Next day he was buried on his mountain alongside his father Mokhachane and his first wife 'MaMohato. Jousse and his Protestant colleagues conducted a funeral service in the presence of Letsie, Molapo, Masopha, and 4,000 other BaSotho.[4]

A week later, in Cape Town, Sir Philip Wodehouse and a representative of the Orange Free State exchanged the final ratifications of the Treaty of Aliwal North.[5]

A tradition has been handed down in the lineage of Molapo. In 1965 it was related by Jameson, son of Qhobela, son of Joel, son of Molapo:

Before he died, Moshoeshoe had a vision that LeSotho would remain in the hands of his sons as the inheritance of his people. He asked how the territory would remain in the hands of his children, as will now be explained. He took an egg, threw it up in the air, and said: 'If it breaks when it falls, my form of government will collapse; if it does not break, it will remain firm.'

[1] *Leselinyana*, Apr. 1870.
[2] Gérard, 11 Mar. 1870.
[3] Report of Missionary Conference, March 1870, *JME* xlv (1870), 242. Years later Gérard told a colleague that towards the end Moshoeshoe asked him to concert with the Protestant missionaries and have him baptized in a joint ceremony, and Gérard refused. Some BaSotho have maintained that Gérard baptized Moshoeshoe in secret, but Gérard denied this (Roche, p. 223 n. 30). Another version current in Lesotho is that Moshoeshoe expressed a desire to be baptized by the Catholics and should therefore be considered to have died a Catholic, in the sense that he had received 'baptism by desire'; but Archbishop 'Mabathoana (Informant 12), a descendant of Majara, son of Moshoeshoe, denied this.
[4] Report of Missionary Conference, March 1870, *JME* xlv (1870), 242; Gérard, 11 Mar. 1870; *Leselinyana*, Apr. 1870.
[5] Wodehouse to Granville, Secretary of State, 19 Mar. 1870, *Further Despatches*, *C.-99*, p. 3.

And in fact it did not break. Then he died, satisfied with the government he had left behind. This was his last act. He died in peace. As he died the earth trembled. The pots in the houses started moving but did not break, and my grandmother (who told me this) was unable to go over to the crawly child (my father). Immediately afterwards, messengers arrived announcing the death of Moshoeshoe.

Thereafter a song was composed by Molapo's poets at Leribe. It spread through LeSotho. People were sent to Leribe from all over to learn the song. This is what is said:

> Whose are we BaSotho?
> When Moshoeshoe is dead?
> Whose [people] shall we be?
> The leopard had died with its colours —
> Thesele, son of Mokhachane —
> BaSotho, whose [people] are we [now]?[1]

---

[1] Re ba mang BaSotho?
Ha Moshoeshoe a shoele?
Re tla sala re le ba mang?
Bata se shoele le mabala —
Thesele oa Mokhachane —
BaSotho re ba mang?

Informant 5, Jameson Qhobela Joel Molapo. 'The praise-name Thesele is formed from the verb *he thesela* (to thump, butt, smash)—an indication of the way in which he dealt with his enemies in battle.' M. Damane and P. B. Sanders, *Lithoko: Sotho Praise-Poems*, Oxford, 1974, p. 66 n. 2.

EPILOGUE

WHEN Lesotho became independent again on 4 October 1966, several of Moshoeshoe's hopes and expectations had been fulfilled. The colonial government had maintained his ban against the ownership of land by Whites and the surviving Nguni communities posed no threat to the integrity of the state, so that the new Lesotho had a much more homogeneous population than most countries in post-colonial Africa.[1] The people were predominantly Christian[2] and most of the children were receiving at least a little primary education in church schools; but the structure of society remained largely intact. Moreover, members of Moshoeshoe's family occupied most of the positions of power and prestige. Six of the nine Cabinet offices and eighteen of the twenty-two principal chieftainships were held by his patrilineal descendants. Two other principal chiefs were descended from his brothers and the remaining two from his allies.[3] The Prime Minister was a grandson of Molapo, the king a great-great-grandson of Letsie; and the king, recognizing that the name was a potent symbol of national unity, assumed the title Moshoeshoe II.

Nevertheless, the prospects of the newly independent Lesotho were daunting. As Moshoeshoe had foreseen, the boundary which Wodehouse, the High Commissioner, had

---

[1] In 1966 Basutoland had a *de jure* population of about 970,000 BaSotho, of whom about 117,000 were absent in the Republic. There were also about 3,000 Whites in Basutoland, most of them traders and administrators and members of their families.

[2] In 1956 34 per cent of the BaSotho were Roman Catholics, 37 per cent were Protestants, and 29 per cent were not Christians. Moshoeshoe II was brought up as a Catholic.

[3] At the time of independence, two principal chieftainships were held by the king and one each by eleven other descendants of Letsie, three descendants of Molapo, and one descendant of Masopha, Majara, Makhabane, Mohale, Moletsane (Taung), and Lethole (Khoakhoa). *The Lesotho Independence Order, 1966*, Schedule 2, correlated with [G. I. Jones], *Basutoland Medicine Murder*, Cmd. 8209, Table opposite p. 78.

accepted in his negotiations with President Brand had left later generations without enough land to support themselves. By 1966 most people had forgotten that Moshoeshoe's subjects had once been a self-sufficient peasantry, producing a surplus of grain for sale to Whites in exchange for manufactured goods. The population had increased to nearly a million and Basutoland had become a net importer of food, in spite of the fact that people were making heroic efforts to grow wheat and pasture livestock high in the Maloti as well as in the lowlands. Land shortage and soil erosion were grave problems and all the political parties declared that the conquered territories beyond the Caledon River should be returned.

The decline from a food surplus to a food deficiency had not been remedied by economic diversification. The territory lacked natural resources to attract private capital investment.[1] Moreover, until well after the end of the Second World War the British Government had assumed that it was the destiny of Basutoland to be incorporated by its white-controlled neighbours.[2] Consequently, Britain had behaved as a temporary caretaker in Basutoland. It had spent very little money there and Moshoeshoe's hope that British over-rule would promote economic growth had not been realized.

The Malthusian situation had been ameliorated by the export of labour—the territory's only significant marketable commodity—with the result that its declining rural economy had become meshed in a subordinate relationship with the burgeoning economy of white-controlled South Africa. In the regional context, colonial Basutoland became a dormitory for migrant workers, who commuted between their rural homes and white South Africa's farms, mines, and factories, where they encountered such rigid colour bars in

[1] Lesotho has considerable hydroelectric potential, but it had not been tapped by 1966.

[2] The British Government transferred Basutoland to the Cape Colony in 1871, but the Colonial Government so completely mismanaged the territory that it became involved in a war it could not win and begged Great Britain to resume responsibility for Basutoland. Britain did so, reluctantly, in 1884. Leonard Thompson, *OHSA*, ii. 267–71.

employment and wage levels that they could not acquire sufficient skills nor earn enough money to generate economic growth at home.

In 1962 a report of the World Health Organization estimated that two-thirds of the BaSotho were seriously undernourished. At the time of independence about half of the men of working age were employed in the Republic and about 80 per cent of the population were dependent on the wages they earned there. The total revenue for 1965–6, including British aid, was about 12 million Rand, which was less than half of 1 per cent of the revenue of the Republic. Moreover, the largest item in the regular revenue was a share in the customs duties collected by the Republic, which set the tariff to suit its own interests.[1] Basutoland used the Republic's currency and was served by republican banks. All its external communications lay through the Republic and its internal as well as its external trade was still dominated by Whites. These ineluctable facts were not altered by the advent of formal independence.

Nor were Lesotho's economic weaknesses offset by political strengths. Instead of assisting Moshoeshoe's successors to reform his political system (as Moshoeshoe himself had desired), the British officials, constrained by lack of funds, had confined themselves to keeping the peace and suppressing serious crime, and left the chiefs to deal with the routines of local administration—settling disputes, allocating land, and collecting taxes—with little supervision or advice. In colonial Basutoland, a British commissioner observed in 1935, the indigenous and the colonial governments worked 'in a state of detachment unknown in tropical Africa'.[2] Furthermore, the British had treated the indigenous institutions as an autocratic hierarchy, with the result that the

[1] South Africa and the High Commission Territories (Basutoland, Bechuanaland Protectorate, and Swaziland) formed a free trade area under an agreement made in 1909, with each Territory receiving a fixed percentage of the customs revenue collected by South Africa. Basutoland's share was 0·88575 per cent until 1965 when it was reduced to 0·47093 per cent, in spite of BaSotho opposition.

[2] Cmd. 4907, cited in Sandra Wallman, *Take Out Hunger: Two Case Studies of Rural Development in Basutoland*, London and New York, 1969, p. 12.

democratic features of the indigenous system atrophied: a colonial *pitso* was an occasion for transmitting orders from white officials to black subjects, rather than for two-way communication between chiefs and followers. Also, successive Paramount Chiefs created territorial jurisdictions for several of their sons, and as their numbers multiplied the territorial chiefs felt more and more insecure and Moshoeshoe's political system became riddled with internal conflicts.

In 1960 the young Moshoeshoe II assumed the paramountcy at the time when the British Government had finally abandoned the prospect of transferring Basutoland to South Africa and was beginning tentatively to prepare the territory for self-government. He had been educated at Catholic schools in Basutoland and England and at Oxford University and he aspired to become a modernizing ruler with real executive powers. However, his powers were whittled away in the political manœuvres that took place during the transitional period and Lesotho was launched into independence with a constitution based on the Westminster model. It created a Cabinet responsible to a legislative body elected by adult suffrage and left the principal chiefs with seats in a modified version of the House of Lords and the king as a constitutional monarch.[1]

These institutions were not a viable solution to the problem of the relations between the indigenous and the imported systems, which the British had kept apart. The chieftainship—and especially the monarchy—was still regarded as a legitimate authority by most BaSotho, in spite of the shortcomings of many incumbents.[2] Political parties and mass electoral processes were recent innovations and very few BaSotho had occupied senior positions in the colonial bureaucracy. So in Lesotho, as in nearly every state that emerged from the disintegration of the colonial empires, independence was followed by a period of political insta-

---

[1] *The Lesotho Independence Order, 1966*. The politics of the transitional period have been ably analysed by J. H. Proctor in 'Building a Constitutional Monarchy in Lesotho', *Civilizations*, 1969, and by Richard F. Weisfelder in *Defining National Purpose in Lesotho*, Athens, Ohio, 1969, and *The Basuto Monarchy: A Spent Force or a Dynamic Political Factor?*, Athens, Ohio, 1972.

[2] Wallman, p. 25.

bility, partly because the political institutions did not accurately reflect the symbiosis that had developed between the 'traditional' and the 'modern' elements in SeSotho society.[1]

Although Moshoeshoe's political system has been superseded and his country impoverished, his legacy endures. He has been vindicated for opting for colonial rule in preference to the only available alternative—rule by white settlers. In spite of Britain's failure to perform the creative functions that he had desired, the BaSotho possess significantly more cultural integrity and social cohesion than Blacks who became subjected to white South Africans. When they work in the Republic, BaSotho have to submit to the discriminations and humiliations experienced there by other Blacks, but at home in their villages they have preserved an atmosphere of freedom. To cross the Caledon River is to witness a striking contrast between the bearing of the BaSotho and that of the black inhabitants of the Republic of South Africa.

Moreover, the memory of Moshoeshoe is still an inspiration to his people. In the context in which he lived—confronted first by Nguni invasions and then by escalating white power—he secured the best options that were available. Although the modern context is radically different and calls for different methods and goals, the BaSotho cherish the knowledge that in Moshoeshoe there was a rare combination of political wisdom, personal integrity, and respect for human dignity.

[1] See C. S. Whitaker, *The Politics of Tradition*, Princeton, 1970, for a perceptive discussion of the interaction between 'traditional' and 'modern' elements in African societies. Whitaker refutes the ethnocentric idea that African societies must necessarily 'develop' in a single direction towards a 'modern' western model.

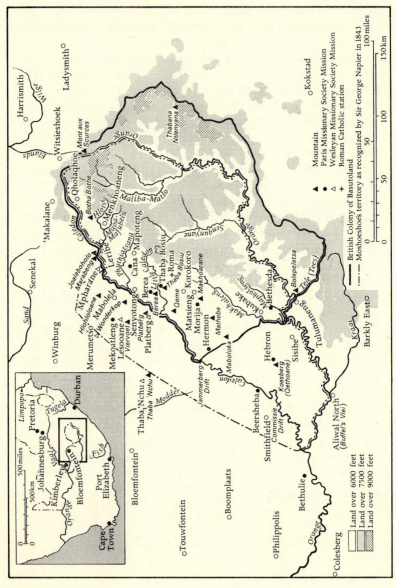

Map 2. Lesotho and vicinity in the time of Moshoeshoe

ADDITIONAL NOTES

1. (See above, p. 3 n. 1.)

D. F. ELLENBERGER's longer list of Mokhachane's wives and children from a manuscript in the Ellenberger Papers:

1. By Kholu, daughter of Ntsukunyane (*Fokeng*): 'Ma-Tšoeunyane (f), Moshoeshoe (d. 1870), Makhabane (d. 1835), 'MaNtoetse (f), Posholi (d. 1868).
2. By Mpinyane, daughter of RaChoshosane, son of Mokhethi (*Fokeng*): 'MaMahloana (f) and several other daughters.
3. By Nkoti, daughter of Monyalo (*Hlakoana*): Mohale (d. 1861), Mpepuoa (f).
4. By 'MaNtšebo (*Fokeng*: full sister of 5 and 6): Ntšebo (f), Mopeli, Mpusa, Nyebe, Nthotha (died in infancy), Nkata.
5. By 'MaKoena: Koena, Lelosa, Tšiame.
6. By 'MaMoima: Moima, Mphoto.
7. By 'MaMokheseng: Mokheseng (adopted child), Lebeoana, Lenkoana, Mokhameleli.
8–10. Nthokoleng, 'MaMokhoaki and Tlalane are also named as wives of Mokhachane. 4–6 were sisters, daughters of a man named Mokoteli and of the same mother.

2. (See above, p. 8 n. 3.)

The three principal Houses of Moshoeshoe (birth dates approximate):

1. Mabela ('MaMohato) Seepheephe Ntahli Molise Kata (*Fokeng*) (d. 1834):
   A. Letsie (Mohato) 1811–91
   B. Molapo 1814–80
   C. Mathe (f), b. 1817, married Lesaoana, senior son of Makhabane, full brother of Moshoeshoe
   D. Masopha 1820–98
   E. Majara 1829–58.
2. 'MaNneko Masheane (*Hlakoana*) (d. 1833):
   A. 'Neko, died young
   B. Mahlape (f), married Molumo, senior son of Mohale

C. Makhobalo b. 1821.
3. Mosula 'MaSekhonyana Molise Kata (*Fokeng*) (Cousin of 1):
   A. Sekhonyana (Nehemiah) 1828–1906.

Later wives and children included:

4. 'MaNtsane Molise Kata (*Fokeng*) (sister of 3), died 1839, mother of Ntsane.
5. 'MaTlali, mother of Tlali and Tlaliyane.
6. 'MaMosebetsi (*Sia*), mother of Sofonia and Tsekelo.
7. 'MaJohannes, mother of Johannes.
8. 'MaSetefane, mother of Setefane (Stephen).
9. 'MaMatsoso, mother of Matsoso (Samuel).
10. 'MaNtsela Tsoali Raphule Mochekoane Sekhume (*Tloung*).
11. 'MaNkomote (*Sia*), no children.
12. 'MaKibinyane Letšeka Masekoane Molise Kata (*Fokeng*).
13. 'MaPumane, mother of Letlala and Namane.

There were also wives named 'MaKimela, 'MaTlapane, Ra-Mosebatu, and Sefora; and sons named Fohloane, Kena, Mateleka, Monethi, 'Mota, Sekhebetlelo, and Selebalo.

Sources: E & M, p. 379; *BR* ii. lxx; D. F. Ellenberger in *Livre d'Or*, p. 676; Journal of Father Gérard, O.M.I., archives of Catholic Archdiocese, Maseru; a list prepared by Professor I. Schapera; and comments of informants in Lesotho, especially Informant 39.

3. (See above, pp. 12–13 n. 4.)

The terms Sotho and Nguni

There is no historically authentic terminology to distinguish the two major sub-cultures among the Bantu-speaking farming peoples of southern Africa. The people themselves recognized different levels of identification and differentiation, and in several areas, as in LeSotho, there had been interactions over many generations between peoples whom modern scholars call 'Sotho' and 'Nguni'.

During much of the nineteenth century white people often used the word 'Bechuanas' (Tswana) as a generic name for the peoples who predominated on the high veld, and the word 'Kaffirs' or 'Caffers' as a comparable generic name for the peoples who predominated in the coast region below the mountain escarpment (e.g. Casalis (1), p. xviii; Arbousset (1), p. 165 n. 2). The first time the word BaSotho is known to have been written down was in 1824 when John Melvill, Cape Colonial Agent at Griqua Town, applied it, in the form 'Bushootoo', to the people who lived in the Caledon valley (Melvill to Government Secretary, Cape Town, 17 Dec. 1824, SA B9 F2 PF, LMS). The French missionaries, Thomas Arbousset and Eugène Casalis, who reached LeSotho in 1833, applied it to the subjects of Moshoeshoe. But Arbousset was ambivalent about its scope. In his book which was published in 1842 he wrote that the 'natives' on the high veld sometimes 'extend the designation ... of *Basuta* to the Bechuanas generally', and that the Zulu of Dingane used the word 'Basutos' to 'comprise all the Bechuanas in their neighbourhood, the subjects of Moshesh, the Mantetis [Tlokoa], the Lighoyas [Hoja], &c.' (Arbousset (1), p. 271 and p. 157 n. 9). Thereafter, BaSotho gradually replaced 'Bechuana' as the generic name for the peoples who predominated on the high veld, including the Tswana and the Peli. See Martin Legassick, 'The Sotho-Tswana Peoples before 1800', in Leonard Thompson, ed., *African Societies in Southern Africa: Historical Studies*, London and New York, 1969, and R. S. Webb to Morena A. A. Moletsane, 3 May 1954, Lesotho Archives.

By a similar process, the word 'Nguni' supplanted 'Kaffirs' and other terms as a generic name for the peoples who predominated on the coastal side of the mountain escarpment. In the 1830s Dr. Andrew Smith used it, in the form 'Abingoni', in precisely the same sense as it was used later by Bryant and modern scholars (Andrew Smith Papers, vol. 4, p. 100). In 1842, Arbousset's book included the statement that he had seldom (but therefore sometimes) heard the 'natives' on the high veld 'extend the designation *Bakoni* to all the Caffers which they knew' (Arbousset (1), p. 271). Shula Marks is therefore incorrect in claiming that Bryant, publishing in the twentieth century, was responsible for imposing a generalization where none had existed in the minds of Africans ('The Traditions of the Natal "Nguni": A Second Look at the Works of A. T. Bryant' in L. Thompson, ed., *African Societies*, pp. 126–7); likewise Shula Marks and Anthony Atmore, 'The Problem of the Nguni: An Examination of the Ethnic and Linguistic Situation in South Africa before the Mfecane', in David Dalby, ed., *Language and History in Africa*, London, 1970, pp. 120–32.

I conclude that the two African cultures were clearly distinct (in spite of many similarities and overlaps), that it is not anachronistic for a historian to recognize this, and that the roots Sotho and Nguni, which were used by Africans in this sense in the 1830s and 1840s, and probably earlier, are the most appropriate.

4. (See above, p. 13 n. 3.)

Sotho Tribal Relationship

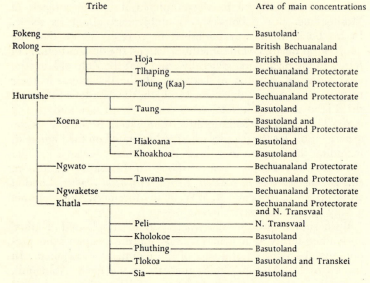

Tribe	Area of main concentrations
Fokeng	Basutoland
Rolong	British Bechuanaland
Hoja	British Bechuanaland
Tlhaping	Bechuanaland Protectorate
Tloung (Kaa)	Bechuanaland Protectorate
Hurutshe	Bechuanaland Protectorate
Taung	Basutoland
Koena	Basutoland and Bechuanaland Protectorate
Hiakoana	Basutoland
Khoakhoa	Basutoland
Ngwato	Bechuanaland Protectorate
Tawana	Bechuanaland Protectorate
Ngwaketse	Bechuanaland Protectorate
Khatla	Bechuanaland Protectorate and N. Transvaal
Peli	N. Transvaal
Kholokoe	Basutoland
Phuthing	Basutoland
Tlokoa	Basutoland and Transkei
Sia	Basutoland

Note: I have brought Jones's spellings into conformity with the usage in this book.

5. (See above, p. 38 n. 2.)

The main sources for Moshoeshoe's career in the *lifaqane* are numerous articles that were published in *Leselinyana* more than sixty years after the events by the BaSotho authors Azariel Sekese, Mareka Nchakala, S. F. Mlapokaze, and Abram Ra-Matšeatsana; the *Cape Monthly Magazine* article by Nehemiah [Sekhonyana] Moshoeshoe; articles by French missionaries in the *JME*, vols. ix (1834) ff.; and the books by Arbousset (1842) and Casalis (1859 and 1882) and unpublished papers by Arbousset (1840), Tlali Moshoeshoe (1858), and Sekhonyana Moshoeshoe (1905). The standard synthesis is E & M (1912): it is based on most of the sources mentioned above and on additional information Ellenberger obtained orally in LeSotho. But there are many inconsistencies among and within these sources, most of which take the form of disconnected accounts of separate episodes. The relationships between the episodes are often unclear, even in Ellenberger's synthesis. Informants whom I saw in 1965 and 1968 were not able to untangle these problems. Consequently, any synthesis that purports to follow Moshoeshoe and his chiefdom through the *lifaqane* is bound to be at variance with some of the evidence. It would be pedantic to footnote every detail. In the following Note (6) I mention the most significant variation from the synthesis I have made in the text.

6. (See above, p. 42 n. 1.)

Botha Bothe

In the text I have followed the version in E & M, pp. 143–6, which is based largely on Nehemiah [Sekhonyana] Moshoeshoe's letter to J. M. Orpen, 4 Dec. 1905, Ellenberger Papers, and is compatible with articles in *Leselinyana* by Sekese (1 and 15 Sept. 1892; 1 Apr. and 15 Dec. 1893), Nchakala (1 July 1891), Mlapokaze (May 1903), and RaMatšeatsana (1 May 1891). There is a completely different version in Arbousset (2), an unpublished paper which Ellenberger may not have seen. On 22 February 1840 Moshoeshoe, Arbousset, and others were deep in the Maloti mountains, about twenty miles east-south-east of Botha Bothe, on an expedition to the Mont-aux-Sources. They spent that night in a vast cave and Arbousset recorded ((2), pp. 105–7):

For my part, I gathered several new parts of the history of the Bassoutos. For example, Moshesh related to me that in 1821 or 1822, at the time of the irruption of the Mantatis [Tlokoa] into his country, he had sought refuge in this immense cavern wherein we were now, and he remained there for five or six months with a part of his people and his herds. Having been pursued up to this retreat by his enemies, he evacuated it and climbed a neighbouring mountain ridge for his security. The Mantatis did not dare follow him there, and they withdrew after a few days of delay. But precisely at the moment when they were turning back, a Matabele [Nguni] chief by the name of Sepeka fell upon the Bassoutos from the eastern side and forced them to flee. They descended the mountain and gave battle to the Batlokuos (former name of the Mantatis) who had hastened to this place upon seeing them on the western slope of those harrowing peaks. Moshesh, always noted as much for his parental love as for his military valour, directed the battle through his advice, inspired his soldiers, and encouraged them by his shouts and by the brandishing of his assagai. At the same time, he carried his son Molapo on his shoulders. Mammagaton ['MaMohato], the queen, held Massoupa [Masopha] to her bosom, and one of the officers of the king led the princess, Tsomate [Mathe], by the hand. The breaking forth of a rain and hail storm, accompanied by thunder, weakened the ardour of the assailants. But it was not entirely to the advantage of the Bassoutos: several of them plunged into an abyss from the top of the mountain; also, a considerable portion of the cattle trundled into one or other of the enemy camps, especially into Sepeka's; night finally came to cover this vast field of horror and carnage with its shadow. Moshesh, taking advantage of the darkness, retreated to a neighbouring mountain which was at once opposite to the Mantatis and the Matebeles. Contented with the booty that they had just obtained, the enemies withdrew on the following day, some towards the east, others towards the west, each group perhaps fearing the other, anxious in any case to secure the cattle they had captured. Thus were the Bassoutos left in peace.

If Moshoeshoe was speaking the truth, and if Arbousset understood and recorded him correctly, the synthesis that I have adopted, following all the other evidence, is wrong.

7. (See above, p. 174 n. 1.)

The Vundle

The Vundle chiefly lineage have a remarkable tradition. They claim that they originated in the 'Belgian Congo' thirty-three generations ago; that they migrated southwards to Ntsoana-Tsatsi on the South African high veld (about twenty miles east of Frankfort, O.F.S.) eleven generations ago and to southern Nguni country seven generations ago; and that they returned northwards to LeSotho in the time of chief Tyhali, the great-grandfather of the present (1968) chief, Mhamha Vova, while Moshoeshoe was still at Botha Bothe (i.e. before 1824). They also claim that they were the first Bantu-speaking settlers of south-eastern LeSotho and that they were not subjects of Moorosi, but independent allies of Moshoeshoe. (Testimony of Thembane Zonamzi and Mhamha Vova, Informants 49 and 50.) However, all the names in Chief Mhamha's genealogy are Nguni names and Vundle culture seems to be unadulterated Nguni, which could scarcely have been so if the Vundle chiefs had lived among the southern Nguni for no more than four generations. Moreover, D. F. Ellenberger, who founded a mission at Masitise in Moorosi's country in 1866, was sure that Tyhali and his followers had settled in southern LeSotho under Moorosi in 1847–8, and documents written in the 1860s confirm that Tyhali was subordinate to Moorosi. (D. F. Ellenberger, *Leselinyana*, 4 Feb. 1911; Jno. Austen, Superintendent of the Wittebergen Native Reserve, to the Civil Commissioner of Aliwal North, 8 July 1865, *BR* iii. 387.) In my field work in 1968 I found that several other chiefs whose ancestors had been incorporated by Moshoeshoe or his allies were smarting under the treatment they had received in the colonial period, when paramount chiefs descended from Moshoeshoe had 'placed' their sons over them in successive generations, thereby reducing their status and their landholdings, so that they had an interest in claiming that their ancestors were independent allies of Moshoeshoe. Nevertheless, the traditions of the Vundle warrant more thorough investigation than they have yet received.

SOURCES

THE sources for this book are uneven. The first documents written by people who had met Moshoeshoe are dated 1833, by which time he was about forty-seven years old, and although the volume of evidence then grows rapidly, most of it has been refracted through the minds of people whose culture was radically different from his own.

There are five main types of primary documentary sources. The Protestant missionaries who settled in LeSotho in and after 1833 sent frequent reports to their headquarters in Paris. A high proportion of these reports was published *in extenso* in the *Journal des Missions Évangéliques*, which contains about two hundred pages from LeSotho in each year from 1834 onwards. The Paris missionaries also wrote numerous other works, notably the several books by Eugène Casalis, who was a first-class ethnographer and had excellent rapport with Moshoeshoe, a book and an unpublished travel account by Thomas Arbousset, and the journals of Louis Cochet and Pierre-Joseph Maitin.

Second, various other white people visited Moshoeshoe from time to time. The most useful surviving accounts include those by Dr. Andrew Smith, who led a large Cape colonial expedition through the high veld in 1834–5, and Joseph Orpen, an Irish settler, who got to know Moshoeshoe well in the 1850s. Smith's unpublished Journal is much more detailed than his *Diary*, which P. R. Kirby edited for the Van Riebeeck Society.

Third, during the last three decades of his life Moshoeshoe conducted an extensive correspondence with colonial and republican officials. These letters form a high proportion of the contents of several British *Parliamentary Papers*, which were called for as a result of the annexation and abandonment of the Orange River Sovereignty and the annexation of Basutoland, and of the *Basutoland Records*, which George McCall Theal compiled while Basutoland was a dependency of the

Cape Colony. Three volumes of the *Basutoland Records*, terminating on 3 March 1868, were published in 1883, but the rest, continuing to 1872, have not been published.

Fourth, D. F. Ellenberger, who joined the Protestant mission in LeSotho in 1861, collected numerous historical statements. Most of his works were first published as articles in the SeSotho mission journal *Leselinyana*; many were then revised and incorporated in *Histori ea BaSotho*; and finally, after further revision, some were translated into English by J. C. Macgregor and published in 1912.

Fifth, there are a number of writings by BaSotho who knew Moshoeshoe. Several essays have been preserved that were written by two sons of Moshoeshoe, Tlali and Tsekelo, when they were at school in Cape Town in 1858. Another son, Sekhonyana (baptised Nehemiah), published historical articles in the *Cape Monthly Magazine* in 1880 and wrote supplementary letters to Joseph Orpen in 1905. And Azariel Sekese and other BaSotho published numerous historical articles in *Leselinyana*, especially during the period 1890 to 1916.

All these sources present problems for the historian. White peoples' perceptions of Moshoeshoe and SeSotho society were profoundly influenced by their own interests and norms. The numerous letters that are attributed to Moshoeshoe were written in English (occasionally in French or Dutch) by missionaries or mission-educated sons and marked X by Moshoeshoe, and it is not possible to determine how accurately they reflected the king's intentions as expressed in SeSotho. Ellenberger did not preserve records of his discussions with informants and his major work, *History of the Basuto: ancient and modern*, ends with the arrival of the first missionaries in 1833. Finally, the literate BaSotho who knew Moshoeshoe and his contemporaries were educated in the mission schools and when they wrote for *Leselinyana* they were constrained by the fact that they were using a journal edited by white missionaries. Indeed, in so far as the primary documentary sources shed light on Moshoeshoe's personality and the internal history of his kingdom, most of them do so from the evangelical point of view. Individuals who became

Christians or co-operated with the missionaries are prominently and favourably reported on, while those who opposed them are generally ignored or criticized. Moshoeshoe himself emerges with considerable credit as the patron of the mission, but people like Posholi and Tšapi rarely receive their due.

The secondary literature includes numerous books and articles written to commemorate the work of the Protestant and Catholic missions (the latter was founded in 1862), and others written by British colonial administrators and traders and white South African journalists with Eurocentric assumptions. There are also several studies by anthropologists, including a comprehensive account of SeSotho culture by Hugh Ashton and an analysis of the impact of the missionaries in the nineteenth century by Claude-Hélène Perrot. Captain R. S. Webb has compiled an admirable *Gazetteer for Basutoland*, giving the coordinates of practically every historical site, and Daniel Kunene and Samson Guma have written excellent commentaries on SeSotho oral literature. Recent books, articles, and dissertations by John Omer-Cooper, William Lye, Peter Sanders, and Anthony Atmore are among the first interpretations of the primary sources by modern white historians. So far, few BaSotho have had opportunities for historical training and research, but it is to be expected that Mosebi Damane and other members of the history department on the Roma campus of the University of Botswana, Lesotho and Swaziland will soon be producing significant works.

I have classified the documentary sources in the usual way in Sections A, B, and C of the bibliography. Section D is a list of the informants whom I interviewed in Lesotho. I selected them partly for their reputations as knowledgeable persons and also to obtain evidence from members of as many different descent groups as possible, including the lineages of several of Moshoeshoe's sons and also the lineages of chiefs who became Moshoeshoe's allies and subjects. Appointments were made in advance and open-ended discussions lasted between one and five hours. A few informants preferred to converse in English; discussions with the majority were in SeSotho and were interpreted by Esau Moroa Sehalahala (or, in some cases, Samson Guma). I made notes in my workbook during a discussion and typed cards from the notes the same evening. In the bibliography, informants are classified by their descent, starting with descendants of Letsie, Moshoeshoe's eldest son. I list the name of each informant, his age, his status, and the time and place of the interview(s). In the footnotes accompanying the text, an informant is identified by the letter I and the number against his name in the Bibliography: thus 'I. 22' is Principal Chief Tumane Thaabe Matela, a descendant of Moshoeshoe's first ally, Lethole, the pre-*lifaqane* chief of the Khoakhoa.

In most cases, whether they realize it or not, BaSotho informants' knowledge and interpretation of the events of Moshoeshoe's times are influenced, at least to some extent, by the published works of Casalis and Arbousset, and Ellenberger and Macgregor; but the informants added immensely to my understanding of SeSotho custom, Moshoeshoe's methods and objectives, and the structure of his kingdom. It is sad to record that more than a dozen of these informants have died since I met them.

There is much about Moshoeshoe and his career—especially during the first forty-seven years of his life—that is still obscure and is likely to remain so. I have discussed several of the major problems in the text (e.g. the status of Mohlomi and his relations with Moshoeshoe, pp. 24–7) and in the footnotes and end-notes (e.g. Moshoeshoe's movements during the *lifaqane*, pp. 334–6).

A. Unpublished Documents

1. Official

Orange Free State Archives, Bloemfontein:

Orange River Sovereignty, BR 1/4, 1/5, 3/1; SC 3/1, 3/3.
Orange Free State, GS 1155, 1338–56.
Public Record Office, London:
C.O. 48, 179, 879; H.L. 12, 20.

2. *Unofficial*

Mission Archives

Catholic Archdiocese, Maseru:
  Journal of Father Joseph Gérard, O.M.I., 1864–1871
  Missions 1862–1868.
London Missionary Society, London:
  South Africa 1797–1849, Boxes 9–20.
  Revd. John Philip correspondence.
  Revd. J. J. Freeman correspondence.
Société des Missions Évangéliques, Paris:
  Correspondence from missionaries.
  Excursion Missionnaire de M. Thomas Arbousset dans les
    Montagnes Bleues, 1840.
  Notes et souvenirs du missionaire Louis J. Cochet.
  Journal du missionaire Pierre-Joseph Maitin, 1855–1856.
Lesotho Evangelical Church, Morija (formerly Société des
  Missions Évangéliques): Sundry papers.
Wesleyan-Methodist Missionary Society, London:
  South Africa, Boxes 5, 7, 12; Boxes labelled S.A. Kaffraria
  1858–1864, Grahamstown, Queenstown, and Bechuanaland
  1864–67, S.A. Bechuanaland 1868–76; and Journal of W.
  Impey 1838–1847.

Others

Colonial Office Library, London:
  Vol. 13015, Private Correspondence of Sir Philip Edmond
    Wodehouse, 1861–1869.
Durham University Library:
  Papers of the third Earl Grey.
Library of the Revd. Paul Ellenberger (at Masitise, Lesotho, in
    1965: now in France):
  Papers of the Revd. D. F. Ellenberger.
Lesotho Archives, Maseru:
  George McCall Theal, ed., Basutoland Records, vols. iv–vi
    (MSS.).
  Manuscripts by Captain R. S. Webb.
Orange Free State Archives, Bloemfontein:
  P.A. 11.2 Letter-Book of the Revd. James Cameron.
  P.A. 221.1–2 Revd. W. Illsley papers.
Rhodes University Library, Grahamstown:
  J. M. Orpen documents in the Cory Collection.

South African Museum Library, Cape Town:
  Andrew Smith papers.
South African Public Library, Cape Town:
  Grey Collection, vol. 265; SeSotho MSS. by Hlali and Tsekelo
  Moshesh (Tlali and Tsekelo Moshoeshoe) *c.* 1858.
  Vol. 572968 FOL-STO G. W. Stow, 'The Intrusion of the
  Stronger Races Continued'.
Library of Captain R. S. Webb, Paarl:
  Sundry papers.

B. Publications

1. Official

Great Britain

C.O. 879/1 *Confidential*: *Assumption of Sovereignty over the Territory between the Vaal and Orange Rivers, and British Kaffraria*; and related printed documents.

C.O. 879/2 *Private letter from Sir P. E. Wodehouse, December 11, 1865* and related printed documents.

H.L. 12/1113 *Correspondence relative to Assumption of Sovereignty between the Vaal and Orange Rivers . . . presented to Parliament May 19, 1851.*

H.L. 20/1182 *Further Correspondence relative to the State of the Orange River Territory . . . presented to Parliament, May 31, 1853.*

H.L. 13 *Further Correspondence relative to the State of the Orange River Territory . . . presented to Parliament, April 10, 1854.*

23719 *Despatches . . . on the Subject of the Recognition of Moshesh, Chief of Basutos, and of his Tribe, as British Subjects . . . presented to Parliament,* July 1869.

C.-18 *Further Despatches . . . on the subject of the Recognition of Moshesh . . . presented to Parliament, 21 February 1870.*

C.-99 *Further Despatches . . . on the subject of the Recognition of Moshesh . . . presented to Parliament, May 1870.*

Cmd. 8209 [G. I. Jones] *Basutoland Medicine Murder: A Report of the Recent Outbreak of 'Diretlo' Murders in Basutoland,* 1951.

Cape of Good Hope

Evidence taken at Bloemhof before the Commission appointed to investigate the claims of the South African Republic, Captain N. Waterboer, Chief of West Griqualand, and certain other Native Chiefs, to portions of the territory of the Vaal River now known as the Diamond-Fields, 1871.

Report and Evidence of the Commission on Native Laws and Customs of the Basutos, 1873.

Union/Republic of South Africa
South African Archival Records, Orange Free State, vols. 1–4 (1854–9), 1952–65.

Lesotho
The Lesotho Independence Order 1966.

2. *Unofficial Books and Pamphlets*

AMBROSE, David P., *Oxfam Guide to Thaba Bosiu*, Lesotho, 1968.

ARBOUSSET, T., and DAUMAS, F., *Relation d'un voyage d'exploration au nord-est de la Colonie du Cap de Bonne-Espérance . . . 1836*, Paris, 1842. (Reprint of the English 1846 edition, *Narrative of an Exploratory Tour to the North-East of the Colony of the Cape of Good Hope*, Cape Town, 1968.)

ASHTON, Hugh, *The Basuto*, London, 1952.

BACKHOUSE, James, *A Narrative of a Visit to the Mauritius and South Africa*, London, 1844.

BALFET, Frantz, *Un Pionnier de la Mission du Lessouto: Samuel Rolland (1801–1873)*, Paris, 1914.

BANQUIS, Jean, *Origines de la Société des Missions Évangéliques de Paris*, 2 vols., Paris, 1930–1.

BIRD, John, ed., *The Annals of Natal: 1495–1845*, 2 vols., Pietermaritzburg, 1888.

BOEGNER, M. A., et al., *Livre d'Or de la Mission du Lessouto*, Paris, 1912.

BROADBENT, Samuel, *A Narrative of the First Introduction of Christianity among the Barolong Tribe of Bechuanas*, London, 1865.

BRYANT, A. T., *Olden Times in Zululand and Natal*, London, 1929.

—— *The Zulu People*, Pietermaritzburg, 1949.

—— *A History of the Zulu and Neighbouring Tribes*, Cape Town, 1964.

CAPLAN, Gerald L., *The Elites of Barotseland, 1878–1969*, London, 1970.

CASALIS, Eugène, *Études sur la langue sechuana*, Paris, 1841.

—— *Les Bassoutos ou vingt-trois années d'études et d'observations au sud de l'Afrique*, Paris, 1859. (English edition, *The Basutos or twenty-three years in South Africa*, London, 1861, reprint, Cape Town, 1965.)

—— *Mes souvenirs*, Paris, 1882. (English edition, *My Life in Basutoland*, London, 1889, reprint Cape Town, 1971.)

CLAVIER, Henri, *Thomas Arbousset*, Paris, 1965.

COLLINS, Wm. W., *Free Statia: Reminiscences of a Lifetime in the Orange Free State*, Cape Town 1965.

COPE, Trevor, ed., *Izibongo: Zulu Praise Poems*, Oxford, 1968.

CORY, George, ed., *The Diary of the Revd. Francis Owen*, Cape Town, 1926.

CUNYNGHAME, General Sir Arthur Thurlow, *My Command in South Africa 1874–1878*, London, 1879.

DAMANE, Mosebi, *Peace, The Mother of Nations*, Morija, 1947.

—— *Morena Moorosi*, Morija, n.d.

DE KIEWIET, C. W., *British Colonial Policy and the South African Republics, 1848–1872*, London, 1929.

DE KOCK, W. J., ed., *Dictionary of South African Biography*, i, Cape Town, 1968.

DIETERLIN, H., *Adolphe Mabille (1836–1894)*, Paris, 1898.

—— *Eugène Casalis (1812–1891)*, Paris, 1930.

EDWARDS, John, *Reminiscences of the Early Life and Missionary Labours of the Revd. John Edwards*, 2nd ed., London, 1886.

EKSTEEN, M. C., *Lesotho in Uitwaartse Beweging*, Johannesburg, 1962.

ELLENBERGER, D. Fred, *Histori ea Basotho*, 4th ed., Morija, 1956.

—— (comp.) and MACGREGOR, J. C. (trans.), *History of the Basuto: ancient and modern*, London, 1912.

ELLENBERGER, V., *Un Siècle de Missions au Lessouto (1833–1933)*, Paris, 1934. (English ed., trans. Edmond M. Ellenberger, *A Century of Mission Work in Basutoland (1833–1933)*, Morija, 1938.)

—— *La Fin tragique des Bushmen*, Paris, 1953.

EYBERS, G. W., *Select Constitutional Documents illustrating South African History 1795–1910*, London, 1918.

FAGAN, Brian M., *South Africa*, London and New York, 1965.

FAVRE, Édouard, *François Coillard: Missionnaire au Lessouto 1861–1882*, Paris, 1910.

FINNEGAN, Ruth, *Oral Literature in Africa*, Oxford, 1970.

FRASER, John George, *Episodes in My Life*, Cape Town, 1922.

FREEMAN, J. J., *A Tour in South Africa*, London, 1851.

GALBRAITH, John S., *Reluctant Empire: British Policy on the South African Frontier 1834–1854*, Berkeley, Calif., 1963.

GALLIENNE, Georges, *Thomas Arbousset (1810–1877)*, Paris, 1931.

GERMOND, Robert C., *Chronicles of Basutoland*, Morija, Lesotho, 1967.

GOIRAN, H., *Une Action Créatrice de la Mission Protestante Française au sud de l'Afrique*, Paris, 1931.

GOODY, Jack, *Technology, Tradition, and the State in Africa*, London, 1971.

GUILLARMOD, A. Jacot, *Flora of Lesotho*, Lehre, 1971.

GUMA, S. M., *Morena Mohlomi, 'Mora Monyane*, Pietermaritzburg, 1960.

HAILEY, Lord, *The High Commission Territories*, Part V of *Native Administration in the British African Territories*, London, 1953.

—— *The Republic of South Africa and the High Commission Territories*, London, 1963.

HALPERN, Jack, *South Africa's Hostages: Basutoland, Bechuanaland, and Swaziland*, Baltimore, 1965.

HARRIS, Captain William Cornwallis, *The Wild Sports of Southern Africa*, 5th ed., London, 1852. (Reprint, Cape Town, 1963.)

HOW, Marion W., *The Mountain Bushmen of Basutoland*, Pretoria, 1970.

IKIME, Obaro, *Merchant Prince of the Niger Delta*, London, 1968.

ISAACS, Nathaniel, *Travels and Adventures in Eastern Africa*, ed. L. Herrman, 2 vols., Cape Town, 1935–6.

JOUSSE, Théophile, *La Mission Française Évangélique au sud de l'Afrique*, 2 vols., Paris, 1889.

KHAKETLA, B. Makalo, *Moshoeshoe le Baruti*, Morija, 1954.

—— *Lesotho 1970: An African Coup under the Miscroscope*, London and Berkeley, Calif., 1972.

KIRBY, Percival R., ed., *The Diary of Dr. Andrew Smith, director of the 'Expedition for exploring Central Africa', 1834–6*, Van Riebeeck Society, 2 vols., Cape Town, 1939–40.

KUNENE, D. P., *Heroic Poetry of the Basotho*, Oxford, 1971.

—— DANIEL, P., and KIRSCH, Randal A., *The Beginning of South African Vernacular Literature*, African Studies Association, n.d. (*c.* 1970).

LAGDEN, Sir Godfrey, *The Basutos*, 2 vols., London, 1909.

LAYDEVANT, F., *Histori ea Lesotho*, Mazenod, 1961.

—— *The Basuto*, Mazenod, n.d.

LEE, D. N., and WOODHOUSE, M. C., *Art on the Rocks of Southern Africa*, Cape Town, 1970.

LEOATLE, Edward Motsamai, *Morena Moshoeshoe Mor'a Mokhachane*, Morija, 1952.

LLOYD, Peter C., *The Political Development of Yoruba Kingdoms in the Eighteenth and Nineteenth Centuries*, London, 1971.

LOW, D. A., *Buganda in Modern History*, Berkeley, Calif., 1971.

LUCAS, T. J., *Cape Life and Sport*, London, 1878.

MACGREGOR, J. C., *Basuto Traditions*, Cape Town, 1905.

MACKINTOSH, C. W., *Coillard of the Zambesi*, London, 1907.

MACMILLAN, W. M., *The Cape Colour Question*, London, 1937.
—— *Bantu, Boer, and Briton*, 2nd ed., Oxford, 1964.
MAJARA, Simon N., *Morena oa Thaba*, Mazenod, 1963.
MAKORO, J. C. K., *Histori ea Batlokoa*, Mazenod, n.d.
MALAN, J. H., *Die Opkoms van 'n Republiek*, Bloemfontein, 1929.
MANGOAELA, Z. D., *Lithoko tsa Marena a Basotho*, Morija, 1957.
MARAIS, J. S., *The Cape Coloured People*, London, 1939.
—— *Maynier and the First Boer Republic*, Cape Town, 1944.
MASON, R. J., *The Pre-History of the Transvaal*, Johannesburg, 1962.
MEARS, W. G. A., *Wesleyan Barolong Mission in Trans-Orangia 1821–1884*, Cape Town, n.d.
MOLETSANE, Morena Abraham Aaron, *An Account of the Auto-biographical Memoir*, Paarl, 1967.
MOPELI-PAULUS, A. S., *Moshweshwe Moshwaila*, King William's Town, n.d.
MORRELL, W. P., *British Colonial Policy in the Mid-Victorian Age*, Oxford, 1969.
MORRIS, DONALD R., *The Washing of the Spears*, New York, 1965.
MULLER, C. F. J., *Die Britse Owerheid en die Groot Trek*, 2nd ed., Johannesburg, 1963.
OMER-COOPER, J. D., *The Zulu Aftermath*, Evanston, 1966.
ORPEN, J. M., *Principles of Native Government*, Cape Town, 1880.
—— *Reminiscences of Life in South Africa*, Cape Town, 1964.
—— Special Commissioner of the *Cape Argus*, *History of the Basutos of South Africa*, Cape Town, 1857.
PAROZ, R. A., *Southern Sotho–English Dictionary*, Morija, 1961.
PELLISSIER, S. H., *Jean Pierre Pellissier van Bethulie*, Pretoria, 1956.
PERROT, Claude-Hélène, *Les Sotho et les missionnaires européens au xixe siècle* (Annales de l'Université d'Abidjan, 1970, Série F, Tome 2, Fascicule 1), Dijon, 1970.
PERSON, YVES, *Samori: Une Révolution Dyula*, 2 vols., Dakar, 1968.
RANGER, T. O., and KIMAMBO, Isaria, eds., *The Historical Study of African Religion*, London, 1972.
RITTER, E. A., *Shaka Zulu*, London, 1955.
ROCHE, Aimé, *Clartés Australes: Joseph Gérard, O.M.I. (1831–1914)*, Lyons, 1951.
RUTHERFORD, J., *Sir George Grey, 1812–1898*, London, 1961.
SCHAPERA, I., *The Khoisan Peoples of South Africa*, London, 1930
—— *The Ethnic Composition of the Tswana Tribes*, London, 1952.
—— *Government and Politics in Tribal Societies*, London, 1956.
—— *Tribal Innovators: Tswana Chiefs and Social Change 1795–1940*, London, 1970.

SCHOLTZ, G. D., *Die Konstitutie en die Staatsinstellinge van die Oranje Vrystaat*, Amsterdam, 1937.

—— *President J. H. Brand*, Johannesburg, 1957.

SHAW, William, *Memoirs of Mrs. Anne Hodgson*, London, 1836.

SHEDDICK, Vernon, *The Southern Sotho*, London, 1953.

—— *Land Tenure in Basutoland*, London, 1954.

SIMONS, H. J., *African Women: Their Legal Status in South Africa*, London, 1968.

SMIT, P., *Lesotho: a Geographical Study*, Pretoria, 1967.

SMITH, Edwin W., *The Mabilles of Basutoland*, London, 1939.

SOUTHALL, A. W., *Alur Society*, Cambridge, 1956.

SPENCE, J. E., *Lesotho—The Politics of Dependence*, London, 1968.

STEEDMAN, Andrew, *Wanderings and Adventures in the Interior of Southern Africa*, 2 vols., London, 1835.

STOW, G. W., *The Native Races of South Africa*, London, 1905.

STUART, J., and MALCOLM, D. M. K., eds., *The Diary of Henry Francis Fynn*, Pietermaritzburg, 1950.

THEAL, George McCall, ed., *Basutoland Records*, vols. i–iii, Cape Town, 1883. (Reprint with index, Cape Town, 1964.)

—— *History of South Africa*, 11 vols., London, 1888–1919. (Reprint, Cape Town, 1964.)

THOMPSON, Leonard, ed., *African Societies in Southern Africa: Historical Studies*, London and New York, 1969.

THORNTON, R. W., *The Origin and History of the Basuto Pony*, Morija, 1936.

TYLDEN, G., *A History of Thaba Bosiu, 'A Mountain at Night'*, Maseru, 1945.

—— *The Rise of the Basuto*, Cape Town, 1950.

UYS, C. J., *In the Era of Shepstone*, Lovedale, 1933.

VAN DER MERWE, P. J., *Die Noordwaartse Beweging van die Boere voor die Groot Trek*, The Hague, 1937.

VAN JAARSVELD, F. A., *Die Eenheidstrewe van die Republikeinse Afrikaners: i. Pioniershartstogte (1836–1864)*, Johannesburg, 1951.

VAN WARMELO, N. J., *History of Matiwane and the Amangwane Tribe as told by Msebenzi to his kinsman Albert Hlongwane*, Union of South Africa, Department of Native Affairs, Ethnological Publications, vii (1938).

VENTER, I. S. J., *Die Ruilkontrakte in 1833–34 aangegaan tussen Mosjesj en die Wesleyane*, Communications of the University of South Africa, C. 20, 1960.

—— *Die Sendingstasie Thaba 'Nchu 1833–1900*, Communications of the University of South Africa, C. 18, 1960.

WALKER, Eric A., *A History of Southern Africa*, 3rd ed., London, 1957.

—— *Historical Atlas of South Africa*, Cape Town, 1922.

—— *The Great Trek*, 4th ed., London, 1960.

WALLMAN, Sandra, *Take Out Hunger: Two Case Studies of Rural Development in Basutoland*, London and New York, 1969.

WALTON, James, *African Village*, Pretoria, 1956.

—— *Early Ghoya Settlement in the Orange Free State*, Bloemfontein, 1965.

WEBB, R. S., *Gazetteer for Basutoland*, Paarl, 1950.

WEBER, Max, *The Theory of Social and Economic Organization*, New York, 1957.

WEISFELDER, Richard F., *Defining National Purpose in Lesotho*, Athens, Ohio, 1969.

—— *The Basuto Monarchy: A Spent Force or a Dynamic Political Factor?* Athens, Ohio, 1972.

WELSH, David, *The Roots of Segregation, Native Policy in Colonial Natal, 1845–1910*, Cape Town, 1971.

WHITAKER, C. S., *The Politics of Tradition*, Princeton, 1970.

WILLIAMS, John C., *Lesotho: Three Manpower Problems*, Pretoria, 1971.

—— *Lesotho: Land Tenure and Economic Development*, Pretoria, 1972.

WILSON, Monica, *The Thousand Years Before Van Riebeeck*, Johannesburg, 1970.

—— *Religion and the Transformation of Society*, Cambridge, 1971.

—— and THOMPSON, Leonard, eds., *The Oxford History of South Africa*, 2 vols., Oxford, 1969, 1971.

ZOLBERG, Aristide R., *Creating Political Order*, Chicago, 1966.

3. Articles

ALPERS, Edward, 'Re-thinking African Economic History: a contribution to the discussion of the roots of under-development', *Ufahamu*, Los Angeles, iii (3) (Winter 1973), 97–129.

AMBROSE, David P., 'Jeremiah Libopuoa Moshoeshoe (1839–1863)', *Lesotho*, viii (1969), 24–9.

ASHTON, Hugh, 'Political Organisation of the Southern Sotho', *Bantu Studies*, xii (4) (1938), 287–320.

ATMORE, Anthony, 'The Passing of Sotho Independence', in Leonard Thompson, ed., *ASSA*, pp. 282–301.

—— and SANDERS, Peter, 'Sotho Arms and Ammunition in the Nineteenth Century', *JAH* xii (1971), 535–44.

BARNARD, B. J., ''n Lewensbeskrywing van Majoor Henry Douglas Warden', *AYB*, 1948, i.

BOWKER, T. H., 'The Cave Cannibals of South Africa', *South African Magazine*, ii (1868), 641–5.

BREITENBACH, J. J., 'Sir Philip Edmond Wodehouse', in W. J. de Kock, ed., *Dictionary of South African Biography*, i.

BRUTSCH, Albert, 'The visit of Basotho chiefs to the Cape Colony in 1845', *Lesotho*, viii (1969), 5–12.

BUNDY, Colin, 'Emergence and Decline of a South African Peasantry', *African Affairs*, lxxi (Oct. 1972), 369–88.

CLARKE, M., 'Unexplored Basutoland', *Proceedings of the Royal Geographical Society*, x (1888), 519.

CORY, Sir George, 'The Rise of South Africa', vi, *AYB*, 1940.

DAVENPORT, T. R. H., 'The Move towards Responsible Government', *OHSA* i. 311–33.

DORNAN, S. S., 'The Basuto—Their Traditional History and Folklore', *Proceedings of the Rhodesian Scientific Association*, viii (1) (1908), 65–94.

FAGAN, Brian M., 'The Later Iron Age in South Africa', in L. Thompson, ed., *ASSA*, pp. 50–70.

FAIRCLOUGH, T. L., 'Notes on the Basuto, Their History, Country, etc.', *Journal of the African Society*, iv (1904–5), 194–205.

FERNANDEZ, James W., 'The Shaka Complex', *Transition*, 29 (1967), 11–14.

G. ST. V. C., 'A Page in Colonial History', *Cape Quarterly Review*, i (1882), 684–8.

GLANVILLE, T. B., 'A Pisto', *The Gentleman's Magazine*, Sept. 1876, 428–46.

GLUCKMAN, Max, 'The Kingdom of the Zulu in South Africa', in M. Fortes and E. E. Evans-Pritchard, eds., *African Political Systems*, London, 1940.

—— 'The Rise of a Zulu Empire', *Scientific American*, ccii (4) (Apr. 1960), 159–69.

GROBBELAAR, J. J. G., 'Die Vrystaatse Republiek en die Basoe-toevraagstuk', *AYB*, 1939, ii.

GUMA, S. M., 'Some Aspects of Circumcision in Basutoland', *African Studies*, xxiv (3–4) (1965), 241–9.

HAMMOND-TOOKE, David, 'The "Other Side" of Frontier History: a Model of Cape Nguni Political Process', in L. Thompson, ed., *ASSA*, pp. 230–58.

HAMNETT, Ian, 'Koena Chieftainship Seniority in Basutoland', *Africa*, xxxv (3) (1965), 241–51.

HIRSCHMAN, Albert O., 'Underdevelopment, Obstacles to the

Perception of Change, and Leadership', *Daedalus*, Summer 1968, 925–37.

HOW, Marion, 'An Alibi for Mantatisi', *African Studies*, xiii (2) (1954), 65–76.

HUET, P., 'Reisjournaal—Verhaal van een uitstapje uit Aliwal naar de Fransche Zendelingstatien in het Basutooland', *Elpis*, i (1857), 149–87.

INNSKEEP, R. R., 'The Archeological Background', *OHSA* i. 1–39.

JACOTTET, E., 'Mœurs, Coutumes et Superstitions des Ba-Souto', *Bulletin de la Société Neuchateloise de Géographie*, ix (1896–7), 107–51.

JONES, G. I., 'Chiefly Succession in Basutoland', in Jack Goody, ed., *Succession to High Office* (Cambridge Papers in Social Anthropology, No. 4), Cambridge, 1966.

JOUSSE, Théophile, 'Moshesh, roi des Bassouto', *Le Chrétien Évangélique: revue religieuse de la suisse romande*, 1867, pp. 7–17, 67–78, 122–32.

LAYDEVANT, F., 'La Poésie chez les Basuto', *Africa*, iii (1930), 523–35.

—— 'Étude sur la famille en Basutoland', *Journal de la Société des Africanistes*, i (1931), 207–57.

—— 'Le Sceptre des chefs Basuto', *Africa*, xviii (Jan. 1948), 41–4.

—— 'Les Rites de l'initiation au Basutoland', *Anthropos*, xlvi (1951), 221–54.

LEGASSICK, Martin, 'The Sotho-Tswana Peoples before 1800', in L. Thompson, ed., *ASSA*, pp. 86–125.

LLOYD, Peter C., 'The Political Structure of African Kingdoms: an exploratory model', in M. Banton, ed., *Political Systems and the Distribution of Power*, London, 1965.

—— 'The Political Development of West African Kingdoms', *JAH* ix (1968), 319–29.

LYE, William F., 'The Difaqane: the Mfecane in the southern Sotho area', *JAH* viii (1967), 107–31.

—— 'The Ndebele Kingdom South of the Limpopo River', *JAH* x (1969), 37–54.

—— 'The Distribution of the Sotho Peoples after the Difaqane', in L. Thompson, ed., *ASSA*, pp. 190–206.

MACGREGOR, J. C., 'Some Notes on the Basuto Tribal System, Political and Social', *Report of the South African Association for the Advancement of Science*, vi (7) (1910), 276–81.

MARKS, Shula, 'The Nguni, the Natalians and Their History', *JAH* viii (1967), 529–40.

MARKS Shula, 'The Traditions of the Natal "Nguni": A Second Look at the Works of A. T. Bryant', in L. Thompson, ed., *ASSA*, pp. 126–44.

—— 'Firearms in Southern Africa: a Survey', *JAH* xii (1971), 517–30.

—— and Atmore, Anthony, 'The Problem of the Nguni: An Examination of the Ethnic and Linguistic Situation in South Africa before the Mfecane', in David Dalby, ed., *Language and History in Africa*, London, 1970.

[MHLANGA, Platje] AN AGED FINGO, 'A Story of Native Wars', *Cape Monthly Magazine*, 2nd series, xiv (Jan.–June 1877), 248–52.

MIDGLEY, John Franklin, *The Orange River Sovereignty 1848–1854*, *AYB*, 1949, ii.

MOHAPELOA, J. M., 'The Essential Masopha', *Lesotho*, v (1965–6), 7–17.

MOLOJA, 'The Story of the "Fetcani Horde" by one of themselves', *Cape Quarterly Review*, i (1882), 267–75.

MOSHESH, Nehemiah [Sekhonyana], 'A Little Light from Basutoland', *Cape Monthly Magazine*, 3rd series, ii (Jan.–June 1880), 221–33, 280–92.

MULLER, C. F. J., 'The Period of the Great Trek', in C. F. J. Muller, ed., *Five Hundred Years: A History of South Africa*, Pretoria, 1969, pp. 122–56.

'MZIKI [A. A. Campbell], '*Mlimo: The Rise and Fall of the Matabele*, Pietermaritzburg, 1926.

OMER-COOPER, J. D., 'Aspects of Political Change in the Nineteenth-century Mfecane', in L. Thompson, ed., *ASSA*, pp. 207–29.

PERROT, Claude-Hélène, 'Premières années de l'implantation du christianisme au Lesotho, 1833–1847', *Cahiers d'Études Africaines*, xiii (4) (1963), 97–124.

—— 'Un Culte messianique chez les Sotho au milieu du XIXᵉ siècle', *Archives de Sociologie des Religions*, ix (18) (July–Dec. 1964), 147–52.

PHILLIPSON, D. W., 'Early iron-using peoples of southern Africa', in L. Thompson, ed., *ASSA*, pp. 24–49.

PROCTOR, J. H., 'Building a Constitutional Monarchy in Lesotho', Duke University Reprint from *Civilizations*, Brussels, 1969.

RAMSEYER, Paul, 'La Circoncision chez les Bassoutus', *Revue d'Ethnographie et des Traditions Populaires*, xxxiii (1928), 40–70.

RAUM, Johannes W., 'Die Jünglingsweihen der Süd-Sotho-Stämme', *Wiener Völkerkundliche Mitteilungen*, Vienna, xvi–xvii (11–12) (1969–70), 7–69.

SANDERS, PETER, 'Sekonyela and Moshweshwe: Failure and Success in the Aftermath of the Difaqane', *JAH* x (1969), 439–55.

SECHEFO, Justinus, *The Twelve Lunar Months among the Basuto*, Mzenod, n.d. (reprinted from *Anthropos*, iv–v (1909–10)).

—— *Customs and Superstitions in Basutoland*, Mazenod, n.d.

SMITH, Alan, 'The Trade of Delagoa Bay as a Factor in Nguni Politics, 1750–1835', in L. Thompson, ed., *ASSA*, pp. 171–89.

SMITS, Lucas G. A., 'The Distribution of the Population in Lesotho and Some Implications for Economic Development', *Lesotho*, vii (1968), 19–35.

STONE, Lawrence, 'The Disenchantment of the World', *The New York Review of Books*, xvii (9) (Dec. 1971), 17–25.

STUIVER, Minze, and VAN DER MERWE, Nicolaas J., 'Radiocarbon Chronology of the Iron Age in Sub-Saharan Africa', *Current Anthropology*, ix (1) (1968), 48–58.

THOMPSON, Leonard, 'South Africa's Relations with Lesotho, Botswana, and Swaziland', *African Forum*, New York, ii (2) (Fall 1966), 65–77.

—— 'The Zulu Kingdom', *OHSA* i. 334–64.

—— 'The Difaqane and its Aftermath, 1822–1836', *OHSA* i. 391–405.

—— 'The Subjection of the African Chiefdoms, 1870–1898', *OHSA* ii. 244–86.

VAN DER POEL, Jean, 'Basutoland as a Factor in South African Politics (1858–1870)', *AYB*, 1941, i.

VAN SCHOOR, M. C. E., 'Johannes Henricus Brand', in W. J. de Kock, ed., *Dictionary of South African Biography*, i.

—— 'The Orange Free State', in C. F. J. Muller, ed., *Five Hundred Years*, pp. 203–20.

VANSINA, JAN, 'A Comparison of African Kingdoms', *Africa*, xxxii (1962), 324–35.

WALTON, James, 'Villages of the Paramount Chiefs of Basutoland: I. Butha Buthe', *Lesotho*, i (1959), 15–21.

—— 'Villages of the Paramount Chiefs of Basutoland: II. Thaba Bosiu, the Mountain Fortress of Chief Moshesh', *Lesotho*, ii (1960), 11–19.

WHITE, Gavin, 'Firearms in Africa: an introduction', *JAH* xii (1971), 173–84.

WILSON, Monica, 'Changes in Social Structure in Southern Africa', in L. Thompson, ed., *ASSA*, pp. 71–85.

—— 'The Hunters and Herders', *OHSA* i. 40–74.

—— 'The Nguni People', *OHSA* i. 75–130.

Wilson, Monica, 'The Sotho, Venda, and Tsonga', *OHSA* i. 131–82.
—— 'Co-operation and Conflict: the Eastern Cape Frontier', *OHSA* i. 233–71.

4. Newspapers and Periodicals

Journal des Missions Évangéliques, Paris: i (1826)–xlvii (1872).
Leselinyana, Morija: 1863–5, 1869 ff.
Annales de l'Association de la Sainte-Famille: iii–v (1866–70).
South African Commercial Advertiser: 25 Feb., 1 and 4 Mar. 1843.
Cape of Good Hope and Port Natal Shipping and Mercantile Gazette: 6, 13, and 27 Dec. 1844, 7 Feb. 1845.

C. Unpublished Dissertations, Seminar Papers, and Other Manuscripts

Elphick, Richard Hall, 'The Cape Khoi and the First Phase of South African Race Relations', Ph.D. dissertation, Yale, 1972.
Gluckman, Max, The Rise of the Zulu Kingdom.
Guma, Samson Mbizo, 'The Forms, Contents and Techniques of Traditional Literature in Southern Sotho', D.Litt. and D.Phil. dissertation, University of South Africa, 1964.
Legassick, Martin C., 'The Griqua, the Sotho-Tswana, and the Missionaries, 1780–1840: The Politics of a Frontier Zone', Ph.D. dissertation, U.C.L.A., 1970.
Lye, William F., 'The Sotho Wars in the Interior of South Africa, 1822–1837', Ph.D. dissertation, U.C.L.A., 1969.
Schapera, Isaac, Genealogies of the House of Moshoeshoe.
Van Aswegen, H. J., 'Die Verhouding tussen Blank en Nie-Blank in die Oranje-Vrystaat, 1854–1902', D.Phil. dissertation, University of the Orange Free State, 1968.
Webb, R. S., The History of the LiHoja.
Zarwan, John, 'The Xhosa Cattle Killings, 1856–1857', Seminar Paper, Yale, 1973.

D. Basotho Informants

A MoSotho's name is his genealogy: thus no. 1 is Matlere, son of Lerotholi, son of Letsie, son of Moshoeshoe.

In the footnotes, Informants are referred to by the numbers in the following list.

Descendants of Letsie, First Son of Moshoeshoe's First House

1. Matlere Lerotholi Letsie. Aged. Chief of Motsitseng, Mokhotlong District: Assistant Minister of Local Government. Interviewed by Rivers Thompson in Maseru, 1966. (Died in 1973.)

2. Makhobotlela Bereng Letsie. Born *c.* 1907. Chief of Thupali-Kaka. Interviewed on 2 Apr. 1965 in the District Office, Mohale's Hoek, where he is employed.

3. Kelebone Nkuebe Letsie. Born *c.* 1902. Chief of Mphaki. Educated Lovedale. Secretary, Council of Chiefs, Matsieng. Interviewed at Matsieng on 5 Mar. 1965. (Died in 1972.)

Descendants of Molapo, Second Son of Moshoeshoe's First House

4. Molapo Qhobela Joel Molapo. Born *c.* 1898. Chief of Khukhune. Interviewed at his home about 15 miles north-east of Botha Bothe on 23 Feb. 1965.

5. Jameson Qhobela Joel Molapo. Born *c.* 1895. Chief of 'Muela. Half-brother of no. 4 by a junior wife. Interviewed at the Crocodile Inn, Botha Bothe, on 23 Feb. 1965 and at his home, about 19 miles from Botha Bothe, on 7 Aug. 1968. Interested in history: claims to have been a member of the last authentic initiation school and to be the sole surviving custodian of secret initiation songs (*likoma*). (Died in 1971.)

6. Mopeli Jonathan Molapo. Born *c.* 1904. Chief of Mohobollo. Educated Lovedale. Assistant to the Paramount Chief at Matsieng. Interviewed at the Leribe hotel, 25 Feb. 1965. (Died in 1970.)

7. Motsarapane Jonathan Molapo. Born *c.* 1881. Chief of Hleoheng. Educated Lovedale, and speaks a little English in the Scots accent of his teacher, the Revd. David Hunter, father of Professor Monica Wilson. Interviewed at the Leribe hotel, 25 Feb. 1965. (Died in 1969.)

8. Lishobana Mpaki Molapo. Born *c.* 1898. Chief of Mokhejane. Interviewed at his home in the Botha Bothe District on 24 Feb. 1965. Has historical knowledge independent of the published works.

9. 'Mako Moliboea Molapo. Born *c.* 1895. Chief of Likhakeng. Interviewed at the Leribe hotel on 25 Feb. 1965 and in his village at Likhakeng on 13 Aug. 1968. Exceptionally well informed and deeply interested.

Descendants of Masopha, Third Son of Moshoeshoe's First House

10. Moorosana Masopha. Perhaps the last surviving grandson of Moshoeshoe's First House. Claims to have been born *c.* 1865. Interviewed at his home in Tsikoane village near Leribe on 14 Aug. 1968, but he was in his dotage. (Died in 1970.)

11. 'MaMoorosi Masopha. A granddaughter of Moshoeshoe's First House. Born *c.* 1879. Interviewed at her home in Thupa Kubu village, Maseru District, on 11 Sept. 1968. Interesting on Masopha and domestic arrangements in his household.

Descendant of Majara, Fourth Son of Moshoeshoe's First House

12. (Emmanuel) 'Mabathoana . . . Majara, O.M.I., C.B.E. Born *c.* 1906. Catholic Archbishop of Maseru and head of the Catholic Church in Lesotho. Interviewed at his home in Maseru on 21 Feb. 1965. (Died in 1966.)

Descendant of Selebalo, a junior son of Moshoeshoe

13. Halejoetse Selebalo Moseneke Leabua Selebalo. Born *c.* 1933. Chief of 'Mate, near the ruins of the village of Menkhoaneng, Moshoeshoe's birthplace. Interviewed at his home in the presence of ten councillors on 9 Aug. 1968. Interesting on Moshoeshoe's placement of Selebalo.

Descendants of Makhabane, full brother of Moshoeshoe

14. Makhabane Boshoane Mitchell Peete Lesaoana Makhabane. Middle-aged. Principal Chief of Koeneng and Mapoteng. Interviewed at his village, Bela-Bela, Leribe District, in the presence of twelve councillors, on 19 Aug. 1968. Interesting on his ancestor Lesaoana (see Index).

15. Malefetsane Lebaho Khomo-ea-Leburu Makhabane. Born *c.* 1896. Interviewed at the Blue Mountain Inn, Teyateyaneng, on 14 Aug. 1968.

Descendants of Mohale, half-brother of Moshoeshoe

16. Goliath Malebanye Potsane Mohale. Born *c.* 1883. Ward Chief of Likoeneng, near Mohale's Hoek. Claims to be the true heir to the BaSotho paramountcy by virtue of descent through Senate, daughter of Letsie's First House. Interviewed in his village, with councillors present, on 3 Apr. 1975. (Died in 1972.)

17. Bolokoe Malebanye Potsane Mohale. Born *c.* 1900. Chief of Maqhena. Full brother of no. 16. Interviewed in his village,

5 miles from Mohale's Hoek, on 6 Sept. 1968. Refutes Goliath's claim to the paramountcy.

Descendants of Monyane, son of Monaheng

18. Konyama Cheba Tsolohi Mokoatsi Ramakhetheng Nkopane Monyane. Born *c.* 1905. Headman of Senqunyane South. Formerly a member of the Paramount Chief's staff. Lives at Bela-Bela, attached to the chieftainship of no. 14. Interviewed at Bela-Bela on 19 Aug. 1968 and in Maseru on 1 Sept. 1968.

19. Ntai Lepae Motopela Mokheseng Ntai Mohlomi Monyane. Note his descent from Mohlomi. Interviewed in the Blue Mountain Inn, Teyateyaneng, on 14 Aug. 1968; lives near Teyateyaneng. Interesting on traditional rituals.

20. Nkopane Maxim Mahanoe Makhetha Monyane. Born *c.* 1900. Minister of the Lesotho Evangelical Church. Interviewed at his home, 17 miles from Maseru on the Mafeteng road on 31 July 1968.

Another Koena Informant

21. Boikanyo Sefako RaMaiketse. Born *c.* 1942. Interviewed at the home of the Revd. Osmers, Quthing, 3 Sept. 1968.

Descendant of Moshoeshoe's Ally, Lethole, Chief of the Khoakhoa

22. Tumane Thaabe Matela Letsika Matela Lethole. Born 1916. Principal Chief of Makhoakhoeng. Interviewed at his home, about 20 miles north-east of Botha Bothe, on 24 Mar. 1965 in the presence of about fifteen councillors. Concerned to emphasize his status by virtue of Lethole's alliance with Moshoeshoe.

Hlakoana Informants

23. Frank Joase Akim Mapetla Kholane. Born *c.* 1879. Headman of Masianokeng. Educated Lovedale. Interviewed at his home, Masianokeng, 8 miles from Maseru on the Mafeteng road on 30 July 1968. His grandson, Mr. Mapetla, is a lawyer—Secretary to the Cabinet (1968) and Chief Justice (1973).

24. Tšitso Tjobase 'Mote RaMatšeatsana. Born *c.* 1890. Descendant of Moshoeshoe's councillor, RaMatšeatsana (see Index). Interviewed in the Mafeteng District office on 23 Aug. 1968.

25. Nathaniel Liphapang 'Mote RaMatšeatsana. Born *c.* 1900. Interviewed at his home at the foot of Thaba Bosiu on 12 Aug. 1968.

Fokeng Informants

26. Matheala Letafa Ntsekhe Seaja Ntsekhe. Born *c.* 1898. Headman of Malimong. Interviewed at the Blue Mountain Inn, Teyateyaneng, on 14 Aug. 1968. Well informed on Fokeng history.

27. Molise Molingoane Tsolo. Born *c.* 1880. Headman of Methalaneng. Formerly on the staff of the Paramount Chiefs down to 'MaNtsebo. Interviewed at his village Likhoele near Mafeteng on 7 Mar. 1965. (Died in 1968.)

28. Makalo Peter Matee Motsoloane Mokolokolo. Born *c.* 1912. A descendant of Moshoeshoe's military councillor and warrior Mokolokolo (see Index). Is responsible for farming the King's lands. Interviewed at his home 18 miles from Maseru on the Mafeteng road on 1 Aug. 1968. Interested in family history.

Taung Informants

29. Abraham Aaron Moletsane. Born 1878 in Moletsane's village. Educated Lovedale. Formerly a teacher in French mission schools. Author of *Autobiographical Memoir*; worked with R. S. Webb in the preparation of the *Gazetteer for Basutoland*. Interviewed at his home, Kalime, 12 miles from Likhoele, on 7 Mar. 1965 and 22 Aug. 1968. Excellently informed on Taung history. (Died in 1969.)

30. Lati Tigeli Monare Moletsane. Born *c.* 1905. Chief of Sekhutlong. Formerly in the Bechuanaland Protectorate Police. Interviewed in the District Office, Mohale's Hoek, on 2 Apr. 1965.

31. Pett Khitšane Khampepe Moletsane. Born *c.* 1874. Wesleyan minister (retired). Interviewed at the village of Monare, Principal Chief of Taung, 12 miles north of Mohale's Hoek, on 9 Apr. 1965. (Died in 1971.)

32. Seeiso Mokhele Khashane Mokhele Moletsane. Born 1913. Interviewed in the District Office, Mohale's Hoek, on 6 Sept. 1968.

33. Lepau Sesoai Sesoai Tšukulu Thotobolo. Middle-aged. Interviewed at his village below Botha Bothe mountain and on the mountain on 8 Aug. 1968. A well-informed guide to the mountain.

Kubung Informant

34. Mpho, Chief of Kolo ha Sebatana; widow of Mabitso Seokoana Masareletse Ntsie Sebatana. Interviewed in her

village of Ntsie, north of Mount Kolo, on 21 Aug. 1968, with councillors present. Claims Moshoeshoe placed the Kubung under Letsie at Mount Kolo after they had been driven from their homes by Whites.

Tloung Informant

35. Lelosa Pokane Hlouhla. Born *c.* 1879. Formerly assistant to Joel, son of Molapo. Interviewed at the Crocodile Inn, Botha Bothe, on 24 Feb. 1965 and 25 Mar. 1965. Well informed.

Kholokoe Informants

36. 'MaTeletse, widow of Mpotla Teletse Tlhaka Molope Phoka. Born *c.* 1923. Interviewed in her village, Tlhaka, on the south side of the Hololo River, about 20 miles from Botha Bothe, in the presence of six councillors, on 7 Aug. 1968. Interesting on the incorporation of the Kholokoe by Moshoeshoe.

37. Matsimela Lesiba Mokebe Molope. Young man. Well educated. Participated in discussion with no. 36, stressing status and achievements of the Kholokoe under Moshoeshoe.

Tlokoa Informant

38. Petlane Motseletsele Mpaololi Petlane Ts'oeu. Middle-aged. Headman of Kolo ha Petlane. Interviewed in his village, Likhaleng, south of Mount Kolo, on 21 Aug. 1968. Claims that Ts'oeu separated from Sekonyela and joined Moshoeshoe voluntarily at Botha Bothe at the time when Sekonyela assumed the Tlokoa chieftainship; but no. 34 declares Ts'oeu came under Moshoeshoe after Moshoeshoe routed Sekonyela in 1853. According to Sekese, Ts'oeu was an uncle of Sekonyela and he and many other Tlokoa joined Moshoeshoe at Thaba Bosiu in about 1831, after a Kora band had attacked the Tlokoa at Joalaboholo (A. Sekese, *Leselinyana*, 15 June 1905).

Sia Informants

39. Mosebi Phori Mokubisane Damane (known as Mosebi Damane). Born 1918. Educated Lovedale and Fort Hare. Schoolmaster till 1973; Lecturer in History at the University of Botswana, Lesotho, and Swaziland 1973–5. Numerous discussions in Paris in November 1964 and in Lesotho in August 1968 and November 1972. The oustanding MoSotho historian. See Acknowledgements.

40. Tlhabeli Sekolong Lekhafola Selengoane Tsikoane. Born *c.* 1913. Headman of Lekhafola. Interviewed at the Blue Mountain Inn, Teyateyaneng, on 15 Aug. 1968.

41. Ramanyo Lefa Sekhaupane Lesoma Ramanyo. Born *c.* 1918. Headman of Matelile ha Sekhaupane. Interviewed in his village, Lefa, south of Matelile mountain, Mafeteng District, on 22 Aug. 1968, in the presence of councillors.

Rolong Informant

42. Mositooeng Rapiti Sehunelo Chake. Middle-aged. Headman of Sekameng. Interviewed in his village near Thulo, Mount Kolo area, Mafeteng District, in the presence of five councillors on 21 Aug. 1968. His family moved to Lesotho from Thaba 'Nchu in 1885 as a result of the succession dispute following the death of Moroka. (Died in 1969.)

Tsoeneng Informants

43. Khiba Josias Amos Pati Khiba (known as Knight Khiba). Born *c.* 1882. Interviewed in the District Office, Quthing, on 4 Sept. 1968. (Died *c.* 1969.)

44. Khupiso Tubatsi Manamolela Khokoane. Middle-aged. Assistant Minister attached to the Quthing District (1968). Interviewed in the District Office, Quthing, 4 Sept. 1968.

Phuthi Informants

45. Tumo Danyele . . . Moorosi. Headman of Maqoqo. Interviewed by Rivers Thompson at Quthing in January 1971.

46. Seeqela Phafoli 'Muso Motsoanakaba Phafoli Moorosi. Born 1928. Interviewed in the District Office, Mohale's Hoek, 6 Sept. 1968.

47. Teboho Pitso Mocheko Letuka Moorosi. Born 1916. Has worked in Johannesburg. Interviewed in village 2 miles below Quthing on 5 Sept. 1968. Nos. 45, 46, and 47 are all well informed on Phuthi culture and history. Note that no descendant of Moorosi is a Principal or Ward Chief in modern Lesotho (cf. the Khoakhoa and Taung Principal Chieftaincies).

Hlapo Informant

48. 'MaMazibuku Manizulu Mazibuku. Chief of Makong ha Chona, widow of Nokochona Belo. Middle-aged. Interviewed in her village near Botha Bothe in the presence of about ten

councillors on 8 Aug. 1968. This community is still culturally Nguni; the chief herself was born in Natal and she and her councillors speak Zulu.

Vundle Informants

49. Thembane Zonamzi Mateisi Tyhali. Middle-aged. Interviewed in the District Office, Mohale's Hoek, on 6 Sept. 1968.

50. Mhamha Vova Stokhwe Tyhali. Born *c.* 1893. Chief of Mjanyane. Interviewed with two councillors in the District Office, Quthing, on 4 Sept. 1968. This community is still culturally Nguni. They speak Xhosa. They claim they were Moshoeshoe's allies, not subordinates, and they resent the inferior status to which their chiefdom has been reduced under Moshoeshoe's descendants. See p. 336 n. 7.

Zizi Informants

51. Esau Moroa Sehalahala. Born 1903 in the village of no. 23. Educated Healdtown, South Africa, and matriculated by private study. Interpreter in Judicial Commissioner's Court. Numerous discussions in March and April 1965 and August and September 1968. See Acknowledgements. His ancestor, a refugee from Shaka, was incorporated in Moshoeshoe's kingdom. (Died in 1975.)

52. Buzini Senekal Pinda Mbengola Monethi (known as Stephen Pinda). Born *c.* 1885. Retired schoolmaster (PEMS). Interviewed in the District Office, Mafeteng, on 6 Mar. 1965, and there and in his home in Mafeteng on 20 Aug. 1968. Very well informed on many aspects of the history of Lesotho. His ancestor, a refugee from Shaka, was incorporated in SeSotho society in the time of Moshoeshoe; claims relationship to Makoanyane (see Index).

53. Makoloane Mothibi Lichaba Mothibeli Tlaroli (known as Philemon Lichaba). Born *c.* 1880. Formerly a schoolmaster (PEMS). Interviewed in the District Office, Quthing, on 4 Sept. 1968.

54. Pheello Mothibi Ramoea Mqedlane Msithi. Born *c.* 1896. Retired Sergeant-Major, Basutoland Mounted Police; headman of Waterfall, 8 miles from Quthing. Interviewed in the Quthing District Office on 4 Sept. 1968.

55. Lekhabunyane Nchakha Lehau Rapeoana Mobe Nyanye. Born *c.* 1900. Claims his great-grandfather Rapeoana joined Moshoeshoe during the *lifaqane*. His grandfather Lehau was in charge of Moshoeshoe's cattle and lands. Interviewed in his

village near Qiloane, below Thaba Bosiu, on 2 Aug. 1968. Interesting anecdotes *re* Moshoeshoe.

56. Dickson Fora Rafutho Jara (known as Rafutho). Aged. Custodian of Thaba Bosiu. Lives in village at the foot of the mountain. Guided Dr. Guma and me over the mountain on 3 Feb. 1965 and interviewed again in his village on 23 July 1968. Well informed. His grandfather and great-grandfather, refugees from Shaka, joined Moshoeshoe at Botha Bothe and stayed with him, 'because they loved Moshoeshoe'.

Addenda to Publications

DAMANE, M., and SANDERS, P. B., eds., *Lithoko: Sotho Praise-Poems*, Oxford, 1974.

MASON, R. J., 'Background to the Transvaal Iron Age—new discoveries at Olifantspoort and Broederstroom', *Journal of the South African Institute of Mining and Metallurgy*, lxxiv (6) (Jan. 1974).

CHRONOLOGY

c. 1786	Birth of Lepoqo (Moshoeshoe)	Birth of Shaka
1795		Britain conquers the Cape Colony
1803		Britain cedes the Cape Colony to the Batavian Republic
c. 1804	Moshoeshoe is initiated; birth of Sekonyela, heir to the Tlokoa chiefdom	
1806		Britain reconquers the Cape Colony
c. 1810	Moshoeshoe marries 'MaMohato	
c. 1811	Birth of Letsie	Britain begins the conquest of the southern Nguni chiefdoms
c. 1816	Death of Mohlomi	Shaka seizes the Zulu chieftainship
c. 1820	Moshoeshoe founds his own village at Botha Bothe; Matiwane raids LeSotho from Zululand	
c. 1821	Mpangazitha and Matiwane invade LeSotho—beginning of the *lifaqane* wars	
c. 1822	Sekonyela's Tlokoa drive Moshoeshoe into the mountains	
c. 1823	Moshoeshoe besieged on Botha Bothe mountain by Sekonyela	Mzilikazi defies Shaka and invades the Transvaal
c. 1824	Moshoeshoe occupies Thaba Bosiu	
c. 1825	Matiwane's Ngwane defeat Pakalita's Hlubi; beginning of raids by	

		Coloured bands of armed horsemen	
c.	1827	Moshoeshoe repels Matiwane	
	1828		Shaka assassinated and succeeded by Dingane
c.	1829	While Moshoeshoe raids the Thembu, Sekonyela attacks Thaba Bosiu	Trekboers from Cape Colony begin to settle north of the Orange River
c.	1831	Moshoeshoe repels Mzilikazi	
	1833	French Protestant missionaries reach LeSotho	
	1834	Rolong and Coloured groups settle north of the Caledon; Andrew Smith's expedition visits Moshoeshoe	Slaves emancipated in Cape Colony; Xhosa at war with Cape Colony
	1835	Moshoeshoe's last raid on the Thembu—death of Makhabane	
	1836		Voortrekkers begin to settle on the high veld
	1837		Voortrekkers drive Mzilikazi beyond the Limpopo
	1838	Moletsane's Taung settle north of the Caledon	Dingane kills Retief's party and is defeated at Blood River
	1840		Mpande defeats and succeeds Dingane
	1843	Governor Napier makes a treaty with Moshoeshoe	Britain annexes Natal
	1845	Governor Maitland modifies Napier's treaty	
	1846–7		Xhosa at war with Cape Colony; Governor Smith annexes Xhosa territory to the Kei River
	1848	Governor Smith annexes all territory between the Orange and the Vaal	
	1849	Major Warden makes	

boundaries reducing Moshoeshoe's territory

1851	Moshoeshoe defeats Warden at Viervoet	Xhosa at war with Cape Colony (till 1853)
1852	Moshoeshoe repels General Cathcart	Britain recognizes independence of voortrekkers north of the Vaal
1853	Moshoeshoe conquers Sekonyela	
1854	Britain abandons Orange River Sovereignty and renounces treaties with Moshoeshoe	White inhabitants found the Orange Free State republic; a Parliament created in Cape Colony
1857		Millennial movement among the Xhosa
1858	War with the O.F.S.: BaSotho victory; Grey arbitrates O.F.S.–LeSotho boundary	White inhabitants of the Transvaal found the South African Republic
1861	Moshoeshoe asks for British protection	
1865	War with the O.F.S.	
1866	Molapo surrenders, Moshoeshoe signs Treaty of Thaba Bosiu	
1867	War resumed: O.F.S. victories, Moshoeshoe repeatedly requests British protection	
1868	Governor Wodehouse annexes 'Basutoland'	
1869	Wodehouse and O.F.S. representatives settle boundary between Basutoland and O.F.S.	Diamond rush to alluvial diggings near the Vaal–Harts confluence
1870	Moshoeshoe abdicates in favour of Letsie, and dies	Diamond rush to the dry diggings (Kimberley)
1871	Basutoland incorporated in Cape Colony	
1872		Cape Colony obtains Responsible Government

1877		Britain annexes the Transvaal
1879	Moorosi rebels	Zulu War
1880–1	BaSotho rebellion	White Transvaalers rebel and regain independence
1884	The Cape Colony relinquishes Basutoland, Britain resumes control	
1885		Discovery of Witwatersrand main gold reef
1898		The last African chiefdoms in southern Africa brought under white control
1899–1902		Britain conquers the O.F.S. and the Transvaal
1910	Basutoland remains a British Colony	Cape Colony, Natal, O.F.S., and Transvaal unite to form the Union of South Africa
1961		South Africa becomes a Republic and leaves the Commonwealth
1966	Lesotho becomes independent under King Moshoeshoe II and Prime Minister Leabua Jonathan	

GENEALOGICAL TABLES

The Putative Ancestry of Moshoeshoe

```
                        Napo
                          |
                      Motebang
                          |
                       Molemo
                          |
                      Tšoloane
                          |
                      Monaheng
```

Ntsane	Motloheloa	Motloang	Mokoteli	Mokheseng	Monyane
Khojane	Sekake	Peete	Thamae	Mabitle	Mohlomi

Libe	Mokhachane
Ramakha Moshoeshoe	Makhabane Posholi

The First Houses of Mokhachane and Moshoeshoe

```
              Mokhachane    =    Kholu (f)
               (d.1855)          (d.1860)
```

'MaTšoeunyane (f)	Moshoeshoe =	'MaMohato	Makhabane	'MaNtoetse (f)	Posholi
	(1786–1870)	(d.1834)	(d.1835)		(d.1868)

Letsie	Molapo	Mathe (f)	Masopha	Majara
(1811–91)	(1814–80)	(b.1817)	(1820–98)	(1829–58)

The Royal Succession

```
                      Moshoeshoe
                          |
                   Letsie I (1870–91)
                          |
                  Lerotholi (1891–1905)
                          |
             Letsie II (1905–13) – Griffith (1913–39)
                                       |
                               Seeiso (1939–40)
                                       |
                           Moshoeshoe II (1960 –    )
```

Notes: These tables are derived from E & M, pp. 374–81, and Claude- H. Perrot, *Les Sotho et les missionnaires européens au XIXᵉ siècle*, Dijon, 1970, p. 18, as amended by Mosebi Damane, Informant 39.

The dates of the births of Moshoeshoe and his children, and of the death of his mother, are approximate.

Between 1940 and 1960 'MaNtsebo, first wife of Seeiso, was Regent.

INDEX

In the index M = Moshoeshoe, PEMS = Paris Evangelical Missionary Society, and WMS = Wesleyan Missionary Society

1. Moshoeshoe in 1833

2. Moshoeshoe in 1845

3. Mokhachane, Moshoeshoe's father (1845)

4. Kholu, Moshoeshoe's mother (1845)

6. Molapo, Moshoeshoe's second son (1845)

5. Posholi, Moshoeshoe's brother (1844)

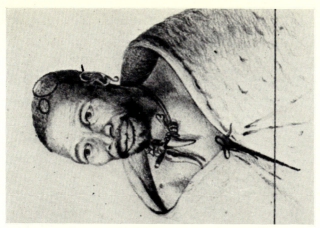

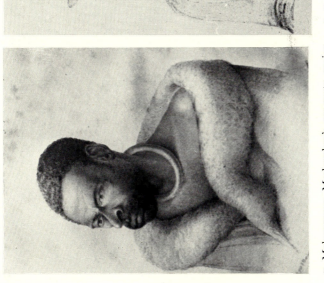

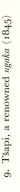

7. Makoanyane, Moshoeshoe's age-mate, senior warrior, and councillor (1845)

8. RaMatšeatsana, baptized Abraham, a councillor (1845)

9. Tšapi, a renowned *ngaka* (1845)

11. Mopeli, baptized Paul, a half-brother of Moshoeshoe (1845)

10. Sekhonyana, baptized Nehemiah, eldest son of Moshoeshoe's third wife (1845)

12 and 13. Eugène Casalis and Thomas Arbousset in 1833, the year in which they first met Moshoeshoe

14. Marabeng, the mountain stronghold of Sekonyela, the Tlokoa chief; captured by Moshoeshoe in 1853; from the south

15. Marabeng, from overhead; the modern road and railway pass on the northern side

16. Botha Bothe mountain, Moshoeshoe's first stronghold, from the north-west

17. Botha Bothe mountain, from the north

18. Thaba Bosiu, from the south-west; Moshoeshoe's mountain home from 1824 until his death

19. Thaba Bosiu: the western cliff face, looking southwards from the Khubelu of Rafutho pass

20. Thaba Bosiu, from the east-north-east: the conical hill in the foreground is Qiloane

21. Thaba Bosiu, from the south-east

22. Thaba Bosiu: the Khubelu or Rafutho pass which Orange Free State burghers under Louis Wepener tried to storm in 1865

23. The ruins of Moshoeshoe's village on Thaba Bosiu, looking eastwards towards the Maloti; the pinnacle of Qiloane is in the middle distance, left of centre